The Globalization of Childhood

The Globalization of Childhood

The International Diffusion of Norms and Law against the Child Death Penalty

Robyn Linde

For Steve —
with gratitude
— Robyn

OXFORD
UNIVERSITY PRESS

OXFORD
UNIVERSITY PRESS

Oxford University Press is a department of the University of Oxford. It furthers
the University's objective of excellence in research, scholarship, and education
by publishing worldwide. Oxford is a registered trade mark of Oxford University
Press in the UK and certain other countries.

Published in the United States of America by Oxford University Press
198 Madison Avenue, New York, NY 10016, United States of America.

Library of Congress Cataloging-in-Publication Data
Names: Linde, Robyn, author.
Title: The globalization of childhood : the international diffusion of norms and law against
the child death penalty / Robyn Linde.
Description: New York, NY : Oxford University Press, 2016. |
Based on author's thesis (doctoral - University of Minnesota), 2010. |
Includes bibliographical references and index.
Identifiers: LCCN 2015046239 (print) | LCCN 2015047775 (ebook) |
ISBN 9780190601379 (hardcover : alk. paper) | ISBN 9780190601386 (Updf)
Subjects: LCSH: Capital punishment—United States. | Juvenile corrections—United States. |
Law—United States—Foreign influences. | Capital punishment. | Juvenile corrections. |
Law and globalization. | Children (International law)
Classification: LCC KF9227.C2 L56 2016 (print) | LCC KF9227.C2 (ebook) |
DDC 345/.0773—dc23
LC record available at http://lccn.loc.gov/2015046239

1 3 5 7 9 8 6 4 2
Printed by Sheridan Books, Inc., United States of America

For Holly at Lake Harriet and everything after

CONTENTS

LIST OF FIGURES

LIST OF TABLES

ACKNOWLEDGMENTS

It is a great privilege to have the opportunity to thank the individuals who were important to the writing of this book. First, I would like to express my most sincere gratitude to my dissertation adviser and mentor, Kathryn Sikkink, whose commitment to human rights and intellectual acumen are a testament to the ability of scholars to carry out meaningful work on social and political change. Additionally, I was fortunate to have the advice and guidance of other esteemed professors (and former professors) at the University of Minnesota—Twin Cities: Barb Frey, Dan Kelliher, Dara Strolovitch, and Sally Kenney. I am very lucky for their continued support of my scholarship and career. I would also like to thank my dissertation group at the University of Minnesota, whose members were helpful in reading and offering input on early drafts of this manuscript: Susan Kang, Jennifer Rutledge, David (Hun Joon) Kim, Carrie Walling, Sandra Borda, Tuba Inal, Rock (Zhenqing) Zhang, Darrah McCracken, Veronica Michel, and Martin Kifer. Additionally, great appreciation is extended to Stephen Ropp and the anonymous reviewers at Oxford University Press, whose careful reading and excellent suggestions have greatly improved this book. I am also immensely grateful to my editor, Angela Chnapko, whose guidance, encouragement, and help in navigating the review process at Oxford have been invaluable. I am honored to have had such a remarkable group of people devote time to my project.

I am indebted to friends, old and new, for whose love, support, and advice I am very thankful: Ayten Gündoğdu, Cigdem Cidam, Vicky Lichtman, Mikaila Muriel Lemonik Arthur, Ben Ledsham, Jason Stegemoller, Brooke Protko, Holly Dygert, and Zhen Wang. My parents and in-laws, Michael and Mary Linde and Bob and Jackie Shapiro, and brothers, Ryan and Reid Linde, have likewise cheered me on for many years. Thanks especially to my mother who took me to the library.

Additionally, there have been many other people and institutions that lent support to this project: the Amnesty International USA (AIUSA) archives at the University of Colorado Boulder, and Ellen Moore and

David Hays who helped me to access them; Columbia University's Rare Book and Manuscript Library, now the AIUSA archives' new home; New York University Law Library; a number of current and former AIUSA activists, including especially Rick Halperin and Ali Miller; the University of Minnesota Law Library and Professor David Weissbrodt for access to his personal AIUSA archives; and Rhode Island College Vice President Ron Pitt and Dean of the Faculty of Arts and Sciences Earl Simson, who granted me time off from teaching to finish drafts of this book. Thanks are also due to Sage Publications and the *European Journal of International Relations*, and to Brill Publishing and the *International Journal of Children's Rights*, for allowing me to republish parts of my articles as chapters in this book.

Finally, and most importantly, much love and gratitude is extended to my happy little family. My two lovely daughters—Bug and Scout—may have substantially lengthened the time it took to write this book, but they have been the sweetest distraction. This book would not be possible without my co-conspirator, political agitator, part-time vandal, secret weapon, co-author, partisan, first and last reader, and true love, Holiday Shapiro. From prospectus to publication, there is no person whose input and opinion I value more; there is no one I'd rather have in my corner. This book is infinitely better for her quick wit, patience, and mad editing skills. She is the source of everything good in my life. Everyone should have a Holly.

The Globalization of Childhood

CHAPTER 1

༄

Introduction

When we speak of children in the field of international relations, we tend to speak of them as war victims, child soldiers, and child laborers. They have been the bystanders, beneficiaries, or casualties of the changing international order in the post–World War II era. Children inhabit a specific narrative in global society, their image invoking ideas of innocence, vulnerability, and the need for protection. As a result, children became the symbols of many international institutions devoted to advancing human rights and democracy around the world in the last few decades of the twentieth century, yet they have been historically absent from the international relations literature itself.[1]

I seek in this book to theorize children as an important part of state consolidation and international order and as worthy recipients of greater attention in the field of international relations. I examine the development of domestic and international law forbidding the death penalty for child offenders as a point of entry into the history of children, childhood, and the international system. I argue that the widespread process of state consolidation that took place in the late nineteenth century and throughout the twentieth century—a process whereby the state began

---

1. In recent years, a number of scholars have begun to examine the role of the child in international relations and have made important contributions to the field. Please see the "state of the field" following this section.

to regulate large swaths of civil and private life, including children's lives—was aided by the development of the *global child*, a figure that required steadily increasing levels of protection by the state, and later, by the international community. These protections were extended even to the least sympathetic children, those who committed the most egregious crimes, making the diffusion of norms and law about the child death penalty particularly illustrative of wide-scale state consolidation around the world. Protections for child criminals over the last century and a half were also illustrative of international consolidation—or the merging of disparate sources of authority over children into more centralized international institutions, such as the United Nations Children's Fund or UNICEF.

For society to protect infants, toddlers, youth, and even teenagers who pose no physical threat to the community at large,[2] there is little public controversy or debate. For society to protect child offenders whose crimes, if committed by an adult, could result in the death penalty, however, is far more expressive of a common construction of children and childhood. The abolition of the death penalty for child offenders—a ban found in 96 percent of states at the end of the twentieth century—is therefore a bold policy position, suggesting that the boundaries of childhood are inviolable and that there is nothing that a child can do, no crime too brutal or too violent, to revoke the protection childhood affords.

In this book, I argue that the global model of childhood that emerged after World War II was important to the development of the international system, serving to consolidate power and legitimize international institutions. I further examine the growth of this model, one codified today in international law and developed primarily in Europe and the United States in the late nineteenth and early twentieth centuries and diffused from these points of origin throughout the world. Regarding the abolition of the child death penalty, norms and law forbidding the penalty for child offenders were specifically advanced by the British and French colonial powers. I present in this book my dataset consisting of dates of abolition of the penalty and thereby explain the process by which a specific construction of childhood emerged, spread through bureaucratic methods of state organization, and was globalized. Yet in tracking the

---

2. The 1990 Convention on the Rights of the Child defines a child as "every human being below the age of 18 years." Teenagers can be children (below the age of 18) or legal adults (18- and 19-year olds). The age limits of the child death penalty varied over time and among states, ranging from age seven (in early common law systems) to age 18.

development of a global or universal model of childhood, I do not suggest that the model is found everywhere, only that it was and is presented to world society *as if* it were universal, as though it applies to all, regardless of locality or context.

Although the global diffusion of a specific construction of childhood is compelling as both a historical study and political exercise, why should international relations scholars care about the evolution of childhood in society or about the international diffusion of norms and law protecting children? In an age marked by terrorism, war, and economic uncertainty—a period when security and economic matters would seem to trump all other issues—why should we concern ourselves with children and international efforts to protect them? I suggest that we should not underestimate or give short shrift to the dramatic social promotion of childhood over the last century and a half. Children were reimagined and redefined from the legal property of their fathers to internationally protected and even 'sacralized' citizens of the international community—their position enshrined in dozens of international legal texts and in national law.[3] The transformation of children from legal nonentities into a distinct, cloistered, and highly protected class was remarkable, challenging and ultimately serving to alter many of the core precepts of law and social organization in societies around the world. In effect, the promotion of childhood triggered such profound changes in family structure and state organization that by the end of the twentieth century, legal distinctions between children by race, class, and gender were discarded in favor of a universal model of children's rights.

The State of the Field

Unlike other social science that focus on children, international relations has yet to fully theorize the position of children and the development of norms and law about childhood in global society. Children are largely absent from the international relations literature apart from the child conflict[4] and

3. Hugh Cunningham, *Children and Childhood in Western Society since 1500* (New York: Longman, 1995); Viviana A. Zelizer, *Pricing the Priceless Child: The Changing Social Value of Children* (Princeton, NJ: Princeton University Press, 1994).

4. See for example, Frank Faulkner, "Kindergarten Killers: Morality, Murder, and the Child Soldier Problem," *Third World Quarterly* 22, no. 4 (2001): 491–504; Vera Achvarina and Simon F. Reich, "No Place to Hide: Refugees, Displaced Persons, and the Recruitment of Child Soldiers," *International Security* 31, no. 1 (2006): 127–164; Carol B. Thompson, "Beyond Civil Society: Child Soldiers as Citizens in Mozambique," *Review of African Political Economy* 26, no. 80 (1999): 191–206; Steve Hicks, "The

child labor literatures,[5] and more recently from the emerging body of litera-ture on child citizenship and the Convention on the Rights of the Child.[6] The children in these literatures are mostly victims—of war, poverty, abuse, and neglect. Relatively little scholarship has been produced about children as rights holders or about the role that ideas about children and childhood have played in the shaping of international order. Important work in recent years has begun to remedy this exclusion, especially research identifying a link between norms and law about childhood and power in the interna-tional system.[7] This book is situated within this discourse. It seeks to reveal

Political Economy of War-Affected Children," *The Annals of the American Academy of Political and Social Science* 575 (2001): 106–121; Jo de Berry, "Child Soldiers and the Convention on the Rights of the Child," *The Annals of the American Academy of Political and Social Science* 575 (2001): 92–105; R. Charli Carpenter, "Surfacing Children: Limitations of Genocidal Rape Discourse," *Human Rights Quarterly* 22, no. 2 (2000): 428–477; Siobhán McEvoy-Levy, ed., *Troublemakers or Peacemakers? Youth and Post-Accord Peacebuilding* (Notre Dame, IN: University of Notre Dame Press, 2006); Helen Brocklehurst, *Who's Afraid of Children: Children, Conflict, and International Relations* (Surrey, UK: Ashgate, 2006).

5. See for example, William E. Myers, "The Right Rights? Child Labor in a Globalizing World," *The Annals of the American Academy of Political and Social Science* 575 (2001): 38–55; Sudharshan Canagarajah and Helena Skyt Nielson, "Child Labor in Africa: A Comparative Study," *The Annals of the American Academy of Political and Social Science* 575 (2001): 71–91; Geeta Chowdhry and Mark Beeman, "Challenging Child Labor: Transnational Activism and India's Carpet Industry," *The Annals of the American Academy of Political and Social Science* 575 (2001): 158–175.

6. See for example, Elizabeth Bartholet, "Ratification by the United States of the Convention on the Rights of the Child: Pros and Cons from a Child's Rights Perspective," *The Annals of the American Academy of Political and Social Science* 633 (2011): 80–101; James Bohman, "Children and the Rights of Citizens: Nondomination and Intergenerational Justice," *The Annals of the American Academy of Political and Social Science* 633 (2011): 128–140; Felton Earls, "Children: From Rights to Citizenship," *The Annals of the American Academy of Political and Social Science* 633 (2011): 6–16; Anna Holzscheiter, *Children's Rights in International Politics* (New York: Palgrave Macmillan, 2010); Allison James, "To Be(Come) or Not to Be(Come): Understanding Children's Citizenship," *The Annals of the American Academy of Political and Social Science* 633 (2011): 167–179; Andrew Rehfeld, "The Child as Democratic Citizen," *The Annals of the American Academy of Political and Social Science* 633 (2011): 141–166; Geraldine Van Bueren, "Multigenerational Citizenship: The Importance of Recognizing Children as National and International Citizens," *The Annals of the American Academy of Political and Social Science* 633 (2011): 30–51.

7. Paula Fass, "A Historical Context for the United Nations Convention on the Rights of the Child," *The Annals of the American Academy of Political and Social Science* 633 (2011): 17–29; Holzscheiter, *Children's Rights*; Norman Lewis, "Human Rights, Law, and Democracy in an Unfree World," in *Human Rights Fifty Years On: A Reappraisal*, ed. Tony Evans (Manchester, UK: Manchester University Press, 1998): 77–104; Vanessa Pupavac, "Misanthropy without Borders: The International Children's Rights Regime," *Disasters* 25, no. 2 (2001): 96; Geraldine Van Bueren, *The International Law on the Rights of the Child* (Boston: Martinus Nijhoff, 1995); Alison M.S. Watson, "Children and International Relations: A New Site of Knowledge?" *Review of International Studies* 32, no. 2 (2006): 237–250; Alison M.S. Watson, *The Child in International Political Economy: A Place at the Table* (New York: Routledge, 2009).

the importance of the construction of children and childhood to the development of the international system after World War II, and specifically considers the impact of children as rights holders on the process of state consolidation and on international institutions.

On the broader topic of children in general, sociological institutionalists argue that childhood is a social construction, one that has been built (and continues to be built) on a global scale. This view is consistent with that of scholars in international relations and law, constructivists and international legal theorists included, who contend that citizens and legal subjects are constructed over time.[8] There is strong support for the argument that childhood is a social construction because its meaning has been understood differently at different times and places. Moreover, attitudes or moral positions about the nature and capabilities of children have likewise varied markedly.

Despite these diverse constructions, a body of international law has developed that prescribes a detailed model of childhood, delineating children's needs and the requirements for a healthy, safe, productive, and successful life as global citizens. This model has several defining features, including the immaturity, vulnerability, and reduced capability of children (biologically, psychologically, intellectually); the upper age limit of 18 years; and a relationship between the state and the child in which the state assumes responsibility for the child's welfare. Consensus on this model evolved and eventually could be found in many areas of law, including those governing access to primary school education and protection from exploitative labor practices. Although differences remain *in practice*, the position of children *in law* is remarkably similar around the world. An important aspect of this universal model is a lesser standard of culpability for children and their exclusion from adult criminal penalties.

8. Margaret E. Keck and Kathryn Sikkink, *Activists Beyond Borders* (Ithaca, NY: Cornell University Press, 1998); Michael Barnett, "Social Constructivism," in *The Globalization of World Politics*, eds. John Baylis and Steve Smith (New York: Oxford University Press, 2005): 149–165; Emanuel Adler, "Constructivism and International Relations," in *Handbook of International Relations*, eds. Walter Carlsnaes, Thomas Risse-Kappen, and Beth Simmons (London: Sage, 2002): 112–154; Nicholas Onuf, "Worlds of Our Making: The Strange Career of Constructivism in International Relations," in *Visions of International Relations*, ed. Donald J. Puchala (Columbia, SC: University of South Carolina Press, 2002): 119–141; Nicholas Onuf, *World of Our Making: Rules and Rule in Social Theory and International Relations* (Columbia, SC: University of South Carolina Press, 1989); Ted Hopf, "The Promise of Constructivism in International Relations Theory," *International Security* 23, no. 1 (1998): 171–200; Franklin E. Zimring, *The Changing Legal World of Adolescence* (New York: Free Press, 1982).

Herein lies the central puzzle of this book: This overwhelming consensus on the meaning and boundaries of childhood did not always exist. Childhood is a historical construct developed over centuries. Before the nineteenth century, children were afforded little, if any, *legal* protection from abuse, neglect, and exploitation. In many parts of the world, there were no age-based limits on criminal penalties such as the death penalty. In some states, including the United Kingdom and states that share its legal heritage, children as young as seven could be executed if intent or *mens rea* could be demonstrated; this was true in the United States well into the twentieth century.[9] Yet by the century's end, almost all states in the international system had either ended the death penalty for all crimes and all offenders or limited the penalty to those 18 years and older. What caused this profound shift? How did the position of children in society evolve from one in which children were legally indistinguishable from adults to one in which they were a separate, distinct, and protected class, shielded from familial, societal, and state abuse? How did this particular construction of childhood come about?

Indeed, by the end of the twentieth century, a predominantly Western model of childhood—characterized by the age parameters of birth (or conception)[10] to 18—had become an international idea, one that included protection from adult criminal penalties, and principally from the death penalty. This is not to suggest that all states have adopted this norm and no longer execute child offenders. Indeed, there have been several holdouts in the twenty-first century: China, the Democratic

---

9. As late as the 1988 US Supreme Court ruling in *Thompson v. Oklahoma*, some US states did not have a minimum age for the death penalty. As such, the minimum age for the penalty was taken from British law as seven or 14, depending on the demonstration of *mens rea*. No US state codified seven as the minimum age, although some states had set their age limits younger than 14 at the time of the *Thompson* ruling: Indiana set its minimum age for the penalty at 10; Mississippi's minimum age was 13; and Montana's was 12. Arizona, Delaware, Florida (if the defendant had prior convictions), Oklahoma, Pennsylvania, South Carolina, South Dakota, and Washington had no minimum age at the time of the *Thompson* ruling. Sources indicate there was no minimum age by statute for Idaho or Utah, either. No executions of children under the age of 13 were recorded in the United States in the twentieth century. See Amnesty International, "United States of America: The Death Penalty and Juvenile Offenders," AMR 51/23/91 (1991): 64; Hugo Adam Bedau, ed., *The Death Penalty in America: Current Controversies* (New York: Oxford University Press, 1997); Tom Seligson, "Are They Too Young to Die?" *Parade Magazine*, 1986, 5.

10. Since some predominantly Catholic countries argue that life begins at conception, the beginning of childhood is therefore still a contested part of the model. See Geraldine Van Bueren, *The International Law,* for a more detailed discussion of this issue.

Republic of the Congo (DRC), Iran, Iraq, Saudi Arabia, Sudan, the United States, Pakistan, and Yemen. All of these states, including the United States, have been at odds with international human rights law in general.[11] Of this group, only the United States is currently believed to be compliant with international law regarding the child death penalty. Other states have continued to sentence child offenders to death, including the Maldives, Nigeria, and the United Arab Emirates.[12]

Varying age limits apply to different aspects of childhood across issue areas. As this and other chapters attest, most countries historically excluded very young children from the death penalty. In Great Britain and in states that inherited its legal system, children under the age of seven were excluded from the penalty; this limit was progressively raised to 14, 16, and finally to 18. Other criminal penalties, such as eligibility for life without parole, have likewise seen a similar increase in age limits over time. Other issue areas, like marriage eligibility, alcohol consumption, driving, recruitment into the armed forces, and others have different age limits; chapter 4 discusses these limits in postcolonial Africa. Why then does this book focus on the age 18 as the near universally accepted upper boundary of childhood? The age 18 has come to be a threshold point or "evolutionary concept" separating childhood from adulthood in international law.[13] Anna Holzscheiter argues that with the exception of the 1980 Hague Convention on the Civil Aspects of International Child Abduction and the European Convention on the Recognition and Enforcement of Decisions Concerning Custody of Children of 1980, international treaties had not established the upper age limit of childhood before the Convention on the Rights of the Child (CRC).[14] With the widely shared acceptance of 18 as the age of separation between children and adults in the convention, the international community has reached and expressed a consensus on the boundaries of modern childhood. And, importantly, *age* is now the defining quality of childhood. This book lays out the process by which age, as opposed to other qualities, became the *single* measure of childhood, and it considers how this process was

11. Andrew Moravcsik, "The Origins of Human Rights Regimes: Democratic Delegation in Postwar Europe," *International Organization* 54, no. 2 (2000): 217–252.

12. Human Rights Watch, "Iran, Saudi Arabia, Sudan: End Juvenile Death Penalty," Oct. 9, 2010; Michael Borchenek, Human Rights Watch, "Dispatches: Executions Down, But Not for Juvenile Offenders," April 1, 2015.

13. Holzscheiter, *Children's Rights*, 131.

14. Holzscheiter, *Children's Rights*, 132.

related to the development of the modern liberal state and the international system.

Finally, this is a study of childhood, not of children per se. Although the model of childhood reflects beliefs about children, the terms are not synonymous or coterminous. The global model of childhood includes certain understandings about the nature of children, their morality, their potential, how they should be raised, and what environment fosters their development. As states consolidated power over children and began to regulate ever more areas of their lives over the course of the nineteenth and early twentieth centuries, the state became the principal arbiter of the appropriate treatment of children. The result of consolidation was the emergence of a single model of childhood, one standard, one idealized, globalized—and increasingly scrutinized—period of human life.

HISTORICAL BACKGROUND OF THE DEATH PENALTY

The history of the abolition of the death penalty for child offenders is best contextualized within the history of abolition in general. Concerns about state practice, the promise of rehabilitation, and questions about the role of punishment in society all shaped the penalty's application for both adults and children. Campaigns to end the child death penalty drew on multiple social issues to make their arguments compelling, uniting humanitarian concerns for child welfare with concerns about abolition and state-sanctioned violence—a combination unique to child justice issues. This section demonstrates the historical links between efforts to reform the use of the death penalty by excluding child offenders and efforts to abolish the penalty for everyone.

Different states have taken different paths to abolition, and limitations on the death penalty by age represent only one means of reform. States can also limit the penalty on the basis of gender, intent, advanced age, condition (such as pregnancy), the nature of the crime, or the method of execution. One common method of limiting the penalty has been to disallow it for ordinary crimes but to maintain it for crimes against the state, such as treason or war crimes. States can also end the penalty altogether, as many states around the world have done. By banning the penalty outright, states also, obviously, end the penalty for children. Additionally, a state may have banned the penalty for those under the age of 18 at one point in its history and abolished it for all offenders at a later date; the United Kingdom and France are examples of this order of abolition. As the data (presented in chapter 2) attest, the norm against the child death penalty was part of a larger trend that included abolition of the penalty in general (for all crimes and all offenders). A highly unusual quality of this historical process, and one discussed at length in this book, is the pattern whereby general abolition subsided for many decades while abolition of the penalty for child offenders widely diffused. This is discussed in more detail in chapters 2 and 7.

While the practice of the death penalty long predates the modern era, the abolitionist movement in the Western world is fairly recent. The modern movement really began with the publication in 1764 of Cesare Beccaria's treatise *On Crimes and Punishment*, a seminal text that influenced figures including Voltaire, Thomas Jefferson, Thomas Paine, the Marquis de Lafayette, and Maximilien Robespierre.[15]

Although the European system is today widely considered among the most advanced with regard to abolition, it was the United States that blazed an abolitionist trail in the nineteenth century.[16] Michigan was the first US state to abolish the death penalty in 1846 for all crimes except treason, before any state in the world and more than twenty years before any state in Europe.[17] Wisconsin abolished the penalty for *all* crimes in 1853, ten years before any state in the world and twelve years before the first European state, San Marino, abolished it in 1865.[18] Moreover, Wisconsin abolished the penalty for all crimes 119 years before any current member state in the European Union.[19]

Opposition to the death penalty outside of the few countries that abolished it outright was focused on certain practices or else sought to limit the

15. William Schabas, *The Abolition of the Death Penalty in International Law* (Cambridge, UK: Cambridge University Press, 2002): 5.

16. Tuscany, Austria, and Russia all suspended the death penalty for periods during the eighteenth century. See Roger Hood, *The Death Penalty: A Worldwide Perspective* (Oxford: Oxford University Press, 2002).

17. Franklin E. Zimring and Gordon Hawkins, *Capital Punishment and the American Agenda* (Cambridge, UK: Cambridge University Press, 1986); Amnesty International, "Facts and Figures on the Death Penalty" (Amnesty International, 2005). Outright abolition of the death penalty in the modern era began in Austria, Brazil, Russia, and Tuscany, all of which suspended the use of the penalty for a period of time in the eighteenth and nineteenth centuries. Additionally, other states such as Portugal and the Netherlands abolished for ordinary crimes in the nineteenth century, but retained the penalty for extraordinary crimes, such as those committed during war.

18. Venezuela was the first country to abolish in 1863. Wisconsin restored the death penalty in 2006.

19. Amnesty International, "Facts and Figures." Sweden and Finland were the first countries in the European Union to abolish the death penalty for all crimes in 1972.

penalty's application rather than end it altogether. Concerns about public executions (and the unruly crowds they attracted), limitations on the penalty for the very young, and an ever-shrinking list of capital crimes characterized reform in the nineteenth and early twentieth centuries. Efforts to eradicate the death penalty for child offenders began in earnest in the nineteenth century, and abolitionists capitalized on a few executions of children that were especially disturbing, as described in chapter 3.[20] In England, at least, the abolitionists' intent was not to end the death penalty only for children, but to end it for everyone. Although these abolitionists had a broader agenda, they recognized child executions as particularly reprehensible and seized upon these executions to spotlight the penalty's inhumanity. Their reform efforts succeeded. A number of states abolished the penalty for child offenders age 17 and younger. The nineteenth century saw an end to public executions in England and elsewhere. Moreover, Venezuela (1863), San Marino (1865), Costa Rica (1877), and Brazil (1882) ended the penalty for all crimes during the nineteenth century. Ecuador (1906) followed in the early years of the twentieth century. France (1906), Paraguay (1914), Trinidad (1925), and the United Kingdom (1933) ended the penalty only for child offenders under the age of 18 in the early twentieth century.

The pace of abolition accelerated after World War II, but not before some states carved out exceptions for war crimes even though the penalty was already prohibited in their domestic law.[21] This postwar period was notable for the creation of international human rights law and the establishment of the United Nations, and it marked a turning point in how the penalty was viewed. The events of the war made the danger of the penalty's abuse by individual states starkly evident.[22] The period was equally notable, however, for trials for war crimes and collaboration that allowed for and resulted in executions of the convicted.

These competing forces—a dawning global recognition of the right to life versus the continued pursuit of the long-held idea of

20. See in particular the John Any Bird Bell execution in 1831 and the Joseph Morely execution in 1887. Sir Leon Radzinowicz and Roger Hood, *A History of English Criminal Law*, 5 vols., vol. 5, *The Emergence of Penal Policy* (London: Stevens & Sons, 1948–1986); *The London Times*, "Execution of John Any Bird Bell, for Murder," August 2, 1831, 14(606), 4a.

21. Norway in 1946 is a good example. William Schabas, *The Abolition of the Death Penalty*, 1.

22. Ibid., 6.

retributive justice—shaped the human rights law that would emerge from this period.[23] The 1948 Universal Declaration of Human Rights (UDHR) does not mention the penalty at all, and the 1976 International Covenant on Civil and Political Rights (ICCPR) limits but does not ban the penalty, forbidding it only for child offenders under the age of 18 and for pregnant women. Not until the Second Optional Protocol to the ICCPR in 1989 do we see a call for complete abolition. The 1990 CRC unequivocally banned the practice for child offenders who commit their crimes when they are under the age of 18.

By the end of the twentieth century, almost 37 percent of all countries had abolished the death penalty for all crimes and all offenders.[24] By 2010, almost 50 percent of countries had abolished for all crimes and all offenders, children included.[25] Some of these countries had previously abolished the penalty only for child offenders. This group included Albania, Armenia, Australia, Azerbaijan, Bulgaria, Cook Islands, Denmark, France, Hungary, Italy, Latvia, Mauritius, the Netherlands, New Zealand, Paraguay, the Philippines, Poland, Romania, Rwanda, Serbia,[26] South Africa, Ukraine, the United Kingdom, and Uzbekistan. The profound shift in death penalty law and policy during the last half of the twentieth century is captured by the changes between the Nuremberg trials after World War II and the international criminal trials at the end of the century. When Uruguay objected to death sentences at the Nuremberg Trials, it was accused of sympathizing with the Nazis. In contrast, neither the recent international criminal tribunals, including those for the former Yugoslavia and Rwanda, nor the rules established for the International Criminal Court permit the penalty.[27]

With countries that fall into one of two sets or categories—those that abolished the death penalty altogether and those that abolished only for child offenders who commit their crimes when under the age of 18—both *in practice* end the death penalty for child offenders. However, states that abolished the penalty outright are of little use in an analysis of the child death penalty because it is not clear what motivations or collection of

23. Kiyoteru Tsutsui and Christine Min Wotipka, "Global Civil Society and the International Human Rights Movement: Citizen Participation in Human Rights International Nongovernmental Organizations," *Social Forces* 83, no. 2 (2004): 590.

24. Based on United Nations membership of 189 countries in 2000. The number of abolitionist countries was 69 in 2000.

25. Based on United Nations membership of 192 countries in 2010. The number of abolitionist countries for all crimes and all offenders was 95 in March 2010.

26. Serbia abolished for child offenders in 1992 as the Federal Republic of Yugoslavia.

27. Schabas, *The Abolition of the Death Penalty*, 1–2.

factors led to abolition. In these cases, it is not immediately evident that the protected status accorded to children or the special legal and cultural significance of childhood had any impact whatsoever on death penalty policy.

In contrast, when a state limits the penalty to those who commit their crimes when they are older than 18, it says something specific about that state's actions. First, the limitation creates a law and policy distinction between adults and children and may indicate a social and cultural distinction as well. Second, it signifies acceptance of the age 18 as a point of demarcation between childhood and adulthood. In short, the abolition of the death penalty for child offenders may suggest a widespread acceptance of societal responsibility for children and their actions, a responsibility not accepted for adult criminals. I say '*may*' because the legal limitation of the death penalty to criminals who commit their crimes when they are older than 18 actually says nothing *prima facie* about the motivations for or processes behind the reform. States may adopt these reforms for a host of reasons, including pressure from the international community, regional norms, or adherence to international law, in place of (or in addition to) ideas about children's vulnerability, need for protection, and reduced culpability for their actions.

In this book, I focus on several phenomena: First, I trace the international adoption of death penalty reforms for those under the age of 18, presenting data from all states that abolished for child offenders, including those that abolished the penalty for all crimes and all offenders. I map the arc of reform by identifying the global pattern of adoption, the diffusion of the norm against the child death penalty. Second, I consider this diffusion pattern in light of other historical events: colonialism, World War II, the wave of postwar democratization and decolonization, and the founding and development of international institutions. Third, I contextualize death penalty reform for children within movements toward children's rights in general. Finally, I select case studies that offer a window on the micro-level processes of death penalty reform for children and the motivations of states for abolition.

By restricting case study analyses to those states that abolished the death penalty only for child offenders under the age of 18, I can better target and examine the advent, spread, and acceptance of the norm against executing child offenders. While I recognize that some states that abolished the penalty for all crimes and all criminals may have been influenced by the norm against execution of child offenders, this broader phenomenon is beyond the scope of this book.

THEORIES OF NORMATIVE DIFFUSION

According to constructivists in international relations, norms have life-cycles consisting of stages of emergence, spread (or acceptance), and internalization. The emergence period is distinguished from the internalization period (or period of widespread adoption) by a stage of rapid spread and acceptance or support for the norm. This intermediate stage is commonly called the *cascade* or tipping point, when large clusters of norm adoption are observable.[28] States that do not adopt a norm during the cascade period are called *laggards*. This process of normative spread is known as diffusion, and there are many theories as to how norms diffuse, who diffuses them, the causal pathways of the different stages of diffusion, and why diffusion is often not entirely complete.

Norm Emergence

Constructivists and liberal theorists posit that norms emerge in particular cultures because of principled individuals who develop new ideas and successfully advocate for them in their communities.[29] As norms gain purchase, more individuals, groups, sectors, and communities adopt them, encouraging and influencing other communities, the state, and possibly even other states to adopt the norms as well. Sociological institutionalists have explored at length the process by which state institutional models have diffused internationally. Their findings suggest that domestic factors are most influential at early stages of the normative lifecycle and that they are less influential as norms spread.

Since liberal theories of international relations seek domestic explanations for international developments, these theories are especially suited to studies of norm emergence. Constructivist and liberal theories are, in fact, the *only* theories capable of explaining the emergence of norms. Although sociological institutionalists recognize that key parts of the global cognitive framework have their origins at the domestic

---

28. Martha Finnemore and Kathryn Sikkink, "International Norm Dynamics and Political Change," in *Exploration and Contestation in the Study of World Politics*, eds. Peter J. Katzenstein, Robert O. Keohane, and Stephen D. Krasner (Cambridge, MA: MIT Press, 1999).

29. Andrew Moravcsik, "The Origins of Human Rights Regimes"; Martha Finnemore and Kathryn Sikkink, "International Norm Dynamics"; Keck and Sikkink, *Activists Beyond Borders*.

level,[30] they do not offer a theory of emergence apart from the proposition that norms emerge from powerful Western cultures and are emulated by other actors. How, for example, can theories of emulation account for peripheral innovators, such as the Latin American states that abolished the death penalty in the nineteenth century? Realists as well have little to say about the emergence of a norm considered to be low politics and epiphenomenal to international organization.[31] Only constructivist and liberal theories account for the agency exercised by *norm entrepreneurs*, principled actors who create and push for the adoption of new norms.

One area of scholarship especially conducive to investigating norm emergence is political network theory,[32] with its focus on the relationship between norm emergence and power. Political network theory assesses the climate or environment for sociopolitical change, suggesting that the presence of principled actors or resonant issues creates "permissive"[33] or "enabling"[34] conditions for emergence. To understand how norms emerge, according to these theorists, researchers need to look at intra- and inter-network dynamics, network power and politics, the organizational structure of nongovernmental organizations (NGOs), and the ability of social movements to effectively target (or market to) more powerful actors.[35] While network

30. Tsutsui and Wotipka, "Global Civil Society," 589; Francisco O. Ramirez, Yasemin Soysal, and Suzanne Shanahan, "The Changing Logic of Political Citizenship: Cross-National Acquisition of Women's Suffrage Rights, 1890 to 1990," *American Sociological Review* 62, no. 5 (1997): 735–745; Wade M. Cole, "Sovereignty Relinquished? Explaining Commitment to the International Human Rights Covenants, 1966–1999," *American Sociological Review* 70, no. 3 (2005): 472–495; John W. Meyer, "Globalization: Theory and Trends," *International Journal of Comparative Sociology* 48, no. 4 (2007): 261–273; Emilie Hafner-Burton and Kiyoteru Tsusui, "Human Rights in a Globalizing World: The Paradox of Empty Promises," *American Journal of Sociology* 110, no. 5 (2005): 1373–1411.

31. Stephen D. Krasner, "Sovereignty, Regimes, and Human Rights," in *Regime Theory and International Relations*, ed. Volker Rittberger (Oxford: Clarendon, 1993).

32. I use the term "political network theory" to differentiate the literature in political science and sociology from the more established literature in physics, engineering, and computer science. In this sense, I utilize Wendy Wong's distinction between the "application" of network theory and an "extension" of network theory; she frames her study as the latter. See Wendy Wong, *Internal Affairs: How the Structure of NGOs Transforms Human Rights* (Ithaca, NY: Cornell University Press, 2012): 55.

33. R. Charli Carpenter, "Setting the Advocacy Agenda: Theorizing Issue Emergence and Nonemergence in Transnational Advocacy Networks," *International Studies Quarterly* 5, no. 1 (2007): 100.

34. Wong, *Internal Affairs*, 112.

35. Clifford Bob, *The Marketing of Rebellion: Insurgents, Media, and International Activism* (Cambridge, UK: Cambridge University Press, 2004); R. Charli Carpenter, "Setting the Advocacy Agenda"; R. Charli Carpenter, "Studying Issue (Non)-Adoption in Transnational Advocacy Networks," *International Organization* 61, no. 3 (2007): 99–120; David Lake and Wendy Wong, "The Politics of Networks: Interests, Power,

theory itself holds no allegiance to any particular school of thought in international relations, it is useful as a complement to constructivist efforts to understand how ideas develop and which successfully diffuse. Chapter 3 evaluates the principled activism that first led to the enactment of protections for child criminals and shows how an early or nascent network of intellectuals and child advocates fostered and diffused norms of child welfare and protection. Network theory is particularly useful for the study of the abolition of the child death penalty during the late period, when an international advocacy network successfully campaigned to end the penalty in the United States and elsewhere. This is discussed in more detail in chapters 5 and 6.

Norm Cascades

As stated, the early period of norm emergence and the later period of institutionalization are separated by a cascade—a time of rapid spread during which a critical mass of states adopt the new norm. Constructivists and sociological institutionalists contend that the cascade ushers in a new stage of widespread acceptance, whereby the primary motivation for states to adopt the law or norm is to emulate other states. A distinguishing quality of the cascade period is that states may adopt a norm even without domestic pressure to do so. Thus, the sole impetus for the adoption of a norm may be external, the result of international or regional pressure. Sociological institutionalists expect isomorphism across the system of states precisely because of cascades. They would expect that as the norm protecting child offenders from the death penalty continues to gain ground, the pressure on states that have not yet adopted the norm should increase, resulting in a cascade of legislative or policy spread and death penalty reform.

Sociological institutionalists argue that within world culture, there are 'scripts'—akin to norms in the international relations literature—that are created through the joint production of individuals, societies, and states.[36] Yet the contributions of members of world society and world polity[37] to

and Human Rights Norms," in *Networked Politics: Agency, Power, and Governance*, ed. Miles Kahler (Ithaca, NY: Cornell University Press, 2009): 127–150; Wong, *Internal Affairs*.

36. Frank J. Lechner and John Boli, *World Culture: Origin and Consequences* (Malden, MA: Blackwell, 2005): 44.

37. Sociological institutionalists consider world polity to consist of states and IGOs. World society consists of nongovernmental organizations (similar to what others may refer to as civil society). Cole, "Sovereignty Relinquished?" 480.

global scripts or norms are not adopted equally as part of world culture, as will be discussed, because members do not all exhibit the same degree of progress and justice—important measures of legitimacy in modern world culture.[38]

Sociological institutionalists further contend that between the end of the eighteenth century and the beginning of the twentieth century, certain profound changes took place in the international system. The world exhibited more unity, expressed symbolically through the drafting and development of international law, for example.[39] By the beginning of the twentieth century, a single world culture—one primarily "made in and by Europe"—had "coalesced."[40] Accordingly, for more than a century now, we have understood the world as a "unitary social system," "a singular polity" in which actors view the entire world "as their arena of action and discourse."[41]

By joining institutions committed to global ideals of progress and justice, states win legitimacy in world society and, as a result, are invited to participate in the global market and take part in elaborate ceremonies that celebrate a commitment to justice (often spoken of as human rights) and economic progress (often referred to as development), such as global forums and conferences. Through the cognitive frames of progress and justice, the goals of world society are thus diffused, triggering in states a desire for legitimacy and peer pressure to conform to global standards. This process makes the adoption of these goals and forms of organization 'appear' voluntary and, at times, even indigenous.

Interestingly, however, sociological institutionalists do not necessarily see this global peer pressure as requiring action, such as compliance with international human rights law, but often only as needing to 'appear virtuous' in order to gain legitimacy.[42] The need to appear virtuous to neighbors and other states in the international system (by ratifying the necessary treaties, for example), rather than to 'be virtuous' (by complying with the treaties ratified) explains, to some degree, the presence of laggards in the twenty-first century regarding the norm against the child death penalty. In fact,

---

38. Meyer, John, "The Nation as Babbitt: How Countries Conform," *Contexts* 3, no. 3 (2004): 43.

39. Lechner and Boli, *World Culture: Origin and Consequences*, 69–70.

40. Ibid., 65.

41. John Boli and George M. Thomas, *Constructing World Culture: International Nongovernmental Organizations since 1875* (Stanford, CA: Stanford University Press, 1999): 14.

42. Meyer, "Globalization: Theory and Trends," 264.

sociological institutionalists even *expect* laggards, a problematic position, as will be argued.

In the case studies of this book, state models and law and policy regarding children were originally adopted and implemented in British and French colonies through coercion. Sociological institutionalists have little to say about the coercive nature of colonialism as a method of diffusion.[43] As Martha Finnemore argues, "Violence is a fundamentally different mechanism of change than cognition."[44] Although sociological institutionalists recognize the unique role of the British Empire in shaping world culture, they tend to downplay the coercive nature of that process. Even considering that the violence inherent to the colonial enterprise preceded independence and that cognitive approaches can explain patterns of adoption in the postindependence and cascade periods, there remains an agency problem. The primary mechanism of diffusion for world society, cognitive processes, only applies after the initial violence of acculturation. Cognitive processes alone cannot explain the norm's spread.

Moreover, sociological institutionalists tend to underemphasize the role of law in the diffusion of world cultural models. For these theorists, law and national policy are seen as the dependent variable, as evidence of the isomorphism of state models.[45] Yet the case studies in this book demonstrate that legal diffusion is in fact a primary *method* of norm diffusion and that it should be recognized as an independent variable that can explain isomorphism both in state organization and in the values of newly independent states.

Coercion through law is likewise a different type of coercion than that theorized by realists; it is not material coercion like military power or economic pressure. Rather, it is a method of organizing society by determining permissible behaviors, legitimate petitioners (as subjects under law), contracts, and consequences. Only constructivists acknowledge this kind of power. Michael Barnett and Raymond Duvall suggest that many approaches in international relations suffer because they employ a too simple or narrow understanding of power derived from realist analysis.[46] Indeed, colonial power via law, according to Barnett and Duvall, is

---

43. Martha Finnemore, "Norms, Culture, and World Politics: Insights from Sociology's Institutionalism," *International Organization* 50, no. 2 (1996): 325–347.
44. Ibid., 343.
45. Meyer, "Globalization: Theory and Trends." John Meyer et al., "World Society and the Nation-State," *The American Journal of Sociology* 103, no. 1 (1997): 144–181.
46. Michael Barnett and Raymond Duvall, "Power in International Politics," *International Organization* 59, no. 1 (2005): 43.

compulsory and institutional, representing a direct form of power that works through the interactions of specific actors (the traditional way we understand power), and through the social relations that constitute the capacities of subjects (as either colonizers or the colonized), respectively.[47] Furthermore, a simplistic or inadequate conception of power is not limited to international relations scholars. Legal positivists likewise expect that international treaties and norms are meaningless because they lack means of coercion capable of securing compliance with international law.[48]

Legal diffusion also wields a "productive power" that is indirect.[49] Barnett and Duvall contend that productive power works by constituting "all social subjects with various social powers through systems of knowledge and discursive practices of broad and general social scope."[50] *Coercive socialization* through law, as a form of productive power, discursively produces legal subjects, attaches legal meanings, and defines the scope of judiciable actions.[51]

I argue that the mechanics of diffusion for the norm against the child death penalty are best understood through a hybrid of sociological institutionalist and agentic constructivist approaches.[52] Sociological institutionalists can explain the global spread of a particular model of childhood with similar or identical features, while constructivists can explain the unique type of power at work in coercive socialization. These schools of thought, however, disagree about the play of competing norms in the international system: Constructivists claim that norms compete and that some succeed over others because they are more persuasive, backed by powerful actors, better framed, or nested better within already adopted norms or because of the organizational structure and interaction

47. Ibid., 43–48.

48. Benedict Kingsbury, "The Concept of Compliance as a Function of Competing Conceptions of International Law," *Michigan Journal of International Law* 19, no. 345 (1998): 345–372; Anthony Clark Arend, Robert J. Beck, and Robert van der Lugt, eds., *International Rules: Approaches from International Law and International Relations* (Oxford: Oxford University Press, 1996); John Austin and Sarah Austin, *The Province of Jurisprudence Determined*, 2nd ed. (London: J. Murray, 1861–1863); John Austin and Wilfrid E. Rumble, *The Province of Jurisprudence Determined*, Cambridge Texts in the History of Political Thought (New York and Cambridge, UK: Cambridge University Press, 1995); John Austin, Robert Campbell, and Sarah Austin, *Lectures on Jurisprudence, or, the Philosophy of Positive Law*, 3rd ed. (London: J. Murray, 1869).

49. Barnett and Duvall, "Power in International Politics," 43.

50. Ibid., 55.

51. Ibid., 56.

52. Also known as liberal constructivism.

of networks that promote or oppose particular norms. This is certainly all true, but sociological institutionalists (and realists) would take these assertions further by claiming that the competition was rigged from the beginning.

A more significant point of contention, however, concerns agency. Human agency, for sociological institutionalists, is strictly limited. International NGOs and principled activists merely embody or carry out world culture by following established scripts. While sociological institutionalists grant actors a degree of agency by allowing them to "actively draw on, select from, and modify shared cultural models, principles, and identities," the choices available to these actors are few.[53] Although more recent efforts by sociological institutionalists have sought to address the agency issue,[54] a structural theory of diffusion, like traditional sociological institutionalism, cannot recognize the power of nonstate and non-Western actors against foundational Western ideas.[55] Our movements, ideals, goals, and achievements are forged out of and bound by existing world culture. We can innovate, but not create anew.

Other studies support this understanding of coercive diffusion. Carsten Anckar, one of the few social scientists to address the death penalty on a global scale through a cross-national, quantitative study, found that:

> Former colonies have simply incorporated the death penalty statutes of their former mother countries into their own legislation. The other explanation follows the same line of reasoning that applied to the discussion on the link between a history of slavery and the death penalty. The inhabitants of the colonies grew accustomed to the use of force and cruel punishments in the colonial era. . . .Of these two explanations, diffusion is probably more important.[56]

Although Anckar examines death penalty use rather than abolition, he agrees that statutes regarding the penalty were copied or adopted through emulation, and that states "grew accustomed" to the penalty

---

53. Boli and Thomas, *Constructing World Culture*, 18.
54. Meyer, "The Nation as Babbitt"; Tsutsui and Wotipka, "Global Civil Society."
55. Boli and Thomas, *Constructing World Culture*.
56. Carsten Anckar, *Determinants of the Death Penalty: A Comparative Study of the World*, Routledge Research in Comparative Politics 8 (London and New York: Routledge, 2004): 167.

through its practice, an argument that credits processes of socialization or habitualization.[57] Anckar's argument, taken together with
mine, suggests that colonial powers that used the child death penalty
diffused the penalty, and that those that abolished the penalty diffused
abolition.

The diffusion literature, predominantly coming out of international
relations and comparative politics, is useful for organizing the causal
mechanisms of law and policy cascades. There are three main schools of
thought in this area: the normative imitation (or emulation) approach
that houses both sociological institutionalists and constructivists; the
rationalist approach that typically includes neoliberal institutionalists and some "weak" constructivists (to cite Hasenclever et. al);[58] and a
cognitive-psychological approach that suggests that the use of cognitive
shortcuts may lead to suboptimal decision making and bounded ration-
ality.[59] There are also two principal 'classes' of mechanisms of diffusion,
learning and adapting, which straddle the three schools of thought, but
which fit most comfortably within a rationalist approach.[60] A fourth,
more recent, addition to the diffusion literature is network theory,
discussed below.

The problem with these typologies is that they tend to disregard
methods of diffusion that are both coercive *and* rely on the socializing
effects of policy adoption. Kurt Weyland, for example, makes a distinction between external pressure and domestic initiative, suggesting a
strict dichotomy between forces distinct from the state (such as international institutions), and those within it.[61] Yet Weyland's analysis is
not easily reconciled with the dynamic described in this book between
international and domestic forces. In my argument, domestic actors
(principled activists, norm entrepreneurs) pushed for the adoption of
protections for children before a global model of legitimate statehood
diffused. Once this model existed, it exerted a powerful pull on states

57. Ibid.

58. Andreas Hasenclever, Peter Mayer, and Volker Rittberger, *Theories of International Regimes*, vol. 55, Cambridge Studies of International Relations (Cambridge: Cambridge University Press, 1997).

59. Kurt Weyland, "Theories of Policy Diffusion: Lessons from Latin American Pension Reform," *World Politics* 57, no. 2 (2005): 262–295; Kurt Weyland, "The Diffusion of Innovations: How Cognitive Heuristics Shaped Bolivia's Pension Reform," *Comparative Politics* 38, no. 1 (2005): 21–42.

60. Zachary Elkins and Beth Simmons, "On Waves, Clusters, and Diffusion: A Conceptual Framework," *The Annals of the American Academy of Political and Social Science* 598, no. 1 (2005): 33–51.

61. Weyland, "Theories of Policy Diffusion."

to adopt policies respecting human rights, the rights of children included. Domestic actors of other states were then socialized to the rapidly globalizing model through legal acculturation to a Western system of rights and liberties. This process was not, strictly speaking, external and purely coercive; nor was it mere emulation. Rather, it was a combination of brute force (realism), socialization through law (constructivism), and the pull of an increasingly international model of legitimate statehood (sociological institutionalism and international legal theory). Yet the diffusion literature in international relations tends to ignore the first and second processes, and to gloss over the third. When normative considerations are taken seriously, as in the work of some rationalists, they tend to be utility-driven as opposed to ideologically based.[62] Other authors reduce normative approaches to the perception of legitimacy without investigating the genealogy of legitimacy (how certain state characteristics come to be perceived as legitimate at the expense of other characteristics) or the processes by which legitimacy derives its power.[63]

Liberalism and much of the literature on children and childhood do not explain well the process of international legal diffusion that led to the ban on the child death penalty. First, liberal theories of international relations suggest that domestic bargaining shapes policy outcomes, but there is no evidence that issues of child protection were a point of contention in colonialism, with one glaring exception: child marriage. The British, especially, but also the French, extended their civilizing mission to child brides, and passed a number of laws and protections throughout the colonies dictating the legal age of consent. This intrusion into family law, discussed in detail in chapter 4, met with considerable resistance, but was seen by the British (at least) as a necessary burden. The colonial powers enacted laws that raised the eligibility age for marriage for girls throughout the colonies, and all the countries here included as case studies maintained these age-based restrictions, give or take a year, after independence—in most cases, the age restrictions for marriage were *raised* shortly after independence.

Second, historians, psychologists, curricula and education scholars, and others have developed a young, yet thriving, scholarship on childhood and the history of the family. Drawing on the work of Hugh

---

62. Elkins and Simmons, "On Waves."
63. Weyland, "Theories of Policy Diffusion"; Weyland, "The Diffusion of Innovations."

Cunningham and Michael Anderson, we can create categories within this literature: the "sentiments" approach, the demographic approach, the socioeconomic approach, and (I would add another), the globalized childhood approach. First, a number of early scholars understood historical changes to childhood as changes in sentiment or attitude toward children.[64] Second, a demographic approach has sought to understand changes in families through changes in the age of eligibility for marriage and in family size over time.[65] Third, historians and social scientists have argued that socioeconomic factors played a critical role in the diffusion of protections for children around the globe.[66] Cunningham and others stress the structural opportunities of capitalism, especially wealth accumulation and competition among labor forces, to explain the introduction of protections for children.[67] In particular, Cunningham and others claim that compulsory schooling took away children's economic value and was the "key change which made possible the spread of the idea that all children should have a proper childhood."[68]

Like liberal theories in international relations, the scholarship of childhood and the family does little to explain the international isomorphism of law and policy related to children. An evolution of sentiment toward children cannot account for how most countries in the international system developed nearly identical child policies, although it may shed light on how changing attitudes in powerful states produced shifts in policy that were then forced upon other states. Demographic changes merely suggest convergence in (or divergence of) policies and family structure, and socioeconomic factors cannot explain how states with widely varied resources and levels of material wealth adopted similar state structures and policies toward children within one hundred years of one another. The globalized childhood approach, addressed in the next section, commonly draws on sociological institutionalist

---

64. Philippe Ariès, *Centuries of Childhood* (New York: Knopf, 1962); Norbert Elias, *The Civilizing Process*. vol. 1, *The History of Manners* (New York: Urizen, 1978); Lloyd De Mause, ed., *The History of Childhood* (New York: Psychohistory Press, 1974); Edward Shorter, *The Making of the Modern Family* (New York: Basic, 1975); Lawrence Stone, *The Family, Sex, and Marriage in England, 1500–1800* (New York: Harper & Row, 1977).

65. Cunningham, *Children and Childhood in Western Society since 1500*, 13.

66. Ibid.; Ferdinand Mount, *The Subversive Family: An Alternate History to Love and Family* (New York: Free Press, 1982).

67. Cunningham, *Children and Childhood in Western Society since 1500*.

68. Ibid., 203; Vivianna Zelizer, *Pricing the Priceless Child: The Changing Social Value of Children* (Princeton, NJ: Princeton University Press, 1994).

literature and suggests that the creation of a single, universal standard of childhood explains the isomorphism in law and policy toward
children as well as the problems in achieving positive, lasting change
for children.[69]

Network approaches to diffusion come closest to addressing the in-
tersection of power and socialization. David Lake and Wendy Wong
argue that disparities in power among and within networks are a
variable missing from the literatures on transnational advocacy networks and norms.[70] Elsewhere, Wong examines Amnesty International
as a scale-free network (a hub-and-spokes network), arguing that
Amnesty's particular combination of centralized agenda setting and
the enforcement of veto power with a decentralized system of campaign implementation (carried out by national sections) is the most
effective organizational structure for NGOs seeking to promote normative change.[71] In my research on the child death penalty, I found
that the British Empire, with its centralized bureaucracies and single,
common legal system, was highly effective in diffusing norms of child
welfare and protection. As chapter 3 illustrates, the British Empire
sought to create a single system of law and institutions throughout its
colonies, but allowed for minor variation to account for local cultural
contexts. Through the establishment of state institutions and administration addressing children, as well as through the creation of a legal
category of children, British colonialism diffused the norm abolishing
the child death penalty.

Finally, coercive socialization as a mechanism of diffusion did not occur
in every type of colonial enterprise. Spain, Portugal, and Belgium all abolished the child death penalty significantly *after* their colonies had ended
the penalty. John Gerard Ruggie's distinction between American *hegemony* and *American* hegemony is relevant here.[72] It was not hegemony that

69. Marianne N. Bloch, *Governing Children, Families, and Education: Restructuring
the Welfare State*, 1st ed. (New York: Palgrave Macmillan, 2003); Marianne N. Bloch,
Devorah Kennedy, Theodora Lightfoot, and Dar Weyenberg, eds., *The Child in the
World/the World in the Child: Education and the Configuration of a Universal, Modern, and
Globalized Childhood*, 1st ed. (New York: Palgrave Macmillon, 2006); Nikolas S. Rose,
Governing the Soul: The Shaping of the Private Self (New York: Routledge, 1990); Roberta
Lyn Wollons, *Kindergartens and Cultures: The Global Diffusion of an Idea* (New Haven,
CT: Yale University Press, 2000).

70. Lake and Wong, "The Politics of Networks: Interests, Power, and Human Rights
Norms," 127–150.

71. Wong, *Internal Affairs*, 25.

72. John Gerard Ruggie, "Multilateralism: The Anatomy of an Institution,"
International Organization 46, no. 3 (1992): 593.

explained the postwar institutional arrangement, but the particular hegemony of the United States.[73] Likewise, it was not *colonialism* that was responsible for the diffusion of norms of child protection, but the particular goals and concerns of the *British* and *French* colonial powers.

Laggards

After norms have diffused successfully, there are often a few laggards—or states that reject the norm and/or fail to comply with it entirely. Although sociological institutionalists expect hegemonic laggards and the "radical decoupling" of global models and state practices, this expectation presents a theoretical contradiction not easily reconciled.[74] Indeed, radical decoupling is exactly what we find in the international system with regard to human rights. Emilie Hafner-Burton and Kiyoteru Tsutsui found that:

> ... in no instance does state ratification of any of the six core UN human rights treaties predict the likelihood of government respect for human rights. Rather, state ratification of all six treaties has a negative effect on signatories' behavior: treaty members are more likely to repress their citizens than nonratifiers.[75]

Sociological institutionalists explain that social movements, like the movement for children's rights, are fueled by liberal ideas that may come out of the West, but that powerful actors (such as the United States) tend to resist core aspects of world culture.[76] Beth Simmons offers a more nuanced approach, suggesting in a study of international monetary affairs that states comply with international norms because of reputational concerns. Economics often factor in as well, as states face off against their neighbors for competitive advantage within a particular region.[77]

The theoretical contradiction of expecting hegemonic laggards is two-fold: First, if liberal ideas about children came from the West as sociological institutionalists claim, and these ideas were fashioned in part in

---

73. Ibid., 592.
74. Hafner-Burton and Tsusui, "Human Rights in a Globalizing World," 1383.
75. Ibid., 1398.
76. Meyer, "Globalization: Theory and Trends," 266.
77. Beth A. Simmons, "International Law and State Behavior: Commitment and Compliance in International Monetary Affairs," *American Political Science Review* 94, no. 4 (2000): 819–835.

the United States in particular, how can a theory of global emulation of Western ideas tolerate hegemonic laggards? Sociological institutionalists provide a structural approach to norm diffusion whereby norms or scripts are created and spread by powerful countries, especially by the hegemon. The presence of hegemonic laggards in this case suggests that sociological institutionalist theories are inadequate to explain the successful diffusion of the norm against the child death penalty. Second, sociological institutionalism attempts to explain both the role of the British and French, as global colonizers of the nineteenth and early twentieth centuries, in diffusing the norm, *and* the presence of hegemonic laggards such as the United States in the late twentieth century. But sociological institutionalism cannot account for both phenomena.

In effect, by expecting hegemonic laggards, sociological institutionalists seek to explain everything, and end up undermining their own approach to diffusion. If nothing could disprove a sociological institutionalist approach, then it is too adaptive as a theory of diffusion and cannot serve as a reliable guide to explain and understand the international system. I suggest instead that sociological institutionalism has much to offer as an interdisciplinary approach to diffusion, but that the school suffers from overreach. In particular, the expectation of hegemonic laggards through decoupling challenges the core assumptions of the theory and should be reconsidered.

Like sociological institutionalists, realists expect a compliance gap between international human rights law and state practice because human rights norms are epiphenomenal to states' interests.[78] Even legal scholars and neoliberal institutionalists suggest that states comply with human rights law and norms only when it is in their interest to do so, although proper management can aid cooperation with treaties and international regimes.[79] However, even though realists expect laggards, they do not expect hegemonic laggards, since realists propose that the normative framework in global society should reflect the goals and values of the

78. Krasner, "Sovereignty, Regimes, and Human Rights"; Hafner-Burton and Tsusui, "Human Rights in a Globalizing World," 1380.

79. Hafner-Burton and Tsusui, "Human Rights in a Globalizing World," 1377; Robert O. Keohane, *After Hegemony: Cooperation and Discord in the World Political Economy* (Princeton, NJ: Princeton University Press, 1984); George W. Downs, David M. Rocke, and Peter N. Barsoom, "Is the Good News About Compliance Good News About Cooperation," *International Organization* 50, no. 3 (1996): 379–406; Abram Chayes and Antonia Handler Chayes, "On Compliance," *International Organization* 47, no. 2 (1993): 175–205.

hegemon. Additionally, realists overlook the effects that human rights norms and law can have domestically through NGOs.[80]

Liberal theories also cannot account for the isomorphism of law and policy across the international system, since policy is thought to be based on state preferences.[81] Additionally, there is a great deal of scholarship that investigates the domestic use of the death penalty in the United States and elsewhere, much of which shares a theoretical kinship with liberalism. Case studies on the United States and other countries tend to examine the role of domestic factors, including social and cultural factors,[82] political institutions,[83] race relations,[84] and norms and identities.[85]

80. Hafner-Burton and Tsusui, "Human Rights in a Globalizing World," 1380–1381.

81. Moravcsik, "The Origins of Human Rights Regimes."

82. Michael Mitchell and Jim Sidanius, "Social Hierarchy and the Death Penalty: A Social Dominance Perspective," *Political Psychology* 16, no. 3 (1995): 591–619; Austin Sarat, *When the State Kills: Capital Punishment and the American Condition* (Princeton, NJ: Princeton University Press, 2001); Mark Peffley and Jon Hurwitz, "Persuasion and Resistance: Race and the Death Penalty in America," *American Journal of Political Science* 51, no. 4 (2007): 996–1012; David Jacobs and Jason T. Carmichael, "The Political Sociology of the Death Penalty: A Pooled Time-Series Analysis," *American Sociological Review* 67, no. 1 (2002): 109–131; Stephen Garvey, *Beyond Repair? America's Death Penalty* (Durham, NC: Duke University Press, 2003); Franklin E. Zimring, *The Contradictions of American Capital Punishment*, Studies in Crime and Public Policy (New York: Oxford University Press, 2003); David Jacobs and Stephanie L. Kent, "The Determinants of Executions since 1951: How Politics, Protests, Public Opinion, and Social Divisions Shape Capital Punishment," *Social Problems* 54, no. 3 (2007): 297–318; Frank R. Baumgartner, Suzanna De Boef, and Amber E. Boydstun, *The Decline of the Death Penalty and the Discovery of Innocence* (Cambridge and New York: Cambridge University Press, 2008).

83. See for example, Ellen Benoit, "Not Just a Matter of Criminal Justice: States, Institutions, and North American Drug Policy," *Sociological Forum* 18, no. 2 (2003): 269–294; Curtis A. Bradley, "The Juvenile Death Penalty and International Law," *Duke Law Journal* 52, no. 3 (2002): 485–557; David F. Greenberg and Valerie West, "Siting the Death Penalty Internationally," *Law & Social Inquiry* 33, no. 2 (2008): 295–343; Sangmin Bae, "The Death Penalty and the Peculiarity of American Political Institutions," *Human Rights Review* 9, no. 2 (2008): 233–240; Biko Agozino, "The Crisis of Authoritarianism in the Legal Institutions," *Journal of Contemporary Criminal Justice* 19, no. 3 (2003): 315–329; Paul Brace and Brent D. Boyea, "State Public Opinion, the Death Penalty, and the Practice of Electing Judges," *American Journal of Political Science* 52, no. 2 (2008): 360–372; Stephen F. Smith, "The Supreme Court and the Politics of Death," *Virginia Law Review* 94, no. 2 (2008): 283–383; Brent D. Boyea, "Linking Judicial Selection to Consensus," *American Politics Research* 35, no. 5 (2007): 643–670; Jacobs and Kent, "The Determinants of Executions since 1951"; Sangmin Bae, "The Right to Life vs. the State's Ultimate Sanction: Abolition of Capital Punishment in Post-Apartheid South Africa," *International Journal of Human Rights* 9, no. 1 (2005): 49–68; Sangmin Bae, *When the State No Longer Kills: International Human Rights Norms and Abolition of Capital Punishment*, SUNY Series in Human Rights (Albany, NY: State University of New York Press, 2007); Eric

Like constructivists, many international legal theorists expect compliance with international human rights law.[86] Law, for these theorists, represents a powerful normative framework that when endowed with legitimacy, can draw or "pull" states toward compliance, in a manner akin

Neumayer, "Death Penalty: The Political Foundations of the Global Trend Towards Abolition," *Human Rights Review* 9, no. 2 (2008): 241–268; Eric Neumayer, "Death Penalty Abolition and the Ratification of the Second Optional Protocol," *International Journal of Human Rights* 12, no. 1 (2008): 3–21.

84. See for example, Timothy V. Kaufman-Osborn, "Capital Punishment as Legal Lynching?" in *From Lynch Mobs to the Killing State: Race and the Death Penalty in America*, eds. Charles Ogletree Jr. and Austin Sarat (New York: New York University Press, 2006): 21–54; Charles Ogletree, Jr. and Austin Sarat, eds., *From Lynch Mobs to the Killing State: Race and the Death Penalty in America* (New York: New York University Press, 2006); Howard W. Allen, Jerome M. Clubb, and Vincent A. Lacey, *Race, Class, and the Death Penalty: Capital Punishment in American History* (Albany, NY: State University of New York Press, 2008); Amnesty International USA, *Killing with Prejudice: Race and the Death Penalty* (New York: Amnesty International USA, 1999); Barry C. Feld, *Bad Kids: Race and the Transformation of the Juvenile Court*, Studies in Crime and Public Policy (New York: Oxford University Press, 1999); Jesse Jackson, Jesse Jackson, Jr., and Bruce Shapiro, *Legal Lynching: The Death Penalty and America's Future* (New York: New Press, 2001); Carsten Anckar, *Determinants of the Death Penalty: A Comparative Study of the World*, Routledge Research in Comparative Politics 8 (New York: Routledge, 2004); James D. Unnever and Francis Cullen, "The Racial Divide in Support for the Death Penalty: Does White Racism Matter?" *Social Forces* 85, no. 3 (2007): 1281–1301; Mark Peffley and Jon Hurwitz, "Persuasion and Resistance: Race and the Death Penalty in America," *American Journal of Political Science* 51, no. 4 (2007): 996–1012; Jacobs and Carmichael, "The Political Sociology of the Death Penalty: A Pooled Time-Series Analysis"; Joe Soss, Laura Langbein, and Alan R. Metelko, "Why Do White Americans Support the Death Penalty?" *The Journal of Politics* 65, no. 2 (2003): 397–421; James D. Unnever and Francis T. Cullen, "Reassessing the Racial Divide in Support for Capital Punishment: The Continuing Significance of Race," *Journal of Research in Crime & Delinquency* 44, no. 1 (2007): 124–158.

85. See for example, Jeffrey Fagan and Valarie West, "The Decline of the Juvenile Death Penalty: Scientific Evidence of Evolving Norms," *Journal of Criminal Law and Criminology* 95, no. 2 (2005): 427–500; Zimring, *The Contradictions of American Capital Punishment*; Schabas, *The Abolition of the Death Penalty*; Benjamin D. Steiner, William J. Bowers, and Austin Sarat, "Folk Knowledge as Legal Action: Death Penalty Judgments and the Tenet of Early Release in a Culture of Mistrust and Punitiveness," *Law & Society Review* 33, no. 2 (1999): 461–505; Ridvan Peshkopia and Arben Imami, "Between Elite Compliance and State Socialisation: The Abolition of the Death Penalty in Eastern Europe," *International Journal of Human Rights* 12, no. 3 (2008): 353–372; Marika Lerch and Guido Schwellnus, "Normative by Nature? The Role of Coherence in Justifying the EU's External Human Rights Policy," *Journal of European Public Policy* 13, no. 2 (2006): 304–321; Bae, "The Right to Life vs. the State's Ultimate Sanction: Abolition of Capital Punishment in Post-Apartheid South Africa." Bae, *When the State No Longer Kills*; William Schabas, "Life, Death and the Crime of Crimes: Supreme Penalties and the ICC Statute," *Punishment & Society* 2, no. 3 (2000): 263–285; Katie Lee, "China and the International Covenant on Civil and Political Rights: Prospects and Challenges," *Chinese Journal of International Law* 6, no. 2 (2007): 445–474.

86. Chayes and Chayes, "On Compliance"; Louis Henkin and the Council on Foreign Relations, *How Nations Behave; Law and Foreign Policy* (New York: Published

o the power of domestic law over individuals.[87] According to the international legal scholarship, both domestic and international law function differently than many realists and legal positivists claim: For example, as demonstrated in chapter 6, individual states in the United States complied with compulsory education laws for children and other norms regarding children long before (sometimes fifty to one hundred years before) the federal government sought to enforce these laws. This suggests that norms of compulsory education in the United States were highly successful in shaping the behavior of individual states, in many cases decades before they were backed by coercion—a defining quality of domestic law and one notably lacking in international law. Since legal positivists are skeptical of law that lacks teeth, this finding suggests that even domestic law is not as dependent upon coercion as legal positivists argue. It may even suggest that international and domestic law have many mechanisms in common.

THE CHILD AND THE STATE

The abolition of the death penalty for child offenders under the age of 18 was part of a larger and longer-term trend of law and policy reform to protect children. The protection of children *in law* first emerged in the West around the sixteenth century—in the form of regulation of poor and vagrant children as well as laws governing apprenticeships in England—but protections greatly increased both in force and scope in the nineteenth and twentieth centuries.[88] This reformist trend was in turn part of a

for the Council on Foreign Relations [by] F.A. Praeger, 1968); Harold Koh, "How Is International Human Rights Law Enforced?" *Indiana Law Journal* 74, no. 4 (1999): 1397–1417; Harold Koh, "Review Essay: Why Do Nations Obey International Law?" *Yale Law Journal* 106, no. 8 (1997): 2599–2659; Thomas M. Franck, *Fairness in International Law and Institutions* (New York: Oxford University Press, 1995); Thomas M. Franck, "Legitimacy in the International System," *The American Journal of International Law* 82, no. 4 (1988): 705–755; Martha Finnemore and Stephen J. Toope, "Alternatives To 'Legalization': Richer Views of Law and Politics," *International Organization* 55, no. 3 (2001): 743–758.

87. Franck, "Legitimacy in the International System." On the other hand, Jack Goldsmith and Eric Posner argue that while compliance may offer reputational benefits, a state's reputation will not necessarily be important for compliance. See Jack L. Goldsmith and Eric A. Posner, "A Theory of Customary International Law," *University of Chicago Law Review* 66, no. 1113 (1999): 1113–1177.

88. In Britain, see the 1536 Apprenticing of Parish Poor Children (27 Hen. VIII, c. 25); the 1562 Apprenticeship under the Elizabethan Statute of Artificers (5 Eliz., c. 4); the 1572 Poor Law Act (14 Eliz., c. 5); the 1601 Further Provision for Apprenticing Pauper Children (43 Eliz., c. 2); and the 1661 Poor Relief Act (13 & 14 Car. 2, c. 12).

broader pattern of humanistic reform in Western societies that also produced a specific type of liberal state after the Enlightenment.[89] The goal
of the liberal state was national progress, defined principally by economic
growth (and driven by the harnessing of available resources for profit and
gain), and, eventually, by a higher quality of life for the state's citizens.[90]

A global trend in national policies toward progress and justice naturally
shaped the application of the death penalty. Types of torture accompany-
ing the penalty were limited in the West in the latter half of the eighteenth
century,[91] and death penalty reform began in earnest in the nineteenth
century, as many states, especially in Latin America, abolished the penalty for all crimes and all offenders. States also began to limit the penalty
by age in the nineteenth century. As discussed, in the United Kingdom
(and in states that inherited or were influenced by its legal system), the
penalty was limited to those older than seven, or 14 if *mens rea* or intent
could not be demonstrated. Many states in Europe, especially, raised the
age of eligibility for the penalty to 16 by the early twentieth century, as
did many colonies of the United Kingdom and France.[92]

A new wave of colonialism in the nineteenth and early twentieth centuries demanded a broadening of the idea and application of rights from the
national to the universal in order to confer legitimacy on the colonial enterprise.[93] Nineteenth-century colonialism was justified under the guise
of spreading 'civilization'; a prelude to this effort was a return to thinking

89. Cole, "Sovereignty Relinquished?" 473; Jack Donnelly, *Universal Human Rights in Theory and Practice*, 2nd ed. (Ithaca, NY: Cornell University Press, 2003).

90. Meyer, "The Nation as Babbitt," 43.

91. Lynn Hunt, *Inventing Human Rights: A History* (New York: W.W. Norton, 2007): 76.

92. Bahamas (17), Bahrain (14), Bangladesh (16), Barbados (16), Belgium (16), Bulgaria (17, later 21), Burma (16), Cape Verde (16), Ceylon (16), Chile (16), China (16), Columbia (12 before abolition in 1910), Comoros (16), Cyprus (16), Democratic Republic of the Congo (16), Egypt (16, then 17), Figi (16), France (16), Gambia (16), Ghana (16), Greece (14, later 15 and 16), Grenada (7, later 16), Guinea (13), Guyana (16), Honduras (16), Hong Kong (16), Iran (9 and 15), Irish Free State (16), Israel (17), Jamaica (16), Japan (16), Liberia (16), Luxemburg (16), Madagascar (16), Malaysia (16), Mauritania (16), Mauritius (16), Morocco (16), North Korea (17), Nyasaland (16), Poland (17), Qatar (16), Seychelles (16), Somaliland (16), Southern Rhodesia (16), St. Vincent and Grenadines (16), Tanganyika (16), Thailand (15), Togo (16), Trinidad (16), United Kingdom (16), Virgin Islands (16), Zaire (15), and Zanzibar (12). This list was compiled from UN data from Human Rights Commission reports and from Amnesty International's archives in Boulder, Colorado, as well as from reports from Save the Children Fund: Edward Fuller, *The International Handbook of Child Care and Protection*, vol. 3 (London: Longman, 1928); Edward Fuller, *The International Year Book of the Child Care and Protection*, vol. 2 (London: Longman, 1925).

93. Anthony Pagden, "Human Rights, Natural Rights, and Europe's Imperial Legacy," *Political Theory* 31, no. 2 (2003): 171–199.

of rights in terms of the laws of nature, such that cultures that did not exhibit the same norms or customs held by 'civilized' people could be "dispossessed by those who do."[94] The result was that rights could only be understood within the context of 'civilization,' as defined by the Europeans, and by a particular political order, representative government.[95] This trend toward universalism was still limited, however, by citizenship in a state. As such, the laws of nature could be applied to the colonies, via the expansion of colonialism, but the colonized themselves had no say in the matter.

The dual goals of progress and justice were made explicit in the colonialism that defined the period: British and French colonialism were justified on these pillars. Empires would acquire colonies and (ostensibly) prepare them for entry into the global market, while harvesting their resources to enrich themselves. These empires also felt a duty to confer cultural 'enlightenment' through the imposition of Christianity and metropolitan customs, norms, and values. This was the civilizing mission, and it involved children in important ways, as will be seen.

Death penalty practice provides an interesting lens through which to examine colonialism's civilizing mission. The British, for example, used the death penalty in their colonies to instill fear and the rule of law. But apart from the Mau Mau rebellion—when an anticolonial force in British East Africa rose up against the British in the 1950s—they were careful to distance themselves from the act of capital punishment.[96] The British were sensitive to criticism of the death penalty and its savage nature and sought to sanitize it through reforms, even while complete abolition was being sought at home.[97] These pressures originated from the metropole, or mother country, because "those who believed themselves to be civilized had a duty not to behave towards 'backwards' or 'barbarian' peoples in a cruel and 'inhuman' manner."[98] In other words, the British had to walk a fine line between fear and charity.

It was precisely this unsustainable conflict between the need to instill fear and to demonstrate imperial benevolence that led both to the demise

---

94. Ibid., 183–184.
95. Ibid., 190.
96. Stacey Hynd, "Killing the Condemned: The Practice and Process of Capital Punishment in British Africa: 1900–1950s," *Journal of African History* 49, no. 3 (2008): 416.
97. Ibid., 417.
98. Pagden, "Human Rights," 191.

of the British Empire in Africa and to the protection of children. Both the British and French empires felt growing pressure from their citizens to do more for the people of the colonies, and this pressure especially concerned young girls who were in "moral danger."[99] Compulsory marriage, genital mutilation, and child marriage upset metropolitan sensitivities and ultimately forced colonial governments to intervene in traditional and family law, something they had long sought to avoid.[100] Colonial intervention in family law further inflamed tensions between the colonizers and the colonized. After World War II, colonialism was exposed as morally bankrupt, and its disintegration meant that a new international order was needed, one based on human rights that could be ensured *against* states or regimes.

The Liberal State and the Child

The development of a liberal state devoted to national progress and the welfare of its citizenry was aided by the promotion of the natural and social science in the nineteenth and twentieth centuries. The emergence of a professional class of scientists as well as a preoccupation with objectivity through scientific methods in the nineteenth century drove efforts toward progress in the liberal state.[101] These experts claimed the ability to separate the normal from the abnormal, the desirable from the undesirable, and the moral from the amoral.[102] As a result, a single standard of normality emerged that allowed states to develop national policies to ensure the 'normal' and to address the 'abnormal' child.

In delineating a class of persons, the model of childhood fostered by Europeans and Americans was co-constitutive of ideas about how children should be treated. As concerns were raised by child advocates

99. Saheed Aderinto, " 'The Girls in Moral Danger': Child Prostitution and Sexuality in Colonial Lagos, Nigeria, 1930s to 1950," *Journal of Humanities and Social Science* 1, no. 2 (2007): 1–22.

100. Antoinette Burton, "From Child Bride To 'Hindoo Lady': Rukhmabai and the Debate on Sexual Respectability in Imperial Britain," *The American Historical Review* 103, no. 4 (1998): 1119–1146; Laurent Fourchard, "Lagos and the Invention of Juvenile Delinquency in Nigeria," *Journal of African History* 46 (2006): 115–137; Ann L. Stoler, "Making Empire Respectable: The Politics of Race and Sexual Morality in 20th-Century Colonial Cultures," *American Ethnologist* 16, no. 4 (1989): 634–660.

101. Bloch, *Governing Children*; Lorraine Daston and Peter Galison, "The Image of Objectivity," *Representations* 40 (1992): 81–128.

102. Bloch, *Governing Children*, 16.

(increasingly in the nineteenth century but also much earlier) about child abuse and neglect, the state intervened. The new interest in child welfare validated and institutionalized ideas about childhood as a vulnerable period of life when children need protection, structure, and guidance. Protection came in the form of statutes that outlawed abuse and neglect; structure and guidance were provided by educational institutions, reformatories, industrial schools, church, and, decreasingly, places of employment.

State institutions were established to determine the extent of abuse and neglect and the required manner of intervention. Abuse and neglect, however, were difficult to gauge without benchmarks. Child advocates, quick to use science to inform their actions, encouraged and supported the attention paid to children by science. Doctors established guidelines for nutrition, hygiene, welfare, and psychological well-being.[103] Social scientists developed curricula; investigated the effects of child labor; and advanced theories about children's distinct nature. Developmental psychology "offered new, scientifically constructed indices by which 'normal development' could be quantitatively as well as qualitatively distinguished from the 'subnormal' or 'abnormal.'"[104] These guidelines progressively became part of the dogma of childhood as competing norms, especially those not legitimized by science, were discarded.

Michel Foucault's work on "biopower" is useful for understanding the relationship between the child and the state.[105] Biopower can be understood as the effort to control life in order to maximize individual potential. According to Foucault, biopower began with measures to monitor the life process through birth and death registrations.[106] The use of the death penalty, Foucault suggests, was replaced by other means of controlling the body.[107] Controlling the processes of life required justification by science and the establishment of state institutions to monitor populations.[108]

103. Harry Hendrick, *Children, Childhood and English Society, 1880–1990* (Cambridge, UK: Cambridge University Press, 1997): 12; Karen Baistow, "From Sickly Survival to the Realisation of Potential: Child Health as a Social Project in Twentieth Century England," *Children & Society* 9, no. 1 (1995): 22.

104. Baistow, "From Sickly Survival," 26–27.

105. Michel Foucault, *The History of Sexuality*, vol. 1. *An Introduction*. Translated by Robert Hurley (New York: Vintage Books, 1981).

106. Michel Foucault, *The Birth of the Clinic: An Archeology of Medical Perception* (London: Routledge, 1963): 211; David Armstrong, "The Invention of Infant Mortality," *Sociology of Health and Illness* 8, no. 3 (1986): 211–232.

107. Foucault, *The History of Sexuality*, 140.

108. Ibid., 144; Baistow, "From Sickly Survival," 21.

In line with theories of agentic constructivism, standards of behavior toward children evolved as ideas about childhood evolved. One of the principal ideas that developed in the West in the nineteenth and early twentieth centuries was that children were less culpable for the crimes they commit and should not be given adult penalties such as the death penalty. As scientific methods to study children were applied outside the West, the global model of childhood began to crystallize. Western studies of children in the periphery provided support for the contention that all children experience the same stages of development, and have the same requirements for good health, education, leisure, and need for labor restrictions.[109]

The state became the most competent diffuser of norms in general. Network theory suggests that certain types of organizational structure are particularly conducive to successful norm diffusion, and a centralized state developing standards of childhood across institutions worked to spread a single and increasingly complex model of childhood.[110] Eventually, a model of childhood was constructed, predominantly in the West: the model of a global child with the same needs, abilities, desires, and limitations regardless of citizenship. Yet the idea that childhood is a social construction says little about how it came to be the particular social construction enshrined in state and international law today or about how a specific aspect of the model, such as reduced culpability, came to be integral to our understanding of children's capacities. Sociological institutionalists have argued that since all states share the goal of economic progress, they are highly susceptible to new ideas about how best to achieve this progress.[111] A focus on children as a tool of development became common in the nineteenth century, as states such as England and France recognized a connection between children's health and the ability of the empire to win wars.[112] The interest in children and childhood also served the goal of progress, as educating and caring for children as the heirs of the nation

109. Bloch, "The Child in the World"; Erica Burman, "Developing Differences: Gender, Childhood and Economic Development," *Children & Society* 9, no. 3 (1995): 121–141; Satadru Sen, "The Orphaned Colony: Orphanage, Child and Authority in British India," *Indian Economic & Social History Review* 44, no. 4 (2007): 463–488; Satadru Sen, *Colonial Childhoods: The Juvenile Periphery of India 1850–1945* (London: Anthem, 2005); Satadru Sen, "A Separate Punishment: Juvenile Offenders in Colonial India," *The Journal of Asian Studies* 63, no. 1 (2004): 81–104; Satadru Sen, "A Juvenile Periphery: The Geographies of Literary Childhood in Colonial Bengal," *Journal of Colonialism and Colonial History* 5, no. 1 (2004).

110. Wong, *Internal Affairs.*

111. Meyer, "The Nation as Babbitt," 43.

112. Baistow, "From Sickly Survival."

came to be seen as a sound investment in the stability and prosperity of the state. By the 1960s, a focus on children as a key part of national development had become global wisdom.

Children were also a tool of empire, as missionaries, travelers, and scientists used Western ideas about children and families to measure the "'civilization' and 'culture,' and the 'nature' of primitive families and childhood in exotic places."[113] According to Marianne Bloch, in her research of curricula, studies of children in the colonies and other cultures outside the West "produced 'new' types of 'advanced' and 'progressive' knowledge about childhood, the family, and schooling" that resulted in the discovery of "universal truths" about children and their development.[114] Satadru Sen has shown in his studies of juvenile orphanages and reform schools in nineteenth- and twentieth-century India that the children in government facilities became the subjects of countless studies and experiments designed to identify the core, natural, universal child by separating the child from his or her racial identity.[115] In a study of the British in Nigeria, Laurent Fourchard argues that the establishment of the Social Welfare Office in 1941 created juvenile delinquents as a distinct group of criminals.[116] The colonial administration and judicial system in Nigeria actually "legislated 'juvenile delinquency' into existence."[117] Moreover, the construction of juvenile delinquency and the preoccupation with the 'moral danger' of young girls was not unique to Nigeria or even to the British colonies, as "special judicial machinery for the 'treatment of juvenile offenders' was also established" in the empires of the French, Belgians, and Portuguese in the 1940s and 1950s.[118]

By the twentieth century, the model of childhood diffused to the colonies was age-specific, meaning that it was not defined by behavior, ritual, race, class, status, or gender, but rather by age alone. The age of 18 became widely accepted as the upper age limit of childhood in criminal codes after World War II, and this boundary was extended to areas of child protection even outside criminal matters. The model of childhood that took shape after World War II was not initially one that bestowed many rights upon children, but rather one that imposed duties upon adults. Children were, however, important to national identity, considered vulnerable and in

113. Bloch, *The Child in the World*, 16.
114. Ibid.
115. Sen, "The Orphaned Colony"; Sen, *Colonial Childhoods*; Sen, "A Separate Punishment"; Sen, "A Juvenile Periphery."
116. Fourchard, "Lagos and the Invention of Juvenile Delinquency in Nigeria," 115.
117. Ibid., 116.
118. Ibid.

need of care, and were increasingly seen as less culpable for their actions than adults.

The acculturation of colonies to Western norms and legal systems, carried out most extensively by the French in Algeria, included an inherent logic of state consolidation of authority over citizens, including children. Laws prohibiting the child death penalty were commonly found in criminal codes, and the British took the lead in standardizing criminal procedures and sanctions. At independence, many former colonies had laws prohibiting the death penalty for child offenders under the age of 18. These colonies maintained after independence, at least initially, the state organizational structure they had inherited, including the prohibition of the child death penalty and other protections for children. Many even increased protections for children in the first few decades of statehood. These states had internalized aspects of the colonial state model that not only recognized the validity of children's protection, but also could not imagine a solution to issues of child welfare outside of law. They were, in effect, socialized to predominantly Anglo-French ideas of child protection (including protection from adult criminal penalties), and to the role of the state in guaranteeing it.

The widespread standardization of the treatment of young criminals by the British (especially) helped cast the model of childhood that would form the basis for the international children's rights regime in the second half of the twentieth century. The same connection between children's welfare and civilization, made explicit in the British and French colonial enterprises, was used by international governmental organizations (IGOs) and international NGOs to promote a particular type of development that emphasized a single, common standard for children's education, health, and welfare, a standard that came to include the norm against the death penalty for child offenders.

CHAPTER OVERVIEW

Over the next six chapters, I examine the global diffusion of the norm against executing child offenders. In chapter 2, I present my dataset, along with an evaluation of key findings in the diffusion and death penalty literatures as well as a summary of the dominant mechanisms of diffusion—or the mechanisms to which the norm's adoption can be principally attributed. In chapter 3, I focus on the early adoption of the norm through the English and French case studies—and determine that the primary mechanism of diffusion in these states was the work of principled domestic actors.

In chapter 4, I examine the effects of colonialism and legal acculturation on the former colonies of Algeria, Kenya, Tanzania, and Tunisia,
and the influence of the West on the enactment of protections for children in Japan and Ethiopia. I argue that legal acculturation was the main
socializing mechanism in these states to Western ideas of childhood. In
chapter 5, I use the case studies of UNICEF and Amnesty International to
demonstrate how international law and institutions spread the Western
construction or model of childhood to developing states and how the child
death penalty was chosen as a human rights campaign at the turn of the
twentieth century. Chapter 6 evaluates the role of laggards through an
examination of the cases of the United States, Pakistan, and China. In
chapter 7, I consider limitations to the global model of childhood, assess
ongoing issues of compliance with norms of child protection, and discuss
critical theory approaches to children's human rights.

CONCLUSION

International law on children's rights, in important ways, usurps state
authority over the ideology of childhood, establishing complicated and
exacting standards that all states should adopt. Although international
law concerning children lacks an enforcement mechanism, it nonetheless serves as a means of confronting states about their child policies and
forces them to address these norms as they participate in international
institutions. The international community's enshrinement of children as
rights holders and consolidation of power over the boundaries and standards of childhood mirror international consolidation of human rights in
general after World War II, as the international community increasingly
became the arbiter of acceptable treatment of citizens by states.

Although I am certain that the idea of childhood did *not* originate in the
West, as at least some type of recognition of the differences between very
young children and adults appears to be common across cultures, it is evident that numerical, age-based legal norms about children diffused globally from the West. The British and French, in particular, advocated for
and enforced legal norms against the child death penalty in their colonies.
These norms expressed ideas about the nature of children that formed
the basis of a model of childhood. This model, characterized by the immaturity, vulnerability, and reduced culpability of children; by the upper
age limit of 18; and by a relationship between the state and the child in
which the state assumed responsibility for the child's welfare, became the

international model found in the 1990 CRC and advanced by UN agencies such as UNICEF.

After World War II, children became part of the civilizing rhetoric of the international community, and the rapid postwar decolonization and democratization helped to spread protections for children, even though international law was slow to develop in this area. An international children's rights regime began modestly with the series of conventions and declarations about children and with the ICCPR in the 1960s and 1970s, and was then bolstered and broadened in scope with the ratification of the CRC in the 1990s. The development of rights and protections for children in international law meant that states no longer had complete control over the way children were treated. Childhood was now an international idea. In a very real way, the state was divested of full authority over children, since state policies and practices were now seen as a legitimate international concern.

The shift in authority over children from the state to the international community marked the completion of a greater and more gradual pattern of divestment from the father, who was sovereign of the family, to the state, and finally from the state to the international community. This power over childhood is ideological. By articulating standards of childhood, the international community assumes the power to define childhood, which includes identifying areas of protection, setting the scope of protections, identifying violations of those protections, and establishing processes of adjudication when violations occur. This postwar pattern, whereby the international community took ideological control over the content, scope, and measure of human rights norms and principles, created what would become the modern rights regime.

CHAPTER 2

✿

Data and Case Selection

INTRODUCTION

In this book, I track the diffusion of the global norm against the death penalty for child offenders through national law and legal histories. Law serves many purposes in society, as discussed in chapter 1, but most importantly for this study, it is a clear and binding expression of norms, values, policies, or procedures. While states generally have excluded different classes of people from punitive measures through various means, the exclusion of children under a specific age from the death penalty *in law* communicates shared and specific ideas about childhood and the limits of child culpability. Written law in particular is compulsory in a way that oral law or social understanding may not be, and it is durable: While written laws can be subsequently repealed, revoked, or annulled, they are nonetheless indelible, leaving a permanent trace of their passage or enactment. For these reasons, among others, I trace the cascade of the norm abolishing the child death penalty through law, and through written law specifically.

The dataset that I have compiled includes all the states for which I have verifiable dates of abolition and/or laws or cases. These dates refer to the *first instance* of the abolition of the death penalty for child offenders, usually found in penal codes or in codes of criminal procedures, although these can also be found in national case law or in the accession of previous codes and laws by newly formed states. Although both general abolition and abolition of the death penalty solely for child offenders serve to end the penalty for child offenders in practice, only the latter is useful for researching trends in norms regarding children.

The norm against the child death penalty spread rapidly through the international system, becoming firmly institutionalized by 2005. Efforts to trace this progression are made difficult by the paucity of research on children outside of the West, in general, and on child offenders and the death penalty, in particular. It is therefore nearly impossible to determine precisely how many child offenders have been put to death by their respective governments. Many governments themselves, NGOs, and academics did not keep records of these deaths prior to the 1970s and 1980s, when human rights NGOs such as Amnesty International began to take an interest in the subject.[1] This chapter will explore some of the theories cited in chapter 1, including my claims of how the norm abolishing the death penalty for child offenders diffused globally.

METHODOLOGY

When a state chooses to restrict its application of the death penalty, it can do so in many ways: First, it can limit the penalty by abolishing it for classes of people, such as women; second, for types of crimes; third, by age, such as for children or the elderly; and fourth, for all crimes and all offenders (general abolition). When a state chooses this route—general abolition—it can be difficult to pinpoint the motivation behind the policy change. In contrast to abolition for child offenders only, the motivation behind general abolition may be less clear or unknown. However, since general abolition applies to children, the outcome is the same: The state has stopped executing children. This study therefore includes both states that abolished the penalty altogether and those that abolished it only for child offenders, albeit in different ways.

To analyze the legal diffusion of the norm against the child death penalty, I first had to compile its history. I created three datasets. The first is

---

1. Save the Children Fund conducted research into the child death penalty in the 1920s and found ten countries that had abolished the penalty for child offenders under the age of 18. These states were all in Europe: Albania, Belgium, Bulgaria, Czechoslovakia, Estonia, Germany, Latvia, Lithuania, Switzerland, and Hungary. However, Save the Children did not supply names or dates of passage of these laws. The data are therefore difficult to confirm. Edward Fuller, *An International Yearbook of Childcare and Protection* (London: Longmans, 1925); Edward Fuller, *The International Handbook*, vol. 3 (London: Longmans, 1928); Edward Fuller, *The International Year Book*, vol. 2 (London: Longmans, 1928); Edward Fuller, *The Right of the Child: A Chapter in Social History* (London: Victor Gollancz, 1951).

the list of states that abolished the death penalty for all crimes and all offenders (general abolition). Second is the list of states that abolished the penalty for child offenders *only*, regardless of whether they would later abolish the penalty outright. This second list required the identification of the date of the case or code by which states *first* excluded child offenders under the age of 18 from the penalty. I looked at national penal and criminal codes in the nineteenth and twentieth centuries and examined the development of death penalty jurisprudence as it (most commonly) narrowed over time to apply only to adults convicted of violent (and usually deadly) crimes.

These national laws express a key characteristic of modern childhood, namely, that age is an identifier of childhood, and that childhood is bound by age limits. In particular, these laws employ the age of 18 as the upper age limit of childhood, the *modern* point of demarcation between children and adults. At this age or above, criminal offenders may be treated as adults and become eligible for adult penalties. The cases and codes included in this second list employ the age limit of 18 in their death penalty statutes, without qualification such as intent or *mens rea*. Primary source material was used where possible, insofar as it (or a reliable translation) could be found in French, Spanish, or English. Some legal codes are simply not available in American libraries, thus limiting the research.

Third, I compiled the complete universe of cases that includes the dates when states first abolished the child death penalty *plus* dates for general abolition, minus any duplication. If, for example, a state abolished the child death penalty in 1933 and then abolished the penalty outright in 1965, as happened in the United Kingdom, only the 1933 abolition was counted. Altogether, this third dataset consists of 137 states since the mid-nineteenth century that either abolished the penalty specifically for child offenders under the age of 18 or banned the penalty for all crimes and all offenders. It was also from the smaller dataset (states that abolished only for child offenders) that I drew my cases, since this type of abolition conveyed a particular intention regarding children and their protection from adult criminal penalties.

A highly unusual feature of the diffusion pattern for the norm against the child death penalty is its *two cascades*—two periods of rapid adoption— as presented in Figure 2.1. The second cascade is larger than the first, with more states adopting the norm and a higher rate of adoption.

Beginning in the 1960s, a first cascade of states outlawed the penalty for child offenders (either by limiting the penalty to those 18 and older or by abolishing it outright). This trend was driven by the decolonization that took place around the globe at this time, as almost half of states that

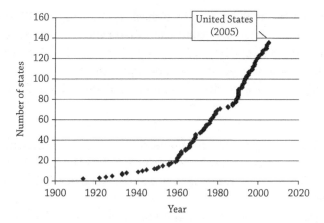

Figure 2.1 The Number of States that Abolished the Death Penalty for Child Offenders, by Year.
This figure includes both general abolition and abolition for child offenders only. Illustration reproduction courtesy of Sage Publications.

abolished during this period were recent colonies or trustees. Following a brief pause in this abolitionist trend, from 1982–1984, the second cascade began in 1985 and ended in 2005. The data suggest that the period after 2005 can be thought of as the late period of norm diffusion, or the period when the norm abolishing the child death penalty has been widely adopted or institutionalized. Even though more states could ban the child death penalty, the norm had successfully cascaded by the late period and been enshrined as international law.

From the smaller dataset of states that abolished the death penalty solely for child offenders, I selected case studies according to the time period in which states abolished, taking into account geographical diversity and colonial history. The history of childhood outside of the West is a grossly underresearched area, which, when compounded with another underresearched area (the child death penalty), results in many hurdles to accurate historical information. Accordingly, my choice of case studies (especially those of former colonies) was also based on the availability of material. These case studies include *early adopters*—states that abolished between 1863 and 1959—(Ethiopia, France, Japan, Tunisia, and England); *first cascade adopters*—1960–1981—(Algeria, Kenya, and Tanganyika/Tanzania); and *second cascade adopters* and *laggards*—1985–2005—(China, Pakistan, and the United States).

With the datasets collected and the norm's lifecycle mapped, I then organized these states into categories by dominant mechanism of diffusion—or the mechanism to which the norm's adoption can be principally attributed. I determined these mechanisms of diffusion based on the findings of the case studies and their types of law (common, civil, religious); colonial influence; temporal period of abolition; and participation in international legal regimes and institutions.

Through the case studies, three mechanisms of diffusion became evident:

1. *Principled activism*: Primarily domestic (but also cross-national) principled actors petitioned states for changes in law and for policies of child protection. Cases: France, Japan, Pakistan, England, and the United States
2. *Coercive socialization*: British and French colonialism led to the forced adoption of child protection laws in some colonies and to the legal acculturation that followed. Cases: Algeria, Kenya, Tanganyika/Tanzania, Tunisia, and Japan (under US occupation)
3. *Globalized childhood*: Western norms about children in terms of age, development, maturity, and competence became a universal model applied to children in all states, economies, and cultures after World War II. This model derived its authority from the natural science and later, from the social science and international law. Cases: China, Pakistan, the United States

In addition, there was one outlier, Ethiopia, which underwent a process of *voluntary socialization*, whereby the country's leaders enthusiastically invited Western legal scholars to draft laws that included restricting the death penalty to those 18 and older, as discussed in more detail below.

Although the causal mechanisms listed above correspond roughly with the temporal periods of early-, cascade-, and late-period adoption, this book is organized by mechanism of diffusion. This method offered a more efficient way of presenting the findings, as different mechanisms of diffusion were evident across periods. Furthermore, there was no period—early, cascade, or late—that was associated with a single mechanism (See Figure 2.2), although some were more commonly found in certain periods. For example, coercive socialization was more important during the cascades (1960–2005) than in any other period. Principled activism was critical to diffusion in both the early and late periods of the norm's lifecycle.

Finally, the book traces the model of childhood as it diffused internationally through *law*—specifically, criminal law addressing child offenders, usually those convicted of murder or rape. Legal diffusion may be

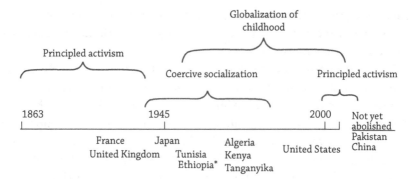

*Ethiopia is an example of 'voluntary socialization,' as discussed in the text above.

Figure 2.2 Case Studies by Date and Mechanism of Diffusion.
Illustration reproduction courtesy of Sage Publications.

different from other types of diffusion. Law gives us important information about a state's attitude toward children by revealing the parts of
childhood the state chooses to regulate. The exclusion of criminal offenders from the death penalty based on age sends a powerful message of
protection for children, as the ban applies to all children, murderers and
rapists included.

DATA

Based on data from the archives of Amnesty International USA, reports
to the UN Human Rights Committee (HRC), and the Committee on the
Rights of the Child, and research into penal and criminal procedure codes,
I found that at least 137 countries have national laws prohibiting the
death penalty for child offenders. Although there are other cross-national
legal studies of childhood, these studies tend to examine national constitutions, which is less complicated than examining national legislation, as
this can be difficult to compile, translate, and analyze, and may employ
diverse legal terminology.[2] Moreover, norms about children and childhood tend to emerge in domestic legislation long before they appear in
national constitutions. The scarcity of literature on children and the death

2. See for example, John Boli-Bennett and John W. Meyer, "The Ideology of
Childhood and the State: Rules Distinguishing Children in National Constitutions,
1870–1970," *American Sociological Review* 43, no. 6 (1978): 800.

penalty required me to rely on data and information collected by NGOs like Amnesty International to measure compliance with the norm against the child death penalty.[3]

It is worth pointing out some of the broad contours of the database, which, as stated, consists of the first instance when states abolished the death penalty for child offenders. States did this either through general abolition or through abolition specifically for those under the age of 18 (or even older). In my database of 137 countries, presented in Table 2.1, seventy-four abolished solely for child offenders either *in lieu of* general abolition or *before* general abolition. An additional sixty-three states abolished the penalty for all crimes and all offenders without first abolishing for child offenders. Another seventeen states have abolished since 2005, when abolition by the United States cemented the norm's place in international law. These seventeen states are: the Philippines (2006), Albania (2007), Cook Islands (2007), Kyrgyzstan (2007), Rwanda (2007), Argentina (2008), Uzbekistan (2008), Burundi (2009), Togo (2009), Gabon (2010), Latvia (2012), Benin (2012), Mongolia (2012), Madagascar (2012), Chad (2014), Fiji (2015), and Suriname (2015).[4]

The data support the finding that the norm abolishing the child death penalty has been institutionalized throughout the world, even

---

3. As such, I assume that countries that have national legislation are in compliance with that legislation unless evidence is discovered to the contrary. Some states, like Iraq and Nigeria, adopted legislation many decades ago and may have been compliant at one time. I have left these states (those that might not have been compliant in the second cascade, but that abolished during an earlier period) in the database, since their adoption of laws abolishing the death penalty for child offenders, usually shortly after independence, says something about the national mood, the zeitgeist surrounding independence, and the acceptance of international norms. Other states, like Pakistan, Sudan, and China, have adopted laws restricting the application of the penalty according to different age limits more recently (during the second cascade), but have continued to execute child offenders under the age of 18 and therefore are not included in the dataset. Moreover, since this dataset draws heavily on UN reports, these dates are taken from the self-reporting of countries, replete with all of the problems this system entails. Whenever possible, I have searched for supporting documentation to increase confidence in these reports. Overall, I have found few examples of false reporting. However, when I did find evidence that calls into question the veracity of UN reports or Amnesty documents, I excluded these states from the dataset. See Amnesty International, "Stop Child Executions!" (New York 2006; reprint). Hands Off Cain reports that Pakistan executed a child offender in 2004. Hands Off Cain, "The 2005 Report," http://www.handsoffcain.info/bancadati/index.php?tipotema=arg&idtema=6000633; Amnesty International, "USA: Supreme Court Outlaws Executions of Child Offenders" (New York 2005; reprint). The report can be found in AIUSA archives at UC Boulder, now at Columbia University.

4. A number of these states—Albania, Benin, Latvia, Madagascar, the Philippines, Rwanda, and Uzbekistan—had previously abolished for child offenders.

Table 2.1 LIST OF STATES THAT ABOLISHED THE DEATH PENALTY FOR CHILD OFFENDERS UNDER THE AGE OF 18, WITH DATES OF ABOLITION IN LAW; WHERE (G) MEANS GENERAL ABOLITION OR ABOLITION FOR ALL CRIMES AND ALL OFFENDERS.

VENEZUELA (G)	1863
SAN MARINO (G)	1865
COSTA RICA (G)	1877
BRAZIL (G)	1882
ECUADOR (G)	1906
France	1906
URUGUAY (G)	1907
COLOMBIA (G)	1910
Paraguay	1914
PANAMA (G)	1922
Trinidad	1925
ICELAND (G)	1928
United Kingdom	1933
Mauritius	1935
Italy	1941
Lebanon	1943
Denmark	1945
Japan	1949
Jamaica	1951
Grenada	1953
HONDURAS (G)	1956
Tunisia	1956
Ethiopia	1957
Nigeria	1959
Azerbaijan	1960
Ghana	1960
Kuwait	1960
Ukraine SSR	1960
Armenia	1961
New Zealand	1961
Tanganyika	1961
Madagascar	1962
MONACO (G)	1962
USSR	1962
Tanzania	1964
Uganda	1964
Sierra Leone	1965
Algeria	1966
DOMINICAN REPUBLIC (G)	1966

(continued)

Table 2.1 CONTINUED

Gambia	1966
Cameroon	1967
Kenya	1967
AUSTRIA (G)	1968
Bulgaria	1968
Jordan	1968
Belarus	1969
Benin	1969
Poland	1969
VATICAN CITY STATE (G)	1969
Israel	1971
FINLAND (G)	1972
SWEDEN (G)	1972
Australia	1973
Czechoslovakia	1973
Hungary	1973
Egypt	1974
Iraq	1974
Syria	1974
Bahrain	1976
PORTUGAL (G)	1976
United Arab Emirates	1976
Yemen People's Republic (south)	1976
Albania	1977
Rwanda	1977
Congo	1978
Netherlands	1978
Romania	1978
LUXEMBOURG (G)	1979
NICARAGUA (G)	1979
NORWAY (G)	1979
Sri Lanka	1979
Cook Islands	1980
CAPE VERDE (G)	1981
Singapore	1985
Vietnam	1985
GERMANY (G)	1987
HAITI (G)	1987
LIECHTENSTEIN (G)	1987
South Korea	1988
Barbados	1989
CAMBODIA (G)	1989
SLOVENIA (G)	1989

(continued)

Table 2.1 CONTINUED

Tunisia	1989
ANDORRA (G)	1990
CROATIA (G)	1990
CZECH REPUBLIC (G)	1990
IRELAND (G)	1990
MOZAMBIQUE (G)	1990
NAMIBIA (G)	1990
SAO TOME AND PRINCIPE (G)	1990
SLOVAK REPUBLIC (G)	1990
South Africa	1990
MACEDONIA (former Yugoslav Republic) (G)	1991
ANGOLA (G)	1992
Former Republic of Yugoslavia	1992
Peru	1992
SWITZERLAND (G)	1992
GUINEA-BISSAU (G)	1993
Myanmar	1993
Philippines	1993
Russia	1993
SEYCHELLES (G)	1993
Uzbekistan	1994
Zimbabwe	1994
DJIBOUTI (G)	1995
MOLDOVA (G)	1995
North Korea	1995
SPAIN (G)	1995
BELGIUM (G)	1996
GEORGIA (G)	1997
Indonesia	1997
NEPAL (G)	1997
Tanzania	1997
CANADA (G)	1998
ESTONIA (G)	1998
Latvia	1998
LITHUANIA (G)	1998
Tajikistan	1998
TIMOR-LESTE (G)	1999
TURKMENISTAN (G)	1999
UKRAINE (G)	1999
COTE D'IVOIRE (G)	2000
India	2000
MALTA (G)	2000
BOSNIA-HERZEGOVINA (G)	2001

(continued)

Table 2.1 CONTINUED	
CYPRUS (G)	2002
MONTENEGRO (G)	2002
SERBIA (G)	2002
St. Vincent and the Grenadines	2002
Thailand	2003
BHUTAN (G)	2004
GREECE (G)	2004
SAMOA (G)	2004
SENEGAL (G)	2004
TURKEY (G)	2004
MEXICO (G)	2005
USA	2005

Table reproduction courtesy of Sage Publications.

though more states may yet ban the practice. The norm's globalization is evident because customary law now applies to the penalty and because very few states have executed child offenders in the twenty-first century. Moreover, with abolition by the United States in 2005, legal scholars and laggard states no longer challenge the norm's status of *jus cogens*, meaning that the norm is now the subject of such widespread international consensus that it does not require states to have signed a treaty or convention in order to be bound by it, that it "permits no derogation," and that it can only be modified by the emergence of a new norm "of the same character" and caliber.[5] Once a norm becomes *jus cogens*, it is preemptory, and it immediately renders all treaties in contradiction with it void.

What is clear from the research conducted by human rights organizations since the late twentieth century is that there is de facto abolition of the death penalty for child offenders in most countries, save for the handful of laggards discussed below. Thus, even though my research identified 137 states that have national laws or judicial decisions prohibiting the child death penalty, *almost no states apply the penalty regardless of whether they have a national ban in place.* The overwhelming compliance with the norm even in the absence of law enshrining it underscores its global legitimacy.

5. David Weissbrodt, Joan Fitzpatrick, and Franck Newman, *Human Rights: Law, Policy, and Process*, 3rd ed. (Anderson, 2001): 23.

Table 2.2 EARLY ADOPTERS (IN
ORDER OF ABOLITION).

Venezuela	United Kingdom
San Marino	Mauritius
Costa Rica	Italy
Brazil	Lebanon
Ecuador	Denmark
France	Japan
Uruguay	Jamaica
Colombia	Grenada
Paraguay	Honduras
Panama	Tunisia
Trinidad	Ethiopia
Iceland	Nigeria

Additionally, there is one state, Mexico, which likely abolished the penalty for child offenders under the age of 18 before 1960, although I do not have an exact date of abolition.

Diffusion of Abolition of the Death Penalty for Child Offenders

The diffusion of the norm against the child death penalty can be divided into three periods—early, first cascade, and second cascade, as described in chapter 1. Each of these is taken in turn below.

Early Period: Norm Emergence

Laws abolishing the death penalty for child offenders under the age of 18 were first codified in the national laws of Venezuela, San Marino, Costa Rica, and Brazil in the nineteenth century. These first adopters would be joined in the early period by a wide variety of states from around the world (see Table 2.2), before the period ended in 1959 and the first norm cascade began.

Social scientists and legal theorists that study diffusion argue that states that adopt norms early tend to be influenced by domestic actors, or norm entrepreneurs, who campaign to spread new ideas or norms within the state.[6] These actors and entrepreneurs build and foster relationships and connect with one another, creating networks of support that facilitate

---

6. Finnemore and Sikkink, "International Norm Dynamics"; Cass Sunstein, *Free Markets and Social Justice* (New York: Oxford University Press, 1997); Ramirez, Soysal, and Shanahan, "The Changing Logic of Political Citizenship."

the spread of new ideas in society, and among legislators and institutions. Norm entrepreneurs are more likely to be successful if their society is democratic and tolerates the influence of nongovernmental actors on issues of government policy.

The First Cascade

As stated in chapter 1, a norm's development from emergence to acceptance or institutionalization is separated by a threshold period, commonly called a norm cascade, when "a critical mass of relevant state actors adopt the norm."[7] Social scientists cite a number of explanations for cascades, including international pressure or recent political transition. For abolition of the child death penalty, the norm cascades twice, first from 1960–1981 and then from 1985–2005. See Figure 2.1 for a visual depiction of this phenomenon. These two cascades have different features, including different regional clustering. The first cascade occurred mainly in Africa and the Middle East and appears to have been triggered primarily by the sweeping decolonization and democratization that took place in the 1960s and 1970s, as well as by the ideological cascades in the former Soviet Union. The second cascade exhibits regional clustering in Europe and occurred in response to the fall of the Soviet Union and the rise of the European Union as a new moral authority.

There are other points of difference between the cascades. The first cascade was a period of particularly rapid adoption. In the twenty-one years between 1960 and 1981, forty-nine states and territories abolished the penalty for child offenders (through specific measures for child offenders or for all offenders)—more than twice as many as abolished in the previous ninety-six years. The list of first cascade adopters is presented in Table 2.3.

The Second Cascade

The second cascade occurred between 1985 and 2005. States that abolished the child death penalty during the second cascade are listed in Table 2.4.

As for cause, I suggest that this second cascade was the result of a unique sequence of events: the third wave of democratization (as documented by

---

7. Sunstein, *Free Markets and Social Justice*, 38; Finnemore and Sikkink, "International Norm Dynamics," 255.

Table 2.3 FIRST CASCADE ADOPTERS
(IN ORDER OF ABOLITION).

Azerbaijan	Vatican City State
Ghana	Israel
Kuwait	Finland
Ukraine SSR	Sweden
Armenia	Australia
New Zealand	Czechoslovakia
Tanganyika	Hungary
Madagascar	Egypt
Monaco	Iraq
USSR	Syria
Tanzania	Bahrain
Uganda	Portugal
Sierra Leone	United Arab Emirates
Algeria	Yemen People's Republic (south)
Dominican Republic	Albania
Gambia	Rwanda
Cameroon	Congo
Kenya	Netherlands
Austria	Romania
Bulgaria	Luxembourg
Jordan	Nicaragua
Belarus	Norway
Benin	Sri Lanka
Poland	Cook Islands
	Cape Verde

Ten additional states likely abolished during the first cascade, but I do not have specific dates and/or laws for them. These are: Afghanistan, Botswana, Georgia, Guyana, Guernsey, Lesotho, Libya, Samoa, St. Lucia, and Swaziland.

Samuel Huntington) beginning in 1973; the fall of the Soviet Union in 1989 and the independence of former Soviet states; and the rise and expansion of the European Union. Moreover, as the Cold War fizzled, security and military concerns decreased, allowing for human rights issues and humanitarian reform to figure more prominently in state policy. In 1990, nine states abolished the death penalty for child offenders, more so than in any other year in history; all of these except South Africa chose to abolish for all crimes and all criminals.

As mentioned earlier, there are an additional eight laggard states that are not in compliance with international law abolishing the penalty for child offenders, meaning that they maintain the penalty in practice

Table 2.4 SECOND CASCADE ADOPTERS (IN ORDER OF ABOLITION).

Singapore	Slovak Republic	Djibouti	India
Vietnam	South Africa	Moldova	Malta
Germany	Macedonia (former	North Korea	Bosnia-Herzegovina
Haiti	Yugoslav Republic)	Spain	Cyprus
Liechtenstein	Angola	Belgium	Montenegro
South Korea	Former Republic of	Georgia	Serbia
Barbados	Yugoslavia	Indonesia	St. Vincent
Cambodia	Peru	Nepal	Thailand
Slovenia	Switzerland	Tanzania	Bhutan
Tunisia	Guinea-Bissau	Canada	Greece
Andorra	Myanmar	Estonia	Samoa
Croatia	Philippines	Latvia	Senegal
Czech Republic	Russia	Lithuania	Turkey
Ireland	Seychelles	Tajikistan	Mexico
Mozambique	Uzbekistan	Timor-Leste	USA
Namibia	Zimbabwe	Turkmenistan	
Sao Tome and Principe		Ukraine	
		Cote D'Ivoire	

In addition to these sixty-four second-cascade states, there are another six states that likely abolished the child death penalty during the period, but for which I do not have exact dates: Brunei Darussalam, Kyrgyzstan, Mauritania, Morocco, Tonga, and Turks and Caicos.

(according to Amnesty International). These are: China, the DRC, Iran, Iraq, Pakistan, Sudan, Saudi Arabia, and Yemen.[8] Additionally, Gaza's Hamas government likely executed Hani Abu Aliyan (a child offender) in early October 2013. Constructivist scholars, especially, vigorously debate the reasons that laggard states ultimately comply with international law and norms, suggesting causes ranging from international soft pressure to hegemonic coercion to the intrinsic power of international law.[9]

Trends in the Data

The diffusion pattern both for general abolition and for child offenders *only* is compared with the complete universe of cases in Figure 2.3.

8. Amnesty International, "Executions of Juvenile Offenders since 1990," 2007, http://www.amnesty.org/en/death-penalty/executions-of-child-offenders-since-1990.
9. As an example: John Gerard Ruggie, "What Makes the World Hang Together?" *International Organization* 52, no. 4 (1998): 855–885; Franck, "Legitimacy in the International System"; Krasner, "Sovereignty, Regimes, and Human Rights."

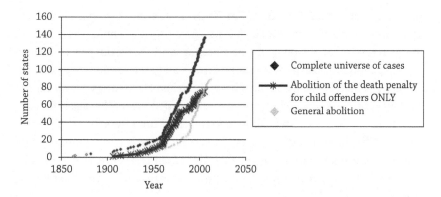

Figure 2.3 The Number of States that Abolished the Death Penalty for Child Offenders Only; the Number that Abolished in General; and the Complete Universe of Cases (States that Abolished in General and Those that Abolished for Child Offenders Only), by Year.
The complete universe of cases used in this figure consists of 137 states. This includes states that abolished for the child death penalty only, as well as those that abolished in general. However, this total excludes states that abolished in general if they first abolished for the child death penalty. In other words, I used the date of first abolition in the complete set of cases. For "abolition of the death penalty for child offenders ONLY," I used the seventy-four states listed in Table 2.1. For general abolition, I used the eighty-nine states that abolished for all crimes and all offenders from 1863–2012, even if they had previously abolished for the child death penalty. This was done to accurately reflect the cascade of general abolition apart from the cascade of abolition for child offenders.

The data mapped in Table 2.1 and Figure 2.3 permit a couple of observations: One, in contrast to other cases of norm diffusion, the first states to abolish the death penalty for child offenders did so by abolishing for all crimes and all criminals (general abolition), arguably the most radical type of abolition. The trend began in Venezuela, San Marino, Costa Rica, Brazil, and Ecuador, and in a handful of other countries that followed shortly afterward. Ramirez et al. argue, in their study of the diffusion of the norm of women's suffrage, that suffrage was first extended to men in most states and was only later extended to women, until a point was reached when most states that introduced suffrage automatically conferred it on both women and men.[10] This is the typical progression of human rights norms: First, they are narrowly granted to some social groups (the most vulnerable, elites, dependents, etc.) before being offered more broadly to the population at large.[11]

The diffusion of the norm against the death penalty for child offenders progressed differently, however. First, it began in Latin America in the nineteenth century with general abolition for all crimes and all offenders. It then narrowed in the mid-twentieth century to apply to child offenders

10. Ramirez, Soysal, and Shanahan, "The Changing Logic of Political Citizenship."
11. See Lynn Hunt for a broad survey of this trend. Hunt, *Inventing Human Rights*.

only (from about 1933 until 1978). Then, in the last two decades of the twentieth century and into the twenty-first century, there was a sudden spike in general abolition again, as states around the world, particularly in Europe, abolished the penalty for all crimes and all offenders in quick succession. In fact, seventeen states have abolished the penalty for all crimes and all offenders since the United States ended the child death penalty in 2005; no state has since abolished for child offenders alone. This pattern of diffusion during and after the second cascade corresponds to that seen in Ramirez et al.'s study on suffrage, when over time states broadly conferred the franchise on both men and women, rather than extending it piecemeal.

Another observation from the data is that when the complete universe of cases is divided into two categories, general abolition and abolition solely for child offenders, it is apparent that the norm abolishing the penalty for child offenders cascaded two to three decades *before* the norm of general abolition (see Figure 2.1). There are different possible explanations for this phenomenon: The norm cascade in the 1960s and 1970s abolishing the child death penalty might have foretold more radical abolition later in the century. The notion of limitations to the penalty serving as prelude to total abolition could have played out in a couple of different ways: One, excluding children from the penalty might have underscored the penalty's inhumanity, leading some states to abolish outright. Two, limiting the penalty to adults might have braced a skeptical public for later, more wholesale, reforms. Another possible explanation for the sequence of cascades, with general abolition trailing abolition of the child death penalty, is that the trend toward general abolition that began in the early 1990s was primarily the result of a single regional cascade, the outcome of European convergence on the death penalty and other human rights issues. This regional cascade can be attributed to many causes, including the fall of the Soviet Union and the integration of the European Union and other regional institutions. I found evidence that all of these developments partly explain the cascade of general abolition beginning in the 1990s.

Finally, the norm against the death penalty for child offenders is particularly interesting because the trend itself began in the periphery, in Latin America in the nineteenth century. The hegemon at the time, the United Kingdom, and one of the most powerful states, France, adopted the norm relatively early in the first third of the twentieth century, but were not the norm's places of origin. Peripheral emergence provides a challenge to theories of international relations, law, and sociology that suggest the West should lead norm emergence and drive diffusion.

STAGES OF DIFFUSION

The following sections will present the primary mechanisms of diffusion for the norm against the child death penalty: principled activism, coercive socialization, and the globalization of childhood. I will also discuss laggards, or states that resisted or rejected the norm.

Principled Activism

The norm against the death penalty for child offenders emerged through the efforts of child advocates and death penalty opponents in a handful of countries in the nineteenth and twentieth centuries. The movement was especially strong in England, where norm entrepreneurs served as government ministers, social workers, intellectuals, scientists, and lawyers, although I found comparable evidence of activism in France, Japan, and the United States. These norm entrepreneurs advanced ideas about children's vulnerability, need of care, and reduced culpability under law. As described in chapter 1, these conclusions about children were justified by scientific studies on the nature, characteristics, and capabilities of children, studies that diagnostically separated 'normal' from 'abnormal' childhood and legislated accordingly.

Concern for the treatment of child offenders was also part of the broader humanistic trend toward progress and justice, since children represented the future of the nation as well as reflected its sense of compassion and its regard for the welfare of its citizens. Reforms for children in England, for example, came out of state reforms that limited the authority of the monarchy and the ruling class, and prescribed change in numerous aspects of society, including its penal system.

Although principled activism for children was present in all of the cases, it was especially important for early and late adopters. Some late adopters like the United States and Pakistan required additional late-stage principled activism against the child death penalty to bring these states closer to compliance with international law and with the globalized model of childhood.

In the US case, the combination of two distinct mechanisms of diffusion—principled activism and the globalization of childhood—is attributable to the United States' unique history of child protection efforts. Under the leadership of child advocates, the United States became a laboratory for the development of norms of child protection in the late nineteenth and early twentieth centuries, especially in the area of juvenile justice, before losing ground as the twentieth century progressed.[12] The pattern of US diffusion then came full circle, with a new generation of domestic activists applying pressure in the late twentieth century for compliance with the international norm against the child death penalty. These activists successfully leveraged the global model of childhood, which included the ban on the penalty for child offenders.

The necessity of principled actors in both the early and late periods of the norm's diffusion attests to the power of agency by both individuals and NGOs in ideational spread and challenges highly structural theories of global sociopolitical change. Yet principled actors are not themselves sufficient to produce change. Both Charli Carpenter and Wendy Wong, for example, have shown that principled actors and worthy causes create the enabling conditions for norm emergence but do not, on their own, account for the emergence of particular norms.[13] Indeed, as chapters 3 and 5 discuss, principled actors and organizations mobilized networks of intellectuals, NGOs, lawyers, politicians, and activists to secure protections for child criminals. The passage of child-protective laws and policies in England, France, the United States, and Pakistan demonstrates the power of networks to advance new norms.

Coercive Socialization

The colonies of the British and French underwent a process of *coercive socialization*, whereby norms, law, and rubrics of state organization were diffused to them. The British and French established bureaucracies that administered colonial law and drafted and enforced public policy based on their own legal principles. These laws and policies specified the relationship between the state and the child, one that would include criminal sanctions. In the four Middle Eastern and North African cases (Algeria, Kenya, Tanzania/Tanganyika, and Tunisia), I found four steps of coercive socialization that were not necessarily linear: First, the British and French colonial powers built bureaucracies that allowed them to efficiently achieve their goals, primarily the goals of progress (wealth accumulation) and justice (*mission civilisatrice* or the white man's burden).

---

12. Robyn Linde, "From Rapists to Superpredators: What the Practice of Capital Punishment Says about Race, Rights and the American Child," *International Journal of Children's Rights*, 19, no. 1 (2011): 127–150.

13. Carpenter, "Setting the Advocacy Agenda," 100; Wong, *Internal Affairs*, 112.

The second step of coercive socialization was a form of legal imperialism, whereby the British and French enforced laws derived from their own legal systems in which *individuals* were the central legal subjects. As stated, the British were especially motivated to develop a single criminal code and procedure throughout their colonies. French colonial law was much more complicated. It varied to a far greater extent by colony, time period, offence, and offender. In some cases, French law was applied directly to the colony; in others, there were a number of different legal sources for a particular area.

Third, child law and policy developed, straddling disparate areas of law, government, and custom. Invariably, these laws and policies produced a relationship between the state and the child that would eventually (in many former colonies) usurp parental, tribal, or community power over children. Law governing children's lives developed primarily in two areas: criminal law and family law. Restrictions to the death penalty by age were typically found in criminal codes or criminal procedure codes and, with a brief lag of a few decades in some cases, eventually reflected the penalty's age limit in the metropole. Family law mandated birth and death registrations and regulated marriage, divorce, and child support. Although both the British and the French were hesitant to impinge upon family law, they eventually did so to some degree.

Fourth, colonial society was socialized over time to the goals of the British and French colonial powers (to the twin goals of progress and justice); to the method of state organization (bureaucracy); and to other predominantly Western legal norms. These societies were thus socialized to the authority of the state over children and to the various protections and guarantees that state authority entailed, prohibitions of the child death penalty among them. Evidence for socialization is found in the choice by many colonies to continue the protections for children begun under the empire, and even to increase them upon independence. Although some countries, such as Tunisia and Tanzania, would eventually revoke some of these protections, this reversal would not come until later.

One case study, Japan, had some similarities with the colonial cases. Under occupation after World War II, Japan reformed its criminal law based largely on its occupiers' Anglo-American legal systems. The occupation period resulted in an unprecedented number of legal advisers that set out to reconstruct the Japanese state and reshape its legal practices.[14]

---

14. Weixia Chen, "The Death Penalty in Japan and China: A Comparative Study" (MA thesis, University of California, 2003): 52–53.

Although different in circumstances from the colonial cases, Japan's acculturation to Anglo-American legal norms (but not the common law system) was nonetheless coercive. Although the child death penalty had at the time only been abolished in England and not in the United States, Japan's abolition of the penalty corresponded with child protection trends in the West in general and complemented child protection efforts from Japan's prewar history.

Coercive socialization through law and state organization is not the typical way we understand coercion or socialization in international relations. Legal coercion is different from military force or economic aid. Law imposes a society's values; defines legitimate and illegitimate behavior; creates social units and levels of authority; and, to a degree, establishes the agency of actors within the system by recognizing (or failing to recognize) their legal status as individuals (or groups) with a given identity. In my study, I found that the British and French colonial powers established an identity for children apart from that of their parents, kin, clan, religion, and even gender in Algeria, Kenya, Tanzania/Tanganyika, and Tunisia. The legal category 'child,' as a Western construction, was universal and applied equally (in law) to all children below the age of 18 in these colonies. Although law as a type of coercion may seem less distasteful or violent at first blush than other forms of coercion, it can be more powerful than an occupying force. By defining and organizing social relations in the Western image, colonial powers socialized the colonies in a way that dictated, to a large degree, their structure and characteristics after independence.

As mentioned, there was one anomalous case study, Ethiopia. The norm of abolition in Ethiopia diffused through a process best thought of as *voluntary socialization*, whereby the state proactively sought out Western aid in the development of its legal system. The postwar period was a vibrant time of legal development in Ethiopia, with the drafting of a new constitution and six codes in the decade that followed.[15] The penal code, which included the ban on the child death penalty, had numerous foreign influences. Large parts of the code, for example, were based on the US Constitution.[16]

---

15. J. Vanderlinden, "Civil Law and Common Law Influences in the Developing Law of Ethiopia," *Buffalo Law Review* 16 (1966–1967): 257; Stanley Z. Fisher, *Ethiopian Criminal Procedure: A Sourcebook* (Addis Ababa, Ethiopia: Haile Selassie University, 1969): ix.

16. Franklin F. Russell, "The New Ethiopian Penal Code," *American Journal of Comparative Law* 10 (1961): 267.

Through colonialism and the diffusion of Anglo-French law, legal systems, and principles, children were given a place in the state order as individuals. State authority over children usurped parental, clan, kinship, or tribal control and created children as legal subjects that were equal to one another under the law throughout the state. As these laws and policies created child subjects in the image of the metropolitan child, the beliefs of child advocates and a growing corps of specialists that *all* children possess the same nature, needs, and characteristics were confirmed. This evolving consensus on the common nature of children reinforced the efforts of international institutions, such as UNICEF, to make children a prominent part of development initiatives and inspired the modern movement for international children's rights that would begin in the 1970s. Former colonies of the British and French thus entered an international system in which the only legitimate model of statehood was the Western liberal model that created children as legal subjects; advanced the notion of a universal childhood; established the state (and increasingly, the international community) as the rightful guardian of children's interests; and affirmed the role of the fast developing international community in promoting and securing children's welfare.

Globalized Childhood

In the second half of the twentieth century, the global model of childhood—based on the consensus on children's universal vulnerability, limited culpability, and need of care in several areas—became more complex and specific. The diffusion of this model of childhood occurred on many levels. First, an increasingly global community of child advocacy and a set of norms protecting children emerged through early-twentieth-century efforts by organizations such as the League of Nations and the International Save the Children Union (hereafter Save the Children), eventually finding sure footing in the United Nations, especially within UNICEF. The agency was the single most important actor in the promulgation of Western norms about children and childhood throughout the world, especially in the Global South after World War II. Established in 1946 primarily as an aid organization, UNICEF expanded its mission to include campaigns focusing on health, sanitation, education, and child care, eventually adopting a comprehensive child approach that looked at multiple areas of child development. UNICEF and other organizations were central to the internationalization of childhood, promoting Western norms of child welfare through their development programs.

Second, world conferences, meetings, special sessions, and summits, some sponsored by the United Nations, were also key to diffusing a global model of childhood to states. These prestigious and influential events "display world culture under construction."[17] These meetings and events became common in the nineteenth century, but since World War II, they have taken on a more symbolic, prominent, and global role, offering an authoritative stance on a wide range of issues relevant to international institutions.[18] Through the mobilization, organization, assessment, and follow-up they entail, UN meetings in particular have become a type of "secular ritual," expressing a global consensus on global matters.[19] The most important meeting on children in the last fifty years was the 1990 World Summit on Children, corresponding with the 1990 CRC. At this summit, the largest assembly of world leaders ever convened (at that time) participated in what was heralded by UNICEF as a "dramatic affirmation of the centrality of children to our common future."[20] Moreover, Anna Holzscheiter argues that the Convention itself is held in such high esteem that UN publications about it "convey the impression that not talking about children as the most vulnerable part of society ... is a societal taboo—not only in Western societies but also on an international level."[21]

Finally, the growth and increasing complexity of international law have gradually produced a still expanding and ever more detailed model of childhood, one that is in fact *globalized*. Three declarations and one convention about children were drafted during the twentieth century: the 1924 Geneva Declaration, the 1948 Declaration on the Rights of the Child, the 1959 Declaration on the Rights of the Child, and the 1990 CRC. Each of these documents is a window onto the model of childhood as it then existed and reflects contemporary ideas about children and the role of the state and of parents (and, in the case of the 1990 CRC, of the international community) in ensuring children's welfare (see Table 2.5). Taken together, they show the shifting boundaries and growing substance of the global model of childhood.

Of the four declarations and conventions *specifically addressing children*, only the CRC prohibits the death penalty for child offenders. Yet other international conventions and treaties also ban the penalty for those under

17. Lechner and Boli, *World Culture: Origin and Consequences*, 84.
18. Ibid.
19. Ibid., 89.
20. UNICEF, "United Nations Special Session on Children: The World Summit for Children," http://www.unicef.org/specialsession/about/world-summit.htm.
21. Holzscheiter, *Children's Rights*, 87.

Table 2.5 THE CHANGING GLOBAL MODEL OF CHILDHOOD, AS EVIDENT IN FOUR INTERNATIONAL DOCUMENTS RELATED TO CHILDREN.

Early-Period Norms Found in Law/1924 Declaration	First-Cascade-Period Norms Found in Law/1959 Declaration and 1976 ICCPR	Second-Cascade-Period Norms Found in Law/1990 CRC
Duties, obligations	Some rights, some duties	Mostly rights
Equality/freedom from discrimination: Race, nationality, or creed (Preamble).	Equality/freedom from discrimination: Broader protections including color, sex, language, political opinion, social origin, property, birth, or other status (1959 Principle 1, ICCPR Article 24).	Equality/freedom from discrimination expanded to include ethnic origin and disability (Article 2).
Material/physical needs: food, health care, shelter (Sections 1, 2).	Protection to develop physically and mentally (1959 Principle 2). Right to adequate nutrition, housing, and medical services (1959 Principle 4).	Health and health care (Article 24). Attainment of standard of living adequate for physical and mental development (Article 27).
Education, training (Sections 2, 4).	Education: free, compulsory primary school (1959 Principle 7).	Education: compulsory and free (Article 28).
Justice: rehabilitation of the child criminal (Section 2).	**No death penalty for those under the age of 18 (ICCPR Article 6).** **Juvenile offenders should be separated from adults (ICCPR Article 10).** **Adjudication should be speedy (ICCPR Article 10).** **Treatment should be appropriate to age (ICCPR Article 10).** **Judgments rendered in criminal cases shall be kept private when it is in the interest of juveniles, matters concerning matrimonial disputes, or guardianship of children (ICCPR Article 14).** **Judicial procedures should take into account the age of the juvenile and the promotion of rehabilitation (ICCPR Article 14).**	**No death penalty or life imprisonment for those under the age of 18 without the possibility of release (Article 37).** **Separated from adult criminals (Article 37).** **Freedom from unlawful or arbitrary deprivation of liberty (Article 37).** **Allowed to maintain contact with family (Article 37).** **Prompt access to legal and other assistance (Article 37).** **Right to challenge a sentence's legality promptly (Article 37).** **Treated in a manner consistent with the child's age (Article 40).**

(continued)

Table 2.5 CONTINUED

Early-Period Norms Found in Law/1924 Declaration	First-Cascade-Period Norms Found in Law/1959 Declaration and 1976 ICCPR	Second-Cascade-Period Norms Found in Law/1990 CRC
		Right to judicial protections: no ex post facto punishment, presumed innocence, speedy hearing, legal assistance, examination of witnesses, access to an interpreter, privacy in all stages of the process (Article 40). A minimum age of criminal responsibility (Article 40).
Moral guidance: spiritual development (Sections 2, 5).	Happiness (1959 introduction). Protection to develop morally and spiritually (1959 Principle 2).	Attainment of standard of living adequate for spiritual and moral development (Article 27).
	Protection to develop socially (1959 Principle 2).	Attainment of standard of living adequate for social development (Article 27).
First to receive relief in times of distress (Section 3).	First to receive protection and relief (1959 Principle 8).	Right to protection in armed conflict (Article 38).
		Right not to be part of armed conflict if under the age of 15 (Article 38).
		Right not to be recruited if under the age of 15 (Article 38).
		Right to rehabilitation for child victims (Article 39).
Labor: freedom from exploitation; education and training for a livelihood (Section 4).	Labor: limitations in age and type. Protection from hazardous labor. Protection from exploitation (1959 Principle 9).	Protection from economic exploitation (Article 32).
		Protection from hazardous work or work that interferes with physical, mental, spiritual, moral, or social development (Article 32).
		Protection from sexual exploitation (Article 34).
	Best interest of the child (1959 Principle 2).	Best interest of the child (Article 3).

(continued)

Table 2.5 CONTINUED

Early-Period Norms Found in Law/1924 Declaration	First-Cascade-Period Norms Found in Law/1959 Declaration and 1976 ICCPR	Second-Cascade-Period Norms Found in Law/1990 CRC
	Age defined: before and after birth; physical and mental immaturity (1959 Preamble).	Age defined: 18 unless majority is attained earlier (Article 1).
	Child seen not as an isolated unit, but as part of a family: reference to parents, individuals, voluntary organizations, local authorities, and national governments (1959 preamble and introduction).	Recognition of family (Preamble, Articles 2 (1 and 2), 3 (2), 5, 9 (1, 2, and 4), 14, 18, 20).
	Care from parents (1959 Principle 6).	Care from parents (Article 7).
	Protection of children at dissolution of marriage (ICCPR Article 23).	Right to family relations (Article 8).
		Kept with parents when possible (Article 9).
		Right to request family unification (Article 10).
		Contact with family if separated (Article 10).
	Name and Nationality (1959 Principle 3).	Name and Nationality (Articles 7, 8).
	Registered, given name and nationality (ICCPR Article 24).	Identity (Article 8).
	Social Security (1959 Principle 4).	Social Security (Article 26).
	Assistance to families without adequate means of support (1959 Principle 6).	
	Treatment, education, and care for disabled children (1959 Principle 5).	Right of disabled children to enjoy a full and decent life (Article 23).
		Right to special care and assistance (Article 23).
	Recreation and leisure (1959 Principle 7).	Rest, play, recreation, and leisure (Article 31).
	Protection from trafficking, neglect, cruelty, and exploitation (1959 Principle 9).	Freedom from physical and mental violence, abuse, neglect, or exploitation (Article 19).
		Life (Article 6).
		Right to act as a protagonist in best interest cases (Article 9).
		Right to leave any country (Article 10).

(*continued*)

Table 2.5 CONTINUED

Early-Period Norms Found in Law/1924 Declaration	First-Cascade-Period Norms Found in Law/1959 Declaration and 1976 ICCPR	Second-Cascade-Period Norms Found in Law/1990 CRC
		Right to enter own country (Article 10).
		Freedom of expression, including the ability to seek, receive, and impart information (Article 13).
		Freedom of thought, conscience, and religion (Article 14).
		Freedom of association and peaceful assembly (Article 15).
		Privacy (Article 16).
		Alternative care if deprived of a family (Article 20).
		Right to periodic review of treatment and circumstance (Article 25).
		Protection and assistance of refugee children (Article 22).
		Enjoyment of culture (Article 30).
		Use of own language (Article 30).
		Participation in cultural and artistic life (Article 31).
		Protection from illicit drugs and substances (Article 33).
		Freedom from torture and cruel, inhumane, or degrading treatment (Article 37).

the age of 18. The first treaty to ban the execution of some child offenders was the 1949 Fourth Geneva Convention relative to the Protection of Civilian Persons in Time of War. Article 68 states that "protected persons" who commit their crimes when they are younger than 18 cannot be given the death penalty. The ICCPR also bans the penalty in Article 6.

In examining one aspect of the global model of childhood from Table 2.5 (in bold)—justice and punishment—it is evident that protections for children greatly increased in the fourteen years between the 1976 ICCPR and the 1990 CRC, while the age limit applied to the norm of abolition for child offenders remained the same. The model of childhood advanced by the CRC was also significantly more detailed, complex, and wider in scope than previous attempts to enumerate rights and protections for children.

In addition to the CRC and ICCPR, a number of regional treaties forbid the penalty for child offenders. The American Convention of Human Rights, which also entered into force during the first cascade (in 1978), states that children whose crimes were committed when they were below the age of 18 cannot be executed (Article 4§5). Twenty-five countries have ratified the convention. Article 5 of the African Charter on the Rights and Welfare of the Child prohibits death sentences on children under the age of 18 and has forty-seven ratifications. Protocol No. 13 of the European Convention for the Protection of Human Rights and Fundamental Freedoms, which came into effect in 2002, abolishes the death penalty for all crimes and all offenders.

Although children and childhood were part of the human rights agenda in the last half of the twentieth century, the issue of the child death penalty remained obscure until Amnesty International and its American chapter (along with other national and international NGOs) took it up in the 1980s and 1990s. Amnesty's campaign against the child death penalty was international in scope, but the organization focused its resources on the United States and a few other violators. Employing a moral authority derived from its legacy as a champion of human rights and harnessing the legitimacy of the emerging children's rights regime, Amnesty and other NGOs were able to make the child death penalty an international concern. Through the development of a campaign network, Amnesty International's US section (AIUSA) joined other NGOs in an effort to persuade additional US states to ban the penalty for offenders who commit their crimes under the age of 18. The campaign's success increased the perception of a national consensus against the penalty, which was cited by the US Supreme Court in its 2005 ruling in *Roper v. Simmons*, the decision that outlawed the child death penalty in the United States.[22]

The 1990 CRC began a period of intense international consolidation of authority over childhood, as international law and the institutions established to monitor it came to be viewed as the definitive authority on the treatment of children by the state. All states in the international system have ratified the CRC except for the United States. The convention's nearly

---

22. 543 U.S. 551.

universal ratification indicates global acknowledgment of a model of childhood that all states should adopt.

The late twentieth and early twenty-first centuries were the setting for a dramatic contestation between state sovereignty and international law prohibiting the child death penalty, as laggard states, such as the United States, China, and Pakistan, struggled between resistance to and compliance with international principles. While both China and Pakistan have accepted the norm's legitimacy through the ratification of international treaties and the passage of national legislation, domestic factors, such as incomplete birth registration, lack of full control of territory, and government responses to recent terrorism, have hindered compliance. In the US case, the increased citation of international and foreign law in Supreme Court decisions contributed to the United States' vulnerability to international pressure, as did the escalating rebuke of the United States by UN agencies, diplomats, NGOs, and other nations and the successful campaigns at the US state level that helped to create a national consensus on the issue. As stated, the United States abolished the penalty in 2005 with the *Roper* ruling by the Supreme Court. In both Pakistan and the United States, late-stage principled activism reinforced global pressure to end the child death penalty.

Importantly, international law itself concerning children's rights now often serves as the sole justification for bringing states into compliance with the globalized model of childhood and standards of child welfare. Just how quickly that model and the body of law that undergirds it have grown in such a short time is plain. In the early years after World War II, international efforts targeting children were justified as emergency relief—on the basis of children's physical needs for proper nutrition, sanitation, vaccines, etc., needs supported by studies in the natural science. As international efforts expanded in the 1960s and 1970s, the child was increasingly linked (now by the social science) to the development of the nation and to the ushering of states into the international community as economic partners. With the growth of the international children's rights regime in the 1990s, there is no need for further justification to protect children. Children are rights holders, and international law alone serves to justify attention and assistance.

CASE SELECTION

The case studies for this book were selected based on temporal period, yet the book is organized by mechanism of diffusion. From the list of states that abolished the death penalty for child offenders in the early period, I selected two major cases—the United Kingdom and Tunisia—and three minor cases—France, Japan, and Ethiopia. The selection of cases was guided by regional diversity, but ultimately determined by the availability of primary or secondary sources. Major and minor cases were determined based on the availability of scholarly material. Unfortunately, reliable sources could not be found for any of the few Latin American states (in the early period) and former Soviet states (in the second cascade) that abolished the penalty for child offenders only.

Case selection for the cascade periods was more complicated than early-period case selection and requires greater explanation. Of the forty-nine states that abolished during the first cascade, thirteen were from Africa; twenty from Europe and Central Asia; ten from the Middle East and North Africa; three from East Asia; two from Latin America and the Caribbean; and one from South Asia. All together, almost 47 percent of first-cascade states were either in Africa or the Middle East. Although Europe accounted for the largest number of states that abolished during the first cascade, the majority of these were part of the Soviet Union, where diffusion was variably coercive. The majority of the states that abolished during the second cascade were either formerly under Soviet rule or current members of the European Union or Council of Europe, or both. These patterns indicate that the cascades are strongly linked with British, French, and Soviet decolonization as well as the regional integration of Europe.

The data therefore suggest that the story of the first cascade for this norm is a story of colonialism and, specifically, a story of British and French colonialism. As such, I selected two former British colonies from Africa: Kenya and Tanganyika/Tanzania. The former French colonies were more evenly divided between the Middle East and North African region (MENA) and Africa, but I selected Algeria as a MENA state to compare it with the African cases, and with the French MENA state of Tunisia selected for the early period.

The second cascade is a story of general abolition in Europe and in former Soviet territories and the struggle to bring into compliance the remaining few states that maintained the child death penalty in law or practice. Of the thirty states in the second cascade that are in Europe or are former Soviet territories, only four abolished the death penalty specifically for child offenders: the Former Republic of Yugoslavia (1992), Russia (1993), Uzbekistan (1994), and Latvia (1998). The overwhelming majority (about 87 percent) of European and former Soviet states abolished the penalty altogether during this period.

Selection of Cases				Organization of the Book		
Temporal Period	**Case Studies**			**Mechanism of Diffusion**	**Case Studies**	**Chapter**
Early period	England Ethiopia France Japan Tunisia			*Principled activism*	France England	3
First cascade	Algeria Kenya Tanganyika/ Tanzania			*Coercive socialization*	Algeria Ethiopia Japan Kenya Tanganyika/ Tanzania Tunisia	4
Second cascade	China Pakistan United States			*Globalized childhood and Laggards*	China Pakistan United States Amnesty International UNICEF	5, 6

Figure 2.4 Case Study Selection Based on Temporal Period and Organization of the Book Based on Mechanism of Diffusion.

The United States was chosen as a case because of its hegemonic status and its unusually high-profile contestation of the norm during the second cascade. Indeed, international efforts by human rights organizations to bring the United States into compliance with the norm (discussed in chapters 5 and 6) helped to define the second cascade, which ended with US adoption of the norm in 2005. Finally, I selected two smaller cases, China and Pakistan, states that passed national laws banning the penalty during the second cascade but whose compliance with the norm is incomplete. The organization of the book is presented visually in Figure 2.4.

CONCLUSION

This chapter sought to provide a context for the case studies in the following four chapters. The next chapter will address principled domestic activism, a mechanism strongly associated with early-period adoption. Through the case studies of England and France, I explore the actions and motivations of death penalty reformers and child welfare advocates that ended the penalty for child offenders under the age of 18 in those states.

CHAPTER 3

✦

Principled Activism as a Mechanism of Diffusion

INTRODUCTION

Of the three means of diffusion examined in this book—principled activism, coercive socialization, and the globalization of childhood—only the first is chiefly practiced at the domestic or state level. As described in the preceding two chapters, I argue that the norm abolishing the death penalty for child offenders gradually spread through the international system primarily because it was part of the template of the modern liberal state, along with other protections for children. This template became the prevalent form of state organization after World War II, as states around the world gained independence and sought legitimacy in an international system of equal states committed (ostensibly) to democracy and human rights.

In this chapter, I examine the adoption and diffusion of protections for children, including passage of a ban on the death penalty for child offenders, in two Western states: England (1933)[1] and France (1906). Both of these states were key actors in the diffusion of the norm, because both, to varying degrees, enshrined protections for children in the law they crafted for or applied to their colonial empires, and both eventually outlawed the

---

1. In this chapter, the case study is of England, not the United Kingdom or Great Britain. That being said, when it is certain that a law or historical fact is applicable to the United Kingdom or Great Britain, I reference them accordingly.

death penalty for child offenders under the age of 18. France preceded England in abolition by twenty-seven years, and the process of abolition in France appears to have been largely uncontested until World War II and the German occupation.

Driven by their beliefs about children's innate vulnerability, immaturity, and lesser culpability for their actions, principled activists campaigned for child welfare and justice reforms in the late nineteenth and early twentieth centuries in many Western states, including France, the United States, and the United Kingdom. Their successful advocacy culminated in the passage of child-protective laws and policies in these states and led to the development of a set of common standards of childhood. Consequently, state power and control over children came at the expense of parental authority, as the state itself expanded through the growth of bureaucracy and the founding of new state institutions to monitor the developing model of childhood. It is important to note, however, that the principled activism that emerged in England and France specifically targeted issues of shared concern in these states, especially the morality of young girls, the rehabilitation potential of child criminals, and the failure of parents as the direct cause of child criminality.

EXPECTATIONS OF PRINCIPLED ACTIVISM AS A MECHANISM OF DIFFUSION

As described in chapter 1, the literature on norms tends to divide the process of diffusion into three stages: early, cascade/middle, and late.[2] For each of these periods, a different mechanism of diffusion is thought to prevail. For the early period, political scientists, sociologists, and international legal theorists contend that the motivation to adopt law and norms should be the result of domestic factors, such as agency by committed individuals who petition the government and persuade society to adopt new norms. In the later periods, the struggle over norms shifts from the domestic level or the individual state to the international sphere, as the motivation for adoption is determined less by domestic factors and more by a desire to emulate other states in the international system.[3]

2. Finnemore and Sikkink, "International Norm Dynamics."
3. Finnemore and Sikkink, "International Norm Dynamics"; Meyer et al., "World Society and the Nation-State"; Ramirez, Soysal, and Shanahan, "The Changing Logic of Political Citizenship"; Sunstein, *Free Markets and Social Justice.*

This early period of principled activism and normative agency that precedes the cascade is not set against a backdrop of international law or global consensus, as neither the law enshrining the norm nor the consensus leading to codification of law yet exist. In the absence of international law and international pressure, state-level change during the early period results from domestic movements to advance new norms, although many movements consist of networks that link intellectuals and organizations across national borders, as will be seen. In these states at this time, social change comes from within.

That being said, not all states that adopt new norms during the early period of diffusion are isolated or even act of their own volition, driven to change by a few lonely moral campaigners. Some states that abolished the child death penalty early (Ethiopia, Japan, and Tunisia) were sites of foreign activism and/or coercion. Ethiopia voluntarily invited Western legal scholars to draft laws that included abolition of the child death penalty. With its own period of principled activism predating World War II, Japan banned the child death penalty during the foreign occupation that followed the war's end. Tunisia banned the penalty under France's colonial regime and then recommitted to abolition after independence. These states abolished the penalty, however, toward the end of the early period, in 1949 (Japan), 1956 (Tunisia), and 1957 (Ethiopia).

The principled activism that led to abolition of the death penalty for child offenders in England and France began in the nineteenth century. Yet before the penalty could be abolished, dramatic and substantive changes had to take place in the areas of penal reform, limitations to the death penalty, and child welfare. These changes were initiated by groups of dedicated individuals motivated by a variety of considerations, prime among them protections for children and the betterment of society. Over the course of the nineteenth and early twentieth centuries, changes in these areas eventually yielded a model of childhood that both families and the state were obligated to ensure. Science, especially the development of pediatrics and advances in hygiene, legitimated the new standards and led to the substitution of paternal authority with state authority to monitor deviance from the model.

The findings of the English and French cases suggest that, in contrast to some states that abolished the child death penalty during the cascades, the norm of abolition nested easily within other norms already adopted in England and France that defined the purpose of justice, the power of the state, and the nature of the child. In essence, the story of the emergence of a particular understanding of childhood and the changes it demanded is one of shifting authority from the father to the state to the international system, which mirrors and is part of a larger historical trend toward international moral authority that increasingly transcends national boundaries and alters state behavior.

ENGLAND CASE STUDY

Through a case study of England, this section will present the early legislative and cultural history that preceded abolition of the child death penalty. It will begin with a historical introduction to the case, followed by a discussion of empirical evidence of executions of child offenders in the nineteenth century. It will then trace the relevant legislative trends, in the areas of penal reform and child welfare, which led to the abolition of the child death penalty in the 1933 Children and Young Persons Act. Among the many important social reformers and child advocates in England in this period, this chapter focuses on the work of Sir Samuel Romilly, Sir Robert Peel, Mary Carpenter, and Eglantyne Jebb, as well as NGOs like the Howard League for Penal Reform, the National Council for the Abolition of the Death Penalty (NCADP), and Save the Children. It is important to note, however, that I do not attempt to give a complete history of children in England in this chapter. Rather, I offer a working view of the subject in order to understand the origins of state intervention in children's lives and to help explain the shift toward international authority over children in later chapters.

Historical Context

The country that Queen Victoria inherited in 1837 was remarkably different from the one she left upon her death in 1901. The population explosion that began before her reign helped bring about a number of changes, including the growth of industry, the development of an advanced transportation system, and the rise of overcrowded cities and urban slums. Her reign was also notable for the increasing enfranchisement of men over the course of the century. The reform acts of 1832,[4] 1867,[5] and 1884[6] pushed England (and Wales)[7] toward greater democracy as the right to vote was

---

4. 1832 Representation of the People Act (2 & 3 Will. IV, c. 45).
5. 1867 Representation of the People Act (30 & 31 Vict., c. 102).
6. 1884 Representation of the People Act (48 & 49 Vict., c. 3).
7. The 1884 reform act was broader than the 1832 and 1867 acts, applying to all of the United Kingdom.

granted to working-class men and to men in rural areas. Moreover, the nineteenth century was notable for the launch of humanitarian campaigns, including the abolition of slavery, the reform of working conditions in factories and mines, and Parliamentary reform.[8] The British Empire, acquired over five centuries and occupying a vast swath of the world, began to decline in the late nineteenth century as competition for raw materials increased and industrial production by other European states and the United States accelerated. This ushered in a period known as the 'new imperialism,' when Africa became the object of domination and colonialism, often justified by claims of racial superiority.

Although efforts to assist poor and homeless children were first introduced in the sixteenth century in England, it was the nineteenth century that truly marked the birth of the child protection movement. In the nineteenth century alone, at least thirty-five acts addressing children's issues and child welfare were passed.[9] By contrast, the three previous centuries

8. Elizabeth Orman Tuttle, *The Crusade against Capital Punishment in Great Britain* (London: Stevens & Sons, 1961): 140.

9. These were: the 1802 Regulation of the Employment of Apprentices (42 Geo. III, c. 73); the 1819 Cotton Mills and Factories Act (59 Geo. III, c. 66); the 1831 Act to Repeal the Laws Relating to Apprentices and Other Young Persons Employed in Cotton Factories and in Cotton Mills (1 & 2 Will. IV, c39); the 1833 Factory Act; the 1834 Poor Law Amendment Act (4 & 5 Will. 4, c. 76); the 1838 Parkhurst Prison Act (1 & 2 Vict., c. 82); the Act of 1842 Regulating Employment in Mines (5 & 6 Vict., c. 99); the 1847 Juvenile Offenders Act (10 & 11 Vict., c. 57); the 1850 Act for the Further Extension of Summary Jurisdiction in Cases of Larceny (13 & 14 Vict., c. 37); the 1854 Reformatory Schools Act (17 & 18 Vict., c. 74); the 1854 Middlesex Industrial Schools Act (Local) (17 & 18 Vict., c. 169); the 1854 Reformation of Youthful Offenders Act (17 & 18 Vict., c. 86); the 1855 Youthful Offenders Amendment Act (18 & 19 Vict., c. 87); the 1856 Reformatory and Industrial Schools Amendment Act (19 & 20 Vict., c. 109); the 1857 Industrial Schools Act (23 & 24 Vict., c. 108); the 1857 Reformatory Schools Act (20 & 21 Vict., c. 55); the 1861 Industrial Schools Act (24 & 25 Vict., c. 113); the 1866 Reformatory Schools Act (29 & 30 Vict., c. 117); the 1866 Industrial Schools Act (29 & 30 Vict., c. 118); the 1870 Elementary Education Act (33 & 34 Vict., c. 75); the 1873 Regulation of the Employment of Children in Agriculture Act (36 & 37 Vict., c. 67); the 1874 Births and Deaths Registration Act (37 & 38 Vict., c. 88); the 1876 Elementary Education Act (39 & 40 Vict., c. 79); the 1879 Summary Jurisdiction Act (42 & 43 Vict., c. 49); the 1885 Criminal Law Amendment Act (48 & 49 Vict., c. 69); the 1887 Act to Permit the Conditional Release of First Offenders in Certain Cases (50 & 51 Vict., c. 25); the 1889 Poor Law Act (52 & 53 Vict., c 56); the 1891 Reformatory and Industrial Schools Act (54 & 55 Vict., c. 23); the 1891 Custody of Children Act (54 & 55 Vict., c. 3); the 1893 Reformatory Schools Act (56 & 57 Vict., c. 48); the 1894 Prevention of Cruelty to Children Act (57 & 58 Vict., c. 41); the 1894 Industrial Schools Act Amendment (57 & 58 Vict., c. 53); the 1897 Infant Life Protection Act (60 & 61 Vict., c. 57); the 1899 Reformatory Schools Act (62 and 63 Vict., c. 12); the 1899 Summary Jurisdiction Act (62 & 63 Vict., c. 22); and the 1899 Elementary Education (Defective and Epileptic Children) Act (62 & 63 Vict., c. 32).

produced approximately eight major pieces of legislation on children altogether.

The shift in attention to children in the nineteenth century was a precursor of the rights-based approach to child welfare and protection in the twentieth century. During the early period of abolition, over a span of nearly one hundred years, an international movement for children's rights produced countless advocates; established multiple institutions to care for, study, and advance child welfare; and yielded three international declarations on the rights of the child, one for the League of Nations and two for the United Nations. Although these declarations—the 1924, 1948, and 1959 Declaration on the Rights of the Child—were not binding international law, they nonetheless signaled a growing global consensus about the relationship between the state and the child and on the state's responsibility for child welfare and protection.

Empirical Evidence of Child Executions

Prior to the nineteenth century and the routine collection of statistics on crime, no accurate data exist on the rate of child executions in England.[10] When scholars speak about executions of children prior to the twentieth century, they are referencing executions of children under the age of 14, the age of culpability until the reforms of the nineteenth and early twentieth centuries. Children under age seven were not culpable for their crimes, and children between the ages of seven and 14 were only culpable if evidence of malice or *mens rea* (criminal intent) was found.[11] There are virtually no data on the execution of children between the ages of 14 and 17 before the twentieth century because this class of offenders was not characterized as children until child welfare advocates and penal reformers argued in the mid-nineteenth century for their diminished culpability.[12] The only confirmed exceptions to this data gap are the executions of 14-year-old John Any Bird Bell[13] in 1831 and of 17-year-old Joseph Morely in 1887, believed to be the last child under the age of 18 put to death in England.[14] Nor are there data for offenders that committed their crimes as

10. Radzinowicz and Hood, *A History of English Criminal Law*, 91.
11. Arthur Koestler, *Reflections on Hanging* (London: Victor Gollancz, 1956): 20.
12. Mary Carpenter first argued in the mid-nineteenth century that children under the age of 16 could not be held responsible for their actions. See Radzinowicz and Hood, *A History of English Criminal Law*, 168.
13. Alternatively recorded as John Amy Bird Bell.
14. Radzinowicz and Hood, *A History of English Criminal Law*, 679.

children and were executed as legal adults. This is not believed to present a problem in the study of England, however, since there was typically very little time between sentencing and execution, usually only a few days.

A.W.G. Kean has suggested that the search for "age-lines"—or firm distinctions between classes of individuals liable for the penalty and those who were not—in the study of children by modern scholars misunderstands the way childhood was interpreted by British courts prior to the seventeenth century.[15] Judges possessed great discretion when dealing with children, such that:

> in his early years a child was too young to be punished at all, and that later, and until the age of puberty, special *dolus* had to be proved; whether a child was old enough to be convicted or not, and whether he was of the age of puberty or not, were questions of fact to be decided by the judge in each case.[16]

Additionally, without a reliable system of birth registration, age was difficult to determine and there was great incentive to deceive when punishments were so steep.[17] It was not until the sixteenth century that fixed age-lines were sought, although agreement was not reached until the seventeenth century, when criminal liability was fixed at age 7. Kean contends that it was probably not coincidental that age-lines crystallized when birth registration became more routine.[18]

Because it has not been possible to find accurate data on the number of executions of children between the ages of 14 and 17 before the nineteenth century, the number of child offenders put to death in England is unknown. A number of authors, however, contend that the practice of executing children was common prior to the nineteenth century: James Christoph has suggested that the practice "was by no means unusual."[19] V.A.C. Gatrell estimates that approximately 90 percent of 'men' hanged in the 1780s in London were under the age of 21.[20] John Laurence Pritchard writes, "In the days of George II [1727–1760] it was no uncommon thing

15. A.W.G. Kean, "The History of the Criminal Liability of Children," *The Law Quarterly Review* 53 (1937): 368.

16. Ibid.

17. Ibid., 370.

18. Ibid.

19. James B. Christoph, *Capital Punishment and British Politics: The British Movement to Abolish the Death Penalty, 1945–57* (Chicago: The University of Chicago Press, 1962): 15.

20. V.A.C. Gatrell, *The Hanging Tree: Execution and the English People 1770–1868* (Oxford: Oxford University Press, 1994): 8.

for children under the age of ten years to be hanged, and on one occasion ten of them were strung up together, as a warning to men and a spectacle for the angels."[21] Other scholars refute the degree to which children were executed, especially in the eighteenth century. Arthur Koestler claims that toward the end of the eighteenth century, judges demonstrated an increasing uneasiness in sentencing to death children under the age of 14.[22]

Data on the nineteenth century, although relatively better documented, is also in dispute. Several scholars suggest there were at least eleven child executions in the nineteenth century, including the executions of two children age 7 (see Appendix A for the list of possible nineteenth-century child executions in England).[23] On the other hand, Harry Potter and B.E.F. Knell argue that children under the age of 14 were rarely executed in England in the nineteenth century.[24] Knell examined executions at one location, Old Bailey, between the years 1801 and 1836.[25] Knell found no evidence that children under the age of 14 were executed at Old Bailey during these years, although there were a number of death sentences of child offenders that were later reprieved.[26] Systematically, Knell challenges the claims of Christoph, Pritchard, Koestler, and others who contend that child executions were common in the early nineteenth century. On the contrary, Knell states, child executions were rare by this time, and he casts doubt on their frequency in prior centuries as well. Knell is quick to point out, however, that due to the lack of any real data, his findings outside the Old Bailey and prior to the nineteenth century are "inferential."[27]

21. John Laurence Pritchard, *A History of Capital Punishment* (New York: Citadel, 1960): 18.

22. Koestler, *Reflections on Hanging*.

23. Ibid.; Pritchard, *A History of Capital Punishment*; Christoph, *Capital Punishment and British Politics*; Ivy Pinchbeck and Margaret Hewitt, *Children in English Society*, vol. 2, *From the Eighteenth Century to the Children Act of 1948* (London: Routledge and Kegan Paul, 1973); Negley K. Teeters, *Hang by the Neck: The Legal Use of Scaffold and Noose, Gibbet, Stake, and Firing Squad from Colonial Times to the Present* (Springfield, IL: Charles C. Thomas, 1967); Radzinowicz and Hood, *A History of English Criminal Law*.

24. Harry Potter, *Hanging in Judgment* (London: SCM, 1993): 7; B.E.F. Knell, "Capital Punishment: Its Administration in Relation to Juvenile Offenders in the Nineteenth Century and Its Possible Administration in the Eighteenth," *British Journal of Criminology* 5, no. 2 (1965): 198–207.

25. Knell, "Capital Punishment," 199.

26. Ibid.; Knell found 103 cases of children under the age of 14 sentenced to death at Old Bailey between 1801 and 1836, but could not find their deaths noted in the criminal register. Knell found evidence that all but eight had been reprieved. For the eight for whom no record of reprieve was found, Knell concluded that they must have been reprieved since their deaths were not recorded.

27. Ibid., 203.

The one early nineteenth-century execution on which scholars, including Knell, agree was the hanging of John Any Bird Bell, age 14, for murder. Bell was hanged at Old Bailey in August 1831. Newspapers from the period give contradictory impressions of the reaction to his execution and provide insight, albeit limited, into public support for child executions in general.[28] Transcripts from Bell's murder trial documented that the jury rejected a sentence of death "on account of his extreme youth, and the profligate and unnatural manner in which he had been brought up."[29] At the time, children 14 and older were considered adults and fully culpable for their crimes. The fact that this jury challenged the wisdom of this statutory provision and blamed the parents, an idea that would become increasingly prevalent in the nineteenth century, signaled a change in the way child offenders were viewed.

In addition, when the judge sentenced Bell to death anyway, he felt the need to give a lengthy justification for doing so. However, only two newspapers, *The London Times* and *The Kent and Essex Mercury*, covered the story. The *Times* ran two stories, one for the sentence and one for the execution, both toward the middle of the paper. The fact that the sentence and subsequent execution did not inspire any public editorials or commentaries seems to indicate that they did not provoke outrage. The *Times* report of the trial stated that Bell "showed no outward symptoms of feeling," depicted his eyes as "deeply sunk in the head, a strong expression of cunning," and stated, "he showed no marks of feeling [. . .] until the dissection of his body was mentioned, and then dropped a solitary tear."[30] The *Times* article about the hanging, interestingly, waffles between insults to Bell's character, making reference to the "wretched youth" and "wretched malefactor" at different times, and sympathy to his "tender age," his "trembling anxiety" at his impending death, and the "sad spectacle" of his hanging.[31] Although there is little evidence of public outrage, the judge points to the "intense interest" in the case as measured by the "excessively crowded state of the court by all classes."[32]

In sum, it can be concluded that there is evidence of child executions in England in the nineteenth century, but that these executions are probably more rare than many authors suggest. Child executions

28. *The London Times*, July 30, 1831, "Summer Assizes," 14(604), "Execution of John Any Bird Bell." August 2, 1831: 14(606).

29. *London Times*, "Summer Assizes."

30. *London Times*, "Summer Assizes."

31. *London Times*, "Execution of John Any Bird Bell."

32. *London Times*, "Summer Assizes."

prior to the nineteenth century are poorly documented and limit firm conclusions on the practice. It is likely, however, that child executions experienced the same decline in the eighteenth century as other types of executions.

The Creation of Children and Childhood

Unlike the hard-won victories and defeats in the late period of legislative spread, there appears to have been little controversy over the adoption of legislation prohibiting the death penalty for child offenders in the United Kingdom in 1933. This is not surprising given the public reception to previous penal reform efforts for children in the preceding decades. First, the 1908 Children's Act that increased the age limit for the penalty to 16 inspired no written articles or commentary in *The London Times*. Nor did the Children's Bill in 1910, which attempted to raise the age of eligibility for the penalty to 21 but failed, result in any *Times* articles about the penalty. Finally, a study of major newspapers, magazines, penal reform newsletters, and Parliamentary debates of the time reveals that the provision in the 1933 Children and Young Persons Act[33] reserving the penalty for those 18 and older inspired little public criticism or comment.

Even though legislation ending the child death penalty in the United Kingdom did not elicit opposition at the time, the path to abolition was not easy or quick. The consensus that children under the age of 18 are less culpable for their actions and deserve different treatment than adults required the acceptance of preceding norms about children and childhood within which the new norm of abolition could nest. In particular, it required the development of the idea of 'childhood' as a distinct stage of life (distinguished by age) that merits special consideration and protection, including protection from punitive measures.

Although children were not specifically protected in international law until the twentieth century, the groundwork for these advances was laid in the nineteenth century, a prolific period for child law. States enacted extensive reform legislation, including universal compulsory education, limits to employment, punishment for abuse and neglect, separate housing for juvenile criminals, and lighter punitive measures. Two legislative trends led by principled activists resulted in the 1933 act: penal reform and state interest in child welfare. Both trends are taken in turn below.

33. 1933 Children and Young Persons Act (23 &24 Geo. V, c. 12, s. 19).

Penal Reform

Very little is known about child offenders in England in the sixteenth and seventeenth centuries; however, it is evident that there was little legal distinction between vagrancy and delinquency or between children and adults. Adolescents were first distinguished from younger children in terms of punishment in the 1572 Poor Law Act,[34] which assigned lesser penalties to children than to adolescents (those 14 or older) who were "idlers, rogues, and vagabonds."[35] This was the first step toward a penal system that treated children differently from adults. The act also identified 18 as a key age in that repeat offenders older than 18 could have their crimes classified as felonies, whereas those younger than 18 could not.

The eighteenth century saw such drastic increases in the number of capital crimes that, by the century's end, there were more than two hundred of them. The collection of laws that became known as the Bloody Code was a patchwork that was often repetitive and draconian. "Stealing turnips, consorting with gypsies, damaging a fish-pond, writing threatening letters, impersonating out-pensioners at Greenwich Hospital, being found armed or disguised in a forest park, or rabbit warren, cutting down a tree, poaching, forging, picking pockets, and shoplifting" were all capital offences.[36] Yet as the number of capital crimes increased, the number of persons actually executed declined. Interestingly, as capital crimes began to be repealed at the end of the eighteenth century and in the early nineteenth century, death sentences and executions spiked again.[37] Not coincidentally, this spike corresponds with a sharp population increase in England and Wales at the time and with the related perception of a crime wave.[38]

According to Sir James Fitzjames Stephen, it was never the intention of British justice to carry out every death sentence.[39] David Taylor has suggested that reprieves were necessary in order to keep the number of those killed at an "acceptable (and practicable) level."[40] The pardon was thus "supplemental" to the death sentence in England, with the king playing the

---

34. 1572 Poor Law Act (14 Eliz. I, c. 5).

35. Ivy Pinchbeck and Margaret Hewitt, *Children in English Society*, vol. 1, *From Tudor Times to the Eighteenth Century* (London: Routledge & Kegan Paul, 1969): 97.

36. Christoph, *Capital Punishment and British Politics*, 14.

37. Gatrell, *The Hanging Tree*, 7.

38. Ibid., 18.

39. Sir James Fitzjames Stephen, *A History of the Criminal Law of England*, 3 vols. (London: Macmillan, 1883): vol. 1, 7t.

40. David Taylor, *Crime, Policing, and Punishment in England, 1750–1914* (New York: St. Martin's, 1998): 130.

role of pardoner.[41] Taylor contends that the uncertainty of punishment "reinforced or enhanced" the sentence's terror.[42] By arbitrarily selecting some criminals over others for pardon, "the discernment and magnanimity of the ruling elite" was emphasized.[43]

The likely decline in death sentences for child offenders in the eighteenth century can be attributed in part to the increase in the use of transportation as punishment beginning in 1717, when male children between the ages of 15 and 18 could be transported to work on plantations in America.[44] When the American Revolution succeeded, transportation to America came to an end. As a result, large numbers of boys sentenced to transportation were put in the Hulks, old ships moored in the Thames River, which were filled with hundreds of prisoners in squalid conditions. The first calls for the segregation of young prisoners from adults emerged out of these conditions. One early reformer, Sir Robert Peel, the future Prime Minister of the United Kingdom, ordered in 1825 the separation of adult men from boys, who were placed into a separate ship, the Euryalus.[45] Although conditions improved little for these boys, the Euryalus marked only the beginning of a century of institutional reform. In 1835, the Hulks were condemned and a separate penitentiary for young offenders was established.[46]

Although efforts to curb child crime began in the sixteenth century, child crime did not become a serious public concern until the end of the eighteenth century and the beginning of the nineteenth century, when England, Scotland, and Wales experienced a population boom from an estimated 7,250,000 persons in 1751 to more than 16,000,000 by 1831.[47] London's population alone almost doubled between 1801 and 1831, from one to 1.7 million people.[48] This explosive growth resulted in large migrations of rural residents to urban slums and corresponded, at the very least, with the perception that crime was on the rise. These concerns were increasingly directed at youth, who constituted between 48 and 49 percent of the population of England and Wales in 1821.[49]

41. This ended with the reign of William IV. Sir James Fitzjames Stephen, *A History of the Criminal Law of England*, 3 vols. (London: Macmillan and Co., 1882): vol. 2, 88.
42. Taylor, *Crime, Policing, and Punishment*, 127.
43. Ibid.
44. Pinchbeck and Hewitt, *Children in English Society*, 107.
45. Radzinowicz and Hood, *A History of English Criminal Law*, 143.
46. Ibid., 148.
47. Pinchbeck and Hewitt, *Children in English Society*, 387.
48. Gatrell, *The Hanging Tree*, 18.
49. Pinchbeck and Hewitt, *Children in English Society*, 388.

Another important reformer, Sir Samuel Romilly, a Solicitor General under King George III, required the compilation of crime statistics beginning in 1810. By 1820, it was evident that the number of capital offences was in decline.[50] The Bloody Code was repealed in the 1832 Reform Act, which one hundred members of Parliament supported. In 1837, by which time most capital statutes had been repealed, only eight people were executed in England; the next year saw only six executions.[51] Gatrell portrays the collapse of this "ancient killing system" as dramatic, brought on primarily by the Whigs coming into power in 1830.[52]

Early abolitionists adopted a novel strategy, first used by Romilly, that allowed the lengthy list of capital crimes to be reduced to four by the mid-nineteenth century: They allied themselves with merchants, manufacturers, bankers, and businessmen who recognized that the severe punishment of death for minor crimes meant that few of those accused were found guilty. Shifts in public opinion against the death penalty for minor offences meant that juries would not "systematically" convict.[53] As a result, penalties for stealing cloth, for example, were not enforced because the penalty was death. Romilly argued that if punishments were less severe, juries would be more likely to convict.[54] In the words of John Bright, a Quaker abolitionist, the "certainty of punishment was more important than severity" of a punishment that was rarely enforced.[55] Some of these attempts, such as at reducing the penalties for theft of cloth or for pickpocketing, succeeded easily.[56] Others, such as for forgery, were defeated in the first attempt, but some of these defeats had the effect of ending all executions for these crimes (de facto) even if retained in law.[57]

In 1815, the first systematic inquiry into the source of juvenile delinquency was conducted by the Society for Investigating the Causes of the Alarming Increase of Juvenile Delinquency in the Metropolis,[58] launched in response to the perception of a growing problem. The study found that in addition to environmental factors such as poor parenting and lack of employment and educational opportunities, the severity of the criminal

---

50. Steven Lynn, "Locke and Beccaria: Faculty Psychology and Capital Punishment," in *Executions and the British Experience from the 17th Century: A Collection of Essays*, ed. William B. Thesing (Jefferson, NC: McFarland, 1990): 29.
51. Gatrell, *The Hanging Tree*, 9.
52. Ibid.
53. Christoph, *Capital Punishment and British Politics*, 16.
54. Tuttle, *The Crusade against Capital Punishment*, 4.
55. Tuttle, *The Crusade against Capital Punishment*, 10.
56. Ibid., 5.
57. Ibid., 9.
58. Pinchbeck and Hewitt, *Children in English Society*, 431.

code—a product, as discussed, of nineteenth-century reaction to a perceived increase in crime—was the main cause of the perception of delinquency.[59] As the severity of punishments declined (along with the number of death sentences), the role of prisons in the criminal justice system changed as well. Prisons were the "first resort" at the beginning of the nineteenth century, designed to reform the criminal, but by the end of the century, they were considered places of last resort, as society turned to a range of alternatives to control crime.[60]

Early efforts to study crime and criminality in a scientific manner yielded new ideas about children and crime: Children were perceived to be "malleable" and capable of reform.[61] A key advocate of these new ideas toward child offenders was Mary Carpenter, an influential Unitarian legal reformer, who argued that children under the age of 16 could not be held responsible for their crimes.[62] Carpenter was chagrined by the passage of the 1838 Parkhurst Prison Act, which established a separate prison for children.[63] Although an improvement on earlier systems that housed children of all ages with adults and offered little supervision or care, the founding of a prison for children struck Carpenter and her fellow child advocates as draconian. Carpenter spent many years lambasting Parkhurst. Eventually, her efforts paid off.[64] The 1854 Reformation of Youthful Offenders Act[65] and other acts of this period established reform and industrial schools, after which the numbers of boys at Parkhurst steadily decreased until it closed in 1864. Carpenter was a prolific scholar and author and traveled widely, including to the United States and India, to share her research and testimony about the need for juvenile justice reform. When state facilities provided inadequate conditions for juvenile offenders, Carpenter built her own reformatories and industrial schools.[66]

The founding of reform schools in the 1854 Youthful Offenders Act was described by campaigners of the era as the "Magna Carta of Juvenile Delinquents" in that it simultaneously emphasized the rehabilitation of child offenders and communicated the "duty of the parent to maintain his

59. Ibid., 434–437.
60. Taylor, *Crime, Policing, and Punishment in England*, 145.
61. Pinchbeck and Hewitt, *Children in English Society*, 441.
62. Radzinowicz and Hood, *A History of English Criminal Law*, 168.
63. 1838 Parkhurst Prison Act (1 & 2 Vict. c. 82).
64. Radzinowicz and Hood, *A History of English Criminal Law*, 169.
65. 1854 Reformation of Youthful Offenders Act (17 & 18 Vict. c. 86).
66. Francesa Ashurst and Couze Venn, *Inequality, Poverty, and Education: A Political Economy of School Exclusion* (New York: Palgrave Macmillan, 2014): 115.

offspring, and not to cast the burden on the public."[67] Industrial schools, first founded in 1857, offered educational opportunities and were created for children age 7 to 14 who were convicted of vagrancy.[68] Within four years, there were more than fifty reformatories throughout England; however, the quality of the education provided remained poor until compulsory education laws were passed twenty years later.[69]

The last three decades of the nineteenth century were characterized by a series of important reform initiatives that, among other changes, yielded further drastic declines in the number of death sentences and granted discretionary power to magistrates to release juveniles on their own recognizance.[70] In 1836, for example, 3 percent of penalties for indictable offences were death sentences.[71] In 1896, the percentage was even lower (0.8 percent), and by 1912, the percentage of death sentences among all penalties for indictable offences was 0.4.[72]

It was not until the twentieth century that penal policy began to address offenders older than 16.[73] In 1908, the Children's Act[74] established separate courts for child offenders, reflecting a shift in attitude from the preceding period when the child was seen as a "small adult, fully responsible for his crime."[75] Most importantly for this study, the Children's Act abolished the death penalty for children under the age of 16. The Lord Advocate of the Bill declared:

> There was a time in the history of this House when a Bill of this kind would have been treated as a most revolutionary measure; and, half a century ago, if such a measure had been introduced it would have been said that the British Constitution was being undermined. Now a Bill of this kind finds itself in smooth water from the outset. This measure is not the development of the political ideas of one party, but the gradual development of a quickened sense on the part of the community at large of the duty it owes to the Children.[76]

---

67. Matthew Davenport Hill, as qtd. in Pinchbeck and Hewitt, *Children in English Society,* 477.

68. Taylor, *Crime, Policing, and Punishment,* 156.

69. Pinchbeck and Hewitt, *Children in English Society,* 483.

70. 1887 An Act to Permit the Conditional Release of First Offenders in Certain Cases (50 & 51 Victoria, c. 25). Further reforms of the probation system were enacted in the 1901 Youthful Offenders Act (1 Edw. 7, c. 20) and the 1907 Probation Act (7 Edw. 7, c. 17).

71. Radzinowicz and Hood, *A History of English Criminal Law,* 775.

72. Ibid.

73. Ibid., 376.

74. 1908 Children's Act (8 Edw.7, c. 67).

75. Pinchbeck and Hewitt, *Children in English Society,* 492.

76. Ibid., 612.

The passage of the Children's Act was then followed by ongoing activism in the 1920s and 1930s by societies for abolition, such as the Howard League, a charity still active today in England, and the NCADP, a relatively young organization that would be absorbed by the Howard League in 1948. These societies waged a well-orchestrated, multimedia campaign through newspapers, magazines, pamphlets, theatre, and radio broadcasts (among other media).[77] Their efforts led to the "first full-scale debate" on abolition of the child death penalty in the twentieth century in the 1929 Parliament, resulting in the formation of the 1930 Select Committee on Capital Punishment.[78] The Committee recommended, among other things, a five-year moratorium on the death penalty and the abolition of the penalty for those under 21.[79] Finally, in 1933, the Children and Young Persons Act abolished the death penalty for child offenders who commit their crimes when they are younger than 18.[80] The law was not perceived as revolutionary, as it was "merely making statutory what since 1887 had become the standard practice of reprieving all those under eighteen."[81]

The abolition of the child death penalty in England illustrates a larger pattern in English history: the gap between criminal codes and the actual practice of criminal justice. It is evident that the practice of executing children under the age of 18 had ceased forty-five years before it was codified in law.[82] As demonstrated, even when efforts to remove crimes from the list of capital offences failed, the practice of executing individuals who committed these crimes was often discontinued. Statutory reform sometimes lagged changes in practice by as much as fifty years.[83]

Christoph, however, argues that limitations to the death penalty in England in the nineteenth and twentieth centuries were principally the result of "the increased use of the reprieve power" rather than of substantial penal reform.[84] More than 45 percent of death sentences between 1900 and 1949, for example, were pardoned, reprieved, or commuted.[85] Christoph states, "Such modifications of the law were not the product of a groundswell of sentiment favourable to abolition. They came instead in the course of rather routine examinations of the criminal law and were

77. Tuttle, *The Crusade against Capital Punishment*, 31, 45.
78. Ibid., 33.
79. Ibid., 43.
80. Ibid.
81. Potter, *Hanging in Judgment*, 109.
82. Ibid.
83. Ibid., 138.
84. Christoph, *Capital Punishment and British Politics*, 17.
85. Ibid., 25.

unrelated to agitation against capital punishment."[86] Christoph further suggests that public concern over death penalty policy in the 1920s was the result of two influences that "reviv[ed] public interest and encouraged abolitionists to press for renewed action": campaigns by NGOs such as the Howard League and the NCADP; and the rise of the Labour Party, which formed minority governments in 1924 and 1929.[87]

Child Welfare

Advocates for penal reform were part of a larger social movement for children in England, which was in turn part of a general trend toward humanitarian reform.[88] The Industrial Revolution brought a spate of new law affecting children heretofore unseen in English history primarily because an increase in societal wealth made humanitarian legislation "affordable," according to Linda Pollock.[89] Sympathetic portraits of poor and parentless children found their way into English popular culture. Charles Dickens created Oliver Twist and Tiny Tim, children beset by crime and poverty, who had been failed by adults and society. Dickens was a hugely popular writer whose characters struck a chord in English society and became part of the contemporary culture. Through his high profile and mass audience, Dickens raised awareness of child welfare issues, which resonated with social reformers and their prospective audience. Yet Dickens was himself an important and serious voice for social reform, with a particular interest in penal reform and capital punishment.[90]

Reformers sought restrictions on child labor and increased educational opportunities for children in the early nineteenth century, advances that created spaces for children separate from those inhabited by adults. Child labor began to be restricted with the 1819 Factory Act and continued to be limited incrementally throughout the nineteenth and twentieth centuries.[91] These restrictions had support from working-class men, who

86. Ibid., 19.
87. Ibid.
88. Ibid.
89. Linda A. Pollock, *Forgotten Children: Parent-Child Relations from 1500 to 1900* (New York: Cambridge University Press, 1983): 60.
90. Sally Ledger and Holly Furneaux, *Charles Dickens in Context* (Cambridge and New York: Cambridge University Press, 2013): 303–305.
91. Michael Lavalette, "The Changing Form of Child Labour *Circa* 1880–1918: The Growth of 'Out of School Work'," in *A Thing of the Past? Child Labour in Britain in the Nineteenth and Twentieth Centuries*, ed. Michael Lavalette (New York: St. Martin's Press, 1999): 123; Pinchbeck and Hewitt, *Children in English Society*, 404.

believed their wages suffered as a result of child labor, and opposition from those that thought child labor prevented married women from working in factories.[92] Technological improvements also reduced the need for child labor, especially in the mining industry.[93] Formal education became free and compulsory for all children in 1870, separating children from adults during large portions of the day and standardizing their daily routines.[94]

Legislation limiting employment, making education compulsory, and protecting children from abuse entailed increasing state regulation of children and families. State control came at the expense of parental, especially paternal, control. Early in the nineteenth century, paternal rights were "paramount."[95] Mothers had little legal authority over their children. Until the nineteenth century:

> No court in England ever regarded itself as entitled entirely to extinguish a father's right to custody. Moreover, the principle of 'benefit of child' was much more narrowly interpreted than it would be today, and whenever this principle came into direct conflict with the 'sacred right of the father over his own children,' the Court of Chancery came down heavily on the side of the father.[96]

Holly Brewer has suggested, however, that the authority of parents that was usurped in the late nineteenth century by the state had not been recognized for long.[97] Sporadically in the seventeenth and eighteenth centuries, and certainly by the early nineteenth century, paternal authority had become widespread among all classes. Before this, only wealthy children and heirs under the age of 14 had legal custodians.[98] The implication is that childhood and children have repeatedly been naturalized throughout history: Parental authority in the early nineteenth century was asserted by legal commentators, rendering children property of the father, before being reduced by the state.

Before the passage of education and labor laws in the late nineteenth century, state intervention in families was reserved only for certain types

92. Pinchbeck and Hewitt, *Children in English Society,* 405.

93. Lavalette, "The Changing Form of Child Labour," 121; Peter Kirby, "The Historic Viability of Child Labour and the Mines Act of 1842," in *A Thing of the Past? Child Labour in Britain in the Nineteenth and Twentieth Centuries,* ed. Michael Lavalette (New York: St. Martin's Press, 1999): 101.

94. 1870 Education Act (33 & 34 Vict., c. 75).

95. Pinchbeck and Hewitt, *Children in English Society,* 362.

96. Ibid., 364.

97. Holly Brewer, *By Birth or Consent: Children, Law, & the Anglo-American Revolution in Authority* (Chapel Hill, NC: The University of North Carolina Press, 2005).

98. Ibid., 231–232, 250, 260, 271, 277.

of families. Since only poor families tended to have children who were beggars or vagrants, only these families experienced intervention. As a result, protections for children, ironically, were only applied to poor children before the nineteenth century.[99] By contrast, because only the children of wealthy parents attended school before compulsory education was introduced, only wealthy families experienced changes in education through state regulation of its nature, duration, content, and standards.

The first legal limitation to paternal authority in the nineteenth century was the 1839 Infants Custody Act.[100] The 1839 Act had the revolutionary effect of making paternal authority dependent upon the discretion of a judge, and was the "first statutory intervention in the common law rights of a father in [England]."[101] Other acts, such as the Matrimonial Causes Act of 1857, the 1886 Custody of Infants Act, the 1925 Guardianship of Infants Act,[102] and the 1928 Administration of Justice Act, further eroded paternal authority. Not all of these laws that divested paternal authority were based on concerns for child welfare, however; some were in response to a rising women's movement that demanded more protection and rights for women, including the right of women to parent.[103]

Yet the most direct challenge to paternal authority came from child welfare advocates, who successfully petitioned for new laws to prevent cruelty and neglect. The 1889 Prevention of Cruelty to Children Act[104] was the central piece of legislation outlawing abuse. Like the 1870 Education Act, the 1889 Act applied to all children (at least in theory) irrespective of class. These two acts marked a shift in thought about the young: The category of individuals referenced as 'children' was now defined *solely by age*.

The state's interest in children took a new turn in the twentieth century. Lorraine Fox Harding has argued that while public attention to children had waned by the 1920s and 1930s, "officials *were* enthusiastic about tackling juvenile delinquency."[105] The 1933 Children and Young Persons Act not only abolished the death penalty for child offenders, but also codified widespread changes in the treatment of children in the criminal justice system, raising the age of criminal responsibility to 8, for example.[106]

---

99. Pinchbeck and Hewitt, *Children in English Society*, 367.
100. 1839 Infants Custody Act (2 & 3 Vict., c. 54).
101. Pinchbeck and Hewitt, *Children in English Society*, 376.
102. 1925 Guardianship of Infants Act (15 & 16 Geo. 5, c. 45).
103. Pinchbeck and Hewitt, *Children in English Society*, 383.
104. 1889 Prevention of Cruelty to Children Act (52 & 53 Vict., c. 44).
105. Hendrick, *Children, Childhood, and English Society*, 51.
106. 1933 Children and Young Persons Act (23 & 24 Geo.V, c. 12, s. 50).

Regardless of the motivations behind the act,[107] the sections addressing the death penalty passed without debate, indicating the acceptance of norms about children's reduced culpability for their crimes.

Perhaps the most important and widely known advocacy organization for children, Save the Children, was founded in the United Kingdom by Eglantyne Jebb in 1920.[108] Jebb was a pioneer in child protection whose experiences during World War I led her to conclude, "Every war is a war against the child."[109] Dedicated to the causes of child rescue, child welfare, and child development, Save the Children expanded from its London origins to other states, starting with Canada and Australia, and would eventually become an international organization.[110] Travelling to Geneva, Jebb established the International Save the Children Union with the help and support of the International Committee of the Red Cross.[111] The organization's agenda on behalf of the world's children was ambitious and multifaceted: It collected and disseminated information about children and their condition throughout the world; sent teams of doctors and nurses with expertise in children's health and maternity abroad; and solicited support from politicians, church leaders, and society for its efforts.

Shortly after Save the Children was founded, Jebb began work on what would become the first Declaration of the Rights of the Child, otherwise known as the Declaration of Geneva. The declaration's name was in fact a misnomer; it did not grant rights to children, but rather imposed obligations on adults regarding children's welfare. Jebb used her platform from the newly minted international organization and its ties to the Red Cross to promote the declaration. In 1924, the League of Nations adopted the declaration without dissent; it was then reaffirmed by the League in 1934. In 1946, the United Nations "gave it renewed authority by resolution."[112]

107. For a debate of the motivations, implications, and analysis of the Act, please consult Pinchbeck and Hewitt, *Children in English Society*; Jean S. Heywood, *Children in Care: The Development of the Service for the Deprived Child*, 2nd ed. (London: Routledge & Kegan Paul, 1965); Nick Frost and Mike Stein, *The Politics of Child Welfare: Inequality, Power, and Change* (New York: Harvester Wheatsheaf, 1989); Nikolas Rose, *The Psychological Complex: Psychology, Politics, and Society in England 1869–1939* (London: Routledge & Kegan Paul, 1985); Victor Bailey, *Delinquency and Citizenship: Reclaiming the Young Offender, 1914–1948* (Oxford: Oxford University Press, 1987).

108. Fuller 1951, 24–26.

109. Peter Willetts, *"The Conscience of the World:" The Influence of Non-Governmental Organizations in the U.N. System* (Washington, DC: Brookings Institution, 1996): 215.

110. Ibid., 140.

111. Ibid., 141.

112. Fuller 1951, 73.

The first international treaty of its kind, the Declaration of Geneva established universal standards of child welfare and the safeguards to which all children were due. It was, in effect, the first articulation of a global model of childhood.

In sum, the case has shown that principled activists succeeded in changing attitudes toward children and creating norms of childhood in England over the course of the nineteenth and twentieth centuries, and also, importantly, that this attitudinal shift led to legal protections for children. State intervention on issues of child welfare began at a particular point in history, but this in no way implies that state intervention created concerns about child welfare. Rather, as Pollock has suggested, the state "had to learn not so much what a child is, but that its helplessness could be exploited by society and it therefore required state protection."[113]

Driven by the conviction that children are different from adults, that they are more vulnerable, less culpable, and susceptible to rehabilitation, important reformers like Romilly, Peel, Carpenter, and Jebb and NGOs such as the Howard League and Save the Children set standards of child welfare, pursued and won laws and policies of child protection, including the ban on the child death penalty, and through their efforts, formed the basis for the model of childhood that England would subsequently diffuse to its colonies throughout the world.

FRENCH CASE STUDY

France's experience with the death penalty and child offenders was considerably more convoluted than England's, but principled actors were essential in shaping the state's child policies and law. Motivated, like their English counterparts, by humanitarian concerns for children's welfare and for juvenile justice, these reformers traveled widely to observe institutions and facilities in the United States and in other European states. Most importantly, they formed networks for the exchange of ideas, philosophies, and information; for the discussion of new models and best practices; for the pooling of expertise; and for the mobilization of support for reform and advocacy efforts. As with the England case study, this section traces two reformist trends in France: penal reform and child welfare.

113. Pollock, *Forgotten Children*, 64.

Penal Reform

Fears about juvenile crime peaked in France in the early nineteenth century, as they did in many European and American cities.[114] Protections for children both in criminal codes and in practice were first enacted during the Bourbon Restoration (1814–1830), as Louis XVIII established separate quarters for minors within existing prisons.[115] Around the mid-nineteenth century, studies began to suggest that child criminals came from "broken or otherwise 'defective' families," leading advocates to argue for rehabilitation over punishment.[116] Reform schools, largely run by philanthropic societies, were established in the 1850s in response to these studies.[117] Reformers including Charles Lucas and Frédéric-Auguste Demetz worked to reform the penal system, creating colonies for child criminals based on the belief that their behavior was the result of their environment. As in England and elsewhere in the nineteenth (and twentieth) centuries, concern for child welfare in France was mixed with fear of crime and child criminals.[118] Philanthropic societies and charities dedicated to child welfare continued to proliferate in the nineteenth century, working to pass legislation and ameliorate some of the problems of child abuse, prostitution, and vagrancy.[119] *L'Assistance Publique*, the state social welfare system, was institutionalized in 1849 and took a steadily increasing interest in children's issues.[120]

Juvenile penal reform organizations formed in the nineteenth century, such as the Union Française pour le Sauvetage de L'Enfance (French Union for the Rescue of Children) and the Comité de Défense des Enfants Traduits en Justice (Committee to Defend Children in the Justice System). These organizations were influenced by reform initiatives in the United States, in particular, by the founding of the first juvenile court in Illinois in 1899 and in other US states and cities that followed suit.[121] The organizations

114. Ashurst and Venn, *Inequality*.

115. Sarah Fishman, *The Battle for Children: World War II, Youth Crime, and Juvenile Justice in Twentieth-Century France* (Cambridge, MA: Harvard University Press, 2002): 16.

116. Ibid., 32.

117. Philippe Meyer, *The Child and the State: The Intervention of the State in Family Life* (New York: Cambridge University Press, 1983): 19.

118. Fishman, *The Battle for Children*, 18.

119. Rachel Ginnis Fuchs, *Abandoned Children: Foundlings and Child Welfare in Nineteenth-Century France*, SUNY Series in Modern European Social History (Albany, NY: State University of New York Press, 1984): 48.

120. Ibid.

121. Fishman, *The Battle for Children*, 23–24.

called for France to emulate the US juvenile justice system, while advocates in other areas of child protection cited other models in the United States and throughout Europe.[122] The Comité would eventually expand to a number of cities throughout France, monitoring local courts and private and public institutions, along with advising judges and even serving as probation officers.[123]

The July Monarchy (1830–1848) took these early protections further by creating the first prison in France specifically for minors, La Petite-Roquette in Paris, and overseeing agricultural youth reform colonies, Val d'Yevre and Mettray.[124] These colonies were founded by Lucas and Demetz. Lucas advocated for a type of penal discipline known as the Auburn system, premised on the idea that prisoners should live communally (in contrast to the solitary confinement of the Pennsylvania system), and be engaged in productive activities that generated income for the facility.[125] Both the Auburn and the Pennsylvania systems were American innovations that had great influence on European thought on penal reform. Connected through intellectual circles to fellow reformers in the United Kingdom and the United States, Lucas shared ideas and information about new reform initiatives and approaches. Over the course of his lifetime, he shared correspondent membership in prison reform societies in England, Ireland, and several US cities.[126] Like Romilly in England, Lucas viewed the certainty of a penalty as essential to its efficacy, arguing that since the death penalty was used so rarely, it was ineffective.[127] Lucas also called for the separation of adult from juvenile offenders, formally proposing to a state committee in 1831 the founding of reform schools for child criminals.[128] The state would eventually purchase Lucas' agricultural colony, Val d'Yevre, helping to institutionalize the reform of children as a state responsibility.[129]

A commitment to the Auburn system aligned Lucas with other European intellectuals like Dickens and set him in opposition to others, such as Alexis de Toqueville and Demetz, who preferred the Pennsylvania

122. Ibid., 23.
123. Ibid., 23–24.
124. Ibid., 16–17.
125. Andre Normandeau, "Pioneers in Criminology: Charles Lucas—Opponent of Capital Punishment," *Journal of Criminal Law and Criminology* 61, no. 2 (1970): 218–228.
126. Ibid., 219.
127. Ibid., 224.
128. Ibid., 224–225.
129. Ibid., 225.

model of solitary confinement for adults.[130] After a visit to US reform schools, Demetz in 1840 founded the Mettray school of reform, which was later made famous by Foucault. Although Demetz publicly promoted the Pennsylvania model, Mettray functioned under a different philosophy, namely, that children were not permanent members of a criminal class and could be shaped by their environment. Through fresh air, hard work, and discipline, juvenile offenders could be rehabilitated and become productive members of society.[131] Drawing on the example of reform colonies in Switzerland, Holland, Belgium, and Germany, Mettray operationalized a decidedly European idea of child reform.[132]

It was France's defeat in the Franco-Prussian War in 1870 and the beginning of the Third Republic (1870–1940) that elevated state concern for children to a new level. Social theorists in France sought explanation for the defeat and located it in two conditions: depopulation and poor health among army recruits.[133] Although children under the age of 19 made up about one-third of the population and were recognized as a distinct social group, their percentage of the population was on the decline.[134] Concerns about the links between children's health and child labor had been raised as early as the 1820s, but the fear of an unfit military after France's defeat was a powerful catalyst for change.[135] Abandoned children and child criminals, once thought to burden state social programs and the public, were now accorded greater sympathy, their survival linked to the future of a country that could ill-afford to "waste a single child."[136]

The first modern criminal code, which regulated the death penalty, was the Napoleonic Penal Code of 1810.[137] Article 66 of the code specified 16 as the age of majority, but did not establish separate courts or prisons for minors.[138] Although the Code was not the first legal provision for child criminals (since 1719, a "plea of minority"[139] was heard by French courts), it was by far the most significant effort until that time. Progressive reform, however, was not uninterrupted. Historians have argued that Napoleon "was obsessed with reinforcing the father's authority in the family," and

---

130. Ashurst and Venn, *Inequality*, 90.
131. Ibid., 121.
132. Ibid.
133. Fuchs, *Abandoned Children*, 50; Heywood, *Childhood in Nineteenth-Century France*, 146–149; Fishman, *The Battle for Children*, 19.
134. Fuchs, *Abandoned Children*, 50.
135. Heywood, *Childhood in Nineteenth-Century France*, 146–149.
136. Fuchs, *Abandoned Children*, 40; Fishman, *The Battle for Children*, 12.
137. Fishman, *The Battle for Children*, 13; Code Pénal de 1810.
138. Ibid., 14.
139. Meyer, *The Child and the State*, 18.

the 1803 Civil Code, in which civil majority began at age 21, continued to permit paternal correction, whereby a father could order imprisonment for a rebellious child.[140]

The nineteenth-century *Code Penal* defined a minor as an individual younger than 16; this was raised in 1906 to age 18 (Law of 12 April 1906). By raising the age of majority to 18, other articles in the penal code concerning the treatment of minors now applied to those under 18 as well, including the laws governing the death penalty.[141] Thus technically, though not explicitly, the new code abolished the penalty for offenders under the age of 18.[142] The article raising the minimum age was never amended, although the understanding was that offenders under the age of 18 could no longer be legally executed. The public's reaction to the law was negative, but the state nonetheless supported reform over more punitive measures.[143] France would ultimately create its own children's court in 1912.[144]

The passage of Article 66,[145] the provision of the 1906 law that had the effect of prohibiting the child death penalty, was shaped by the practices of other states, much like the entire slate of reforms for children in the nineteenth and twentieth centuries. The French justice system was compared, specifically, with the "more enlightened and modern systems" of the United States and Belgium."[146] The United States was especially influential, "attracting French admiration and jealousy," and guiding the character of juvenile justice reform.[147] Nonetheless, the United States and France would, over the course of the twentieth century, chart opposing trajectories in their systems of juvenile justice.[148] Whereas the United States was a leader in the rehabilitation and reform of child offenders in the early twentieth century, by the century's end, its justice system and policies had become largely punitive, driven by public fear. France, conversely, adopted an increasingly progressive approach, moving from a fear of child offenders to a system based on rehabilitation and reclamation.[149] Although France did not amass the imperial power of the United

140. Fishman, *The Battle for Children*, 14.
141. Dr. Sarah Fishman, July 9, 2008.
142. Ibid.
143. Sarah Fishman, *The Battle for Children*, 25.
144. Meyer, *The Child and the State*, 42.
145. The article abolishing the child death penalty would later become Article 67 in a revision of the Penal Code.
146. Fishman, *The Battle for Children*, 32.
147. Ibid., 224–225.
148. Ibid., 13.
149. Ibid.

Kingdom and had less impact on world society, its diffusion of norms about children was still significant. France had unparalleled influence in North Africa and Southeast Asia, and helped to incorporate law and norms protecting children into the global model or template of legitimate statehood.

The ban on the child death penalty remained unchallenged until World War II, when under the Vichy regime, a new law was proposed that would lower the age of majority (established in the 1906 law) from 18 to 16, making child offenders between the ages of 16 and 18 eligible for the death penalty, among other (previously) adult punishments.[150] When the proposed new law was published in the *Official Journal*, the dean of the law faculty at Toulouse, Joseph Magnol, wrote to the Ministry of Justice expressing his indignation and confusion: "Perhaps it was an oversight of the project's editor or typographical error."[151] "Must I suppose," he continues, "that minors could, under this hypothesis, be sentenced as adults?"[152] Joseph Barhélemy (the Minister of Justice at the time) responded, "such criminal penalties in principle are applicable to minors who have incurred them, without any legal attenuation," but courts "would, however, never apply the criminal penalty."[153] The exchange suggests the extent of the norm's entrenchment or institutionalization in France by this time,[154] as the power of a norm can be gauged not by compliance alone, but also by way of *response* to its violation (or attempted violation).

In any event, the Penal Administration's "assurances must have rung hollow," and no application decree was passed by the regime.[155] Indeed, resistance fighters under the age of 18 were executed by Germany during the war, the most famous being Guy Moquet. Additionally, in the department of Charente-Maritime alone (on France's West coast), the Germans deported sixty-nine individuals under the age of 18 to concentration camps; of these children, forty-seven did not survive the war.[156] The path to death penalty reform in France would eventually end in 1981, when France outlawed the penalty for all crimes and all offenders.

---

150. Ibid., 169.
151. Ibid., 173.
152. Ibid., 173–174.
153. Ibid., 174.
154. Fishman, *The Battle for Children.*
155. Ibid., 174, 185.
156. W.D. Halls, *The Youth of Vichy France* (London and New York: Oxford University Press, 1981): 54.

Child Welfare

The protections for children enacted in France in the nineteenth century came out of a highly contested discourse about children. The country's Catholic tradition held that people were born of original sin, and that children needed punishment and rigid supervision to quell desires to sin. This religious doctrine conflicted with Enlightenment ideas, embodied in the work of John Locke and Jean-Jacques Rousseau, which stressed that human beings are shaped by experience and that education is required to create good citizens.[157] These different ideas about the nature of children competed with other schools of thought as well: Romanticism "idealized childhood as a period of natural innocence," while another posited that children were "precociously perverse."[158]

Prior to the changes in the eighteenth and nineteenth centuries, detailed below, responsibility for the family's welfare was the father's alone, and he had state institutions at his disposal to back up his authority.[159] Restrictions on paternal correction existed before the nineteenth century (based on ordinances passed in 1673, 1678, and 1697), but this system did not involve an outright or permanent transfer of authority from the father to the state.[160] Limits in age (25 being the oldest a rebellious child could be detained) were slowly replaced by class-based restrictions, with poor and working-class fathers unable to remove children from detention. This early form of state intervention, whereby only some fathers were allowed to retain control over their children, became state policy in the mid-eighteenth century as concerns were raised about abuses of paternal correction.[161]

Beginning around 1760, reformers began advocating for a system of public assistance that would make the social welfare of French nationals the responsibility of the state rather than of the Church or private charities.[162] For the most part, however, a laissez-faire ideology that was hostile to social legislation prevailed in the late eighteenth century.[163] The French Revolution brought a sudden and radical shift away from this approach.

---

157. Fishman, *The Battle for Children*, 15.
158. Ibid., 16.
159. Meyer, *The Child and the State*, 28.
160. Ibid., 28–29.
161. Ibid.
162. Fuchs, *Abandoned Children*, 17.
163. Colin Heywood, *Childhood in Nineteenth-Century France: Work, Health, and Education among the 'Classes Populaires'* (New York: Cambridge University Press, 1988): 221.

The Revolution further undermined the role of the private sector and the Church as providers of social welfare, as the wealth of Church and clergy was largely nationalized.[164] The new Constitution of France in 1791 affirmed the state's commitment to caring for abandoned children and codified these practices in the decree of January 19, 1811.[165] This decree articulated the shift in responsibility for child welfare from the father to the state that would become a major theme of social policymaking in the nineteenth century.[166] State intervention on the basis of child welfare was not uncontested, however. Restrictions on child labor were challenged by liberal economists who believed that all economic issues could be resolved by free market policies as opposed to government regulation.[167]

Although we tend to think of child welfare reform as progressively expanding to protect older children, in France, the opposite was the case. Organizing children by *classes d'age* was actually more common before the nineteenth century as young, single men were distinguished from adults during the *ancien regime*.[168] For example, the age of civil majority in France was lowered to 21 (from 25 in 1792).[169] These age categories would slowly be replaced by class and social divisions as the century went on.[170]

As in other countries in the West, France began to take up issues of education and child labor in the early to mid-nineteenth century, and by the century's end, children would mostly cease to be laborers and become students.[171] Colin Heywood, in a survey of French historians, found that many scholars merged economic with humanitarian arguments, suggesting that changes in industry, such as the introduction of steam power, allowed men to replace women and children in factories, and that this shift, together with an emerging ideology of education as a birthright, would change the lives of children in working-class and poor families.[172] Most of these scholars also cite state intervention as the main driver of change.[173] Phillippe Meyer, for example, contends, "Official charity, real compassion, statistics, and study all combined with speculation (also very real) and the industrial boom, to increase massive intervention on the part of the State."[174] The

---

164. Fuchs, *Abandoned Children*, 17.

165. Ibid., 18; Décret du 19 janvier 1811, concernant les enfants trouvés ou abandonnés et les orphelins pauvres.

166. Ibid., 18, 26.

167. Heywood, *Childhood in Nineteenth-Century France*, 221.

168. Ibid., 82.

169. Hunt, *Inventing Human Rights*, 62; Heywood, *Childhood in Nineteenth-Century*, 319.

170. Heywood, *Childhood in Nineteenth-Century France*, 82.

171. Heywood, *Childhood in Nineteenth-Century France*, 3.

172. Ibid., 3–5.

173. Ibid., 6.

174. Meyer, *The Child and the State*, 6.

first child labor law was passed in 1841, but not effectively enforced until the subsequent laws of 1874 and 1892.[175] What is clear is that as early as the 1830s, France was looking to the labor laws and educational practices of European and other states, particularly the United Kingdom, United States, Switzerland, and Germany.[176] In limiting child labor, even though the law was in the beginning only spottily enforced, France was emulating other countries in the West.[177]

The child labor law of 1841 was a top-down measure, and the public response to it was largely hostile.[178] The origins of the law, as with other child protection and welfare measures in France, were "in the minds of a small group of middle-class reformers."[179] The state, meanwhile, also sought to ensure a "quality labour force" with a "rational exploitation of child labour" in order to enhance productivity.[180] Trade competition with Britain in the mid-nineteenth century heightened concerns about industrial education, but here again it was mainly the defeat by the Prussians in 1870 that gave the final push for state intervention in the workplace.[181] The result was that the Third Republic focused more on children "than perhaps any other regime in France's history."[182]

The 1874 law limiting child labor (the second such law passed) actually met with little opposition, as factory owners and parents alike endorsed the belief that "young children were more usefully occupied in schools than in the workshops."[183] The government also regulated the employment of wet nurses (a key health issue for infants) in 1874, and in 1880, created a free, secular educational system that mandated school attendance until the age of 13.[184]

Efforts to protect children led to a significant increase in state intervention in the lives of families.[185] Nowhere was this more evident than in the Law of 14 July 1889, *On the Protection of Ill-Treated and Morally Abandoned*

175. Fishman, *The Battle for Children*, 18; Heywood, *Childhood in Nineteenth-Century France*, 3–6; Loi sur la limitation du travail des enfants, 1841; Loi du 19 mai 1874 sur le travail des enfants et des filles mineures employés dans l'industrie (Bulletin de l'Assemblée nationale, XII, B. CCIV, n. 3094); Loi du 2 novembre 1892 sur le travail des enfants, des filles et de femmes dans les établissements industriels.

176. Heywood, *Childhood in Nineteenth-Century France*, 230.

177. Ibid.

178. Ibid., 228, 231.

179. Ibid., 231.

180. Ibid., 232.

181. Ibid., 262–264.

182. Fishman, *The Battle for Children*, 19.

183. Heywood, *Childhood in Nineteenth-Century France*, 313.

184. Fishman, *The Battle for Children*, 19; Heywood, *Childhood in Nineteenth-Century*, 260; Loi Roussel: Loi du 23 décembre 1874 relative à la protection des enfants de premier âge; Lois scolaires de Jules Ferry: Loi du 27 février 1880 relative au Conseil supérieur de l'instruction publique et aux conseils académiques.

185. Heywood, *Childhood in Nineteenth-Century*, 260.

Children, which gave the state the power to terminate the parental rights of abused children (*decheance de puissance paternelle*).[186] Protection was also extended to children labeled "*moralement abandonnes*," allowing the state to revoke parental authority "in cases of perceived immorality— vice, drunkenness, crime."[187] Children deemed at risk could become wards of the state with an official of *l'Assistance Publique* as their guardian."[188] This law, combined with the Law of 19 April 1898, *On the Suppression of Violence, Assault, and Battery, Acts of Cruelty, and Attempted Murder Committed Toward Children*, demonstrated a willingness to intervene in families where children were threatened.[189]

By the end of the nineteenth century, education was considered neces- sary for both girls and boys, and children were sent to school for longer hours and for more years than in earlier decades.[190] At the same time (be- ginning in 1877), doctors were sent to the countryside and spread new ideas about health and sanitation to parents there, a development that allowed for an increase in supervision of and state and professional in- fluence over families.[191] Compulsory attendance at school also allowed for the supervision of children by teachers, nurses, and school psycholo- gists.[192] The Third Republic expanded its authority in all areas of children's lives "through intermediaries—doctors, teachers, psychologists, social workers, juvenile judges, legislators—who regulated education and the rights of parents."[193] Intervention was also carried out through the sys- tematization of health care, poor relief, and policing.[194]

Through such measures, the state came to be perceived as the "protec- tor of the weak."[195] As in England, state intervention was premised on a fear of parents, as the home came to be seen as the most dangerous place for children. Through the changes institutionalized during the Third Republic, the child was understood to be the "essential part of the family," and parental authority over the child in effect required the approval of the state.[196] The threat to remove children from the family became the state's most powerful weapon of intervention.[197]

---

186. Ibid., Fishman, *The Battle for Children*, 21.
187. Fuchs, *Abandoned Children*, 58.
188. Ibid., 58–59.
189. Fishman, *The Battle for Children*, 21; Loi du 19 avril 1898: Loi sur la répression des violences, voies de faits, actes de cruauté et attentats commis envers les enfants.
190. Ibid., 53.
191. Fuchs, *Abandoned Children*, 57.
192. Ibid.
193. Ibid., 49.
194. Meyer, *The Child and the State*, 6–7.
195. Fuchs, *Abandoned Children*, 49.
196. Meyer, *The Child and the State*, 11–12.
197. Ibid., 12.

As state responsibility for children increased, paternal power over children declined. Almost immediately, the Third Republic restricted parental correction in 1870, and further modified it in 1889 and 1904.[198] The family, during the Third Republic:

> was removed from its pedestal as the all-important socializing agency. To middle-class bureaucrats, not all working-class families—whether biological or foster—could be trusted to raise law-abiding, hard-working citizens without help from 'experts.' The protection of children's health and lives, not the increased expenditures such protection would cost, was the overriding concern of the legislators.[199]

The nineteenth century in France thus ended with an increasingly bureaucratized and highly emboldened state bent on protecting children not only from societal and environmental hazards in the public sphere, such as the dangers of the factory, but most readily from danger at home. Moreover, the trend toward state empowerment would continue apace. The twentieth century began with a strong statement: The Law of 1904 gave the state full responsibility for the welfare and protection of children. This was followed shortly thereafter by the 1906 Law, which raised the age of criminal majority to 18 and, as stated, banned the death penalty for child offenders.[200]

As described above, charities and churches suffered after the Revolution when the state nationalized the Church's wealth. The state gradually assumed many of the responsibilities of these institutions and, as the nineteenth century progressed, became the primary provider of child-saving activities. Philanthropic organizations remained active, however, and were the impetus behind many child protection laws and the ideological home of many child advocates who pushed for their enactment.[201] These organizations served the objectives of state intervention, reporting cases of mistreatment and abuse, as well as absorbing the children removed from 'abnormal' families.[202] Patronage de l'Enfance et de l'Adolescence (Child and Youth Patronage), Société pour l'Enfance Abandonnée et Coupable (Society for Abandoned and Guilty Children), and Union Française pour le Sauvetage de l'Enfance, to name a few, were among the many prominent organizations that worked to protect children from exploitation, abuse,

198. Fishman, *The Battle for Children*, 37; Hunt, *Inventing Human Rights*, 61–62.
199. Ibid., 60–61.
200. Ibid., 60.
201. Ibid., 59.
202. Meyer, *The Child and the State*, 37.

neglect, vagrancy, and prostitution. The emergence and activism of these groups corresponds closely with the child-saving movement in the United States around this time, discussed in chapter 6.[203]

PRINCIPLED ADVOCACY

As the case studies of England and France have demonstrated, a nascent international advocacy network emerged to address issues in child welfare and penal reform over the course of the nineteenth and early twentieth centuries. These national movements mostly moved in concert, sharing information and expertise, influencing one another, and learning from one another's successes and failures. The state's part in bringing about changes affecting children cannot be overstated: The governments of England and France passed reform measures, built bureaucracies, and expanded their administrative capacity to implement and enforce standards of child welfare and protection, displacing the charities and religious organizations that had traditionally been entrusted with children's care.

The work of these norm entrepreneurs was guided and informed by shared ideas of children as vulnerable and in need of care (and, in the case of child offenders, as less culpable for their crimes). This model of childhood, this collection of related ideas of what a child was and what it required of the state, became institutionalized in England and France through the successful advocacy of these early entrepreneurs, whose work resulted in the enactment of penal reform and child welfare measures that set new, higher, state-ensured standards for children's treatment that socialized English and French society to this model of childhood over time.

The abolition of the death penalty for child offenders was part of a larger trend in England toward the development of a standardized childhood, or a childhood whereby most children have similar experiences across class, status, ethnicity, gender, and locality.[204] The passage of universal education, employment limitations, and protections from abuse and neglect meant that children's lives were becoming more homogenous. In France, a similar march toward state intervention occurred as well. The standardization of childhood had two major components: First, childhood, replete with standards of care, health, education, employment, hygiene, and morality, was legitimated and institutionalized by science, the medical

---

203. Fuchs, *Abandoned Children*, 59.
204. C. John Sommerville, *The Rise and Fall of Childhood* (Beverly Hills, CA: Sage, 1982).

profession, schools, and social welfare programs. Second, the creation of children as objects of scientific study and the new consensus that the most dangerous place for children was in the home required a shift in authority over children from the father to the state.

The emergent model of childhood, however, was dependent upon the vision of norm entrepreneurs who introduced and spread new ideas about children. Science merely provided the justification for the standard; the state provided enforcement. In other words, a standardized childhood is only half of the story. The other half belongs to the men and women who advocated for children, shared and spread their ideas, fought to restrict the death penalty, and sought to reform the penal and judicial systems in England and in France.

The Science of Childhood

The scientific study of childhood began most notably in England with an 1815 study on the causes of juvenile crime, which found that delinquency could be frequently attributed to poor parenting, and in France a few decades later. The findings of the 1815 study reveal changing ideas about children and child offenders in the nineteenth century—most importantly, that they are products of their environment. This proposition would lead to concerted efforts over the course of the nineteenth and twentieth centuries to control the environments that shape children and the adults they would become. The home, workplace, school, and even playground were increasingly subject to new regulations enacted to protect children and promote their development.

Through penal reform and new legislation on child welfare, a standardized childhood began to emerge that included children of both genders and all classes. Whereas children in different circumstances (especially in terms of class) led remarkably different lives prior to the nineteenth century, children's experiences were fast becoming more and more the same. These changes were driven by reform advocates and, increasingly, by the state, to end the abuse of children in the home and to provide guidance and structure in schools, churches, and reformatories.

From the outset, natural and social scientists helped to shape these efforts and sought to gauge their success. The field of pediatrics, especially, emerging in the mid- to late-nineteenth century, provided standards for nutrition, hygiene, and physical and psychological well-being.[205] Social

---

205. Hendrick, *Children, Childhood, and English Society*, 12; Baistow, "From Sickly Survival," 22; Fuchs, *Abandoned Children*, 49.

scientists examined the effects of abuse, neglect, and child labor; developed curricula; and studied the nature of children. These studies and the guidelines for child welfare that they informed created a set of expectations of childhood, one free from exploitation and abuse and characterized by good health, a safe environment, and a quality education. Ideas about childhood not supported by the natural and social science were discarded over time.

Schools helped to standardize childhood by providing a routinized space, apart from the adult world (especially the father), where children were made available to science.[206] Education allowed for the monitoring of children for signs of abuse and neglect by school doctors and nurses.[207] Mandatory education also increased the commonalities in children's experiences by making full-time work difficult. The result was that poor and upper-class children, as the twentieth century progressed, had increasingly similar daily routines.[208] The standardization of childhood, according to John Sommerville, provided a "childhood for everyone, even if it meant squeezing some of them into the mould."[209]

Mandatory school attendance propelled the nascent field of pediatrics and its guidelines for nutrition, hygiene, and physical and mental health, as doctors now had captive subjects to study.[210] The child became the "object of the medical gaze," according to David Armstrong, "which provided the intellectual justification for the creation and identification of children's distinctive attributes."[211] Efforts to improve child health were "piecemeal" in the nineteenth century, but were much more systematic by the twentieth.[212]

A new focus on infant mortality helped to create the child as an object of study. Although infant mortality rates had been estimated prior to the

206. Fuchs, *Abandoned Children*, 49; Lavalette, "The Changing Form of Child Labour," 126.

207. Hendrick, *Children, Childhood, and English Society*, 41; Lavalette, "The Changing Form of Child Labour," 126.

208. Lavalette, "The Changing Form of Child Labour," 126.

209. Sommerville, *The Rise and Fall of Childhood*, 189.

210. Fielding H. Garrison and Arthur Frederick Abt, "History of Pediatrics," in *Abt-Garrison History of Pediatrics*, ed. Isaac A Abt M.D. (Philadelphia: W. B. Saunders, 1965).

211. David Armstrong, *Political Anatomy of the Body: Medical Knowledge in Britain in the Twentieth Century* (Cambridge, UK: Cambridge University Press, 1983): 12; Hendrick, *Children, Childhood, and English Society*.

212. Karen Baistow, "From Sickly Survival to the Realisation of Potential: Child Health as a Social Project in Twentieth Century England," *Children & Society* 9, no. 1 (1995): 23.

late nineteenth century, infant mortality only became a widespread public concern in the second half of that century.[213] Some authors have linked declines in infant deaths to a rise in children's social value, but evidence from the English case suggests that this is not completely accurate.[214] Rather, it was the documentation of infant mortality *itself* that indicated a newfound social preoccupation with children. David Armstrong has suggested that the concern with infant mortality also marked the "social recognition of the infant as a discrete entity."[215] Moreover, Harry Hendrick argues that infant mortality was "invented" in the late nineteenth century because "infant deaths only appeared in the Census as 'infant mortality rate' in 1877."[216] Hendrick contends that it was this new "medical problem" that "signified the emergence of the infant as an object of sociological and medical interest."[217]

In England and France, before the emergence of common standards of childhood in the late nineteenth century, laws—both in text and practice—tended to distinguish among classes of children. For the most part, formal education was limited to upper- and middle-class children, and the regulation of education only applied to them.[218] Class also guided state intervention in family life. Intervention principally affected poor families because only children from these families worked or begged outside the home and were thus vulnerable to regulation by the state. Yet the category of "children" that emerged in the late nineteenth century was defined *solely by age*; there were no other qualifiers (at least in law). This model of childhood, one familiar to readers today, truly gave rise to a standardized childhood because it was applied to *all* children regardless of class or status. Twentieth-century laws, including the 1933 Children and Young Persons Act and the 1906 revisions to the *Code Penal*, were borne of this standard.

213. Pinchbeck and Hewitt, *Children in English Society,* 349.

214. Vivianna A. Zelizer, *Pricing the Priceless Child: The Changing Social Value of Children* (Princeton, NJ: Princeton University Press, 1994); Cunningham, *Children and Childhood.*

215. David Armstrong, "The Invention of Infant Mortality," *Sociology of Health and Illness* 8, no. 3 (1986): 212.

216. Hendrick, *Children, Childhood, and English Society,* 43; Armstrong, "The Invention of Infant Mortality," 212.

217. Hendrick, *Children, Childhood, and English Society,* 43.

218. Heywood argues that in the Middle Ages, children were distinguished by age, but that class distinctions slowly replaced these categories. Age then supplants class beginning in the nineteenth century, in a process that is yet to be completed today in some areas of state intervention. See Heywood, *Childhood in Nineteenth-Century France,* 82.

The Role of the State

The history of child welfare is a history of the divestment of paternal authority over children by the state. The early examples of this divestment in English law, as discussed, primarily targeted poor families. Likewise in France, early social welfare measures by the state were focused solely on the poor.[219] It was not until the late nineteenth and early twentieth centuries, with the passage of restrictions on child labor, compulsory education, and efforts to protect children from neglect and abuse that paternal authority was undermined for all families.

As the model of childhood grew more specific and complex in the mid-to-late nineteenth century, the state began to take on a greater role in monitoring it. Compulsory education, for example, created the need for a force of truant officers to monitor attendance.[220] Norms that depicted children as property were discarded through the initiates of norm entrepreneurs and replaced by new norms. Significant among these were the ideas that children were trusts and that the state functioned as trustee. This shift in thought came at the expense of paternal authority. Hendrick writes, "Parental authority began to be reduced as it found itself in conflict with the state over such issues as infant life protection, compulsory schooling, and child rearing practices."[221] The justification for the decline of paternal authority was provided by science. The government assumed oversight in issues of health and safety during the late Victorian era,[222] while parents, the possible source of abuse and criminality, were not to be trusted.[223] Only the state could assess deviance from the standard of childhood.[224]

Restrictions to the child death penalty also required the divestment of paternal authority. For the state to act on behalf of the child, and thus to treat child offenders differently from adult criminals, the state had first to divest the father of his authority. This gradual process began in the early nineteenth century when children's behavior and character, and thus crime, were linked to family life and paternal influence. In order to reduce the culpability of children, in other words, alternative sources of fault had to be identified; the divestment of paternal authority was needed to minimize the guilt of children and thus limit the punishments for which they

219. Fuchs, *Abandoned Children*, 17.
220. Lavalette, "The Changing Form of Child Labour," 126.
221. Hendrick, *Children, Childhood, and English Society*, 45.
222. Taylor, *Crime, Policing, and Punishment*, 44.
223. Fuchs, *Abandoned Children*, 49.
224. Lavalette, "The Changing Form of Child Labour," 126.

were liable. The rise of nationalism and a new understanding of children as the future of the nation had a powerful impact on the relationship between the child and the state, making child welfare a government priority. Children's health was directly linked to the health of the nation.[225] The sorry shape of recruits for the Boer War, when 40 percent had been rejected because they were physically unfit for service, and the defeat of the French by the Prussians underscored the link between healthy children and "the health of the body politic."[226] The family and the child, then, became a focal point of public policy.[227] Infant mortality, for example, was a growing state concern in the late nineteenth and early twentieth centuries because the threat of a declining population was connected to the state's long-term survival.[228] Additionally, Hendrick and others have argued that it was a new push for a "truly *national* childhood" in England that allowed all other divisions of children, such as class and rural/urban distinctions, to fall away.[229]

Norm Entrepreneurs

The above case studies underscore the importance of norm entrepreneurs in changing how children and childhood were perceived in England and France and in the adoption of laws to protect children. The motivations of these advocates were varied and complex, although there is ample evidence from the cases that they shared a view of their actions as humanitarian. Science, for many advocates of penal reform, abolition of the death penalty, and child welfare, was merely a tool for change, a method of informing and empowering their humanitarianism so that it was more effective in achieving particular desired ends. The new science of humanitarianism deplored appeals to emotion. Roy Calvert, a prominent abolitionist and founder of the NCADP, sought, for example, to rid the movement of "futile emotion and sentiment,"[230] and to combine "the passion of the religious humanitarian with the empiricism of the social scientist."[231]

225. Baistow, "From Sickly Survival," 20; Heywood, *Childhood in Nineteenth-Century*, 148–149.

226. Baistow, "From Sickly Survival," 24.

227. Ibid.; Fuchs, *Abandoned Children*, 60–61.

228. Baistow, "From Sickly Survival," 30; Heywood, *Childhood in Nineteenth-Century*, 148–149.

229. Hendrick, *Children, Childhood, and English Society*, 12.

230. Tuttle, *The Crusade against Capital Punishment*, 48.

231. Christoph, *Capital Punishment and British Politics*, 31.

Evidence from the English and French cases indicates that normative changes in penal reform, restriction of the death penalty, and advances in child welfare were dependent upon norm entrepreneurs who framed and marketed their message using scientific findings and humanitarian rhetoric. Reformers like Lucas, Demetz, and Carpenter formed valuable information networks, traveling widely to observe facilities and institutions, identifying new approaches and best practices, and sharing their findings. Organizations, such as Save the Children, conducted international research and spread norms of child welfare and protection between states, developing coalitions of intellectuals, legislators, lawyers, and activists.[232] That the state stepped in to monitor these successful norms, bolstering them in the process, is not in doubt; sociological institutionalists have exhaustively demonstrated the role of state consolidation in strengthening norms and institutions.[233] Foucault and those that employ his theories have illustrated the role of power and knowledge in regulating state subjects through science.[234] These theorists, however, have not fully accounted for emergence—sociological institutionalists can explain the spread of the standard, Foucault the process, but neither approach is complete without an explanation for emergence.

Additionally, science offered qualitative and quantitative benchmarks and the means to construct children by distinguishing them from adults, tools to measure and address deviation from this construction, and legitimacy for state control. Yet while science may have advanced norms about reduced child culpability, shaped them, fostered them, and spread them, and while the state may have regulated and enforced them, it was the norm entrepreneur that created them in the first place.

Modern childhood has its origins in the work of normative agents whose personal sense of morality drove them to press for reform, including restrictions to the death penalty for child offenders, even in the face of rising crime rates in the nineteenth and twentieth centuries. These advocates could have called for compulsory education for middle-class children only, penal reform just for girls, or sought to abolish the death penalty

---

232. See for example, William Tallack, *The Practical Results of Total or Partial Abolition of Capital Punishment in Various Countries* (London: Society for the Abolition of Capital Punishment, 1866).

233. Ramirez, Soysal, and Shanahan, "The Changing Logic of Political Citizenship"; Boli-Bennett and Meyer, "The Ideology of Childhood and the State"; Meyer et al., "World Society and the Nation-State"; Francisco O. Ramirez and Marc Ventresca, "Building the Institution of Mass Schooling," in *The Political Construction of Education*, eds. B. Fuller and R. Rubinson (New York: Praeger, 1992).

234. Hendrick, *Children, Childhood, and English Society*, 5.

only for poor children. Their advocacy on behalf of *all children* created the subjects of both science and the state.

This is not to say that science and humanitarian ideas in nineteenth-century England and France did not, in turn, shape the entrepreneur or her decisions. As with other social movements, ideas about science and humanitarianism co-constituted both childhood and its advocates. Even so, it was the entrepreneur who launched the mission, the entrepreneur who created and diffused the model of childhood amid public fear and rising delinquency.

CONCLUSION

This chapter has examined the emergence of the norm restricting the death penalty to those 18 and older through the case studies of England and France. It has argued that abolition was part of a larger standardization of childhood developed by norm entrepreneurs who depicted children as vulnerable and dependent in order to facilitate greater state control over their lives and the lives of their families. This emergent model of childhood was legitimated by science and enforced by the state. For the state to monitor children, however, the father had to be divested of his authority over the child. This chapter has demonstrated the agency of norm entrepreneurs who campaigned for laws of child protection, including protection from the death penalty, because they believed that children were different from adults; that childhood has distinguishing traits, including heightened vulnerability and reduced culpability; and that society was responsible for children's welfare. These norms in turn reshaped the relationship between the state and the child, and would in time come to comprise a single common model of childhood for all children. It was the start of a path that would eventually lead to international children's rights, as England and France diffused norms about children and childhood through colonialism, as discussed in the next chapter.

Principled activism would come to play an important part at another stage of the norm's diffusion, during the late period when NGOs were working to bring the United States and other laggards into compliance. In their campaigns against the child death penalty, these NGOs would form a more sophisticated network over time, and, in one case from the United States, would eventually form a coalition with a common source of funding. As such, the agency of principled actors was not confined to the early stage of diffusion, before international law developed on the issue of the child death penalty, as will be discussed further in chapter 5.

CHAPTER 4

✧

Coercive Socialization as a Mechanism of Diffusion

INTRODUCTION

Of the three mechanisms of diffusion examined in this book, coercive socialization is, by far, the least explored in the international relations literature. While many studies have been made of plural legal systems, where two or more sources or systems of law exist in a single area, there is little overlap between these studies and the literature on norms and diffusion.[1]

---

1. Sally Falk Moore, "Law and Social Change: The Semi-Autonomous Social Field as an Appropriate Subject of Study," *Law and Society Review* 7, no. 4 (1973): 719–746; Sally Falk Moore, "Legal Systems of the World," in *Law and the Social Science*, eds. Leon Lipson and Stanton Wheeler (New York: Russell Sage Foundation, 1986): 11–62; Gunther Teubner, "The Two Faces of Janus: Rethinking Legal Pluralism," *Cardozo Law Review* 13, no. 1443 (1992): 1443–1462; Brian Z. Tamanaha, "The Folly of the 'Social Scientific' Concept of Legal Pluralism," *Journal of Law and Society* 20, no. 2 (1993): 192–217; Sally Engle Merry, "Legal Pluralism," *Law and Society Review* 22, no. 5 (1988): 869–896; Masaji Chiba, *Legal Pluralism: Toward a General Theory through Japanese Legal Culture* (Tokyo: Tokai University Press, 1989); Jørgen Dalberg-Larsen, *The Unity of Law, an Illusion? On the Legal Pluralism in Theory and Practice*, Mobility and Norm Change, v. 2 (Glienicke/Berlin and Cambridge, MA: Galda + Wilch, 2000); Baudouin Dupret, Maurits Berger, and Laila al-Zwaini, *Legal Pluralism in the Arab World*, Arab and Islamic Laws Series 18 (The Hague and Boston: Kluwer Law International, 1999); Kayleen M. Hazlehurst, *Legal Pluralism and the Colonial Legacy: Indigenous Experiences of Justice in Canada, Australia, and New Zealand* (Aldershot, UK: Avebury, 1995); M.B. Hooker, *Legal Pluralism: An Introduction to Colonial and Neo-Colonial Laws* (Oxford: Clarendon, 1975); Warwick Tie, *Legal Pluralism: Toward a Multicultural Conception of Law* (Aldershot, UK: Ashgate/Dartmouth, 1999); Robert L. Kidder, "Toward an Integrated Theory of Imposed Law," in *The Imposition of Law*, eds. Sandra

Through an examination of four former colonies—Algeria, Kenya, Tanganyika/Tanzania, and Tunisia—and two additional states—Ethiopia and Japan—I investigate two types of diffusion: *voluntary diffusion*, which occurs when states choose to bring in foreign jurists to craft a new legal system or model their legal system after a foreign system of law; and *coercive socialization* or forced socialization. I argue in this chapter that coercive socialization was the primary mechanism by which the norm against the child death penalty spread through the British and French empires. The process of diffusion was gradual and took place in stages. First, through the establishment of bureaucracies that institutionalized Western legal principles and systems, British and French colonial powers spread Western norms about children, including the norm prohibiting the child death penalty. Coercive methods were partly justified, at least in the British Empire, by the treatment of women and children by native men and by cultural restrictions imposed on women and children in native societies. The position of women and children in these societies was held up against Western norms of protection in England and elsewhere in Europe. Native children, especially, were made available for study through various state-run apparatuses, such as orphanages and reformatories, and these studies demonstrated to the colonizers the inability of native people to properly raise and care for children, thus justifying colonial rule.

Second, upon independence, the former colonies of Britain and France maintained protections for children and even increased them in the first few decades of statehood. This occurred because the newly minted states had internalized key parts of the colonial state model that not only recognized the validity of children's protection, but could not imagine a means of ensuring this protection outside of law. Over time, the legal systems developed in the colonies established a legal relationship between the child and the state that was internalized and retained following independence.

B. Burman and Barbara E. Harrell-Bond (New York: Academic Press, 1979): 289–306; Boaventura de Sousa Santos, *Toward a New Legal Common Sense: Law, Globalization and Emancipation*, 2nd ed., Law in Context (London: Butterworths LexisNexis, 2002); Boaventura de Sousa Santos and César A. Rodríguez Garavito, *Law and Globalization from Below: Towards a Cosmopolitan Legality* (Cambridge and New York: Cambridge University Press, 2005); Gunther Teubner, *Global Law without a State*, Studies in Modern Law and Policy (Aldershot, UK: Dartmouth, 1997); John Griffiths, "What Is Legal Pluralism?" *Journal of Legal Pluralism and Unofficial Law* 24, no. 1 (1986): 1–55; William Burke-White, "International Legal Pluralism," *Michigan Journal of International Law* 25, no. 963 (2004): 963–979; Nico Krisch, "The Pluralism of Global Administrative Law," *European Journal of International Law* 17, no. 1 (2006): 247–278; David Sugarman, *Legality, Ideology, and the State*, Law, State, and Society Series 11 (London and New York: Academic, 1983).

Like most former colonies, all four African and MENA countries included in these case studies abolished the child death penalty upon independence, maintaining the British and French colonial policy against the punishment for those under the age of 18. While Algeria and Kenya continued the ban, Tanganyika (which merged with Zanzibar to become the United Republic of Tanzania in 1964) and Tunisia later repealed their statutes and reauthorized the penalty for child offenders under the age of 18. Both Tanzania and Tunisia, however, are currently compliant with the norm.[2] All four cases illustrate the mechanism of coercive socialization. The smaller case studies of Japan and Ethiopia serve as a counterpoint to the colonial cases, demonstrating that different forms of socialization occurred outside the colonies. In Ethiopia, there was a process of *voluntary socialization* whereby the country's leaders invited Western legal scholars to draft laws that included restricting the death penalty to those 18 and older. Although Japan abolished the penalty shortly after World War II while under Western occupation, the policy nonetheless complemented previous efforts in Japan to protect children.

Data Disclaimer

The history of the child death penalty in Africa and the Middle East before and during colonialism is difficult to research. Where criminal law and historical studies mention the death penalty, there is little information about restrictions (such as age) or about prevalence. Before colonialism, African customary law was oral, but there is evidence that the death penalty was used in many precolonial communities.[3] The British and French colonial powers used the death penalty in their colonies to control their empires and, eventually, as the next section will argue, diffused the norm limiting the penalty to adults (among other limitations).[4] The Belgians, Germans, and Spanish also applied the death penalty in their colonies, although there is no evidence that they diffused the norm protecting children from the penalty.[5]

---

2. Tunisia reabolished in 1989 and Tanzania reabolished in 1997.
3. African Commission on Human and People's Rights, Working Group on the Death Penalty in Africa, "Study on the Question of the Death Penalty in Africa," adopted at the 50th Ordinary Session (24 October–7 November, 2011), Banjul, The Gambia, 24.
4. African Commission, "Study on the Question of the Death Penalty," 26.
5. Ibid.

Details about the British and French use of the penalty are spotty. Stacey Hynd has argued, for example, that the death penalty in general was used only about twenty times per year on average by the British (outside of Nigeria, where it was more common).[6] There are even less data on executions of child offenders. As a result, research for this chapter was cobbled together from unlikely sources for an international relations and comparative politics study of Africa and the Middle East: English literature, the study of gender in colonial India, colonial marriage laws, etc. The paucity of primary materials (and rarity of secondary sources) on the child death penalty in these regions indicates that the process of restricting the penalty by age, both during and after colonialism, was perhaps not contentious.[7] I argue in this chapter that intervention in family law by the British and French introduced, among other things, an age–based measurement of childhood into their colonies that preceded restrictions on the penalty. These protections for children established a legal relationship between the child and the state that would become important for child protection policies after independence.

CASE STUDIES

In this chapter, I argue that norms about children spread through British and French colonies in Africa and the Middle East primarily through coercive means. These empires colonized much of these regions and established legal systems modeled on Western norms, law, and methods of bureaucratic organization. These legal systems varied among states and colonial powers, but all, to some degree, established a legal relationship between the state and the child by restricting the age at which children could engage in particular activities such as marriage and at which they could be held liable for crimes committed. These systems, over time, acclimated colonial societies to certain ideas and norms endemic to Western law, ideas and norms about children among them. After independence, many states struggled to rid their societies of Western influence, but certain norms, including the norm against the child death penalty, were difficult to jettison, in part because they had become accepted to the extent that they were simply taken for granted. Socialization, then, was the principal

---

6. Stacey Hynd, "Killing the Condemned: The Practice and Process of Capital Punishment in British Africa: 1900–1950s," *Journal of African History* 49, no. 3 (2008): 406.

7. Fourchard, "Lagos and the Invention of Juvenile Delinquency," 126.

mechanism of diffusion during the cascades, as most states maintained colonial policies limiting the death penalty to those 18 and older.

Next, I will briefly introduce the colonial cases, focusing on the type of colonial rule each state experienced and its path toward independence (as this speaks to post-independence efforts to revise, end, or maintain colonial law regarding children). This will be followed by thematic summaries of the diffusion of colonial law in general and colonial criminal law and family law in particular.

Kenya and Tanganyika

British rule in Kenya began in the nineteenth century and was notably indirect. Although they originally established a presence in Kenya to curb the slave trade, the British controlled the area beginning in 1895, calling it the East African Protectorate.[8] The relatively small number of colonial administrators relied for governance on local intermediaries, usually on indigenous elites that were 'loyal' to the British for various reasons. This method of rule was common throughout the empire and served to establish a highly bureaucratic system that would persist after colonialism.

The annexation of Kenya in 1920 by the British increased the political activity of Africans who sought reform of colonial rule and organized in the interwar years. Protests in Kenya were mostly localized until 1944, but there was widespread resentment of political and economic policies even where there was no organized resistance.[9] The end of World War II brought minor reforms, including some African representation in the Legislative Council (the Kenyan Parliament), but these changes did little to quell the rising anger toward the settlers and the colonial government.[10]

By 1951, opposition to British rule had grown more militant, resulting in the Mau Mau revolt the following year. The government responded with mass arrests and detentions, declarations of emergency, torture, and capital punishment.[11] All told, the British hanged 1,090 men for their part in

---

8. Charles Mwalimu, *The Kenyan Legal System: An Overview* (Washington, DC: Law Library of Congress, 1988): 5.

9. W.R. Ochieng, *A Modern History of Kenya, 1895–1980* (Nairobi, Kenya: Evans Brothers, 1989): 182.

10. Mwalimu, *The Kenyan Legal System*, 9.

11. Joanna Lewis, "Nasty, Brutish and in Shorts? British Colonial Rule, Violence, and the Historians of Mau Mau," *The Round Table* 96, no. 389 (2007): 293; David Anderson, *Histories of the Hanged: The Dirty War in Kenya and the End of Empire* (New York: W.W. Norton, 2005).

the Mau Mau revolt.[12] Of these, only 346 were convicted of murder; the rest were convicted of possessing arms and ammunition, consorting with terrorists, and the administration of oaths (taken under the aegis of tribal spirits declaring loyalty to Mau Mau leaders).[13] Winston Churchill himself gave permission for the mass application of the death penalty.[14] The revolt, which lasted for eight years, is estimated to have taken as many as 50,000 African lives, more than half of them children under the age of 10, through violence, illness, starvation, and displacement.[15] British violence in Kenya was some of the worst in any Anglophone colony, and Britain today is still coming to terms with its inhumanity.[16] David Anderson has argued that violence in Kenya was so widespread because of the bureaucratization of British rule. The order of the system, with its clear and uniform regulations, lent a normalcy to the violence and conferred on it a sense of legality and acceptability.[17] Interestingly, Mau Mau revolutionaries under the age of 18 were given a reprieve from the death penalty—evidence that even the enemy's children were still recognized as children.[18]

A state of emergency was declared during the revolt, and political organization was outlawed. As a result, a peaceful path to independence would not be possible until the right to organize was restored in 1959.[19] The British Empire, weakened by decolonization after World War II, called two new constitutional conferences in 1961 and 1962, the latter establishing a National Assembly.[20] In June 1963, Kenya was granted internal self-government, followed by full independence by the end of the year.[21]

Prior to 1964, what is now Tanzania was in fact two separate territories under British rule, Tanganyika and Zanzibar. The British took control of Tanganyika as a "mandated territory" after the German loss in World War I.[22] As in Kenya, indirect rule allowed the British to maintain traditional social hierarchies and systems of governance and to adapt them to

12. Anderson, *Histories of the Hanged*, 291.
13. Ibid.; Elie Kedourie, *Nationalism in Asia and Africa* (New York: World, 1970): 115.
14. Anderson, *Histories of the Hanged*, 291.
15. John Blacker, "The Demography of Mau Mau: Fertility and Mortality in Kenya in the 1950s: A Demographer's Viewpoint," *African Affairs* 106, no. 423 (2007): 205.
16. Lewis, "Nasty, Brutish and in Shorts?" 208.
17. Ibid.
18. Anderson, *Histories of the Hanged*, 7.
19. Mwalimu, *The Kenyan Legal System*, 11.
20. Ibid.
21. Ibid., 12.
22. Martin Bailey, *The Union of Tanganyika and Zanzibar: A Study in Political Integration* (Syracuse, NY: Syracuse University, 1973): 7; Foreign Area Studies at the American University and Irving Kaplan, *Tanzania: A Country Study* (Washington, DC: American University, 1978): 43.

Britain's needs.[23] The system allowed local chiefs to remain in power, as the British believed they would be more effective administrators than other intermediaries.

The independence struggle in Tanganyika began in 1954 with the rise of a new political party, the Tanganyika African National Union (TANU), led by the future president, Julius Nyerere.[24] Tanganyika had been placed under UN trusteeship in 1946, and this allowed Nyerere to address the Trusteeship Council at the United Nations in person regarding British rule.[25] The British had initiated reforms after World War II, many of these relating to children and education, and also increased African representation in the Legislative Council.[26] African representation further increased through the years before independence, with TANU taking most elected positions.[27] As TANU became more popular, the British stepped up harassment of its leaders, arresting many, including Nyerere.[28] A new governor in 1958 introduced reforms that allowed the opposition to assume many important government positions.[29] Independence in Ghana in 1957 and elsewhere in the British Empire raised the morale of TANU leaders.[30] When general elections were held in 1958 and 1959, only TANU candidates (and TANU-supported candidates) won.[31] Elections in 1960 led to a TANU landslide of seventy out of seventy-one seats.[32] In May 1961, Tanganyika was granted internal self-rule, followed by full independence by the year's end.[33]

At independence, Tanganyika and Kenya were similar in terms of their economic structure and capacity for development and growth; yet the two countries subsequently took widely divergent paths.[34] Tanganyika, which became independent in 1961, two years before Kenya, embarked on a program of socialist development.[35] President Nyerere pursued a policy of

23. Foreign Area Studies, *Tanzania*, 44.

24. Bailey, *The Union of Tanganyika and Zanzibar*, 6; Foreign Area Studies, *Tanzania*, 49.

25. Foreign Area Studies, *Tanzania*, 49.

26. Ibid., 51, 53.

27. Ibid.

28. Ibid., 61; M.H.Y. Kaniki, "The End of the Colonial Era," in *Tanzania under Colonial Rule*, ed. M.H.Y. Kaniki (London: Longman, 1980): 353.

29. Bailey, *The Union of Tanganyika and Zanzibar*, 6–7.

30. Kaniki, "The End of the Colonial Era," 363.

31. Ibid., 366.

32. Ibid., 367.

33. Bailey, *The Union of Tanganyika and Zanzibar*, 7.

34. Joel D. Barkan, "Comparing Politics and Public Policy in Kenya and Tanzania," in *Politics and Public Policy in Kenya and Tanzania*, eds. Joel D. Barkan and John J. Okumu (New York: Praeger, 1979): 3–4.

35. Ibid., 4.

self-reliance and, beginning in 1967, sought a "complete break with the institutional legacies it inherited at independence."[36] It chose nonalignment and military assistance from China, and supported liberation movements in other parts of Africa, to the chagrin of the West.[37] Kenya, on the other hand, sought to develop ties with the West and to win entry to lucrative Western markets, build a tourist industry, and increase foreign investment. Only later did Kenya Africanize parts of the political and judicial systems it had inherited from the British.[38]

In some ways, however, the two countries' objectives were not dissimilar. They both sought to manage political conflict; expand the civil service; build on the existing infrastructure left by the British (and improve relations with the British); develop a social welfare system; and encourage economic growth.[39] Thus, not only were policy goals in the two countries nearly identical, they were also similar to policy goals in almost every other African state after independence, with the exception of Guinea and possibly Ghana.[40]

After independence, Kenya and Tanganyika both maintained the colonial policy against executing those that commit capital crimes while under the age of 18. Kenya abolished the death penalty for child offenders in 1967, in its post-independence Penal Code in Section 25 (2). This provision in the code was challenged by a child death sentence in 1967 and upheld in the case considering the law, *Turon v. R.*[41] The Penal Code of Tanganyika under British rule banned the penalty for child offenders under the age of 18 in Article 26 (2). Upon independence, the code was maintained, but the prohibition would be tested in a 1977 court case, *R v. Lubasha Maderenya and Tejai Lubasha.* This law, too, was upheld and the ban on the child death penalty remained.[42] The ruling was repealed, however, in 1979, reversing the 1977 decision.[43] Tanzania abolished the penalty for children under the age of 18 in 1997.[44]

Kenya maintained much of the bureaucratic structure and law it had inherited at independence. Its criminal code even stipulates interpretation

---

36. Ibid., 6, 10.
37. Ibid., 10.
38. Ochieng, *A Modern History of Kenya*, 194–195.
39. Ibid.
40. Ibid.
41. *Turon v. R* (1969) E.A. 789 (CA). Ibid., 41.
42. High Court of Tanzania at Mwanza Criminal Sessions case no. 143 of 1977.
43. Ibid.; Tanzania Appeal No. 32 of 1979.
44. Issa G. Shivji, Humudi I. Majamba, Robert V. Makaramba, and Chris M. Peter, *Constitutional and Legal System of Tanzania* (Dar Es Salaam, Tanzania: Mkuki Na Nyota, 2004). The most recent abolition is found in the Written Laws (Miscellaneous Amendment) Act No. 31 of 1997.

"in accordance with the principles of legal interpretation obtaining in England," and that the laws themselves should be "used with the meaning attached to them in English criminal law."[45] However, Tanganyika (and later Tanzania) sought after independence to chart a new path. Its interim Constitution of 1965 established one-party rule on the mainland and left Zanzibar legally autonomous.[46] As Tanzania adopted more socialist policies, its relationship with the West became strained, thus increasing calls for self-reliance.[47]

Nonetheless, both Kenya and Tanganyika (Tanzania after 1964) continued their policies of protection for children. In Kenya, the young government initiated a number of measures that demonstrated its "progressive concern" for women and children.[48] Many of these measures, including increased rights for women and illegitimate children, were criticized for their incompatibility with African traditions.[49] Nonetheless, protections were enacted within the first two decades of independence that dealt with issues including age of majority, marriage, education, employment, and child welfare.[50] The minimum age for marriage in Kenya after independence was 16 for girls and 18 for boys.[51] In Tanganyika and Tanzania, a number of laws were passed to protect children and codify norms within the first two decades of independent rule.[52] The new laws addressed such issues as age of majority, marriage, education, employment, adoption,

45. Tudor Jackson, *The Law of Kenya; an Introduction* (Nairobi, Kenya: East African Literature Bureau, 1970): 85.

46. Foreign Area Studies, *Tanzania*, 74, 77–78.

47. Ibid., 81.

48. James D. Keeney, "Review: Report of the Kenya Commission on the Law of Succession," *University of Pennsylvania Law Review* 119, no. 6 (1971): 1074.

49. Ibid.

50. The Children and Young Persons Act of 1964 (Cap 141), Succession Act of 1972 (Cap 160), Education Act of 1968 (Cap. 211), Age of Majority Act of 1974 (establishing 18 as the age of majority) (Cap. 33), Immigration Act of 1972 (Cap. 172), Citizenship Act of 1967 (Cap. 170), Magistrate's Courts Act of 1967 (Cap. 10), Employment Act of 1976 (Cap. 226), and the Matrimonial Causes Ordinance of 1962 (Cap. 152), among others.

51. Arthur Phillips and Henry F. Morris, *Marriage Laws in Africa* (Oxford: Oxford University Press, 1971): 43.

52. The Age of Majority Ordinance (Cap. 410), Age of Majority (Citizenship Laws) Act of 1970 (Cap 170); Law of Contract Ordinance (Cap. 433), Law of Marriage Act (1971) (No. 5), Affiliation Ordinance (Cap. 278), Births and Deaths Registration Ordinance (Cap. 108), Adoption Ordinance (Cap. 335), Employment Ordinance (Cap. 366), Evidence Act of 1967 (Cap. 6), Customary Law Declaration Orders of 1963, National Education Act of 1978, Children and Young Persons Ordinance (Cap. 13), Children's Homes (Regulation) Act of 1968 (No. 4), Prisons Act of 1967 (Cap. 58), and the Probation of Offenders Ordinance (Cap. 247).

child welfare, and criminal procedure.[53] A minor in Tanzania is defined as a person under the age of 18, according to the Interpretation of Laws and General Clauses Act in 1972.[54] A survey of age limits in Kenyan and Tanganyikan (and Tanzanian) law after independence indicates that 18 was a key age in many areas, including majority, definition of a child, and employment, but numerous statutes addressing child criminals specify ages varying from 16 to 21.

Algeria and Tunisia

The French began their occupation of Algeria in 1830, and France came to view Algeria differently than it did other French territories, perceiving it as an extension of France itself. From its annexation in the 1830s, France used force to subdue the territory, only introducing civil rule in 1870 after its defeat in the Franco-Prussian War. Unlike other French colonies, Algeria was a province of France, and it was administered under the Ministry of Interior as opposed to the Ministry of Foreign Affairs.[55] Nonetheless, Algerians were not citizens or nationals, but French subjects.[56] Citizenship reform was enacted after World War II, but affected few Algerians.

Because of the position of Algeria in the French popular imagination, the rule of Algeria was much more direct than the rule of any of the other former colonies examined in this study. The French sought to embed their culture in Algerian society and to accomplish "long-range domination" of the population through the "development of bureaucratic administration."[57] This approach centralized the administration of Algeria and had a profound effect on both the capabilities of and choices available to Algeria after independence.[58] As with many other aspects of its rule, France extended its Penal Code and Code of Criminal Instruction to Algeria and

53. Robert V. Makaramba, *Children's Rights in Tanzania* (Dar es Salaam, Tanzania: Friedrich Ebert Stiftung, 1998): 77, 79; Shivji et al., *Constitutional and Legal System of Tanzania*, 168–169.

54. Makaramba, *Children's Rights in Tanzania*, 79.

55. Jeswald W. Salacuse, *An Introduction to Law in French-Speaking Africa*, vol. 2, *The Legal Systems of Africa* (Charlottesville, VA: Michie Company Law, 1975): 34; Mounira M. Charrad, *States and Women's Rights: The Making of Postcolonial Tunisia, Algeria, and Morocco* (Berkeley, CA: University of California Press, 2001).

56. J.L. Miege, "Legal Developments in the Maghrib: 1830–1930," in *European Expansion and Law: The Encounter of European and Indigenous Law in the 19th- and 20th-Century Africa and Asia*, eds. W.J. Mommsen and J.A. De Moor (New York: Berg, 1992): 103.

57. Charrad, *States and Women's Rights*, 123.

58. Ibid.

applied these codes to all Algerians.[59] France's policy of assimilation in Algeria differed strongly from its less direct and extensive rule over the rest of the Maghreb. Even so, France allowed Algeria to maintain customary law in family matters, such as marriage and inheritance, until the war for independence.

The call for independence began with the fall of the Vichy regime in 1942.[60] From the beginning of their struggle, Algerians sought international recognition. Reforms were granted by Charles DeGaulle after the war, but were deemed insufficient.[61] Even as France was making arrangements to release Tunisia and Morocco, it was gearing up for a decidedly personal war in Algeria.[62] The French interest stemmed largely from the massive cultural investment in Algeria for more than one hundred years and from the belief that Algeria was an extension of France proper. Other considerations increased France's resolve, including the discovery of oil in the Sahara and the promise of empty desert for nuclear experiments. Moreover, France's impending defeat in Indochine meant that Algeria would face a different struggle than other territories in the Maghreb.[63]

The war was brutal and long. It lasted until 1962 and took between one and 1.5 million lives in a country of nine million.[64] More than two million were in war camps by the war's end.[65] The French grew weary of the violence and international criticism and in a 1961 referendum, a large majority approved self-determination for Algeria, resulting in the Évian Accords that ended the war.[66]

In 1962, even with the brutal war for independence over, Algeria still faced a difficult transition to statehood. The French constituted 10–13 percent of Algeria's population before the war, and the nearly one-million strong exodus left only 50,000 Europeans in Algeria by the end of the decade.[67] It was not just the numbers of departing French, but the positions they held in Algerian society that caused the greatest loss. The French were the doctors, administrators, teachers, and judges; large swaths of the professional and state infrastructure were dominated by the French. The war and the European exodus left the state in tatters.

59. Salacuse, *French-Speaking Africa*, 191.
60. Ibid., 42.
61. Ibid., 43.
62. Charrad, *States and Women's Rights*, 171.
63. Ibid.
64. Ibid.
65. Ibid.
66. Salacuse, *French-Speaking Africa*, 48–49.
67. Ibid., 15; Charrad, *States and Women's Rights*, 115.

At independence, a heterogeneous elite took power and, with few resources, attempted to initiate reform and quell conflict.[68] Ahmed Ben Bella was elected president in 1963, with the job of organizing and training an entirely new administration.[69] The Algerian Revolution sought to purge all things French from the country and to destroy the French system of governance, but this proved nearly impossible.[70] The French exodus meant that the Algerians had to quickly reestablish government control and reconstruct bureaucracy in a time of increasing tension. The new government's strategy was to simplify the system of criminal justice so that it could be easily maintained.[71] Jeswald Salacuse has argued, "After some hesitation, independent Algeria decided to maintain its colonial legislation in force provisionally, but at the same time it declared void all legislation of colonialist inspiration."[72] This appears to have been largely cant. Since the French went to great lengths to destroy any vestiges of Algerian traditional law in the administration, the new government merely paid lip service to purging the system of French influence. In many ways, the government not only tolerated French norms in the legal system, but perpetuated them through codification in the first decade of independence. Conflict between different factions intensified after Colonel Houari Boumediene initiated a *coup d'etat* against Ben Bella in 1965.[73] The coup hurt Algeria's reputation abroad and alienated it from many allies, including Cuba and Egypt.[74] Boumediene cared deeply about what the world thought of him and sought to appear progressive and revolutionary,[75] yet he feared radical change and enacted no reforms or new initiatives during the first two years of his rule.[76]

In 1966, as part of reform measures, the Boumediene regime enacted a new penal code and criminal procedure code.[77] Although not a "slavish copy" of the former French code, the new code nonetheless greatly

68. Charrad, *States and Women's Rights*, 180.

69. Ibid., 181.

70. Salacuse, *French-Speaking Africa*, 8.

71. Ibid., 116.

72. Ibid., 8.

73. Ibid., 58; John P. Entelis, *Algeria: The Revolution Institutionalized* (Boulder, CO: Westview, 1986): 61–62.

74. David Ottaway and Marina Ottaway, *Algeria; The Politics of a Socialist Revolution* (Berkeley, CA: University of California Press, 1970): 230–231.

75. Arslan Humbaraci, *Algeria: A Revolution That Failed; A Political History since 1954* (London: Pall Mall, 1966): 249, 262; Ottaway and Ottaway, *Algeria; The Politics of a Socialist Revolution*, 231–232, 246.

76. Entelis, *Algeria: The Revolution Institutionalized*, 60.

77. Salacuse, *French-Speaking Africa*, 192.

resembled the French code and used almost identical language in Article 50, the provision banning the child death penalty.[78] The reasons Algeria maintained many important parts of the Penal Code, even in light of a powerful nationalist movement, probably has as much to do with the French exodus as with norms of child protection. As stated, postindependence Algeria was forced to quickly simplify its judicial system after the war, and large-scale, fundamental changes were likely not feasible at the time.

Tunisia had a very different experience with the French than the Algerians did. French rule in Tunisia began in 1881 with the Al Marsa Convention, after France ended its initial military occupation of Algeria. Learning from its experience in Algeria, France ruled Tunisia less directly. Unlike Algeria, Tunisia was governed by the Ministry of Foreign Affairs as a separate state.[79] In 1883, Tunisia became a French protectorate, and France simply "grafted upon the traditional system new institutions" to facilitate governance.[80]

There were fewer French settlers in Tunisia than in Algeria, and they preferred a more structured system of corporate land development.[81] Government administration was also more centralized, although the French tried in all of its territories to weaken tribal authority so as to advance bureaucratization.[82] The French in Tunisia mainly worked within the existing social structure and hierarchy and installed French directors or supervisors for government services, administration, and the judiciary.[83] France also expanded the Tunisian bureaucracy and further centralized the political system, allowing for better collection of taxes, enforcing the rule of law, establishing a social security infrastructure, and stimulating economic growth.[84] France coopted Tunisian officials and ruled by supervising local leaders.[85] The Tunisian legal system was nonetheless strongly shaped by French rule, as France imposed its own criminal law, enacted a number of legal reforms, and embedded many French legal principles in the Tunisian system.[86]

78. Ibid., 193.
79. Hooker, *Legal Pluralism*, 199.
80. Salacuse, *French-Speaking Africa*, 365.
81. Foreign Area Studies at the American University and Harold D. Nelson, eds., *Tunisia: A Country Study* (Washington, DC: Supt. of Docs, United States Government, 1986): 32.
82. Charrad, *States and Women's Rights*, 143.
83. Salacuse, *French-Speaking Africa*, 366–367.
84. Charrad, *States and Women's Rights*, 119, 143; Foreign Area Studies, *Tunisia*, 32.
85. Charrad, *States and Women's Rights*, 116–117.
86. Salacuse, *French-Speaking Africa*, 356, 393.

Nationalism in Tunisia began in the late nineteenth century and was from the beginning "a movement rooted in the schools."[87] The French-educated, elite character of the Tunisian nationalist movement never waned, drawing much of its inspiration from French liberal thought.[88] Minor reforms were initiated by the French after World War I, but they failed to meet the demand for change.[89] In 1938, the French responded to growing nationalist protests by arresting Habib Bourguiba, the leader of the main nationalist party and Tunisia's future president, on several occasions. Guerrilla movements began in 1954, resulting in repressive measures by the French, including more arrests.[90] Resistance was short-lived, though, and Tunisia was granted self-rule in 1955 and full independence seven months later in 1956.[91]

Bourguiba became Tunisia's first president and, backed by a cadre of French-trained elites, launched widespread reforms affecting most aspects of government and social life.[92] This ambitious reform agenda by European-educated Tunisians aimed to liberate the country from the "beliefs and practices they saw as obsolete in the modern world and as deterrents to development."[93] Economic issues were prioritized, and the state adopted measures to industrialize and modernize the economy.[94] These elite-led changes resulted in many tensions, especially with the powerful nationalists, conservative Muslims, and others that opposed European influence in the young state.[95] In contrast to Algeria, Tunisia was widely well regarded throughout the West and Africa in the early years of independence, and it sought to cultivate these relationships.[96] Tunisia prized its UN membership and, with the support of the French,[97] it sought "associated status" within the European Economic Community.[98]

Following independence, Tunisia worked to reform its legal system, a task that proved difficult, however, after seventy-five years of colonial

87. Foreign Area Studies, *Tunisia*, 38.

88. Ibid., 39.

89. Ibid., 41.

90. Salacuse, *French-Speaking Africa*, 370.

91. Ibid., 370–372.

92. Kenneth J. Perkins, *A History of Modern Tunisia* (New York: Cambridge University Press, 2004): 7.

93. Perkins, *A History of Modern Tunisia*, 7.

94. Ibid., 8.

95. Ibid., 7.

96. Perkins, *A History of Modern Tunisia*, 140.

97. Relations with France would later deteriorate as a result of land reform initiatives by Bourguiba.

98. Foreign Area Studies, *Tunisia*, 53–54.

rule.[99] Its aim was to "modernize, unify, and laicize the judicial system."[100] It not only banned French courts after independence, but *sharia* courts as well.[101] Unlike Algeria, Tunisia did not reaffirm its criminal code after independence, leaving its 1913 Penal Code in force until 1975, although the code was amended several times.[102]

Algeria and Tunisia, like Kenya and Tanganyika, also maintained the colonial policy against child executions following independence. Algeria abolished the penalty for child offenders under the age of 18 in the 1966 Penal Code,[103] based largely on the penal code in effect under the French. Tunisia's experience with the child death penalty was more convoluted. As in Algeria, the colonial penal code in Tunisia banned the penalty for those under the age of 18. After Tunisia gained independence, it retained the ban. In 1966, however, the penal code[104] was changed so that only minors under the age of 16 would be protected, thus lowering the age limit.[105] The 1989 Penal Code restored the age limit for the penalty to 18.[106]

Where Tunisia challenged the norm abolishing the child death penalty, there is ample evidence that Algeria never did and that Algeria even went on to codify other norms about children consistent with Western ideology. The same Algerian law that maintained the prohibition against the child death penalty established that minors between the ages of 13 and 18 could qualify for reduced punishment or reeducation measures.[107] In 1966, the age of criminal majority was established at 18 in the Code of Criminal Procedure.[108] This was then raised to 21 in ordinances in 1972 and 1975.[109] A 1963 law set the minimum marriage age for girls at 16, raising by one year the age established by the French.[110] A 1976 ordinance made education compulsory to age 16.[111] Additionally, under both Ben

99. Salacuse, *French-Speaking Africa*, 356.

100. Ibid., 401, 409.

101. Ibid., 409.

102. Tunisian Penal Code, Decree of July 9, 1913, Oct. 1, 1913; Ibid., 504.

103. Article 50 of the Ordinance no. 66–156 of June 8, E.A, Journal Officiel de la République Algérienne.

104. Loi no. 66–62 du 5 juillet 1966.

105. Salacuse, *French-Speaking Africa*, 508.

106. Loi no. 89–23 du 27 fevrier 1989.

107. Committee on the Rights of the Child, "Second Periodic Report: Algeria Crc/C/93/Add.7" (2003).

108. Ibid.; Code of Criminal Procedure, Ordinance No. 66–155 of 8 June 1966, Art. 442.

109. Ibid.; Ordinance No. 72–03 of 10 February 1972 and Ordinance No. 75–64 of 26 September 1975.

110. Salacuse, *French-Speaking Africa*, 136.

111. Article 5 of the Ordinance of 16 April 1976, Committee on the Rights of the Child, "Second Periodic Report: Algeria Crc/C/93/Add.7."

Bella and Boumediene, education took up the largest percentage of the state budget, at 21.5 percent in 1966 (compared with national security at only 15 percent).[112] The minimum age for employment was 16, according to a 1975 ordinance, and the military call-up age was established at 19 (unless deferred to age 27) by a 1974 ordinance.[113] The age of civil majority was set at 19 in 1975.[114] In May 1976, a Commission for the Protection of Children and Young People was established by decree.[115]

Unlike Algeria, Tunisia enacted a new family code shortly after independence when Bourguiba set out to "eliminate religious regulations and customs that were considered 'obsolete.'"[116] The 1956 Code of Personal Status, the new family code, outlawed polygamy, gave the state more control over marriage, and established the highest minimum age for marriage in the region—at age 20 for both men and women, five years higher than under the French.[117] Although a 1964 amendment lowered the marriage age to 17 for women, the age nonetheless remained higher than it had under the French.[118] Tunisia used family law like the French had, as a tool to marginalize tribal power and to centralize state bureaucracy.[119] Tunisia protected children under the age of 18 from indecent assault in a 1958 amendment to the Criminal Code.[120] The young country also focused on education, especially on increasing educational opportunities for girls.[121] Bourguiba allocated one-fifth of the country's total budget for education and supported universal primary education, although education to age 16 was not made compulsory until 1991.[122] Protection for children also applied to alcohol consumption, as children under the age of 16 were prohibited in a 1959 law from drinking.[123] Adoption and guardianship of

112. Humbaraci, *Algeria: A Revolution That Failed*, 264; Makaramba, *Children's Rights in Tanzania*, 77.

113. Ordinance No. 75–31 of 29 April 1975 and Ordinance No. 74–103 of 15 November 1974. Committee on the Rights of the Child, "Second Periodic Report: Algeria Crc/C/93/Add.7."

114. Ibid.; Civil Code Ordinance No. 75–58 of 26 September 1975 and Ordinance of 16 April 1976.

115. Ibid.; Decree No. 76–101 of 25 May 1976.

116. Foreign Area Studies, *Tunisia*, 51.

117. Salacuse, *French-Speaking Africa*, 7; Charrad, *States and Women's Rights*, 225.

118. Foreign Area Studies, *Tunisia*, 107.

119. Charrad, *States and Women's Rights*, 201.

120. Act No. 58–27 of 4 March 1958. Committee on the Rights of the Child, "Second Periodic Report: Algeria."

121. Perkins, *A History of Modern Tunisia*, 138–139.

122. Perkins, *A History of Modern Tunisia*, 139–140.

123. Act No. 59–147 of 7 November 1959. Committee on the Rights of the Child, "Second Periodic Report: Tunisia Crc/C/83/Add.1" (2001): 38.

children were addressed in the 1958 Personal Status Code, with further protections enacted in 1967.[124]

Colonial Law

The British and French were by no means the first foreign powers to rule in East Africa or the Maghreb. East Africa was ruled at various times by the Portuguese, Omani Arabs, and Germans. The Maghreb was ruled by Rome, Spain, the Ottoman Empire, and numerous Arab dynasties. All of the states here discussed had precolonial experiences with Islam and Islamic law in addition to other types of traditional and indigenous law. This complicated history makes research into precolonial African and Middle Eastern law difficult. The task is all the more complex because the methods used to recognize law have been greatly influenced by legal positivism, with its bias against unwritten law that is not backed by coercive authority.[125] As a result, oral law and culturally embedded duties and social roles may be overlooked by researchers, misunderstood, or even lost. Moreover, a search for African and Middle Eastern law itself implies a monolithic, shared corpus that did not emerge from the many cultures that inhabit these regions. For our purposes, traditional law is defined as the local and/or indigenous law in place at the time that colonial law was introduced.

This section focuses on law and legal systems imposed during colonialism, and it explores the degrees of acculturation the colonies experienced through their interaction with imperial legal codes. It reveals two important processes involving colonial rule: first, the colonial domination of Africa and the Middle East through law and state organization; and second, the internalization by colonial societies of certain Western norms and principles contained within these legal systems and types of state order.

European law was typically not applied to the colonies until the mid-nineteenth century. Rule was mostly limited to coastal areas, and indigenous communities were largely left alone so long as they did not inhibit the colonial extraction of resources.[126] Although there is great variety

124. Act No. 58-27 of 4 March 1958 and Act No. 67-47 of 21 November 1967. Committee on the Rights of the Child, "Second Periodic Report: Tunisia," 39.

125. Werner Menski, *Comparative Law in a Global Context* (Cambridge: Cambridge University Press, 2006): 380-381.

126. W.J. Mommsen, "Introduction," in *European Expansion and Law: The Encounter of European and Indigenous Law in 19th- and 20th-Century Africa and Asia*, eds. W.J. Mommsen and J.A. De Moor (New York: Berg, 1992): 4.

in the degree and nature of colonial law, some generalizations can be made: There typically were dual systems of law in the colonies: one for the colonial powers, their administrators, and other protected persons; and one for the general population.[127] Traditional law was permitted to varying degrees so long as it did not grossly violate colonial law and values (judged in relation to the needs of the colonial power). Although a type of legal pluralism—or a system whereby two or more systems of law exist side by side—was evident in the colonies, laws enacted in the colonies were often not exact replicas of metropolitan law.[128] Colonial law was more often a hybrid of metropolitan law, traditional law, and law adapted to the specific demands of the colonial enterprise. Martin Chanock has suggested that the legal system of the British colonies was not legal pluralism, but more "one language, perhaps spoken with many different accents, rather than a plurality of tongues."[129] It became an "Anglo-colonial system."[130]

English law in the colonies generally began with what was known as the 'reception statute' found in the Order-in-Council, whereby laws in force in England on the day a territory was annexed were made to apply in the colony as well.[131] Laws passed in England after the Order-in-Council had "no extraterritorial application" unless the colony enacted them.[132] The original purpose of law in the colonies was to keep the peace and to allow Britain to extract resources with little resistance. Eventually, law in the British colonies was shaped by the English Dual Mandate (articulated by Lord Lugard, but applicable to French territories as well), according to which there were two imperatives of colonial rule: to benefit the metropolitan economy and to "'uplift the 'savage races.'"[133] Additionally, the British wanted to guarantee that Europeans would not be governed by traditional law.[134] For the most part, the British allowed their colonies to maintain

---

127. Ibid., 5.
128. Ibid., 10; Martin Chanock, "The Law Market: The Legal Encounter in British East and Central Africa," in *European Expansion and Law: The Encounter of European and Indigenous Law in 19th- and 20th-Century Africa and Asia*, eds. W.J. Mommsen and J.A. De Moor (New York: Berg, 1992): 302.
129. Chanock, "The Law Market," 302.
130. Ibid., 303.
131. Robert B. Seidman, "Law and Economic Development in Independent, English-Speaking Sub-Saharan Africa," in *Africa and Law: Developing Legal Systems in African Commonwealth Nations*, ed. Thomas W. Hutchison (Madison, WI: University of Wisconsin Press, 1968): 10.
132. T. Olawale Elias, *British Colonial Law: A Comparative Study of the Interaction between English and Local Laws in British Dependencies* (London: Stevens & Sons, 1962): 35.
133. Seidman, "Law and Economic Development," 15.
134. Menski, *Comparative Law in a Global Context*, 37.

traditional law, especially in areas of family law such as marriage, land tenure, and inheritance, and a legal system quickly developed whereby English law governed non-Africans and traditional law governed Africans, although English criminal law applied to all, as will be discussed.[135]

In Kenya and Tanganyika, the British had full jurisdiction over all persons, all matters, and all civil and criminal law through the Kenyan and Tanganyika reception clauses, with the exception of the coastal strip in what is now Kenya, which was then controlled by the Sultan of Zanzibar.[136] Even where the British had complete jurisdiction, local courts could apply traditional law if it was "not repugnant to justice and morality or inconsistent with any Order in Council or Ordinance, or any regulation or rule made under [these]."[137] But British law would gradually expand into areas of traditional family law as it became increasingly difficult to justify colonial rule without 'liberating' certain classes of society, such as women and children.

As the above case studies make evident, the French method of rule was far more direct than the British method, although this varied by colony. Like the British, though, the French allowed certain aspects of traditional law, especially family law, to remain until late in their rule.[138] As with British colonial law, there were generally two types of law in French colonies, one for French nationals (mostly the French in Algeria and various protected persons), and one for French subjects (most everyone else).[139] In theory, Algerians could become French citizens in Algeria, but in practice, this was very difficult and relatively uncommon.[140] As was the case in the British Empire, there is some evidence that at least in the East Asian colonies of the French Empire, the *mission civilisatrice*—or civilizing mission— revolved around motherhood, adoption, and education, all institutions to which children are central.[141]

Not unexpectedly, Tunisia was allowed to retain its traditional courts while Algeria was not; yet even in Tunisia, customary law and traditional

135. Seidman, "Law and Economic Development," 13; Elias, *British Colonial Law*, 5.
136. J.N.D. Anderson, *Islamic Law in Africa* (London: Colonial Research Publication: Her Majesty's Stationery Office, 1954): 81.
137. Ibid.
138. Salacuse, *French-Speaking Africa*, 77.
139. Ibid., 73.
140. Lauren Benton, *Law and Colonial Cultures: Legal Regimes in World History, 1400–1900* (Cambridge, UK: Cambridge University Press, 2002): 164.
141. Micheline R. Lessard, "Civilizing Women: French Colonial Perceptions of Vietnamese Womanhood and Motherhood," in *Women and the Colonial Gaze*, eds. Tamara L. Hunt and Micheline R. Lessard (New York: New York University Press, 2002).

courts had limited power.[142] The French controlled the legal process and "drafted all legislative proposals."[143] The French also enacted a number of legal reforms based largely on French law and legal principles.[144] Since Tunisia was a protectorate, French law did not automatically apply without additional enactment.[145] It was France, however, that decided which laws should apply within the context of its own interests.[146] An "elaborate jurisprudence developed," since some French laws applied while some Tunisian laws remained in effect.[147] This hybrid system was complicated, and some confusion exists as to the French Parliament's authority over the laws of particular territories. M.J. Hooker, an expert in legal pluralism, contends that it is not clear "how far any individual colony came under the metropolitan laws of France," as this depended on context, temporal period, and the individual territory.[148]

The French were far more ambitious in their acculturation of the colonies than the British were. As stated, the French sought assimilation in Algeria especially, or, at the very least, they sought association, whereby the territory existed for French benefit, but the French had the "duty to the colonial population to develop their institutions and to secure their well-being."[149] The French made attempts in Algeria to codify Islamic law, most famously with the Code Morand.[150] This was done to assist the French courts, especially in issues of family law, although the code never became law itself. The French undertook reforms after World War II that encroached upon family law and other traditional law as part of the *mission civilisatrice,* as will be discussed.

Following independence, most former colonies did not seek to enact traditional law, and rather "preferred state law with its centralized structure . . . as it would help to create a new unified nation."[151] Centralized state law allowed the nascent governments to inherit much of the order and efficiency of the colonial state while engaging in reform, and also served to modernize the new countries by facilitating economic planning. The bureaucracies established by the colonial powers also proved highly useful, as many of

---

142. Salacuse, *French-Speaking Africa,* 109.
143. Ibid., 393.
144. Ibid.
145. Ibid., 394.
146. Ibid.
147. Ibid., 395.
148. Hooker, *Legal Pluralism,* 201.
149. Ibid., 197.
150. Benton, *Law and Colonial Cultures,* 135.
151. Mommsen, "Introduction," 13.

the new countries took advantage of colonial infrastructure to enact elite-driven reforms.

In sum, pragmatism reigned. The British and French empires institutionalized aspects of metropolitan law that suited their needs in the colonies. Newly independent states, in turn, retained aspects of these legal systems that suited their own needs. Importantly, the former colonies maintained the centralized bureaucracies they had inherited—hallmarks of the colonial enterprise—even after winning independence.

Criminal Codes

The coercive diffusion of the norm against the child death penalty was part of a larger process of homogenizing criminal codes in the colonies, as elaborate yet remarkably similar legal codes were institutionalized across the British and French empires. These colonial legal codes would in turn shape the codes of the newly independent states, many of which came to accept the principles, norms, and values embedded in the systems of law they had inherited. This phenomenon explains the retention by former colonies of key parts of their colonial legal systems, including age restrictions on the death penalty. In the case of the British, most of the age restrictions on the penalty would come years after the standardized criminal codes were enacted in many of the colonies, as amendments to the original codes. These codes, and the French practice of directly applying French criminal law (albeit inconsistently), created uniform legal systems across colonies and imbued these systems with many of the principles, norms, and values important in Western law. The gradual internalization of these values within colonies rendered them susceptible to the logic of the Western legal system and led them to maintain many important facets of the system after independence, age restrictions of the death penalty among them.

Criminal law was one of the most widely homogenized types of law advanced in the colonies, especially by the British. Criminal codes were also usually the first type of law to be introduced by colonial powers, whose central goals were to maintain order during their rule, to extract resources, and to help 'the savage races.' Moreover, whereas colonial powers avoided intervention in traditional law, they intervened most in criminal matters in order to police and control the population for effective rule.[152]

152. Ibid., 10.

Although there was pressure on colonial administrations from the metropole to curtail "the brutal justice exercised by allegedly uncivilized indigenous peoples,"[153] criminal law in the colonies was "severe and authoritarian," and, at least in British territories, relied on corporal punishment more so than in England.[154] One of the key legal ideas the colonial powers in Africa sought to impart was that a criminal act was an act against the public, rather than against a private individual.[155] Private wrongs were previously resolved in some compensatory manner, such as exchanges of goods between tribes and families.[156] With public wrongs, punishment was properly carried out by a centralized state.

Colonial criminal codes and criminal procedure codes reflected metropolitan values, priorities, and needs and included age restrictions on the death penalty akin to those found in metropolitan law. Since England limited its death penalty in 1933 to those 18 and older and France abolished the child death penalty in 1906 when it raised its age of majority to 18, prohibitions against the penalty for offenders under the age of 18 were found in the legal corpus of the former colonies examined in this chapter, albeit decades later. There is evidence that many former colonies of the British and French that gained independence in the 1960s and 1970s (and some even earlier) did so with some version of the norm against child executions codified in their law.[157]

One notable quality of criminal law in the nineteenth and twentieth centuries is *how* it spread. Criminal codes written in one part of the world were subsequently adopted as models in another, resulting in a large degree of similarity in criminal codes around the world.[158] This in itself explains much of the identical language found in the colonial criminal codes of both the British and the French. The British, especially, sought a single uniform system of criminal law in all of their colonies and dependencies. A single criminal code applicable to all colonies had great appeal for the British, although it created deep suspicion among the European settlers and African intelligentsia.[159] The British also sought to homogenize their policies and practices regarding child offenders, convening committees to

153. Ibid.
154. Chanock, "The Law Market," 283.
155. Ibid., 282.
156. Shivji et al., *Constitutional and Legal System of Tanzania*, 258.
157. Hynd, "Killing the Condemned," footnote 4, 405.
158. H.F. Morris, "A History of the Adoption of Codes of Criminal Law and Procedure in British Colonial Africa, 1876–1935," *Journal of African Law* 18, no. 1 (1974): 6–7.
159. Ibid., 6.

survey colonial practices, assigning a Social Welfare Officer to the colonies, and applying to the colonies some reforms enacted at home.

The British first introduced criminal law in Africa in the Gold Coast in 1853.[160] The Indian Penal Code was then drafted in 1860, after the Indian Rebellion of 1857, principally by Scottish advocates.[161] Britain then transplanted the Indian Penal Code to the colonies of Kenya, Nyasaland (Malawi), Tanganyika, Uganda, Northern Rhodesia (Zambia), and Zanzibar in the late nineteenth and early twentieth centuries, but allowed for traditional law and local oversight in the case of minor offences so long as they did not conflict with repugnancy standards or with British standards of justice and morality.[162] The settlers and administrators disliked the code at first, but gradually grew to accept it and eventually resisted efforts to change it.[163] After cases in Kenya and Tanganyika in which settlers killed African employees and were given sentences of only a few years, an import from the Indian Penal Code, interest in adopting a new code increased.[164]

In the 1930s, the Indian Penal Code was replaced by the Colonial Office Model Code, adapted from the Queensland Code of 1889, which was, in turn, adapted from the English Criminal Code of 1880 (which never became law) and, interestingly, from the Penal Code of New York.[165] The code was enacted in Kenya, Tanganyika, and other parts of Africa.[166] By 1935, all criminal codes in Africa, except for the Gold Coast, had an original source, the 1889 Queensland Code.[167]

Criminal law in England was concerned with "public redefinitions of class boundaries," a purpose that carried over into the colonies.[168] As seen in chapter 3, beginning in the sixteenth century, English law criminalized poor children and families by declaring public spaces zones where children could be accused of vagrancy and theft. These laws justified intervention in families by the state. There is no doubt that these laws were not aimed at children of wealthy families, but at those who could be mistaken for vagrants and thieves. Criminal law then reinforced class boundaries

---

160. Seidman, "Law and Economic Development," 14.

161. Elias, *British Colonial Law*, 147; Hooker, *Legal Pluralism*, 62.

162. Shivji et al., *Constitutional and Legal System of Tanzania*, 260.

163. Morris, "A History of the Adoption of Codes," 13.

164. Ibid., 14.

165. J.J.R. Collingwood, *Criminal Law of East and Central Africa* (London: Sweet & Maxwell, 1967).

166. Morris, "A History of the Adoption of Codes," 15–16.

167. Morris, "A History of the Adoption of Codes," 23.

168. Benton, *Law and Colonial Cultures*, 14.

under the pretense of civilizing and charitable behavior. Likewise in the colonies, "shifting definitions of criminality" were an important strategy of domination by the British.[169]

French criminal law in the colonies and protectorates followed a similar pattern. French criminal law was introduced in Algeria in 1842 and made applicable to all.[170] The French were much more interested in transplanting French legal principles to Algeria than to other territories, but applied French criminal law everywhere. The Algeria Code of 1902–1903 allowed for French criminal law to be applied directly to Algeria, and the Code was eventually adopted in Tunisia and Morocco as well.[171]

There is evidence that the British (and, to some extent, the French) applied and enforced criminal law in the colonies to a much greater degree than any other type of law. Criminal law serves a unique purpose in society, as it determines what conduct is permitted by the state based on a morality that is highly subjective, but presented as just and universal. In effect, it controls the population by establishing boundaries of legality and illegality (according to the colonizer's interests). Because of its power to shape social organization, it is expected that criminal law has a greater effect on the acculturation of a society to norms than other types of law. Age restrictions on the death penalty were among these norms.

State Intervention in Traditional Law

This section evaluates intervention in traditional law by the colonial powers, which established an age-based system of maturity, introduced Western norms about children and childhood into the colonies, and as time went on, came to justify colonial rule by 'protecting' women and children from native men who would corrupt, exploit, or abuse them. I examine the particular ways these norms were introduced and spread, first coercively by intervention in traditional law, and then through acculturation as intervention became routine and bureaucratized and was continued after independence. I further explore how the protection of child 'brides' from native men became an important part of the legal system of colonial rule, a subject replete with metropolitan concerns about gender, sex, and maturity.

169. Ibid.
170. Hooker, *Legal Pluralism*, 209; Salacuse, *French-Speaking Africa*, 191.
171. Hooker, *Legal Pluralism*.

Both the British and the French avoided family, religious, and traditional law for the most part early on in their rule, but both empires also found it increasingly difficult to do so as time went on. Their intervention in traditional law (such as by setting age limits for marriage) often sparked resistance from colonies and lent fuel to the nascent independence movements. These forays into traditional law, however, established a precedent for state intervention, institutionalizing a particular type of relationship between the state and the family. The relationship between the state and children (and the state and women) took on paternalistic characteristics. By independence, these relationships had been firmly internalized. Ironically, the same state intervention in families that sparked outcries from the general population during colonial rule and that helped to ignite independence movements also acclimated colonial societies to intervention in traditional law and families, thus allowing for the perpetuation and gradual expansion of protections for children (and women) after independence.

It has not been possible to identify with any degree of confidence ideas about children that were common and widely subscribed to in precolonial Africa. More recent history, especially since the introduction of Islam in Africa and the Middle East, suggests that the upper boundary of childhood was between age seven and puberty for boys and age nine and/or whenever married for girls.[172] In Zanzibar, a child was defined by "purpose and context," a highly fluid definition.[173]

Studies of British colonialism in India demonstrate an important phenomenon likely applicable to the cases in this chapter: The British imported an age-based understanding of childhood to India, but the idea did not diffuse easily. Not only were the ages of Indian children difficult to determine with much accuracy, but many colonists, especially those that worked with young criminals, believed that the ages of European children did not correspond with those of Indian children.[174] Rather, there was a "widespread conviction that 'native childhood' was an oxymoron."[175] It was thought that many Indian children, including those who worked as prostitutes, displayed a maturity or corruption that belied their numerical age. Norms of childhood thus clashed with colonial assumptions that 'native' children were "small, perverse adults."[176] Nonetheless,

---

172. Shivji et al., *Constitutional and Legal System of Tanzania*, 167; Salacuse, *French-Speaking Africa*, 453.
173. Shivji et al., *Constitutional and Legal System of Tanzania*, 167.
174. Sen, *Colonial Childhoods*, 67.
175. Ibid., 1.
176. Ibid.

the issue was settled by 1922, when the Indian Jails Committee established a young person to be between the ages of 14 and 16. Childhood was determined by age alone and "not on the 'depravity' of the individual child, the 'heinousness' of the offence, the notoriety or poverty of the child's social environment, or the discretion of the judge or local government."[177] This was not the first time the British government used age to mark the boundaries of childhood, nor was the age limit reached in India the highest for childhood to date: As early as the 1860s, famine relief efforts drew a distinction between adults (those 18 and older) and children (those under 18).[178]

There is a great deal of evidence, presented below, that the British and French imposed an age-based conception of childhood on their colonies in Africa and the Middle East, much as the British had done in India. Since the precolonial history of childhood in Africa and the Middle East is not readily available, I proceed with some modest assumptions. The boundaries of childhood in Africa and the Middle East before colonialism were not based principally on age, but rather on experience or the carrying out of particular rites. The idea of protection for those under the age of 18 likely did not exist; girls and boys tended to marry below the age of 18 and were, in most parts of Africa and the Middle East, allowed to take on many responsibilities that today would be reserved for adults, especially in the West.

Colonial governments faced a predicament with traditional law, or with those aspects of traditional law that typically governed marriages, inheritance, maintenance (of wives and children), and divorce. On the one hand, imperial powers recognized the cultural importance of traditional law to local populations and the links between traditional law and religion. Both the British and the French steered clear of intervention in traditional law for fear of sparking anticolonial sentiment. On the other hand, colonial governments found it increasingly difficult to justify colonial rule and not to intervene in traditional law. Since colonialism was justified (by the colonizers) according to the notion that empires were benevolent enterprises, spreading 'civilization' to the 'uncivilized,'[179] it became impossible to ignore the widespread abuse of women and children, as the issues of child brides and forced marriages began to receive increased attention in Europe.[180] Child labor also raised concerns, as the practice was linked to

177. Ibid., 68.
178. Ibid.
179. Pagden, "Human Rights," 183–184.
180. Mommsen, "Introduction," 4–5.

slavery, a particularly passionate issue for the British.[181] Gender issues, especially, were a sticking point for Europeans.[182] Compulsory marriage, genital mutilation (often performed on young girls), and child marriage upset metropolitan sensibilities and ultimately compelled colonial governments to change the very laws they sought to avoid.

In the British colonies, precedent for changes in traditional law came from the 1857 Indian rebellion, often referred to as the Mutiny. Britain promised after the Mutiny never to intervene in traditional law again.[183] The policy could not be maintained, however, and Britain began to make changes to Indian traditional law toward the end of the nineteenth century in response to concerns about child marriage, as discussed in more detail below. Intervention in African traditional law generally began much later, in the first few decades of the twentieth century.

There is very little written on the norms of childhood under the British or French in Africa and the Middle East. The information available on childhood in the colonies mostly comes from studies on India and child marriage or the practices of orphanages and juvenile reform facilities. Since much of Indian penal law was carried into Africa by the British, especially into East Africa, an argument can be made that at least some scholarly findings are generalizable to British rule there. This is especially true since the treatment of children in the colonies is less important for the argument of this chapter than the colonial justification for intervention based on trends in London and Paris. The objective of the remaining part of this section is thus to demonstrate that protections for women and children increasingly provided a justification for colonialism, as part of the 'civilizing mission' and 'white man's burden.' A propensity to justify colonialism on the basis of protecting women and children came as much from evidence of actual abuse in the colonies as from events and ideas prevalent in Europe, such as fears of sexual promiscuity in young women and a new interest in the science of race. As a result, many of the findings about India are relevant to East Africa. As for the French Empire,

---

181. Beverly Grier, "Invisible Hands: The Political Economy of Child Labour in Colonial Zimbabwe, 1890–1930," *Journal of Southern African Studies* 20, no. 1 (1994): 27–52.

182. Antoinette Burton, "From Child Bride To 'Hindoo Lady': Rukhmabai and the Debate on Sexual Respectability in Imperial Britain," *The American Historical Review* 103, no. 4 (1998): 1119–1146; Fourchard, "Lagos and the Invention of Juvenile Delinquency"; Ann L. Stoler, "Making Empire Respectable: The Politics of Race and Sexual Morality in 20th-Century Colonial Cultures," *American Ethnologist* 16, no. 4 (1989): 634–660.

183. Mommsen, "Introduction," 8–9.

there is little information about French rule and children other than the list of child protection measures the French took in the twentieth century in Algeria and Tunisia (listed below). There is ample evidence, however, that similar protections were enacted in the French colonies in response to concerns about child marriage.[184]

Orphanages and reform schools were places of particular interest in colonial India for those researching children and childhood. They were sites of intense study of children since the researchers had few guardians to contend with who could object to these studies.[185] After the Mutiny of 1857, the colonial state began to take on "overtly paternal functions, identifying and gradually occupying various theatres of child-control."[186] These studies of children allowed the British to scientifically evaluate many of the racial theories that supported colonialism.[187] The results of these studies would often "render colonialism necessary and rewarding."[188]

In the 1860s, race was entering a "scientific–bureaucratic phase."[189] Children were the key to understanding the racial hierarchy that supported colonialism. Satadru Sen argues, "The discovery of a location, a diet, a uniform, a curriculum, and a routine of work, play, sleep and study that might suit the race was a discovery of the race itself."[190] The question that these social scientists were asking gets to the very root of colonial childhood: If "given 'equal advantages,'" would children of color "grow up to be 'nearly as intelligent as Europeans?'"[191] Essentially, these social scientists were trying to "discover the 'childhood' . . . of natives."[192] Whatever the answer, colonial society could not lose: If the children of colonized peoples were inherently less intelligent and capable, then the racial order in colonial society was sound. If they were in fact capable of equal intelligence when separated from their countrymen and raised and educated by Europeans, then the colonial project was not only sound, it was justified. Colonialism would have a *raison d'être* in children.

Mary Carpenter, the child advocate discussed in chapter 3, was interested in reform efforts in the colonies and carried out an 1866 "tour" of

184. Julia Ann Clancy-Smith and Frances Gouda, *Domesticating the Empire: Race, Gender, and Family Life in French and Dutch Colonialism* (Charlottesville, VA: University Press of Virginia, 1998).
185. Sen, "The Orphaned Colony," 465; Sen, "A Juvenile Periphery."
186. Sen, "The Orphaned Colony," 464.
187. Ibid., 463.
188. Ibid., 464, 469.
189. Ibid., 478.
190. Ibid., 471.
191. Ibid., 473–474.
192. Sen, "A Separate Punishment," 83.

orphanages and reform schools in India. Finding the boys in male orphanages apathetic and dependent, she blamed this trait on the hiring of
Indian servants who served as a source of "sexual and racial contamina-
tion."[193] Although optimistic about the white children, Carpenter found
the Eurasian children less than promising.[194] She supported the creation
of a reformatory system in India. Various subsets of Indian society (Parsis,
Brahmins, Christians, and Jews) agreed with Carpenter's proposed reforms for child offenders and "competed for the badges of civilization and
modernity with each other."[195]

Carpenter also found, and salaciously reported, the phenomenon of
child brides, which would become "one of the key ideological and material
sites" for reform with regard to gender.[196] Child marriage was seen as clear
evidence of barbarism and as the greatest obstacle to progress for the colonies while under Western rule.[197]

In England, the age of consent was raised from 13 to 16 in the 1880s.[198]
This change was a direct response to new anxiety about child prostitution in London, a "moral panic"[199] over a phenomenon seen as a greater
"threat to civilization than ... delinquent boys."[200] New concerns about
child marriage in India led some to dismiss British claims to be a civilizing power as "hollow."[201] The juxtaposition of increasing protections for
children and rights for women in England, especially in terms of the age of
consent and efforts to curb child prostitution, against the ongoing problem of Indian child brides on Britain's watch meant that the British could
no longer ignore calls to change traditional law. The campaign to protect
children and women in colonial societies provided a new lens through
which to view the colonies.

By challenging the treatment of Indian young girls and women, Britain
was challenging the Indian man's capacity for self-rule.[202] Only the British,
as 'benevolent' rulers, could protect Indian women and young girls from
Indian men. As a result, British colonialism found a new civilizing mission
to justify British rule. The helplessness of Indian girls and women "shored

193. Sen, "The Orphaned Colony," 471–472.
194. Ibid., 472.
195. Sen, "A Separate Punishment," 94.
196. Burton, "From Child Bride To 'Hindoo Lady,'" 1126.
197. Ibid., 1127.
198. Burton, "From Child Bride To 'Hindoo Lady,'" 1124.
199. Louise A. Jackson, *Child Sexual Abuse in Victorian England* (London;
New York: Routledge, 2000): 41.
200. Sen, "A Separate Punishment," 85.
201. Burton, "From Child Bride To 'Hindoo Lady,'" 1121.
202. Ibid., 1122.

up the need for intervention by a chivalrous English state and appeared to confirm the inadequacies of indigenous political protest."[203] The age of consent was raised from 10 to 12 in the 1891 Indian Age of Consent Act; the reaction in India was "fierce."[204]

Britain also enacted penal reform for Indian children, an essential part of reform measures at home. 'Juvenile offender' became a legal category in India in the mid-nineteenth century, and an apprenticeship act came into force in 1850.[205] Reformatories were also founded in the 1850s. The Reformatory Schools Act of 1876 and 1897 and a children's act in the 1920s demonstrated an increasing concern with young criminals.[206] The idea behind the removal of children from families in India, as in England in the nineteenth century, was that parents were the source of children's delinquency.[207]

Concern for young girls broadened into a concern for children in general in the late nineteenth and early twentieth centuries, as both Britain and France enacted a number of protections for children in their territories in Africa and elsewhere.[208] Education in British colonies was commonly left to missionaries before the twentieth century, who used education to fight African customs considered repugnant, such as genital mutilation.[209] Independent schools were established in Kenya in the 1920s and 1930s after national protests.[210]

There is far less written on the study of childhood in the French colonies. As stated, the French, like the British, steered clear of family law in Algeria and Tunisia for the majority of their rule.[211] France even recognized traditional family law in parts of Algeria, such as the Kabyle law in the Berber region.[212] When France finally intervened in Algerian traditional law, it tried to couch these changes in terms of Islamic law in an attempt to avoid increasing anticolonial sentiment.[213] During the war for independence, France impinged upon traditional law, raising the age of majority to 18 or 21 (depending on the location) in 1957.[214] In a 1959 law, marriage became

203. Ibid., 1144.
204. Ibid., 1120–1121.
205. Sen, "A Separate Punishment," 86. Apprentices Act of 1850.
206. Ibid., 83;
207. Ibid., 89.
208. David Pomfret, "'Raising Eurasia'; Race, Class, and Age in Hong Kong and Indochina," *Comparative Studies in Society and History* 51, no. 2 (2009): 326.
209. Beth Maina Ahlberg, *Women, Sexuality, and the Changing Social Order* (Philadelphia: Gordon and Breach, 1991): 75–78.
210. Ibid., 79.
211. Charrad, *States and Women's Rights*, 114.
212. Ibid., 133.
213. Ibid., 132.
214. Ibid., 137.

a public act that had to be registered, along with births, deaths, and divorces.[215] The same law set the minimum age for marriage at 18 for men and 15 for girls.[216] These changes allowed France to exert greater control over the Algerian population and to prove its concern with child marriage.[217] The 1959 law also required consent of women in marriage, undermining male power and making child marriage more difficult.[218]

Similar changes were enacted in Tunisia, albeit for different reasons and with a different postindependence outcome.[219] France left family law in Tunisia alone during most of the colonial period because it could achieve its objectives without interference.[220] In Algeria, the French had uprooted large swaths of the indigenous population, resulting in changes in family structure and making regulation of family law a necessity.[221] In Tunisia, colonization was primarily carried out by commercial and industrial interests, which did not necessitate intervention in family law.[222] Intervention finally came with the war for independence, as efforts were made to curb child marriage and reduce the power of fathers to consent for women in marriage.[223] Unlike changes in Algeria, intervention in family law in Tunisia was much more modest. The changes were used, however, by Tunisian nationalists to stoke independence efforts.

In Tunisia, as elsewhere, the family was seen as the last vestige of independence from colonial power.[224] The Tunisian nationalist movement opposed French rule and over time was able to unify both the liberal elite and conservative Tunisian forces under the banner of independence. Both liberals and conservatives supported the retention of traditional customs and identity.[225] Upon independence, the ideological differences between these factions came to the fore, and they fought for control of the new sovereign state.[226] Bourguiba, a liberal reformer, received help from the French to establish his rule. To shore up his power, he set up state agencies

---

215. Ibid., 137–138; Ordinance of February 4, 1959; Decree of September 17, 1959.
216. Ibid., 138.
217. Ibid., 137–138.
218. Ibid., 138.
219. Ibid., 132.
220. Yaw Oheneba-Sakyi and Baffour K. Takyi, "Introduction to the Study of African Families: A Framework of Analysis," in *African Families at the Turn of the 21st Century*, eds. Yaw Oheneba-Sakyi and Baffour K. Takyi (Westport, CT: Praeger, 2006): 28.
221. Ibid., 29.
222. Ibid.
223. Charrad, *States and Women's Rights*, 137–138.
224. Oheneba-Sakyi and Takyi, "Introduction to the Study of African Families," 30.
225. Ibid.
226. Ibid., 31.

in rural areas in order to intervene in formerly autonomous communities and to undermine efforts to enforce traditional religious law.[227] Shortly after independence, Bourguiba enacted the Code of Personal Status that enshrined into law much of the liberal vision of a reformed Tunisian society and made a powerful statement about the role of the state in the family; the code had a particular impact on Islamic family law.[228] These reforms continued throughout the 1960s until more conservative forces asserted greater control over family law beginning in the 1970s.[229]

Issues involving children were often a part of these interventions in all four of the colonial cases. Many of the reforms involved registration (birth, marriage, divorce, death) and marriage restrictions. The colonial powers needed registration laws to monitor the population and maintain control. Marriage reform (especially age restrictions and consent laws) was driven to a large degree by discourses about sexuality and women's rights, as previously discussed. Various children's acts were passed establishing juvenile courts and other measures of protection, including ordinances in Kenya in 1933, 1934, and 1948 and amendments to the ordinances in 1935 and 1936,[230] and in Tanganyika in 1937 and 1945.[231] The Kenyan 1934 Ordinance established a young person as between the ages of 14 and 18. A Birth and Registration Act was passed in Kenya in 1928. In Algeria and Kenya, the age of majority was raised to 18 or 21, depending on the location and circumstance: Kenya in the Age of Majority Ordinance 1933;[232] and Algeria in 1957. Marriage registration and age requirements for marriage were also found in both French and British colonies. In Tunisia, marriage registration was required by the 1957 Civil Status Act. In Algeria, the 1959 Marriage Ordinance[233] established the marriage age as 18 for boys and 15 for girls. Before independence, eligibility for marriage in Kenya was set at 16 for both boys and girls.[234] A 1951 amendment to the Marriage Act in Kenya required consent from a parent or guardian for marriages in which one party was under the age of 18.[235] There is also

227. Ibid., 32.
228. Ibid; République Tunisienne, Code du Statut Personnel, August 13, 1956.
229. Ibid., 35–36.
230. A Bill to Amend the Employment of Women, Youg People and Children's Ordinance, No. 14 of 1933; Juvenile Ordinance 1948; Anderson, *Islamic Law in Africa*; Chloe Campbell, "Juvenile Delinquency in Colonial Kenya, 1900–1939," *The Historical Journal* 45, no. 1 (2002): 139.
231. Tanganyika Children and Young Persons Act of 1937, Cap. 13 and the Approved Schools Decree Cap. 59 of 1945.
232. Anderson, *Islamic Law in Africa*, 92; No. 17 of 1933.
233. Ordinance no. 59–274 of February 4, 1959, Journal Officiel de la République Française.
234. Mwalimu, *The Kenyan Legal System*, 30.
235. Act 26 of 1951, Amendment to the Marriage Act.

evidence that rules were established for guardianship and adoption in the British colonies, adoption being a particularly sensitive subject in Islam because it concerns legitimacy. These laws include: the Kenya Adoption of Children Ordinance 1933,[236] the Kenya Guardianship of Infants Act of 1959,[237] and the Tanganyika Adoption of Infants Ordinance 1942.[238]

Attention to delinquent and street children increased after World War II as the justifications for colonialism unraveled, and it became increasingly evident that empires could not be maintained. Young men in particular became a threat to the colonial order in Tanganyika.[239] Unlike the French, who sought to destroy tribal bonds in Algeria, the British in Tanganyika and Kenya feared the widespread urbanization and detribalization that appeared to break down social norms of control by reducing the influence of tribes on young men.[240] Children, previously an important part of the civilizing mission, were now constructed as its greatest enemy. There also appears to have been a gender dimension to Britain's concerns, as young men were constructed as threats while young women were constructed as victims. As stated in chapter 1, Fourchard contends that judicial and administrative machinery in British colonies created 'juvenile delinquency' based largely on metropolitan fears of female promiscuity and child marriage.[241] This development, Fourchard and others argue, took place in the colonies of France, Belgium, and Portugal as well.[242] Indeed, there is a fair amount of literature examining the French concern regarding the *metis*, or children of mixed parentage—implying 'illustrious' relationships, especially in East Asia.[243]

In sum, I have shown that state intervention in traditional law was a key part of the coercive establishment of colonial law, and thus of the establishment of norms about children. Through intervention, colonial powers

236. Anderson, *Islamic Law in Africa*, 92.
237. Mwalimu, *The Kenyan Legal System*, 38.
238. Anderson, *Islamic Law in Africa*, 129.
239. Mario I. Aguilar, *Rethinking Age in Africa: Colonial, Post-Colonial, and Contemporary Interpretations of Cultural Representations* (Trenton, NJ: Africa World Press, 2007): 45–50.
240. Ibid., 46; Campbell, "Juvenile Delinquency in Colonial Kenya," 131–132.
241. Fourchard, "Lagos and the Invention of Juvenile Delinquency," 116, 132–134.
242. Ibid., 116; John Iliffe, *The African Poor: A History* (Cambridge, UK: Cambridge University Press, 1987): 188.
243. Pomfret, "Raising Eurasia"; Ann L. Stoler, "Sexual Affronts and Racial Frontiers: European Identities and the Cultural Politics of Exclusion in Colonial Southeast Asia," *Comparative Studies in Society and History* 34, no. 3 (1992); Owen White, *Children of the French Empire: Miscegenation and Colonial Society in French West Africa, 1895–1960* (Oxford: Clarendon, 1999).

were able to codify a primarily age-based system of child protection and institutionalized a relationship between the state and the child that was paternalistic and decidedly Western. These norms about children often clashed with racial 'scientific' beliefs, and much time was spent deciphering the nature of children, especially by the British. The underlying justification for colonialism, the *mission civilisatrice* of France and the British 'white man's burden,' meant that the colonial powers faced pressures to enact protections for children (especially young girls in the areas of sex and marriage), forcing these powers to justify their rule through these protections, among other ways.[244] Such intervention, however, inflamed resentment toward the empires and hastened calls for independence. Yet intervention also firmly established a role for the state in family life and institutionalized child welfare as a concern of the state, to such an extent that law and norms of children's protection were maintained after the colonies gained independence. Restrictions on the death penalty for child offenders were a part of these norms and law.

Other Cases

This section examines the minor case studies of Japan and Ethiopia and the nature of socialization regarding norms of child protection in each state. It provides a point of comparison to the colonial cases, as Japan had previously enacted measures protecting child offenders before the American occupation, while Ethiopia voluntarily adopted Western law after World War II.

Japan

Efforts to develop a modern legal system in Japan began during the Meiji Restoration, beginning in 1868, when the new Emperor Mutsuhitu sought to replace the shogunate, or military rule, with more democratic rule.[245] The number of capital crimes was reduced during this period with the 1873 Reformed Penal and Administration Laws,[246] a policy change attributed

244. Pomfret, "Raising Eurasia"; Fourchard, "Lagos and the Invention of Juvenile Delinquency"; Saheed Aderinto, "The Girls in Moral Danger"; Burton, "From Child Bride To 'Hindoo Lady'"; Stoler, "Making Empire Respectable"; Jackson, *Child Sexual Abuse in Victorian England.*
245. Chen, "The Death Penalty in Japan and China," 4.
246. 1873 Reformed Penal and Administration Laws (Kaitei Ritsurei), no. 206.

to the influence of European and North American legal principles.[247] The number of capital offenses was further reduced with the 1882 Penal Code, also thought to have been influenced by the American and European legal systems.[248] The legal changes adopted during the Meiji period did not necessarily reflect a desire to emulate the West; they were instead enacted primarily in response to fears of Western domination and "to break away from unequal treaties with western powers [sic]."[249] The militarization of Japan, associated with the rise of nationalism and wars in the first half of the twentieth century, led to the increased use of the death penalty.[250] Since the Meiji period (1868–1912), hanging has been the only method of execution allowed in Japan.[251]

Until 1947, trials in Japan were modeled after the Continental legal system. After 1947, the Japanese trial process began to take on characteristics of the Anglo-American common law system, as a constitution and government structure were developed based on the American model.[252] The criminal procedure code in place before the war was based primarily on German law, but was then "modified to reflect Anglo-American legal concepts in contexts important to the protection of human rights."[253] The occupation period saw an unprecedented number of common law legal advisers set out to reconstruct the Japanese state and reshape its legal practices.[254] The legal system in Japan is now a mix of civil and common law, representing the influence of American, British, and Continental legal sources.[255]

In prewar Japan, there was law distinguishing child offenders from adults, and prosecutors had great discretion, including the choice to consider age as a mitigating factor when it came to types and degrees of punishment.[256] These protective measures began during the Meiji period with the enactment of the 1880 Penal Code, which stipulated that children

247. Chen, "The Death Penalty in Japan and China," 5.
248. Ibid.
249. Ibid., 11.
250. Ibid., 5.
251. Ibid., 15.
252. Minoru Shikita and Shinichi Tsuchiya, *Crime and Criminal Policy in Japan: Anaylsis and Evaluation of the Showa Era, 1926–1988* (New York: Springer-Verlag, 1992): xiii–xiv; Robert E. Ward, "The Origins of the Present Japanese Constitution," *American Political Science Review* 50, no. 4 (1956): 980–1010. General MacArthur ordered that a draft constitution for Japan be created, and the final constitution was very similar to the draft produced.
253. Shikita and Tsuchiya, *Crime and Criminal Policy in Japan*, xviii.
254. Chen, "The Death Penalty in Japan and China," 52–53.
255. Shikita and Tsuchiya, *Crime and Criminal Policy in Japan*, xvii.
256. Ibid. xv.

under the age of 12 were without criminal responsibility (*doli incapax*).[257] In 1900, the Child Reform Law introduced the first public reform schools for those up to the age of 15. This was followed by the 1908 Penal Code, which raised the age of criminal responsibility from 12 to 14. That same year, the Child Reform Law Amendment raised the age limit for reform schools to 18, and in 1917, the National Reform School Ordinance established a separate reform school system for those older than 14.[258] The 1923 Juvenile Law created a legal system for offenders under the age of 18 and exempted those younger than 16 from the death penalty.[259]

The Poor Relief Law of 1929 and the Maternal and Child Protection Law of 1937 both gave assistance to needy children, though the laws' objectives were more "to ensure an adequate supply of high-quality manpower for industrial and military needs, rather than to improve the lives of children as individuals."[260] In 1933, efforts to curb child neglect and abuse culminated in the Law to Prevent Child Abuse and the 1934 Child Education and Training Law, which, among other things, created a state entity for the scientific study of children and child behavior.[261] A more comprehensive child welfare law was passed in 1947.[262] Japan abolished the death penalty for child offenders under the age of 18 in the Juvenile Law of 1948.

Japan also increased protections for child offenders in many other ways: The 1948 law defined juveniles as offenders under the age of 20, established family court procedures separate from procedures for adults, and decreed rehabilitation rather than punishment as the state's penal philosophy toward juvenile offenders.[263] The system to implement the law was developed over the ten years following the war, when, notably, juvenile crime was at its highest.[264]

The death penalty was applied much more frequently at the beginning of the Shōwa period (1926–1989) than at its end. Before World War II, the number of death sentences ranged between twelve and thirty-seven per year.[265] Crime began to rise steadily after the outbreak of the

257. Ibid., 253.
258. Ibid.
259. Ibid., 254.
260. Kathleen S. Uno, "Japan," in *Children in Historical and Comparative Perspective*, eds. Joseph M. Hawes and N. Ray Hiner (New York: Greenwood, 1991): 400.
261. Shikita and Tsuchiya, *Crime and Criminal Policy in Japan,* 255; Jido Fukushi Ho 1933.
262. Ibid., 256. Child Welfare Act, Act no. 164 of December 12, 1947.
263. Ibid., xxvii.
264. Ibid., 258.
265. Ibid., 331.

Sino-Japanese War in 1937, but declined during the war with the exception of rape and sexual assault.[266] The decrease in crime in general during the war can be attributed to the drafting of men in the age group most likely to commit crime.[267] The number of executions during this period is unknown.[268] At the war's end, the death penalty surpassed its prewar rates, reaching a peak of 116 per year in 1948 before declining.[269]

Both juvenile crime rates and general crime rates rose during the chaos of the postwar period. The number of juveniles (age 20 and younger) who were convicted of penal code violations in 1940 was 3,030.[270] By 1946, the number of juvenile convictions had increased to 17,436, despite a relatively constant percentage of juveniles in the total population during the period. By 1951, the number of juvenile convictions had declined to 7,577.[271] The very next year, 1952, the number fell even more, to 2,305.[272] The majority of juvenile offenders convicted during this period were either 18 or 19, old enough to incur a capital sentence, yet only one offender between the ages of 18 and 20 was executed between the adoption of the 1948 Juvenile Law and the end of the Shōwa period.[273]

The surge of violent crime following the war's end and the restraint shown by the Japanese criminal system in punishing these perpetrators without resorting to the death penalty indicates that the institutionalization of the norm against the child death penalty was complete. Japan abolished the penalty even without a consensus on the norm in Anglo-American law. Abolition nested well within previously institutionalized norms of child protection in Japan and, as will be argued in chapter 6, the United States did not vociferously reject the norm until the late 1980s and early 1990s. As a result, Japan adopted a policy that reflected European law and was consistent with norms of childhood already in place.

Ethiopia

Unlike the other African states discussed in this book, Ethiopia was not subject to foreign rule except for Italian occupation during World War II. Yet the influence of foreign law on the Ethiopian legal system after the

266. Ibid., 43.
267. Ibid.
268. Ibid., 1.
269. Ibid., 331.
270. Ibid., 279.
271. Ibid.
272. Ibid., 280.
273. Ibid., 279–281.

war was not new. Foreign influence on Ethiopian law dates back to the reign of Emperor Menilik II (1889–1913), who was advised by foreign jurists, but under whom little law was written that directly referenced foreign legal systems.[274] One exception is the 1908 decree on land registration that cites the French civil code.[275]

The use of foreign law and the influence of foreign jurists on Ethiopian legal development proliferated during the reign of Haile Selassie, both as regent to the Empress Zauditu and as emperor from 1930 to 1974. Selassie set out to modernize his kingdom and to establish ties with Western and African powers; he had a prominent role in the establishment of the Organization of African Unity (the predecessor of the African Union). When asked about the sources and development of Ethiopian law, Emperor Selassie said, "[The Ethiopians] have never hesitated to adopt the best that other systems of law can offer, to the extent that they respond and can be adapted to the genius of our particular institutions."[276]

Before the 1950s, Ethiopian law was an "amorphous mix."[277] Traditional law was commonly employed, but there was no comprehensive source for the drafters of new law to draw from.[278] An important feature of criminal procedure in traditional law prior to the Italian occupation was that there was no prosecutorial agency. As such, the injured party both initiated the complaint and prosecuted the offender. A convicted murderer would be handed over to the victim's family for punishment, which could consist of anything they desired—money or gruesome death.[279] Over time, the Emperor sought more control over the practice, monopolizing capital sentencing and requiring mediation before such blood revenges could occur.[280] Later, the government tried to assert even greater control by limiting the type of punishments allowed and by requiring that they occur at government-supervised locations.[281]

274. J. Vanderlinden, "Civil Law and Common Law Influences in the Developing Law of Ethiopia," 252.

275. Ibid.

276. Steven Lowenstein, *Materials on Comparative Criminal Law as Based Upon the Penal Code of Ethiopia and Switzerland* (Addis Ababa, Ethiopia: Haile Selassie University, 1965): 61.

277. John H. Beckstrom, "Transplantation of Legal Systems: An Early Report on the Reception of Western Laws in Ethiopia," *The American Journal of Comparative Law* 21, no. 3 (1973): 559.

278. Ibid.

279. Stanley Z. Fisher, "Traditional Criminal Procedure in Ethiopia," *The American Journal of Comparative Law* 19, no. 4 (1971): 709–746.

280. Ibid., 742.

281. Ibid., 743.

The influence of foreign legal systems on Ethiopian legislative development was primarily Continental (mostly French) before World War II. During the war, Emperor Selassie went into exile in the United Kingdom for five years. After the war and liberation from Italy, British forces were present in the country, and Ethiopia's legal system became increasingly based on the British common law model. The postwar period was a vibrant time of legal development, with the drafting of the 1955 Constitution and six additional codes in the ten years that followed. All of the codes were either crafted by foreign lawyers or "inspired by foreign sources," including British, French, Indian, Israeli, Italian, and Swiss.[282] The court system took on a particularly British character; English replaced French as the country's second language, and there was a greater reception to British legal thought among Ethiopian jurists.

The penal code was drafted by a Swiss jurist, Jean Graven, and replaced the earlier 1930 Penal Code, written when Emperor Selassie came to power. Although the Penal Code had numerous foreign influences, large parts of it were based on the US Constitution and its safeguards for persons accused of a crime.[283] These provisions were first included in the 1955 Ethiopian Constitution (which influenced the 1957 Penal Code), for which the American jurist Edgar Turlington was a central drafter.[284]

The norm against the child death penalty nested well within emerging ideas of child protection now seen throughout the world: both in Europe and (increasingly) in British and French colonies. Ethiopia abolished the death penalty for offenders under the age of 18 in the 1957 Penal Code, Article 118. The earliest law concerning 18-year-olds that I identified was the Vagrancy and Vagabondage Proclamation of 1947, which established that children under the age of 18 could be placed in detention if they were found to be vagrants or unlawful.[285] The law was repealed with the passage of the 1957 Penal Code, but the age of 18 continued to serve as an important line of demarcation between adult criminals and child offenders.[286]

There remained a number of inconsistencies in the Ethiopian system, as some of the codes, including the Penal Code, were drafted in French by Continental lawyers.[287] Réné David, the French law professor who drafted

282. Vanderlinden, "Civil Law and Common Law Influences," 257; Fisher, *Ethiopian Criminal Procedure*, ix.

283. Franklin F. Russell, "The New Ethiopian Penal Code," *American Journal of Comparative Law* 10 (1961): 267.

284. Ibid.

285. Steven Lowenstein, "Ethiopia," in *African Penal Systems*, ed. Alan Milner, (New York: Praeger, 1969): 49.

286. Ibid., 49–50.

287. Vanderlinden, "Civil Law and Common Law Influences," 258.

the Ethiopian Civil Code, has argued that the Ethiopian system, with its blend of Continental and common law characteristics, was a strategy by the Ethiopians "against the predominant Anglo-American influence on its general development since the liberation."[288] Yet Stanley Fisher has suggested that in some cases, Continental jurists were replaced by drafters that were trained in the common law system. For example, Jean Graven, the drafter of the Penal Code, was also originally asked to draft the Criminal Procedure Code. He was replaced by Sir Charles Matthew, a British jurist, in an effort to "abandon the initial project of an evenly 'mixed' continental-common law procedure for an overall design more substantially adversary and thus less Continental."[289]

Yet Ethiopia was not content to merely copy civil or common law models. The country rejected a juvenile court initially, as well as a number of statutes in the Penal Code that were suggested by Graven. The punishment of flogging, which was left out of the draft 1957 Penal Code, for example, was reinserted by the Parliament and the Codification Commission of the Penal Code.[290] Additionally, Graven recognized that certain provisions, such as the total abolition of the death penalty, could not be enacted because they went against "the very deepest feelings of the Ethiopian people for justice and for atonement."[291]

COERCIVE SOCIALIZATION

The case studies in this chapter demonstrate that there were at least two types of legal acculturation in the diffusion of the norm against the child death penalty: voluntary socialization, as demonstrated by the Ethiopian case, and the more common, coercive socialization, as demonstrated by the cases of Algeria, Kenya, Tanganyika/Tanzania, Tunisia, and (in a different way) Japan. The case studies of Algeria, Kenya, Tanganyika, and Tunisia indicate that abolition of the death penalty for child offenders under the age of 18 was the result of two broad phenomena: First, British and French colonial powers spread norms about children, including the prohibition of the child death penalty, coercively through the enshrinement of protections for children in colonial law. These laws established a relationship between the state and the child that would ultimately be

---

288. Ibid.
289. Fisher, *Ethiopian Criminal Procedure*, xi.
290. Lowenstein, *Ethiopia*, 40.
291. Lowenstein, *Materials on Comparative Criminal Law*, 62.

embedded in the logic of the state itself. Second, states maintained the ban on the child death penalty in their domestic law after independence because they had not only been socialized to accept state responsibility for children, but because state responsibility for children had become part of a larger cosmopolitan legal framework, as discussed in the next two chapters.

Japan and Ethiopia provide interesting points of comparison to the colonial cases. Japan had a history of age-based child protection policies dating to the nineteenth century. The Western norms of child protection and juvenile justice that were imposed during occupation were in fact quite compatible with Japanese norms. Thus, while the Japanese case demonstrates the practice of coercive socialization, it is also an exceptional, stand-alone case. In Ethiopia, on the other hand, it is uncertain what protections traditional law afforded child offenders. Emperor Selassie was interested in Western legal practices before the passage of the 1957 law, and children under the age of 18 had some legal protections as early as 1947.

Coercive Norms in a Cosmopolitan Legal Framework

In the late nineteenth and early twentieth centuries, colonial powers commonly cited the right and duty to "'civilize' the more backward, barbarian places they governed."[292] The development of legal systems in the colonies was seen as a gift and a tool: It was the gift of civilization wrapped in the needs and objectives of colonial power. As Lauren Benton has argued in the context of Spanish law in the Americas, "The formal extension of legal jurisdiction in and of itself created a clear cultural boundary between the colonizers and the colonized by casting only one as the possessor of law, and of civility."[293] This process of legal development involved acculturation to the norms, values, and principles embedded in the law and to colonial bureaucracy. A central part of this acculturation was the idea that the state would serve a paternalistic function, ensuring the protection of subjects under the law.

This Western legal tradition began to include protections for children in British and French colonial law in the late nineteenth and early twentieth centuries. Among these protections were laws limiting the death penalty for children through age limits at or near the age of 18. As such, the norm

292. Hunt, *Inventing Human Rights*, 193.
293. Benton, *Law and Colonial Cultures*, 12.

against executing child offenders as well as other Western norms about children spread through Africa and the Middle East through colonialism in the early-to-mid twentieth century. The diffusion of French and English norms of childhood to the territories of France and Britain was used as justification for the civilizing mission, shoring up support at home for the colonial enterprise. This normative diffusion further established the relationship between the state and the child, acclimating colonial societies to state intervention in traditional law in the name of children.

In a study of the diffusion of sexual harassment law from the United States to Austria, Mia Cahill found that one of the main ideas was that sexual harassment was a legal problem with a legal solution.[294] The diffusion of the legal model gave sexual harassment a legal definition, so that it could not be divorced from a legal framework.[295] Drawing on Cahill's findings, I would argue that the most important idea that England and France diffused to these colonies was that the provision of children's welfare and protection was the responsibility of the state in general and should be ensured through legal means, in particular. In other words, throughout history, societies have resolved issues involving children in numerous ways, through the family, the community, etc. England and France diffused the idea that state bureaucracy, acting through law, was the appropriate location for solutions to children's issues.

Japan's legal acculturation to norms of child protection began well before the US occupation. Beginning in the nineteenth century, Japan had modeled its legal system after those in the West. Although Japan's actions were voluntary, they were nonetheless a result of international pressure. Japan's move was tactical, as the country sought to avoid Western domination and to maneuver adroitly in a world increasingly governed by legal treaties based on Western norms and principles.[296] Death penalty restrictions and child protection policies emerged from these developments. Under occupation, Japan reformed its criminal law based largely on its occupiers' Anglo-American legal system. Although the child death penalty had only been abolished in the United Kingdom at the time and not in the United States, Japan's abolition of the penalty corresponded with child protection trends in the West in general and complemented child protection efforts from Japan's prewar history. The United States, after

294. Mia Cahill, "The Legal Problem of Sexual Harassment and Its International Diffusion," in *How Claims Spread: Cross-National Diffusion of Social Problems*, ed. Joel Best (New York: Walter De Gruyter, 2001): 254.
295. Ibid., 244.
296. Chen, "The Death Penalty in Japan and China," 11.

all, was an anomaly in the West in terms of the child death penalty, as will be discussed in chapter 6.

Legal acculturation to Western norms and principles had a profound impact on the ways that postindependence Africa would construct its new systems of government and criminal justice. J.W. Mommsen has suggested that:

> The introduction of basic principles of European law into colonial society, like equality before the law or free access to the courts by anybody, had a considerable effect at least in the long term. Though effective implementation may well have been minimal, these principles eventually provided arguments for the indigenous elites in their struggle for independence which could not be easily ignored.[297]

These emerging states articulated their claims for independence in rights-based language, drawing on the Universal Declaration of Human Rights (UDHR) and the UN Charter, as well as on other principles in French and English law. Their right to statehood was based on a cosmopolitan legal framework that allowed all legitimate claims to be voiced. Japan also was shaped by Western norms about children, and its end to foreign occupation was dependent upon its embrace of the Western liberal state model.

The Socialization to Childhood

The process of socialization to English and French norms about children, combined with the acculturation to European legal institutions, led to the continuation of child-protective policies in Algeria, Kenya, Tanganyika, and Tunisia after independence. All four countries maintained the provisions in their law banning the death penalty for child offenders, although Tunisia and Tanganyika later reversed their policies, in 1966 and 1979, respectively, only to reabolish later. The puzzle is why, when these countries were contending with rising nationalist pressures and anti-French and anti-British sentiment, did they continue the ban? Many leaders like Boumediene and Nyerere insisted that they would weed out the foreign influence from state institutions and law. Moreover, the establishment of age limits for childhood has long been a sensitive subject in Islamic countries, since *Sharia* law bestows many more responsibilities on children than is common in non-Islamic cultures.

297. Mommsen, "Introduction."

Japan and Ethiopia, as well, were socialized to Western legal norms about children. At least in Japan, these norms did not conflict with pre-occupation norms, but they nonetheless were part of a liberal state model that was imposed upon Japan after the war. The legal socialization of Ethiopia, though voluntary, also had a great effect on the culture of the country and its forays into Western liberalism. Voluntary socialization would become a common method of legal acculturation to norms about children around the world in the first and second cascade periods, although not commonly in the particular way chosen by Ethiopia. As norms of child protection became part of the Western liberal state model required of all members of the international system and as states came to internalize these norms, they would voluntarily adopt measures to protect children.

The end of World War II and the international institutions that emerged from it created a nascent cosmopolitan legal regime that would provide the foundation for independence movements around the world. The building blocks of a cosmopolitan legal framework in Africa and the Middle East were laid when French and British legal norms and principles were embedded in colonial legal systems and when independence movements drew their legitimacy from these very principles. David Hirsch has suggested that there is a "cosmopolitan criminal law" with authority based on "supra-national principles, practices, and institutions."[298] Although certainly not fully formed when these countries gained independence in the 1950s and 1960s, the defining features of a normative framework for criminal justice were taking shape.

Protections for children were included within this framework, as seen in declarations of the period, such as the Fourth Geneva Convention. NGOs and IGOs like UNICEF further carried Western norms about children and childhood into countries seeking assistance. UNICEF's focus on development in the 1960s and 1970s created "a watershed in nations' views on how to help their most vulnerable citizens."[299] Children were powerfully connected with ideas of prosperity, economic growth, and development. Governmental and nongovernmental reports investigated the health and welfare of children in new countries and assisted NGOs and IGOs in monitoring the state of children worldwide. International law called for states to

---

298. David Hirsch, *Law against Genocide: Cosmopolitan Trials* (Portland, OR: Glasshouse, 2003): xiii.
299. UNICEF, "1946–2006 Sixty Years for Children" (UNICEF, 2006): 11.

refrain from imposing the death penalty on children and for other judicial protections.

As the next chapter makes clear, even though children were considered relatively unimportant in the face of Cold War pressures and economic concerns, norms about children nonetheless developed throughout the 1960s and 1970s. These norms would eventually serve as the basis for a powerful international regime that, beginning in the 1990s, monitored the whole child. The leaders of states after World War II were well aware of these norms about children. From the civilizing mission of colonialism, children were becoming part of the civilizing mission of the international community. Any new state drafting a constitution or new laws after World War II had to address such issues as safeguards for children in the criminal justice system, protection against discrimination, including discrimination on the basis of parentage (legitimate versus illegitimate births), and labor restrictions, among other child protection measures.[300]

Laws protecting children in the six countries examined in this chapter were not only retained in the years after independence (or adopted in the case of Ethiopia), they increased. The laws were, in essence, accepted as legitimate by the countries themselves. Ian Hurd defines legitimacy as "the normative belief by an actor that a role or institution ought to be obeyed."[301] Legitimacy cannot be equated with any single norm, according to Ian Clark; rather, it "takes place within an explicitly normative structure," such that "specific international norms become the dominant language through which the practice of international legitimacy is conducted."[302] Law regarding children should thus be seen as a larger cognitive framework containing particular, individual norms. Law and norms of child protection at the time these former colonies became independent possessed legitimacy. This did not necessarily entail, however, that the specific norm against the child death penalty was seen as legitimate. Rather, norms protecting children in general were seen as legitimate. These norms had in common two main features. First, they defined childhood in a way that demanded protection. Second, this need for protection assigned a specific role to the state. Childhood's protected status and the state's role in providing that protection were seen as legitimate. The prohibition of

300. Philip Alston and John Tobin, "Laying the Foundation for Children's Rights," UNICEF Innocenti Research Centre, Florence, Italy (UNICEF, 2005): 24.

301. Ian Hurd, "Legitimacy and Authority in International Politics," *International Organization* 53, no. 2 (1999): 381.

302. Ian Clark, *International Legitimacy and World Society* (New York: Oxford University Press, 2007): 4.

the death penalty for those under the age of 18 had its origins in these two connected and complementary ideas.

In essence, the norm against the death penalty for child offenders was compatible with norms about children and the state's role in protecting children. Jeffrey Checkel contends that diffusion is more likely to occur where there is a cultural match, defined as "a situation where the prescriptions embodied in an international norm are convergent with domestic norms, as reflected in discourse, the legal system (constitutions, judicial codes, laws), and bureaucratic agencies (organization ethos and administrative procedures)."[303] The norm prohibiting the child death penalty found a cultural match in Algeria, Ethiopia, Japan, Kenya, Tanganyika, and Tunisia because these countries had already been acculturated to norms of child welfare and protection and to a legal relationship between the state and the child.

This is *not* to say that the leaders of the newly independent states cared especially about children; indeed, there is no evidence of any domestic pressure to maintain the ban on the child death penalty or other protections for children. The laws themselves may never have been debated or discussed. Child law was likely quite low on the list of priorities as leaders sought to maintain order and govern a new country. The fact that they retained laws about children, however, says something about the power of these norms. As is evident from the long list of protective measures for children following independence, these states, at the very least, had accepted the idea that children deserve protected status under law.

Coercion and socialization explain the adoption and retention of death penalty limitations, but do not explain noncompliance. Tunisia and Tanganyika kept the prohibition of the child death penalty in the 1950s and 1960s before reversing their policies at a later date. This was not unique for the period or region. Other countries, like Nigeria, also maintained the prohibition of the child death penalty in the first cascade period. Yet Nigeria has not only altered its laws, but has actually executed child offenders since 1990.[304] Although some policies were changed during the first cascade (as in Tunisia), most acts of reversal took place during the second cascade, from 1985 to 2005. All the more interesting, Tunisia and Tanzania were some of the earliest states to ratify the ICCPR, the

303. Jeffrey Checkel, "Norms, Institutions, and National Identity in Contemporary Europe," *International Studies Quarterly* 43, no. 1 (1999): 87.

304. Human Rights Watch, "Iran Leads the World in Executing Children" (June 19, 2007).

treaty that first banned the execution of all child offenders, in 1969 and 1976, respectively. This should not come as a surprise. Oona Hathaway has argued that countries with poor democratic practices "will be no less likely to commit to human rights treaties if they have poor human rights records."[305] Without "collateral consequences," or the domestic institutions in place to enforce the treaties, states have little incentive to abide by their obligations.[306]

Finally, Latin American states, where colonialism was also widespread, were less relevant to the diffusion of the norm against the child death penalty. These states largely abolished the penalty for all crimes and all offenders, rather than just for child offenders (in some cases, a century before their former colonial powers did). Although not child-specific, this trend of general abolition nonetheless shaped the diffusion of the norm against the child death penalty by presenting states with policy alternatives when they were reforming their death penalty statutes in the early twentieth century. Why the colonial empires of Spain and Portugal were so different with regard to child law is a subject of further study. One likely explanation has to do with timing: Juvenile justice reform did not emerge and diffuse until the twentieth century, long after most states in Latin America gained independence.

The Soviet Union, however, abolished the child death penalty during the height of the Cold War in 1962, a time when the country was keen on demonstrating the superiority of communism and a more just and fair society in comparison with the United States. How abolition came to be enshrined in the criminal codes of satellite states also deserves further study, but it is clear that many such reforms were imposed upon these governments, although the degree of Soviet influence varied by state and time period. These satellite states gained their independence in the early 1990s, in the afterglow of the victory of the liberal state model, and (with the exception of Latvia),[307] abolished the death penalty for all crimes and all offenders in rapid succession. The European community symbolized legitimacy for these new countries, which saw no need to challenge a norm that was not only widely accepted by Europeans, but had also been part of these countries' own laws since the 1960s and 1970s.

---

305. Oona Hathaway, "Why Do Countries Commit to Human Rights Treaties?" *Journal of Conflict Resolution* 51, no. 4 (2007): 588.

306. Ibid., 602, 613.

307. Latvia abolished for child offenders only in 1998 before abolishing for all crimes and all offenders in 2012.

CONCLUSION

Coercive socialization diffused the norm against the child death penalty both by imposing Western legal norms of child protection upon colonies and by acclimating colonial societies to Western legal systems. Through colonialism, the former colonies examined in this chapter adopted forms of government that included paternalistic methods of regulation of children and protections for children enshrined in law. The legal systems imposed by the British and French colonial powers socialized states to norms about children, childhood, and the relationship between the state and the child, norms that were internalized over time. As I will argue in the next two chapters, these states retained these norms after independence because the legal relationship between the state and the child and the guarantees this relationship entailed were built into the state model itself. Japan, a country with no colonial heritage, also experienced occupation and was subject to Western law after World War II. The socialization was a relatively easy sell, however, since norms of child protection by the state had historical precedent in Japan. Ethiopia voluntarily sought Western input in crafting its legal system, shaping its child policies in the Western image.

The next two chapters investigate the model of the globalized child as a means of diffusion of the norm against the child death penalty. In chapter 5, I examine the historical development of the globalized child through international organizations, NGOs, and law. Through a case study of UNICEF, I consider how organizations introduced a global model of childhood to states, and, through a case study of Amnesty International and its American chapter, how the child death penalty was selected as a key campaign for children's rights in the late twentieth century. I examine, in particular, the role that moral authority played in these efforts and how these organizations fostered and used this authority to advance rights and protections for children.

CHAPTER 5

✑

Globalized Childhood as a Mechanism of Diffusion

INTRODUCTION

The international system as we know it—characterized by global institutions, a growing body of international law, and the prevalence of the liberal democratic state—began in the years following World War II. In the aftermath of the Holocaust, authoritarian rule was discredited, and a state model based on the consent of the governed and a respect for human rights—a decidedly Western construction—emerged at war's end as the ideological winner. The United Nations, with its membership of sovereign and equal states, was the defining institution of the new international order, and the Universal Declaration of Human Rights, adopted by the UN's General Assembly in 1948, was the signature document of a new era premised on the pursuit of human dignity and fundamental freedoms for all. As Lynn Hunt has argued, the UDHR ended the long winter of imperialism and nationalism that characterized the nineteenth and early twentieth centuries and ushered in a sudden spring of decolonization and independence movements.[1] These movements began soon after World War II, with many former colonies gaining independence over the following three decades. Attention to children's issues was a part of the new era, too. Concern for children's welfare was evident in the war relief campaign, as

---

1. Hunt, *Inventing Human Rights*.

the case study of UNICEF explains, and by the end of the 1960s, children were a central focus of international development efforts.

This chapter begins with the role of UNICEF in the creation of the globalized model of childhood, as UNICEF made state protection for children mandatory and universal. It considers how Western norms about children regarding age, development, maturity, and culpability came to shape the model of childhood that would be applied to all children in all states, economies, and cultures. In my findings, I suggest that there were three sources of authority behind UNICEF's postwar initiatives. These were: the natural science (in areas such as child development, nutrition, immunology, etc.); the social science (especially economics, development studies, and education); and international law (particularly the 1990 CRC).

I then examine the activism of Amnesty International (hereafter Amnesty) and particularly of its American chapter (AIUSA) against the child death penalty, a central struggle in the emerging children's rights regime in the last twenty-five years. Amnesty turned its attention to norms of child protection much later than UNICEF did, focusing on the child death penalty only in the mid-1980s, but its initiatives in the United States and abroad made the penalty an important and highly contested issue. In my findings, I suggest that it was AIUSA's moral authority, use of international law, and stark comparisons between 'civilized' and 'uncivilized' countries that allowed it to raise public consciousness of the penalty. Finally, I trace the legislative development of the CRC and the convention's Article 37 (covering children deprived of their liberty), considering how diverse states, IGOs, and NGOs helped to enshrine into law the globalized model of childhood in the last few decades of the twentieth century.

My findings in this chapter are threefold. First, UNICEF's gradual expansion of its mandate to cover ever-increasing areas of child welfare and protection fueled the development and drafting of new international law regarding children beginning in the 1990s. Second, Amnesty and AIUSA called the international community's attention to children's issues through a focus on US noncompliance with the CRC's ban on the child death penalty. By selecting the child death penalty as a key campaign in the 1980s, 1990s, and later, Amnesty and AIUSA directly influenced the *application* of international law. The case demonstrates how NGOs can promote specific aspects of the model of childhood to engender change (at great opportunity cost, however, as discussed below). Finally, this chapter demonstrates that the initiatives, campaigns, and programs of IGOs and NGOs coalesced around a specific construction or model of childhood, a globalized model that affected the laws, policies, and practices of individual states.

UNICEF CASE STUDY

Although other international organizations would direct their energies toward the protection of children after World War II, no organization was more important to the globalization of childhood than UNICEF. Through its aid and development initiatives, UNICEF diffused the model of the global child—one with identical needs of health, sanitation, and education, an idea supported by scientific studies. In this way, the global child that emerged through UNICEF's work was a seemingly "objective" child, one that required a particular kind of childhood with adequate nutrition, sufficient vaccines, and educational opportunities. As the standards for this model were steadily raised—especially as the mandate and interests of the international community in children spread to other areas beyond health, sanitation, and education—the social science and rights-based approaches to child protection supported new claims about the global child, including reduced criminal culpability. This case study investigates this development.

The creation of a UN agency for children began immediately after World War II as a deliberate and cautious enterprise. Although postwar recovery was different throughout Europe, children across the continent suffered particularly in the aftermath of the war. A bitter winter in 1946–1947 contributed to the increased mortality of young children, especially; in some areas, half of all babies born alive died before the age of one.[2] Relief in the final years of the war was carried out by the UN Relief and Rehabilitation Administration (UNRRA), which provided assistance in Eastern and Western Europe. By 1946, hostilities between the East and West had increased to the point that the United States refused to continue funding "neutral relief."[3] At the final meeting of the UNRRA, Poland and Norway, in particular, proposed that the agency's residual funds be put toward assisting children.

UNICEF was then formed in 1946 using the UNRRA's remaining funds. In establishing the fund, the Third Committee of the General Assembly stated that:

---

2. Maggie Black, *Children First: The Story of UNICEF, Past and Present* (New York: Oxford University Press, 1996).
   3. Ibid., 7.

The children of Europe and China were not only deprived of food for several cruel years, but also lived in a constant state of terror, witnesses of the massacre of civilians and of the horrors of scientific warfare, and exposed to the progressive lowering of standards of social conduct. The urgent problem facing the United Nations is how to ensure the survival of these children. . . . The hope of the world rests in the coming generations.[4]

The establishment of UNICEF moved the United Nations beyond its previous role of providing "information, research, and advisory services"[5] to the provision of "practical help."[6] It was the "first instance of the creation of a grant-in-aid program for material assistance and an organizational form in the social field not specifically envisaged in the [1948] Charter."[7] UNICEF was originally conceived as an organization that would facilitate state responsibility for child welfare by providing assistance to states either to develop new or to expand existing national programs.[8]

By 1953, UNICEF was a permanent part of the United Nations, as its mandate was extended indefinitely.[9] UNICEF quickly adopted an "emergency needs approach" and focused its work on providing food and clothing and ensuring children's health, principally in Europe.[10] State contributions were not automatic, and so the young organization had to raise funds, making it "sensitive to the public mood" early on.[11] Maurice Pate, the first executive director, argued that UNICEF's dependency on voluntary contributions of UN member states was a positive arrangement since:

The needs of the world's children speak for themselves. . . . What the governments of the world want, more than anything, is the demonstration that something can be done about those needs. The better we demonstrate, the more they give. I am convinced that it is not only morally imperative, but

4. United States Department of State, and John J. Charnow, "The International Children's Emergency Fund," Department of State Publication 2787. United States—United Nations Information Series (Washington, DC: Government Printing Office, 1947): 1.

5. Ibid.

6. United States Department of State and Charnow, "The International Children's Emergency Fund," 1.

7. Ibid., 2.

8. Ibid.

9. UNICEF, "About UNICEF." Accessed on May 24, 2008, http://www.unicef.org/about/who/index_history.html.

10. United Nations Children's Fund, "The Nobel Peace Prize 1965: History of the Organization." Last accessed October 18, 2013. Nobelprize.org http://www.nobelprize.org/nobel_prizes/peace/laureates/1965/unicef-history.html.

11. Black, *Children First*, 9.

economically and politically essential for the better off countries to help the children of less well favoured nations grow into better, stronger, more able adults.[12]

Fundraising also elevated the organization's profile, as did celebrity endorsements by Hollywood stars like Danny Kaye. UNICEF further developed an innovative method of carrying out its mandate: Rather than giving orders from remote headquarters and governing bodies, UNICEF developed a hands-on, fieldwork-based approach that quickly gave the agency a credibility that many other UN agencies lacked.[13]

The 1950s and 1960s saw a marked shift in UNICEF's approach, as the organization adjusted its focus from disaster relief to support for programs designed to benefit the children of developing countries over the long term.[14] Its mission expanded to include campaigns against diseases like tuberculosis; efforts to raise standards of nutrition and sanitation and to improve education in maternal and child health care; the funding of daycare and youth centers; and the training of mothers in the areas of "child rearing and home improvement."[15] This new and wider set of goals developed partly in response to the large number of former colonies gaining independence throughout the world, and the new mission enjoyed US support because of the Cold War fear that these new states would ally with the Soviets if aid were not forthcoming.[16]

Corresponding with the UN Decade of Development in the 1960s, a new "country approach" allowed the organization to address national development needs by concerning itself with the intellectual, psychological, vocational, and physical needs of children.[17] This "comprehensive view of the child" meant that few aspects of a child's life were beyond the reach of the agency—or of the international community.[18] This comprehensive view promulgated the idea that "children are an integral part of the population," and, at a time when young states were hungry for access to

12. Robert L. Heilbroner, *Mankind's Children: The Story of UNICEF* (New York: The Public Affairs Committee, 1959): 18.

13. Black, *Children First*, 9.

14. UNICEF, "About UNICEF: Who Are We: Maurice Pate Biography," http://www.unicef.org/about/who/index_bio_pate.html. UNICEF, *The Needs of Children: A Survey of the Needs of Children in the Developing Countries*, ed. Georges Sicault (New York: Macmillan, 1963): 3.

15. United Nations Children's Fund, "The Nobel Peace Prize 1965."

16. Black, *Children First: The Story of UNICEF, Past and Present*, 10.

17. United Nations Children's Fund, "The Nobel Peace Prize 1965."

18. Ibid.

international markets and coveting international recognition, children's welfare and progress were directly linked to national development and economic prosperity.[19]

The history of UNICEF is important to the diffusion of the norm against the death penalty for child offenders because as former colonies in Africa and the Middle East were gaining independence, children increasingly became a key focus of development efforts in these regions. As newly minted states set about the business of governance, international organizations like UNICEF were calling attention to the need for standards and systems of child welfare and protection. The new states largely accepted the state-child relationship embedded in the legal systems they had inherited from the colonial powers, as they contended with increasing international interest in their child policies.

Through development programs premised on a "whole child" approach, UNICEF diffused norms about children to new states that were writing their constitutions and drafting civil, family, commercial, and criminal law.[20] UNICEF argued that "national policies for children should embrace all children, and do so across sectoral lines—health, agriculture, education, water, and sanitation."[21] UNICEF's resources were impressive in the 1960s, with 120 governments contributing to the fund. In 1964 alone, private individuals and groups raised $6 million for UNICEF.[22] The organization received a major boost in 1965 when it received the Nobel Peace Prize.

In 1976, UNICEF introduced a new approach to its work, the "basic service approach," whereby it began to train ordinary individuals from host countries to deliver services in the field. This indirect method of service delivery allowed UNICEF to spread norms about children and childhood deeper into societies. The organization also led a new trend in developing and promoting a scientific model of childhood. As with early-period scientists, government workers, and volunteer and aid agencies, UNICEF began early on to select a set of indicators that would assist it in monitoring and evaluating the condition of the world's children. Starting in the 1950s and 1960s, it began to produce reports drawing on the data it had collected about children throughout the world. In 1979, UNICEF first published the

19. Zena Harmen, "UNICEF: Achievement and Challenge," in *Peace: 1951–1970*, ed. Frederick W. Haberman (Amsterdam: Elsevier, 1972).

20. UNICEF, "1946–2006 Sixty Years for Children" (New York: UNICEF House, 2006).

21. Black, *Children First*, 10.

22. Harmen, "UNICEF."

State of the World's Children, a yearly summary of data using hundreds of indicators that has been published every year since.[23]

The *State of the World's Children* publications consider the whole child and analyze countries' success in meeting the organization's standards of child welfare.[24] By 1982, these yearly publications would become UNICEF's "main advocacy platform," with the entire world as its target audience.[25]

The 1970s were a particularly active period for international attention to children's issues. Highlights included the UN–sponsored International Year of the Child in 1979, an initiative of children's NGOs that promoted children's issues as a key concern of the international community.[26] The UN General Assembly suggested that 1979 would be a year of "practical action," and at least 148 countries established national committees for the Year of the Child.[27] Children's issues garnered substantial press that year, and new national and international NGOs were formed.[28] Ironically, UNICEF, despite its leadership in advancing international standards of child welfare and protection, was slow to embrace the new rights-based approach, facilitating the drafting of the CRC but not explicitly supporting it until 1987. Although UNICEF was only lukewarm about the children's rights focus coming out of the drafting committee for the CRC, the Year of the Child was nonetheless a boon to the agency's finances. UNICEF's income rose 25 percent between 1978 and 1979, from $211 to $285 million, and the upward trend continued into the next decade.[29]

UNICEF's profile was further raised when it was given lead agency status in a number of UN emergency efforts, including in Kampuchea in 1979.[30] UNICEF provided disaster relief during the civil war in the Democratic Republic of the Congo in the early 1960s, in Yugoslavia in 1963, and in Morocco in 1969. It provided famine relief in India in the late 1960s and relief from the damage of a cyclone in 1970 in East Pakistan and Bangladesh.[31] UNICEF was able to enter Nigeria to help the victims of that country's civil war in the late 1960s, at a time when other

---

23. Asher Ben-Arieh and Robert Goerge, "Beyond the Numbers: How Do We Monitor the State of Our Children?" *Children and Youth Services Review* 23, no. 8 (2001): 603.

24. Ibid., 612.

25. Black, *Children First*, 19.

26. Black, *Children First*, 13.

27. Ibid.

28. Ibid.

29. Ibid.

30. Ibid.

31. UNICEF, "1946–2006 Sixty Years for Children," 12.

agencies were not allowed entry.[32] As a result, UNICEF gained legitimacy both within the United Nations and in world opinion for its work for children.

UNICEF's advocacy on behalf of the world's children ushered in a profound shift in public attention to children's issues. The proliferation of organizations devoted to children in the last fifty years is astounding. The Child Rights Information Network, a coalition of NGOs and IGOs, counts 2,095 members. And many of the organizations emerging in the last twenty years were founded on the principles of the CRC. Yet despite this recent organizational mass, UNICEF's role in developing and diffusing the now global model of childhood stands apart. Although other NGOs and institutional organs (for example, the UN Committee on the Rights of the Child) have taken the lead in monitoring states' compliance with numerous provisions of international law, including the ban on the child death penalty, UNICEF was the main actor in shaping and globalizing a single model of childhood after World War II.

As far as the child death penalty was concerned, however, UNICEF appears never to have given the issue much, if any, consideration prior to the 1990 CRC and its participation in its drafting in the late 1980s. There is evidence, as the next chapter will demonstrate, that UNICEF helped toward the beginning of the twenty-first century to draft some national laws for children in countries like Pakistan that explicitly forbid the child death penalty. These efforts were likely a reflection of UNICEF'S eventual adoption of the children's rights framework in the 1990s. In subsequent UNICEF handbooks on the implementation of the CRC, the penalty's illegality is mentioned, albeit briefly.[33]

AMNESTY CASE STUDY

While numerous NGOs worked on abolition of the child death penalty both internationally and within the United States (and continue to work on abolition of the penalty in general), I chose Amnesty and AIUSA (the US section of Amnesty) as case studies for three reasons: First, Amnesty and AIUSA were uniquely positioned to petition for change both

32. Ibid.

33. UNICEF, Rachel Hodgkin, and Peter Newell, *Implementation Handbook for the Convention on the Rights of the Child* (New York: UNICEF House, 1998): 494; UNICEF, *Implementation Handbook for the Convention on the Rights of the Child* (New York: UNICEF House, 2002): 547.

internationally and within the United States simultaneously in a way and to an extent that other NGOs were not. Second, Amnesty and AIUSA's evolution toward advocacy for human rights law, a shift away from the organizations' early focus,[34] is illustrative of the larger trajectory of human rights advocacy in general. Third, the AIUSA case, in particular, demonstrates the agency of NGOs in the selection of issue areas, which is important given the myriad human rights violations competing for attention today. Thus, while there are other major abolitionist organizations in the United States (many of them discussed in this chapter), Amnesty and AIUSA helped to shore up the boundaries of the global model of childhood as it entered the twenty-first century by targeting particular violations (the child death penalty) by particular violators (the United States). In short, Amnesty International is a "gatekeeper" among human rights NGOs; its choice of campaigns shapes and helps to set the agenda of other NGOs, activists, and national and global institutions.[35]

Amnesty opposed the death penalty in its original charter, but only for prisoners of conscience.[36] Over the next sixteen years, a growing consensus developed within the organization for the total abolition of the penalty. One early issue regarding abolition concerned advocacy for offenders convicted of violent crime, as Amnesty until that time had only supported prisoners of conscience that had not engaged in violence. Despite some internal resistance, by 1975 the debate was resolved in favor of total abolition, and an amendment was made to Article 1 of the Amnesty International statute. In the 1977 Declaration of Stockholm, which came out of the 1977 Stockholm Conference on the Abolition of the Death Penalty, Amnesty announced the organization's "unconditional opposition" to the death penalty for all crimes and all offenders. Although the idea of working for "groups of people sentenced to death" (such as child offenders and offenders with mental disabilities) was raised in a pre-Stockholm meeting in September 1977, the issue would not become an organizational priority until much later.[37] It would take another decade to begin a sustained effort to end executions of child offenders.

34. Ann Marie Clark, *Diplomacy of Conscience: Amnesty International and Changing Human Rights Norms* (Princeton, NJ: Princeton University Press, 2001): 5, 8.

35. Bob, *Marketing of Rebellion*, 18.

36. Amnesty International USA and A. Whitney Ellsworth, "Background Paper for AIUSA AGM Working Party on Death Penalty" (University of Minnesota: Private Archives of David Weissbrodt, unknown year).

37. Amnesty International, International Council, and Working Party B, "Pre-Council Meeting on Death Penalty Held on Thursday 15 September" (University of Minnesota Law School: Private Archives of David Weissbrodt, 1977).

AIUSA was established in the mid-1960s. Although only a chapter in a larger NGO, AIUSA would grow in size and wealth over the years, and would come to wield disproportionate influence in larger Amnesty politics.[38] AIUSA has often had a contentious relationship with the International Secretariat in London, where Amnesty International is headquartered.[39] In AIUSA's early years, its members tended to be "graduates of the fight for civil rights, civil liberties, and the anti-Vietnam protests," movements with different objectives, philosophies, and strategies from those of Amnesty in general.[40] By the 1980s, AIUSA was a powerful force in the movement, having increased its contribution to the International Secretariat from $1,000 in 1972 to $1,000,000 by 1981.[41] By 1987, AIUSA's membership exceeded membership in Western Europe as a whole, even though its number of chapters (and active members) was only a fraction of Western Europe's.[42] The United States subsequently lost the lead in membership numbers, but remains the largest individual section.

AIUSA members commonly work on issues within the United States as well as outside it. AIUSA began to focus on death penalty practice in the United States in the 1970s, when the International Secretariat began to permit individual sections to request exemptions from the rule prohibiting advocacy within one's own country.[43] Official changes to the prohibition came in 1995, when the International Secretariat allowed individual sections to be consulted on strategy and actions within their own countries. The US section was the principal driver of this shift.[44]

Another key point of contention within Amnesty and AIUSA regarding the death penalty was its proposed incremental strategy of targeting specific applications of the penalty for which a critical mass of opposition already existed, as with executions of children or the mentally ill. For many within Amnesty, the 1977 Declaration meant that the organization opposed the penalty for all crimes and all offenders. Opposition to a ban on executions solely for child offenders was therefore widespread within

---

38. Clark, *Diplomacy of Conscience*, 7–8.

39. Stephen Hopgood, *Keepers of the Flame: Understanding Amnesty International* (Ithaca, NY: Cornell University Press, 2006): chapter 5.

40. Ibid., 107.

41. Ibid., 108.

42. Ibid., 108–109. Hopgood notes a debate within Amnesty about membership, distinguishing between donors—or those that merely give money— and members— those that are active (and may also give money).

43. Linda M. Thurston and Amnesty International USA, "A Strategic Plan for Effective Work to Abolish the Death Penalty" (University of Minnesota Law School: Private Archives of David Weissbrodt, 1995): 8.

44. Ibid., 9; Hopgood, *Keepers of the Flame*, 100.

the organization, and was based largely on concerns that limiting the penalty would have the effect of 'sterilizing' it, watering down support for an eventual total ban and making the execution of less sympathetic groups of offenders more palatable to the American public. Although supporters of incrementalism could be found throughout the international membership, the US chapter expressed greater support for an incremental strategy as well as for a preemptive one.[45]

With preemption, activists sought to end a state's human rights violations by targeting the state proactively and through multiple methods. Preemption went against the grain of Amnesty's particular brand of activism, one captured by the image of the lone member writing letters *in response* to violations around the world. Although it maintained its practice of writing and petitioning for individual victims, the organization sought greater agency in changing state policy. This shift in tactics would be crucial to ending the child death penalty in the United States, as will be seen.

In 1979, AIUSA began calling attention to US death penalty policy and practice, which included the execution of offenders under the age of 18. The International Secretariat also participated in early efforts to create safeguards for particular classes of offenders such as children under the age of 18 and those with intellectual disabilities, but these efforts stopped short of demanding an end to the death penalty *only* for these specific classes.[46] Currents of unrest within the AIUSA Board of Directors laid the groundwork for a shift in strategy away from total abolition and toward incrementalism. The 1984 Strategy Against the Death Penalty, an AIUSA document, called for a "major shift in emphasis . . . to move away from crisis work around individual cases and toward changing policy."[47] The strategy document, which further stated that the "focus will be fixed on eroding death penalty statutes in increments," was approved by the board.[48] The document suggested that legislation limiting the age of eligibility for the penalty be advanced in receptive US states.[49] The Death Penalty Report to the AIUSA Board of Directors for 1984–1985 stated that the incrementalist strategy was designed to "[build] momentum for

45. Thurston and Amnesty International USA, "A Strategic Plan," 8.

46. Amnesty International and International Secretariat, "Death Penalty Handbook: External, Part 2: International Legal Standards on the Death Penalty ACT 05/17/82" (University of Minnesota: Private Archives of David Weissbrodt, 1982).

47. Charles Fulwood, Campaign Against the Death Penalty, and Amnesty International USA, "Strategy against the Death Penalty, Approved by the Board of Directors" (University of Minnesota Law School: Private Archives of David Weissbrodt, November 18, 1984): 2.

48. Ibid., 4–5.

49. Ibid., 17.

total abolition by weakening and restricting state death penalty laws, as well as abolishing such laws where possible."[50]

Further support for an incrementalist approach came from a 1986 study that found that the American public was steadfast in its support for the death penalty, but that most did not favor the penalty for child offenders or the mentally ill.[51] AIUSA, recognizing that not all countries will achieve abolition in the same way, sought to take US public opinion into consideration.[52] Larry Cox, then Deputy Secretary General of the International Secretariat, supported incrementalism, suggesting that it might be the "most effective strategy on certain countries."[53] The plan was to foment public opposition to the penalty for child offenders and the mentally ill while continuing to advocate for total abolition.[54] In 1987, AIUSA hired a full-time death penalty coordinator, committing to a strategy of incrementalism.[55]

The executions of three men in the mid-1980s (Charles Rumbaugh in 1985, J. Terry Roach in 1986, and Jay Pinkerton in 1986) for crimes they committed as children sharpened AIUSA's focus on the child death penalty and served to catalyze its advocacy efforts.[56] A 1988 internal report makes note of Amnesty's strategy in these cases: to raise public awareness of the fact that only five other countries (Pakistan, Bangladesh, Barbados, Rwanda, and possibly Iran) had executed child offenders since 1979.[57] AIUSA began its campaign against the child death penalty in February 1987, after the executions of Rumbaugh, Roach, and Pinkerton. As part of this effort, the campaign widely publicized a 1987 Inter-American Commission on Human Rights decision that found that in executing

50. John G. Healey and Amnesty International USA, "Memorandum: 1984–1985 Death Penalty Report, To: AIUSA Board of Directors" (Archives of the University of Colorado at Boulder Libraries, AIUSA NY 378-171985).

51. Cambridge Survey Research and Amnesty International, "An Analysis of Political Attitudes Towards the Death Penalty in the State of Florida" (Washington, DC: Cambridge Survey Research, 1986).

52. Amnesty International, "Report of the International Meeting on the Death Penalty 27–29 March 1987 ACT 05/24/87" (University of Minnesota Law School: Private Archives of David Weissbrodt, 1987): 20.

53. Ibid.

54. Ibid., 19–20

55. Thurston and Amnesty International USA, "A Strategic Plan," 4.

56. Victor L. Streib, "The Juvenile Death Penalty Today: Death Sentences and Executions for Juvenile Crimes, January 1, 1973–February 28, 2005," Ohio Northern University College of Law, 2005, 4.

57. Amnesty International, "Country: United States of America: Subject Title: The Death Penalty: Developments in 1987 AMR 51/01/88" (University of Minnesota: Private Archives of David Weissbrodt, 1988).

Roach and Pinkerton, the United States had violated its obligations under the American Declaration of the Rights and Duties of Man.[58]

Just four days after the campaign's launch, the US Supreme Court announced that it would hear the case *Thompson v. Oklahoma,* which considered the question of whether the execution of a child offender for a crime committed when he was 15 violated the Eighth Amendment's prohibition of "cruel and unusual" punishment.[59] In Amnesty's *amicus* brief in the *Thompson* case, it cited international law and the death penalty practices of US states. The court in its ruling declared the execution to be unconstitutional, thus reserving the penalty for offenders 16 and older. *Thompson* was followed in 1989 by *Stanford v. Kentucky,*[60] in which the court found that the execution of child offenders who commit their crimes when they are 16 or 17 does *not* violate the cruel and unusual clause.

Amnesty first took up the issue of child executions internationally in its 1989 campaign, which targeted the use of the death penalty in fifty-one countries. Eight of these were selected as sites of high-level campaigns, and an additional forty-three countries were selected for limited-appeals campaigns in two stages over the course of 1989.[61] The eight high-level countries—China, Iran, Iraq, Nigeria, Pakistan, South Africa, the United States, and the Soviet Union—were chosen for their high numbers of death sentences and executions and because of widespread concern over the application of the penalty in these countries.[62] Although a 1988 strategy document about the 1989 campaign did not mention child offenders, it is likely not a coincidence that the countries chosen for high-level campaigns were those that executed child offenders younger than 18, with the

58. See Case 9647, Inter-Am. C.H.R. 147, OEA/ser.L/V/II.71, doc. 9 rev. 1 (1987). A UN Economic and Social Council resolution 1503 complaint was not filed because the child death penalty would likely not have qualified (or received sufficient support) under the procedure's standards, which require that the complaint "appear to reveal a consistent pattern of gross and reliably attested violations of human rights." Mary E. McClymont, "Personal Letter to David Weissbrodt" (Washington, DC: University of Minnesota Law School: Private Archives of David Weissbrodt, September 19, 1985). The rejection of the 1503 procedure was not from McClymont, but was noted in letter format by Weissbrodt. See UN Economic and Social Council resolution 1503, Economic and Social Council Resolution 1503 (XLVIII), 48 UN, ESCOR (No. 1A) at 8, UN Doc. E/4832/Add.1 (1970).

59. 487 U.S. 815 (1988).

60. 492 U.S. 361 (1989).

61. Amnesty International, "Country: United States of America: Subject Title: The Death Penalty: Developments in 1987 AMR 51/01/88" (University of Minnesota: Private Archives of David Weissbrodt, 1988).

62. Ibid. Pakistan was later dropped from the high-level campaign list, leaving only seven high-level targeted countries. See Amnesty International, "1989 Campaign against the Death Penalty: Country Appeals Series, Circular No. 17f: Recommended

exceptions of South Africa and the Soviet Union.[63] The Soviet Union was likely included out of concern for Cold War objectivity, one of the three core principles guiding Amnesty's advocacy, as well as for geographical diversity. South Africa might have been included for similar reasons, although increasing alarm over apartheid measures and police brutality also brought public attention to the country. While the 1988 strategy document did not discuss child offenders, by March 1989 executions of child offenders were included in campaign materials as a specific point of appeal to US state legislatures, on par with other concerns such as racial discrimination in the penalty's application and executions of the mentally ill and those with intellectual disabilities.[64]

AIUSA's commitment to an incrementalist and preemptive strategy was steadfast. This approach, however, was not fully supported by the International Secretariat, which instead pushed for a "traditional emphasis on letter-writing at the clemency stage and . . . cautioned AIUSA about its preemptive work."[65] Nonetheless, AIUSA did not change course; its work included legal research, monitoring court cases, and communication with prosecutors, among other tasks.[66] While Amnesty expressed opposition to AIUSA's preemptive strategy, it too continued its efforts to end the penalty by publishing reports on death penalty practice around the world and producing *amici* briefs (including the brief in the *Thompson* case). The differences over strategy were likely a nuance not felt outside of the organization.

The campaign against the child death penalty in the United States finally gained traction when AIUSA teamed up with other NGOs and philanthropic organizations in 2002, following the Supreme Court decision in *Atkins v. Virginia*.[67] In *Atkins*, the court declared the execution of "mentally retarded" individuals to be unconstitutional, a ruling based in part on the emergence of a national consensus against the practice as measured by policy changes and the passage of legislation at the US state level.

A number of NGOs working on juvenile justice issues recognized the ruling's implications for the constitutionality of the child death penalty. In anticipation of a future Supreme Court case, many of these NGOs,

Actions and Addresses on USA, AMR 51/09/89" (University of Minnesota Law School: Private Archives of David Weissbrodt, March 1, 1989).

63. South Africa abolished the child death penalty in 1959. The Soviet Union abolished either in 1922 or 1958, depending on the source.

64. Amnesty International, "1989 Campaign against the Death Penalty."

65. Thurston and Amnesty International USA, "A Strategic Plan," 13.

66. Ibid.

67. 536 U.S. 304.

nonprofits, and professional groups met to develop a strategy. Participants included the American Bar Association, Juvenile Justice Center, National Coalition Against the Death Penalty (American NCADP), Justice Project, Death Penalty Information Center, American Civil Liberties Union (ACLU), Physicians for Human Rights, National Juvenile Defender Center, and AIUSA.[68] These NGOs drew on and expanded a preexisting network of NGOs already committed to ending the child death penalty. The strategy they devised revolved around one key idea: the recognition of a national consensus against the child death penalty, similar to the consensus found in *Atkins*.

The campaign by the NGO coalition had three parts: messaging, grassroots organizing, and creating a legal strategy. The message was that "kids are different," an idea the Justice Project assumed primary responsibility for promoting and disseminating in the media.[69] The Death Penalty Information Center, along with other nonprofits, conducted public education and outreach.[70] Grassroots organizing was spearheaded by the Juvenile Justice Center, the American NCADP, and AIUSA, with the American NCADP and AIUSA dividing between them the US states that had yet to abolish the child death penalty and launching campaigns in those states. Wyoming and South Dakota changed their policies, at least in part, in response to these campaigns and to the pending *Roper v. Simmons* case.[71]

The coalition's legal strategy involved recruiting a diverse set of *amici* briefs, sixteen in all, including one from Nobel laureates. These briefs made three core arguments: 1) Children are different from adults; 2) International law and human rights norms prohibit the death penalty for child offenders; and 3) Within the United States, a national consensus had developed against the practice. Justice Anthony Kennedy, the court's swing vote, would draw on all three core arguments in his majority opinion in *Roper*.[72]

After the *Roper* case was accepted by the Supreme Court, the coalition approached foundations for project support. The surge in juvenile crime in the early 1990s had already received widespread attention from

68. Adam Conner and Betsy William, "Banning the Juvenile Death Penalty: Success through Funding of Nonprofit Advocacy and Coalition Work," *Responsive Philanthropy: The NCRP Quarterly* (2005): 12. https://ncrp.org/files/rp-articles/PDF/RP-Summer-2005-Banning_the_Juvenile_Death_Penalty.pdf.
69. Ibid., 12–13.
70. Ibid., 12.
71. Ibid., 12–13; 543 U.S. 551.
72. Ibid., 13.

foundations. The John D. and Katherine T. MacArthur Foundation, for example, began funding projects for juvenile justice reform in 1996, and by 2000, had invested more than $23 million in reform initiatives. Smaller funders, like the Tides Foundation, joined in supporting these projects.[73] The MacArthur Foundation, Open Society Institute, JEHT Foundation, and Atlantic Philanthropies also partnered with NGOs to form a rare philanthropic–nonprofit coalition. The grants themselves were mostly general operating grants, allowing the recipient organizations the autonomy to manage their own resources and campaigns. Funding from the Open Society Institute, JEHT, and Atlantic Philanthropies for the campaign totaled $1.55 million, while $4.4 million was set aside for other work to end the child death penalty in the United States.[74]

As Wendy Wong has argued, all nodes (in this case, NGOs) in a given network are not equally powerful, and the coalition against the child death penalty was no exception.[75] However, grants from the MacArthur Foundation, JEHT, and others encouraged partnerships and strategic cross-organizational planning, creating an equalizing effect and making the network flatter or more horizontal than what would be found outside of the coalition. What made the philanthropic–nonprofit coalition unusual was that nonprofit groups, which typically compete with one another for grant funding, joined forces with philanthropic organizations for maximum impact. The collective effort increased the number of states that abolished the child death penalty, mobilized a grassroots constituency in these states as well as nationally and internationally, provided the arguments for abolition, and clearly demonstrated the similarities between *Atkins* and *Roper*. The campaign against the death penalty for child offenders in the United States is a flagship example of the power of collaborative or joint enterprise, in this case, by foundations and nonprofits to achieve shared goals.

THE GLOBAL MODEL OF CHILDHOOD

UNICEF, Amnesty, and AIUSA shaped in different ways the global model of childhood that emerged after World War II. Through its unmatched international reach, programs in the Global South, and expansion into almost all areas of child welfare, UNICEF set and steadily raised standards

73. Ibid.
74. Ibid., 14.
75. Wong, *Internal Affairs*, 12.

of child welfare and protection to be applied to all children, everywhere. These uniform standards would form the basis of the global model of childhood, eventually finding full expression in the CRC. Amnesty and AIUSA's work for prisoners of conscience would eventually come to include children facing capital punishment, as these organizations singled out US noncompliance with a specific aspect of the global model of childhood (the ban on the child death penalty) expressed in the CRC. As such, Amnesty and AIUSA did not affect the content of the model, but sharpened its application and amplified its impact.

This section considers how the global model of childhood served as a mechanism for the diffusion of the norm against the child death penalty. First, I examine the model itself, beginning with the development and drafting of the CRC. I then explore UNICEF's evolving ideas on children and childhood based on the authority attributed to the natural science, later on economics and the study of development, and finally on international law. Second, I analyze the use of moral authority by both UNICEF and AIUSA, beginning with a discussion of moral authority as a means of leverage and influence. Since moral authority is a widely adaptive tool, I then consider the agency of these actors to select their issue areas: Precisely, why did the child death penalty become an important children's rights issue in the late twentieth century? I discuss the roles that international law and arguments about civilization played in diffusing the norm against the penalty.

Third, I suggest that the agency demonstrated by UNICEF and Amnesty, and particularly by AIUSA, marks a return to earlier types of principled activism seen in Europe and the United States (and discussed in chapters 3 and 6). Yet unlike earlier campaigns and initiatives that were motivated by enlightenment ideals and humanitarian impulses, the principled activism of these organizations was inspired by the global model of childhood. Finally, I summarize how UNICEF, Amnesty, and AIUSA shaped the scope, content, and application of the CRC.

The Convention on the Rights of the Child

The road to a convention for children began in 1979 when the United Nations declared the International Year of the Child. The previous year, Poland submitted an agenda request to the United Nations for a convention on the rights of the child that would "take further and more consistent steps" than the 1959 Declaration by enshrining these rights in a convention, or a legally binding international instrument (E/CN.4/1284).

The text suggested by Poland was essentially an updated version of the 1959 Declaration (E/CN.4/L.1366), and was supported in principle by NGOs in a written statement to the United Nations (E/CN.4/NGO/ 225). These NGOs, among them the International Council of Women, the International Federation for Human Rights, and the International Union for Child Welfare, requested that sufficient time be allotted to consider the multiple studies and vast expertise available on child welfare and protection. Not anticipating the enthusiasm and controversy the proposal would cause, Poland's delegate, Adam Lopatka, suggested that a convention be adopted in 1979 during the International Year of the Child, arguing that while he respected the views of the NGOs, he "did not think they needed several years to make their opinions known on questions which they had long had under consideration" (E/CN.4/NGO/225). In response, the International Union for Child Welfare countered that since the 1959 Declaration had been adopted at a time when most states in Africa and Asia were still colonies and therefore had little input in the declaration's drafting, a new convention should acknowledge that many of the principles of child protection "might not be acceptable to them" (E/CN.4/NGO/ 225). The concern was that a hastily drafted convention might fail to be fully comprehensive in terms of rights covered or fully inclusive in terms of region, leaving out children in large swaths of the world.

A number of delegates said that the declaration did not address many current issues confronting children. Among the issues proposed for addition to a new convention was the age of criminal responsibility (E/CN.4/ L.1468). Protection from the death penalty for children under the age of 18 was first included in Article 20 of Poland's revised draft convention in 1979 (E/CN.4/1349). A prior reference to special treatment for "asocial" children was made by Colombia in 1978, although the death penalty was not mentioned specifically (E/CN.4/1324/Add.2). The abolition of the child death penalty in Article 20 (and later, Article 19) would be incorporated into a broader article covering children deprived of their liberty (Article 37). Article 37 was considered and adopted by the CRC Working Group in 1986.[76]

A collection of NGO cosponsors to a joint proposal and an Ad Hoc NGO group supported the ban on the child death penalty in both the 1982 and 1983 Working Group sessions (E/CN.4/1982/WG.1/WP.1, 6; E/CN.4/ 1985/WG.1/WP.1, 12–14). The Ad Hoc NGO group—active from 1983 to 1989—was responsible for the increase, both in number and diversity, of

---

76. United Nations, *Legislative History of the Convention on the Rights of the Child* (New York: United Nations, 2007): 739.

the NGOs now claiming a stake in the drafting of the convention. From an initial twenty NGOs, the group grew exponentially and would eventually include Amnesty, the International Commission of Jurists, and Save the Children, among others.[77] The Ad Hoc group was the first to specify, in 1985, "Capital punishment shall not be imposed for acts committed by persons under the age of 18" (E/CN.4/1985/WG.1/WP.1, 12–14). This language differed from Poland's 1979 revised declaration that stated, "The child shall not be liable to capital punishment" (E/CN.4/1349). The first statement seems to suggest that *child offenders* be protected from the penalty, while the second seems only to protect children, and would thus seem to allow executions to take place after these offenders reach adulthood. A revised article, proposed by Canada in 1986, more closely resembled Poland's revised version: "No child shall be sentenced to death" (E/CN.4/1986/39, para. 90). An informal working group that included interested NGOs, Canada, and other states suggested new language: "The following sentences shall not be imposed for crimes committed by persons below eighteen years of age: (a) capital punishment; (b) life imprisonment" (E/CN.4/1986/30/para. 93).

In its work on Article 37, the Working Group grappled with the definition of a child as a person below the age of 18, an increasingly contentious issue. The US delegation in 1986 voiced its first specific objection to the definition in the drafting of the convention, arguing that the reference, "persons below eighteen years of age," was arbitrary and suggesting it be deleted (E/CN.4/1986/30, para. 105). Citing international agreements and UN resolutions, both Amnesty and the International Commission of Jurists disagreed and argued for the subparagraph to stay as it was. The US delegation backed down, claiming that it:

> would not insist on [its] amendment and block consensus, provided it was understood that the United States maintained its right to make a reservation on this point and that it was implicitly understood that a child committing an offence which, if committed by an adult, would be criminal could be treated as an adult (E/CN.4/1986/30, para. 105).

As it had during the first reading, the definition of a child was disputed in the second reading of the convention, from 1988 to 1989. India suggested that "persons below 18 years of age" be replaced with "a child" with regard to the death penalty—an obviously ambiguous and culturally variable category (E/CN.4/WG.1/WP.15). An open-ended drafting

---

77. United Nations, *Legislative History*, Annex III B.

group was appointed (and included most Working Group countries), and the final version of the text was adopted in 1989: "Neither capital punishment nor life imprisonment [without the possibility of release] shall be imposed for offences committed by persons below 18 years of age" (E/CN.4/1989/WG.1/WP.67/Rev. 1).[78] The United States again reserved its right to enter reservations on the Article (E/CN.4/1989/48, para. 544).

UNICEF did not take a leadership role in the drafting of the CRC, in large part because it believed a rights-based, legal path to children's protection was not the most effective way to achieve its goals. In the early years of the drafting process, UNICEF was focused on its new initiative targeting Children in Especially Difficult Circumstances (CEDC), including victims of violence, trafficking, exploitation, and war.[79] The organization was then largely out of step with NGOs that were more concerned with advocacy and international legislation. Only in 1987 did UNICEF affirm the "potential convergence" between development and child survival *and* children's rights.[80] Eventually, UNICEF would expand the CEDC category to include delinquents.[81] Although it was slow to accept the new rights-based model of child protection, UNICEF had fully embraced the approach by the 1990s. One of the impacts that the nascent children's rights regime had on UNICEF's direction in the 1990s was to refocus its attention on children in the developed world, as the CRC shed new light on violations in these regions.[82]

The hard work of these IGOs and NGOs finally bore fruit in the 1990s, when children assumed new importance in international affairs. Despite the glacial pace of the drafting process, the 1990 CRC came into force quicker than other prior conventions and had almost universal support. For a brief period in September 1990, children's rights enjoyed the undivided attention of world leaders from more than seventy countries attending the World Summit for Children, the largest gathering at the time of heads of state ever convened.[83] The event represented a unique moment

78. There are some minor differences between this version and the final version, namely, the spelling of 18 as eighteen and the removal of the brackets around "without the possibility of parole." Interestingly, the United States was one of the countries that argued that "without the possibility of release" be left in the Article, even though the United States remains one of the Article's worst violators.

79. UNICEF, *1946–2006 Sixty Years for Children*, 21.

80. Ibid.

81. United Nations and Secretary-General Kofi Annan, *We the Children: Meeting the Promises of the World Summit for Children* (New York: UNICEF House, 2001): 79.

82. UNICEF, *1946–2006 Sixty Years for Children*, 26–27.

83. Norman Lewis, "Human Rights, Law, and Democracy," 77–78. Although the United States was present at the summit, its participation was strikingly minimal. Barbara Frey and Mike Brehm, "20 Years Later: An Assessment of the Continuing Reticence of the United States to Ratify the United Nations Convention on the Rights of the Child." Working paper, 2010.

of clear consensus on the now global model of childhood and inspired an increasingly complex system of analysis, oversight, and advocacy designed to study, safeguard, and promote the globalized child. Following its entry into force, the convention became the last word in child welfare and protection. In effect, the CRC codified the globalized child. It is significant that almost all international advocacy on behalf of children today makes reference to it.

However, as discussed in chapters 3 and 4, these ideas and principles about children did not appear out of thin air. The drafting of the CRC took place in the 1980s, by which time the liberal state model was the last legitimate regime type. The expansion of human rights to specific groups—to children, the disabled, refugees, etc.—seemed a natural extension of this phenomenon, as rights-based approaches to human progress and well-being were increasingly seen as successful. The content of some of these norms about children had previously been codified in international law and institutionalized in the international community through the ICCPR, the Geneva Conventions, and, in the case of the child death penalty, in national practice. For most other norms about children, the CRC made them binding international law, and part of the global model of childhood.

The Model as Mechanism

As the case study demonstrates, UNICEF was the single most important actor in the creation, dissemination, and monitoring of the global child. This model was a specific construction of childhood with many, mostly Western attributes, including the upper age limit of 18; dependency upon adults; less developed mental, physical, emotional, and intellectual capabilities; a lack of agency; a need for protection from adults; and a reduced level of culpability for actions taken. The model now includes modern legal protections, including rights against discrimination based on gender, race, ethnicity, religion, and nationality.

In the early years after World War II, the former allies saw their responsibilities as moral agents to be to provide for people's basic needs, such as food, clothing, and health, an interpretation reflected in the emergency focus of UNICEF's early initiatives. During these years, UNICEF's work for children aimed to provide food, water, and shelter, and to ensure a sanitary environment and protection from disease. The first sources of authority cited by UNICEF in its determination of children's needs were scientific, as the organization drew from studies of child development, immunology, and nutrition.[84] Science thus gave UNICEF the authority needed to compel states either to fund these programs or be the recipient of them.

The model of childhood expanded in the 1960s and 1970s, as organizations like UNICEF adopted a 'whole child' approach that included new issue areas. This enlarged interpretation of children's needs thus added new features to the fast diffusing model. The new, wider focus included issues of family, child and youth welfare services, and vocational training to existing concerns of health and sanitation.[85] An interest in the 'girl child,' specifically, also emerged during this period as it became increasingly evident that women and girls were important to development. A girl's education (and that of her mother), health, nutrition, equality, and employment were critical to bringing the developing world into capitalist markets. The model of childhood, once justified by the natural science, was now also justified by the social science. Economics, arguably the most objective of the social science, was especially key to the growth of the model as a whole. As the global model of childhood steadily broadened in scope in the 1960s and 1970s, and as children came to be seen as essential to the progress of nations, the model's adoption and fulfillment increasingly became part of (and were eventually inseparable from) the project of state-building itself.

Linking children's needs to the needs of the state was not a new concept. Chapter 3, for example, examines how both the British and the French recognized the connection between the health of children and the ability to win wars. In the postwar period as well, children were widely viewed as vital to national development, both by proselytizing agencies like UNICEF that diffused the model of childhood and by the countries that adopted the model. The relationship between children's needs and state needs has also been one of the few sub-areas of children's rights to receive attention in the international relations literature. Scholars that have addressed children's rights cite the link between human rights and economic progress in general and between economic progress and children's rights in particular.[86] One common argument in critical theory approaches to childhood

---

84. United Nations Children's Fund, "The Nobel Peace Prize 1965."

85. Ritchie Calder, *Growing up with UNICEF*, Public Affairs Pamphlet No. 330 (New York: Public Affairs Pamphlets, 1962): 13–14.

86. Lewis, "Human Rights, Law, and Democracy"; Watson, "Children and International Relations."

examines the "new moral imperialism" of children's rights, or the "moral rehabilitation of imperialism,"[87] in which the inability of countries in the Global South to protect and provide for children according to the demands of international law exposes them to intervention by powerful Western states and international organizations.[88]

The model of childhood entered its most recent phase with the coming into force of the 1990 CRC. Since then, international law has become the definitive voice and key source of authority in children's protection and rights globally. Although science and economics still serve as sources of authority, the CRC has codified the model and made it binding international law. As is evident in the case studies of UNICEF and AIUSA, international law itself serves to justify initiatives and campaigns on behalf of children. In no campaign to date has this been more evident than in AIUSA's campaign against the child death penalty.

The Role of Moral Authority and International Law

As the model of childhood grew in complexity and diffused globally, the norms contained within the model (such as the ban on the child death penalty) also diffused and gained traction and acceptance. Yet within the international system, these normative pathways flow in more than one direction. Important actors in the international community—both state and nonstate actors—continue to build upon the model by introducing and promoting new norms (the norm against corporal punishment for juveniles, for example). These new norms percolate and diffuse up, becoming part of the global model and growing its boundaries.

This is akin to the process at the state level, where ideas about childhood and its need for regulation shaped state bureaucracy; state bureaucracy, in turn, validated itself by further expanding the idea of childhood and the state's role in its oversight and protection. At the international level, the global model of childhood and the need to ensure state compliance with the model validated the creation (and the growth and consolidation of) international organizations devoted to children's issues, which in turn, shaped the model and its need for regulation. As such, specific norms and the model as a whole have co-constituted each other as norms about childhood, child protection, and children's rights shaped and were

---

87. Pupavac, "Misanthropy without Borders," 107.
88. Ibid.; Lewis, "Human Rights, Law, and Democracy"; Burman, "Developing Differences"; Watson, "Children and International Relations."

shaped by these patterns of diffusion. Organizations like UNICEF and AIUSA held an institutional moral authority based on their own records of accomplishment and principled positions, as well as on the records of their parent organizations, the United Nations and Amnesty International, respectively. The norm against the child death penalty was bolstered by the moral authority of the institutions that diffused the norm by diffusing the model of which it was a part.

Theoretical variants of moral authority as a form of power have been discussed in the international relations literature for some time: Judith Goldstein and Robert Keohane considered the causal power of "principled beliefs," while Kathryn Sikkink cited the power of "principled ideas."[89] The impact of religion on decision making is also a theme of scholarship related to moral authority and principled ideas, although it is grossly neglected in the international relations literature.[90] Richard Price has argued in a review of the transnational civil society literature that activists "derive their authority from three principal sources: expertise, moral influence, and a claim to political legitimacy."[91] As the discussion of UNICEF and Amnesty below attests, activists must demonstrate that they are knowledgeable about their cause (expertise); that they hold the moral high ground and can use their position effectively (moral influence); and that they represent the interests of the public as opposed to private or corporate interests (political legitimacy).[92] Sikkink adds the perception of accountability to this list, as well as the transparency needed to hold groups accountable.[93]

Transnational moral authority is also not a new idea. Rodney Bruce Hall has argued that it has its roots in pre–sovereign Europe, but can be seen

89. Judith Goldstein, Robert O. Keohane, and Social Science Research Council (US). Committee on Foreign Policy, *Ideas and Foreign Policy: Beliefs, Institutions, and Political Change*, Cornell Studies in Political Economy (Ithaca, NY: Cornell University Press, 1993): 591; Kathryn Sikkink, "Human Rights, Principled Issue-Networks, and Sovereignty in Latin America," *International Organization* 47, no. 3 (1993): 411–441.

90. Jonathan Fox, "Religion as an Overlooked Element in International Relations," *International Studies Review* 3, no. 3 (2001): 53–73.

91. Richard Price, "Transnational Civil Society and Advocacy in World Politics," *World Politics* 55, no. 4 (2003): 587.

92. Ibid., 589, 591; Ann Florini, *The Third Force: The Rise of Transnational Civil Society* (Tokyo and Washington, DC: Carnegie Endowment for International Peace, 2000); Clark, *Diplomacy of Conscience*.

93. Kathryn Sikkink, "Restructuring World Politics: The Limits and Asymmetries of Soft Power," in *Restructuring World Politics: Transnational Social Movements, Networks, and Norms*, eds. Sanjeev Khagram, James V. Riker, and Kathryn Sikkink, Social Movements, Protest, and Contention (Minneapolis: University of Minnesota Press, 2002): 301–318.

at work throughout the twentieth century.[94] Beginning with President Woodrow Wilson's justification for entering World War I and throughout the Cold War (in both the East and West), moral authority has been a powerful tool (and coveted prize) for states. After World War II, colonialism lost all pretense of legitimacy, and a struggle ensued for the "allegiance of peripheral peoples" through competing claims of support for "peripheral self-determination."[95] As Price and others have made clear, moral authority has been extremely useful for activists and organizations as well. Hall contends that transnational moral authority has been used by those seeking to affect political outcomes.[96] Drawing on the work of Alexander Wendt, Yosef Lapid, and Friedrich Kratochwil, Hall argues that moral authority is thus a "shared convention . . . one that acquires utility as a power resource to the extent that it is institutionalized as a convention."[97] Moral authority, Hall says, can be a game-changer, with the power to shape political outcomes. Regarding the child death penalty, the international system of states, committed to the goals of progress and justice, provides the context for children's rights, along with the shared convention that the state is responsible for protecting children. This shared convention provides UNICEF and Amnesty with leverage for advocacy from above and below.

The ideal type of moral authority with regard to international law is one whereby states feel compelled to obey law regardless of its content. This sense of obligation is uncommon, however. In practice, norms and law rarely possess this degree of authority. Moral authority often requires persuasion over time to develop the sense of obligation necessary to produce policy change. Even with universal moral principles within human rights, like the right to life, the moral authority to judge the application of these principles within countries must be developed over time. For example, the child death penalty clearly violates the right to life, as the state causes the death of a child offender. Yet even in this case, principled actors had to build moral authority in order to induce compliance with international legal principles.

As difficult as it is to imagine today, Amnesty's original mission was not directed at advancing international legal standards of human rights, and

94. Rodney Bruce Hall, "Moral Authority as a Power Resource," *International Organization* 51, no. 4 (1997): 591–622.

95. Ibid., 619–620.

96. Ibid.

97. Ibid., 593–594; Alexander Wendt, "Anarchy Is What States Make of It: The Social Construction of Power Politics," *International Organization* 46, no. 2 (1992): 391–425; Yosef Lapid and Friedrich V. Kratochwil, *The Return of Culture and Identity in IR Theory*, Critical Perspectives on World Politics (Boulder, CO: Lynne Rienner, 1996).

the organization would not take on this mission until well into its second and third decades.[98] Before the campaign to end the child death penalty in the late 1980s, international law was seen as aligned with Amnesty's objectives, but not necessarily synonymous with them and not part of its core mission to prevent government persecution of individual prisoners of conscience. Amnesty's founder Peter Benenson believed that public condemnation of human rights violations, not international law, would shape states' behavior.[99]

The changing relationship between Amnesty and international human rights law is vividly captured in the campaigns against the child death penalty. International legal arguments by Amnesty and AIUSA were made with increasing frequency and assumed greater importance in campaign documents by the late 1980s and early 1990s, suggesting that these arguments were expected to resonate with the campaigns' target audiences, presumably the American public, legislators, lawyers, and judges. Moreover, several international legal avenues were pursued in the US campaign, and international law was cited in oral arguments and petitions of death penalty cases throughout the country.

Campaign documents suggest that these international legal arguments were made on a selective and strategic basis. In an AIUSA memo from 1986, lawyers from several organizations active in child death penalty cases were advised *not* to include international legal arguments in all US cases.[100] Rather, the memo suggested that AIUSA "seed the argument and pick ... cases very selectively." Lawyers defending child offenders faced with the death penalty should be contacted and asked "to put the international law argument in."[101] In order to make certain that "they do it, and to be sure they do it in the way [AIUSA] want[s]," AIUSA drafted a legal template of pleadings to be used in briefs.[102] Without this template, which included the international law argument, the memo states, "Lawyers won't want to push the argument, take up pages and time, etc., if it's not a good forum." The memo further suggested that AIUSA avoid state courts that were "inherently more resistant to international law arguments."[103]

---

98. Clark, *Diplomacy of Conscience,* 5, 8.

99. Ibid., 5.

100. Jessica Neuwirth and Amnesty International USA, "Memo To: Paul Hoffman, Jane?, David Weissbrodt, Mary Mcclymont, Joan Hartman Fitzpatrick, Re: Meeting with Jack Boger" (New York: University of Minnesota Law School: Private Archives of David Weissbrodt, 1986).

101. Ibid.

102. Ibid.

103. Ibid.

In these cases, federal judges should instead be encouraged to write about the international legal issues to force their consideration.

Another 1986 memo detailing the minutes of an AIUSA Legal Support Network (LSN) meeting identified Mary McClymont of the ACLU as co-counsel in the Roach and Pinkerton case at the Inter-American Court on Human Rights, and Cheryl Polydor, the LSN coordinator in Washington, DC, as the authors of a "paragraph" that would be "distributed to attorneys representing juveniles in capital cases."[104] The paragraph aimed to "preserv[e] the international law issue in the event an attorney-of-record does not want or know how to raise the issue in depth."[105] These memos offer proof of the collaborative nature of the effort to end the child death penalty in the United States, and they underscore the importance of the NGOs, nonprofits, and activists that worked both independently and in conjunction with AIUSA to end the penalty.

I evaluated Amnesty and AIUSA campaigns through campaign documents, particularly publications and memos, from 1987 to 2004. In these documents, four assumptions about international law were made by Amnesty and AIUSA lawyers, researchers, and strategists:

i.   Human rights standards found in international law provide a strong foundation for human rights advocacy and should be supported.

ii. Traditional legal avenues for international human rights norms are valuable in themselves. Now as then, Amnesty and AIUSA advocates continue to use international forums even when these institutions are unsympathetic to certain arguments or are ineffectual at ending human rights violations, because there is a benefit in itself to the pursuit of remedy through these institutions. International legal claims were also "seeded" in oral and written arguments in US cases.

iii. There is a "compliance pull" to international law.[106] AIUSA's choice to "seed" cases with international legal arguments and the prevalence with which both Amnesty and AIUSA used international law in their campaign publications indicate that the organizations believed international legal arguments to be compelling to their target audiences. It is also possible that by using international law

104. Jane Rocamora, "Memo To: LSN Coordinators and Attendees of the LSN Death Penalty Meeting, Re: Minutes of Death Penalty Meeting on October 27, 1986" (University of Minnesota Law School: Private Archives of David Weissbrodt, November 3, 1986).

105. Ibid.

106. Franck, "Legitimacy in the International System."

even when it was not likely to be dispositive, Amnesty and AIUSA were attempting *to create a compliance pull* for international law—to construct a pull through the repeated use of these arguments in legal briefs.

iv. The compliance pull of international law is insufficient to produce change on its own. Instead, international legal arguments were often paired with references to the consensus of the *civilized* (author's term) international community—as evident in the dissemination of lists of violating countries. In other words, evidence of the consensus of the international community was believed to be found not only in the number of states that prohibited executions of child offenders, but also, more importantly, in the types and identity of states that did and did not execute children.

In their campaigns to end the child death penalty in the United States, Amnesty and AIUSA's success was in linking obligation with international law. To do so, they had to draw on their own moral authority, banked over the course of decades of human rights advocacy, and particularly on their expertise on human rights matters, and to use this to wage a campaign that argued the incompatibility of US policy and practice with international law and norms.

The path that the United States took to compliance with the international ban on the child death penalty, although convoluted because of the federal system, responded to critiques by NGOs, IGOs, and other actors in stages over the course of two decades. Compliance was partly the result of Amnesty and AIUSA campaigns that connected the protection of child offenders *with* the United States' belief that it is a champion and advocate of human rights norms, not a violator. Ann Marie Clark contends that the hard part for Amnesty in inducing compliance with human rights norms is not the application of ideas to practice, but rather, the development of a sense of obligation on the part of states.[107] Amnesty sought to elevate the authority of human rights principles by giving them something (the organization believed) international law could not: transcendence over time, ideology, and geographical space, what Clark calls "impartial application."[108] The evolving relationship between Amnesty and international law says something about how human rights change works, or, at the least, how it has been perceived to work by Amnesty strategists. It further testifies to the gradually but significantly expanding role of international law

107. Clark, *Diplomacy of Conscience,* 128.
108. Ibid., 19.

within the international system and to how this shift contributed to the moral authority of Amnesty and AIUSA.

Evidence from a survey of Amnesty and AIUSA documents, discussed above, suggests that the organizations increasingly came to rely on international law as a way to persuade states to end the child death penalty. In fact, it appears that Amnesty and AIUSA were attempting to create a compliance pull of international law, to construct a pull through the systematic inclusion and citation of international law and norms in legal briefs (and to bolster their own moral authority in the process). Moreover, the list of violating states underscores the fact that this prohibition was not in word only, but also in deed; unlike some other prohibitions in international law, no states executed child offenders except for the United States and a handful of other states that were considered to be outside of the international community. International legal prescriptions were reinforced by the association, promoted by Amnesty and AIUSA, between the child death penalty and uncivilized states, as discussed in the next section.

Amnesty's moral authority is rooted in its expertise in a variety of human rights issues both within countries and across regions. Stephen Hopgood suggests this expertise is contingent upon the independence and objectivity characteristic of Amnesty's research.[109] Clark suggests that through its "position as a disinterested and autonomous 'third party' actor," Amnesty "deploys expertise" to support norm creation and development.[110] Expertise is also essential to UNICEF's moral authority. Unlike Amnesty, however, UNICEF's expertise is derived from science: social science for development issues, and the natural science in the areas of child health, nutrition, sanitation, and physical development, as discussed. Although it is clear from the English case study (and the US case study in the next chapter) that the development of the science of childhood was not apolitical, science possesses an aura of objectivity nonetheless. For example, when UNICEF began to focus on the 'whole child,' and health, education, and sanitation issues became an important platform for advocacy, it constructed the global child as one who primarily needed good health, a decent education, and clean living conditions at the expense of other needs. Sarah Holloway and Gill Valentine argue that the child constructed by the West is "less developed, less able, and less competent than adults," and it was this child that UNICEF promoted in development projects in

109. Hopgood, *Keepers of the Flame*, 73.
110. Clark, *Diplomacy of Conscience*, 11.

the second half of the twentieth century.[111] In fact, by choosing to advocate on the basis of certain issues over others, the child that UNICEF
constructed and diffused was decidedly political. But because the model
had scientific support, and was even a scientific construction, it had the
appearance of objectivity and was therefore seen as legitimate.

Another source of UNICEF's moral authority is its parent organization,
the United Nations.[112] The United Nations' role as a representative for its
member states lends it a legitimacy not found with other transnational
IGOs and NGOs. Yet while UNICEF benefits from the UN's institutional
legitimacy, it is also affected by its reputational harms. Scandals involving abuse by peacekeepers and recent lawsuits over the cholera epidemic
in Haiti erode the UN's legitimacy. Attacks on UNICEF staff in Sudan and
Iraq reflect upon the UN's legitimacy in general and suggest reputational
harm to UN agencies at large.

As with Amnesty, UNICEF's effectiveness depends upon its powers of
persuasion. It must convince governments to accept its recommendations
and assistance. Its pillar issues—health, education, and sanitation—have
the *appearance* of impartiality, but UNICEF still struggles to carry out its
programs in the world's most conflict-prone regions. UNICEF, however,
has a carrot that Amnesty does not: money. UNICEF's budget in 2012
was $3.8 billion.[113] This funding is pumped into child health and welfare
programs, which in many ways help those in power by providing services
that governments are unable to provide. Compliance with UNICEF's
recommendations and international law, then, is part of the return on
UNICEF's investment. UNICEF's moral authority is thus buttressed by its
economic power.

Like Amnesty, UNICEF also entered the rights arena somewhat reluc-
tantly. It did not, as the case makes clear, assume leadership on or even
overtly support children's rights initiatives at first, viewing this direction
as ineffectual to its larger mission of international aid and development.
It helped facilitate the drafting of the CRC nonetheless, and now employs
the language of the CRC in its documents as one source of its authority. UNICEF's use of international law to advance its agenda for children
made a great deal of sense, given that law, like science, has a perceived

111. Sarah Holloway and Gill Valentine, *Children's Geographies: Playing, Living,
Learning*, Critical Geographies 8 (London and New York: Routledge, 2000): 2.

112. Kent J. Kille, ed. *The UN Secretary-General and Moral Authority* (Washington,
DC: Georgetown University Press, 2007): 10.

113. UNICEF, "Annual Report 2012 Summary," http://www.unicef.org/publica-
tions/files/UNICEF_Annual_Report_2012_SUMMARY_ENG_2July2013.pdf.

objectivity. International law, especially, carries a legitimacy that is universal; like the laws of gravity, international law applies in every state and to every person. Although UNICEF was initially skeptical about the utility of a convention for children, it nonetheless has used its content as justification for its programs.

Civilization as Critique

Although they never explicitly mention *civilization* in campaign materials, Amnesty and AIUSA repeatedly listed those states that continued to execute child offenders and consistently cited the global consensus against the practice. In campaign documents and death penalty reports from 1987 to 2004, the most common argument was that the United States was in the disreputable company of the DRC, China, Iran, Iraq, Nigeria, Pakistan, and Yemen, among others.

It is reasonable to assume that strategy documents are drafted with care and purpose and that they place arguments in an order that advocates believe will be persuasive to the target audience. Stronger arguments or arguments the organization particularly wishes to advance will be used in multiple documents and made early within publications. The principal arguments made in Amnesty and AIUSA publications addressing the death penalty in general or for child offenders were: The United States is one of a few states that execute child offenders; international law condemns the practice of executing child offenders; children possess unique characteristics, including reduced culpability for their actions; and there are concerns about the way the death penalty is carried out in the United States.

It is revealing that whenever arguments were made in these reports against child executions in the United States, the list of states that carried out these executions was *always* included in the publication. The suggestion was that these states were rogue states that failed to meet international human rights standards. None of these states were highly industrialized; none are in the West. Moreover, only one publication did not assert the incompatibility of US practice with international law and norms.

Since Amnesty and AIUSA used these arguments in almost all of the reports surveyed on the death penalty for child offenders, it can be assumed that the organizations believed they would persuade their target audiences. Although these publications demonstrate Amnesty's commitment to campaign diversity by discussing all countries that continued to execute child offenders, many devoted significantly more page space to the United States than to the other cases. A 1998 report on child executions worldwide since 1990 surveys national practices and customary law before summarizing the practices of each state that continued to execute child offenders. The document, while covering all noncompliant states, clearly focused on the United States. The DRC, Iran, Nigeria, Pakistan, Saudi Arabia, and Yemen are summarized in two and a half pages *altogether*, while the US summary alone takes up four pages.[114]

The clear and consistent message of these publications is that the US practice of executing child offenders violated customary international law, and that its treatment of children was on par with the treatment of children in the world's least developed, least democratic states. That these countries are listed by name is suggestive of reputation and status—or the lack thereof. The resounding message was that only uncivilized states execute child offenders.

Although the use of international law and references to civilization in human rights campaigns such as these have proven successful in ending some abuses, there are inherent trade-offs. Campaigns that cite international law typically emphasize civil and political rights above social and economic rights, and present the international community and its laws and practices in a static manner—one that leaves little room for non-Western and historically weak countries to contribute to or to help shape the community.

Most importantly, the use of these dichotomies—between civilized states that value human rights law and rogue states that reject it—is dangerous. However skillfully or subtly done, the objective of these comparisons is a blunt one: to shock or embarrass a target audience by comparing a given country's practice and law with that of countries that the audience believes to be backward, ignorant, or repressive. While the potential success of this strategy is evident from the case study, the cost is that it risks crystallizing the world into two crudely imagined categories of states— those that respect human rights (typically in the West), and those that reject them (typically in the Global South). Human rights violations by Western governments that do not consider themselves bound by the rules that govern international society, such as the United States in its ongoing operation of Guantanamo prison, use of drone strikes in conflict zones, and conduct in the wider war on terror, illustrate the risk of these flawed and simplistic formulations.

114. This report was first published in 1998 and has been updated several times. Amnesty International, "Children and the Death Penalty: Executions Worldwide since 1990, ACT 50/007/2002" (2002).

That said, the case suggests that human rights change may be driven by comparisons between civilized and uncivilized states and practices. Such change typically relies on the power of ideas and corresponding processes of socialization, processes not always supported by force or money. Socialization and its mechanisms (naming, framing, shaming, and persuasion) attempt change through the dynamism of ideas, interests, and identity. Amnesty and AIUSA's challenge to the United States' perception of itself as a champion of democracy and human rights through a comparison between US policy and practice and those of nondemocratic regimes was not a strategy unique to these organizations or to this campaign. Shaming tactics, for example, would have little impact if there were no reputation to maintain, no identity to burnish or disavow, and no 'other' to set oneself apart from. The choices by Amnesty and AIUSA in the campaign against the child death penalty should therefore not be unfairly singled out for critique. Rather, these campaign choices and their outcome speak to the power of socialization as a vehicle for human rights change, in this case, to the law and practice of a superpower.

As stated, Amnesty and AIUSA are not the only organizations invested in these comparisons. The United Nations, after all, is the ultimate civilizing institution. Emerging out of the Hobbesian chaos of World War II, the United Nations represents the triumph of human dignity over barbarism. Although war and human rights violations clearly did not end with the UN's founding in 1948, its founding was nonetheless an affirmation of liberal values. The United Nations began to focus on children in the Global South through UNICEF. Although these efforts were not coercive, UNICEF brought with it relatively deep pockets (along with milk, food, vaccines, and penicillin), and the promise of lifting young countries out of poverty, famine, and disease. Regardless of intent, these efforts echo the discourse of colonialism and mark the return of intervention in non-Western states through a range of child-saving initiatives, as discussed in chapters 3 and 4.

The (unsubstantiated) belief that child protection in general emerged in the West is apparent in mid-century publications about UNICEF in the United States. In a public affairs pamphlet in 1959 with prefaces by both Dag Hammarskjold (former UN Secretary-General) and Maurice Pate (former executive director of UNICEF), the author asks why it is possible to believe that children of developing countries could one day have the same chance for life and health as children in the West. The pamphlet concludes that one reason is that "the peoples of Asia and Africa and South America have *come to want* for their children the same life horizons that the people of Europe and North America have come to expect [emphasis added]."[115] The implication is that regardless of whether parents in developing regions wanted their children to live healthy lives before Western organizations came on the scene, the notion of universal standards of child welfare had its origins in the West and was introduced and diffused by UNICEF. The pamphlet goes on to implore young countries (in the "backwaters of civilization," to use the pamphlet's words) to "accept the advice and help of more experienced" states.[116] Even UNICEF's own documents express the belief that the model of childhood in general spread from the West to the periphery, from "richer neighbors" to the developing countries of Africa.[117]

The Agency of Organizations: A Return to Principled Activism

Although the death penalty for child offenders had been prohibited in international law since the ICCPR came into effect in 1976, it took another decade for NGOs, child advocates, and death penalty opponents to push the issue into the national spotlight in the United States. Of all the US violations of human rights codified in the ICCPR, the child death penalty seemed an unlikely subject for an international campaign. After all, the number of child offenders sentenced to death in the United States was relatively small, less than seven per year on average between 1980 and 1985. Moreover, prior to the resumption of these executions in the mid-1980s, no child offender had been put to death in the United States since 1964.[118] The benefits of such a campaign seemed to be outweighed by the opportunity costs. Additionally, rising urban crime and juvenile delinquency meant that there was little sympathy for child criminals, especially violent ones. Yet the child death penalty was put on the public agenda in the late 1980s by a group of organizations in the United States and abroad, including Amnesty, AIUSA, the ACLU, and the National Association for the Advancement of Colored People's Legal Defense Fund.

As discussed, a coalition of NGOs, nonprofit organizations, and foundations launched a collective campaign in 2002 directed at a potential ruling by the US Supreme Court. These organizations took up the cause of the child death penalty for different reasons. For Amnesty and AIUSA, the

115. Heilbroner, *Mankind's Children*, 3.
116. Ibid., 4, 13.
117. UNICEF, *1946–2006 Sixty Years for Children*, 10–11.
118. Amnesty International, "United States of America: The Death Penalty and Juvenile Offenders," 62.

motivation was likely more rooted in international strategy, since the on-going US practice of the child death penalty provided cover for other coun-tries to continue the practice as well. Moreover, abolishing the penalty for child offenders in the United States offered a means to 'chip away' at the death penalty at large, and a campaign focused on children was believed to have a greater chance of success than a campaign focused on older, more culpable adults. The issue also possessed a clarity—the killing of child-ren by the state—not seen in other prospective campaigns by Amnesty and AIUSA.

Perhaps most important for Amnesty and AIUSA, a campaign against the child death penalty in the United States reinforced their organizations' independence and impartiality. By targeting a US violation of human rights, in addition to spotlighting violations in the Global South, Amnesty and AIUSA underscored their political neutrality, which was both part of the organizations' core identity and useful in furthering their goals, since the exercise of balance and fairness in the selection of campaigns gave these campaigns credibility.[119]

The 1990 CRC included the prohibition of the child death penalty, ex-pressing international opposition to the practice. Taken together with the execution of three child offenders in the United States in the 1980s, the CRC provided a policy window, or an "opportunity for action on given initiatives," within which Amnesty, AIUSA, and others could orga-nize.[120] John Kingdon contends that "advocates lie in wait . . . waiting for a development in the political stream they can use to their advantage."[121] Through this type of "tactical pluralism"—namely, drafting *amici* briefs; petitioning legislators; seeding arguments; publishing legal theory and crafting defense efforts using international law arguments; initiating studies about the death penalty and children's development; and making comparisons with 'rogue' states—Amnesty and AIUSA took advantage of the policy window that opened in the late 1980s and 1990s.[122]

As the case makes clear, the decision to focus on the child death penalty was the result of many years of organizational handwringing at AIUSA, which took place as international standards of childhood were developing

---

119. This discussion of the motivation of Amnesty and AIUSA in conducting a campaign against the child death penalty in the United States benefited greatly from conversations with Barbara Frey of the University of Minnesota.

120. John W. Kingdon, *Agendas, Alternatives, and Public Policies* (New York: HarperCollins, 1984): 174.

121. Ibid., 173.

122. Dara Z. Strolovitch, *Affirmative Advocacy: Race, Class, and Gender in Interest Group Politics* (Chicago: University of Chicago Press, 2007): 144.

and maturing. The choice to target the child death penalty by Amnesty, AIUSA, and other organizations was itself a social construction of a problem. After all, the legal execution of twenty or so child offenders— all convicted murderers—in a representative democracy over the course of two decades would not seem to constitute a human rights violation on par with the attention the issue received. Yet Amnesty, AIUSA, and others made the child death penalty the subject of a major international campaign between 1987 and 2005.

Here again, the focus on the child death penalty was not an obvious one. International campaigns to redress an injustice or to achieve social or political change are expensive and time-consuming, and their selection involves hard choices or trade-offs. The 1980s was a period of widespread human rights violations in the Americas. A large-scale campaign for a few child offenders siphoned valuable and limited resources that might have been used to address other violations—such as disappearances and scorched-earth campaigns in Latin America—that were much in evidence in the 1980s, and that were occurring on a far greater scale. The resources of time, effort, and money that Amnesty, AIUSA, and other organizations poured into this campaign at the expense of other possible initiatives made the opportunity costs of this choice during these two decades enormous.

Why then focus on child criminals? There are a few reasons Amnesty and AIUSA would make this choice: First, the United States was in violation of human rights norms, and American activists were motivated to bring it to account. American activists chose to engage their government on an issue of widespread international consensus, and the democratic, grassroots nature of AIUSA lent itself to this kind of campaign. Second, American activists could not tolerate such a clear contradiction of already institutionalized ideas about children—namely, the contrast between the practice of the child death penalty and the belief that children are vulnerable, in need of protection, and less culpable for their crimes than adults. Activists, especially those vehemently opposed to the death penalty in any context, honed in on the incompatibility between the execution of child offenders and the state's obligation to protect children. Third, the campaign against the child death penalty nested well with other objectives of the organizations. Charli Carpenter argues that issue adoption can have "more to do with whether the issue fits existing organizational goals" and its prospective or potential impact on issues already within an organization's mandate than with qualities of the subject and of the issue itself.[123]

---

123. Carpenter, "Studying Issue (Non)-Adoption," 662.

For AIUSA, this narrowly drawn campaign offered an opportunity both to promote juvenile justice and to strike against the practice of the death penalty at large.

It was this exercise of agency—the selection of the child death penalty as the subject of an international campaign at the expense of other pressing issues—that reshaped not only the practice of juvenile justice in the United States, but the broader understanding of children's rights. Executions of child offenders became a central point of contention between the United States (along with other countries that continued to execute child offenders) *and* human rights advocates, diplomats, IGOs, and NGOs. Amnesty and AIUSA (and the other prominent NGOs mentioned) successfully framed the debate as one about the civil and political rights of children and their development and reduced culpability.

Understood in this context, AIUSA's agency recalls the principled activism of child advocates in the nineteenth and early twentieth centuries. Early reforms for child offenders and law protecting children from abuse and neglect resulted from the tireless work of norm entrepreneurs, principled actors who during this time took up the cause of children and insisted upon the duty of adults to protect them. Principled activism as a mechanism of diffusion gradually became less important as the norm spread by way of colonial imposition and coercive socialization, discussed in chapter 4. The founding of human rights organizations like Amnesty and AIUSA and their successful campaign against the child death penalty mark the return of principled activism as a key mechanism of norm diffusion, guided by the globalized model of childhood.

There are differences as well, of course, between the early campaigns and the later campaign to end the child death penalty in the United States (and in Pakistan, as discussed in the next chapter). Amnesty and AIUSA's campaign was transnational and referenced international human rights law and norms as its primary source of authority. In fact, one of the main accomplishments of Amnesty and AIUSA's campaign against the child death penalty (and the death penalty in general) was its success at linking the national practice of capital punishment to international human rights law. This contextualization of the issue within international law and norms created new pressure points for decision makers in the United States at both the state and the federal level. While early principled activists cited the nature of children and the moral demands of charity, later activists cited the international order and global norms of child protection.

The Amnesty and AIUSA case yields several insights into the exercise of agency by nonstate actors: First, it demonstrates that even though the global model of childhood has been enshrined in the international system, opportunities for agency remain. Second, the case suggests that nonstate actors seeking human rights change have tremendous leeway to select where they focus their efforts and how they approach, plan, and conduct their campaigns. Third, the case suggests that while the prominent linkage of the idea of civilization to the protection of child offenders was necessary for US compliance, it was not sufficient to produce change. Rather, the organizations' strategy of publicizing and creating a compliance pull of international law, fomenting international opposition and condemnation, commissioning multiple studies, and simultaneously launching actions at both the international and country level resulted in a 'blitzkrieg' approach to catalyzing change. The campaign to abolish the child death penalty likely pushed US policymakers and decision makers to acknowledge, argue against, seek to refute, and ultimately to adopt international standards in the treatment of child offenders. Yet while international law provided the consensus by which to judge US policy and practice, it was the agency exercised by Amnesty, AIUSA, and other organizations that made the child death penalty an international cause.

The CRC, UNICEF, and Amnesty

Although UNICEF largely stood on the sidelines during the long period of the CRC's debate and drafting, it was nonetheless indispensable to the development of state authority and, ultimately, of international authority over children and control of children's lives. Regulatory authority over children and their parents began with narrowly tailored treaties and laws concerning children and grew over time, culminating in the CRC. The progressive expansion of UNICEF's mandate to include new and increasing areas of institutional concern shaped the contours of the regulatory regime, influencing what states, bureaucrats, and diplomats perceived as *possible* areas of protection and, in time, of rights for children. UNICEF's advocacy created the conditions (in the form of national and international law and policy and its corresponding bureaucracy and administration) that enabled the drafting of the CRC. UNICEF, in effect, made the CRC possible.

For their part, Amnesty and AIUSA had no connection to the development of the CRC and no impact on its content, but helped, importantly, to guide its application. Of the dozens of rights and protections afforded children by the CRC, AIUSA (especially) zeroed in on the violation of a single norm (the child death penalty) by a single violator (the United States). The campaign not only focused the attention of the international community on US noncompliance with the CRC, but also, over the course of two decades, brought dozens of other states into compliance with the norm against the penalty. The successful abolition of the penalty came at a high cost, however, siphoning money and resources and diverting public attention from other pressing human rights issues affecting children.

CONCLUSION

This chapter has argued that the global model of childhood was institutionalized through the work of international organizations like UNICEF that drew on the natural and social science and international law to develop and promote a decidedly Western construction of childhood, as measured by a single, universal, and increasingly detailed set of standards of child welfare and protection. Later, Amnesty and AIUSA would use their moral authority to make the child death penalty an important issue in international children's rights. Through claims about civilized and uncivilized behavior, Amnesty and AIUSA (among other organizations) connected the practice of the child death penalty with the practices of rogue states. The case studies suggest the return of principled activism as a key mechanism of norm diffusion. The next chapter considers laggard states that did not adopt the norm against the child death penalty during the first or second cascade and revisits the US case.

CHAPTER 6

༄༅

Laggards in the Global Age of the Child

INTRODUCTION

Through the three mechanisms of diffusion discussed in chapters 3, 4, and 5—principled activism, coercive socialization, and the globalization of childhood—the norm abolishing the death penalty for child offenders successfully diffused in the twentieth century. There remained, however, a handful of states that continued to execute child offenders, including the United States, whose abolition of the penalty in 2005 ended the second cascade.

In this chapter, I discuss one major case study, the United States, and two minor case studies, China and Pakistan. The US case poses a particular puzzle for some theories of international relations because the United States has been the hegemon at least since the end of World War II. The presence of hegemonic laggards in norm diffusion conflicts with the theories of realists and sociological institutionalists, who expect Western states (especially the hegemon) to lead norm diffusion. The other two states considered in this chapter, China and Pakistan, have both made progress toward ending the child death penalty, but are believed to have executed at least five child offenders between them in the twenty-first century.[1] As laggards, these states provide an interesting juxtaposition to the cascades in the last half of the twentieth century.

1. Amnesty International stopped reporting the number of executions by China in 2009 since these are considered to be a state secret and are difficult to confirm. See Amnesty International, "Death Sentences and Executions 2014," ACT 50/01/2015.

As stated, the abolition of the child death penalty in the United States ended the second cascade and ushered in the norm's late period of diffusion. I base this demarcation point on the number of states that continue to execute children; on the importance (expressed by legal theorists) of abolition by the United States on the norm's diffusion as a whole;[2] and on the global consensus on the norm expressed in other forums. For example, there is evidence that states recognize the global consensus against the practice when they conceal their activities. In the past, many states (Barbados, the DRC, Iran, Yemen, and Zaire) have failed to report to the former UN Commission on Human Rights child executions or laws that allow such executions, while others have misstated their laws (Nigeria). The United States, however, has been the only country to openly and routinely admit its execution of child offenders and the only country to defend its right to do so well into the twenty-first century.[3]

This chapter will first examine the United States as the norm's hegemonic laggard, followed by the noncompliant cases of China and Pakistan. A discussion of the domestic and international factors in abolition will follow, including the roles of race, science, and the state.

THE US CASE

In this case, I present the history of the death penalty for child offenders in the United States, including the historical development of American ideas about children and childhood; trends in race and geography; relevant Supreme Court rulings; the role of international law in Supreme Court decisions; and a review of the NGO activities that helped to end the practice. The case will show that the United States was socialized to international standards of juvenile justice by international and domestic actors. These actors drew on norms about children previously adopted by the United

2. Connie de la Vega and Jennifer Fiore, "The Supreme Court of the United States Has Been Called Upon to Determine the Legality of the Child Death Penalty in Micheal Domingues v. State of Nevada," *Whittier Law Review* 215 (1999): 215–230; Geoffrey Sawyer, "Comment: The Death Penalty Is Dead Wrong: *Jus Cogens* Norms and the Evolving Standard of Decency," *Penn State International Law Review* 22, no. 459 (2004): 459–482; Alice Miller and Joan Fitzpatrick, "International Standards of the Death Penalty: Shifting Discourse," *Brooklyn Journal of International Law* 19, no. 2 (1993): 273–366; Weissbrodt, Fitzpatrick, and Newman, *Human Rights: Law, Policy, and Process.*

3. Amnesty International, "The Exclusion of Child Offenders from the Death Penalty under General International Law, ACT 50/004/2003" (July 17, 2003): 7.

States and the international community to demonstrate the incongruity between these norms and the practice of the child death penalty.

Empirical Evidence of Executions of Child Offenders

The first recorded execution of a child offender in the United States was 16-year-old Thomas Graunger of Plymouth, Massachusetts in 1642, although he was hardly considered a child at the time.[4] Since 1642, at least 366 child offenders under the age of 18 have been executed in the United States, according to Victor Streib.[5] The primary dataset for executions in the United States, the Espy data from 1608–1991, only contains information about the 'age at the time of the execution,' not the age of the offender at the time of the crime.[6] Therefore, although Streib identifies at least 366 executions of child offenders in the United States since 1642, the Espy file shows that only 160 children were executed *while* they were still under the age of 18.[7] I have supplemented the Espy data with data on the executions carried out since 1985, resulting in Figure 6.1, which includes 183 of the 366 child executions in US history. Much of the missing data is likely from the mid-twentieth century, as the duration between the time of the crime and the time of execution increased over the century. Although the dataset may not include some nineteenth-century executions of child offenders (mostly 17-year-olds who were not executed until age 18), these omissions are likely few, and the data before the twentieth century are relatively complete. As the period between crime and execution grew in the twentieth century, fewer children were executed while they were still under the age of 18. Even though the Espy data likely miss a number of mid-twentieth-century child executions, they still demonstrate the spike in executions of offenders who were under the age of 18 *at the time* of execution. Robert Hale has argued that the actual number of child executions

4. Victor L. Streib, "The Child Death Penalty Today: Death Sentences and Executions for Juvenile Crimes, January 1, 1973–December 31, 2004" (Ohio Northern University College of Law, 2005): 3.
5. Ibid., 4.
6. M. Watt Espy and John Ortiz Smykla, "Executions in the US: 1608–2002: The Espy File [Computer File]," Interuniversity Consortium for Political and Social Research, 2002.
7. Streib has not published his data. I have supplemented Espy data of offenders with "unknown" ages in the pre-*Furman* period where possible. See Streib, "The Juvenile Death Penalty Today, January 1, 1973–February 28, 2005."

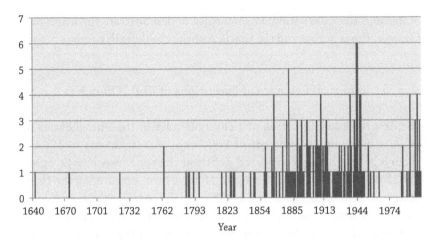

Figure 6.1 Executions of Child Offenders by Year in the United States.

was at least 141 between 1922 and 1962, almost three times the number included in the Espy dataset.[8]

As Figure 6.1 demonstrates, child executions were rare in the seventeenth and eighteenth centuries before becoming more common in the nineteenth century and spiking dramatically in the mid-twentieth century. Yet there were other patterns as well. As in the United Kingdom, the death penalty for child offenders under the age of 14 became increasingly rare in the United States in the eighteenth and nineteenth centuries. The last execution of an individual under the age of 14 in the United States was Fortune Ferguson in 1927, at age 13 for rape.[9] The last execution of a person younger than 18 occurred in 1959, when Leonard Shockley, an African American boy, was executed for murder and robbery committed at age 16.[10]

In 1972, the US Supreme Court ruled in *Furman v. Georgia*[11] that the death penalty as it was then applied was arbitrary and violated the Eighth and Fourteenth amendments to the Constitution. The last child offender executed in the years before the *Furman* ruling was James Andrew Echols,

8. Robert L. Hale, A Review of Juvenile Executions in America, Criminology Studies 3 (Lewiston, NY: Edwin Mellen, 1997): 92.

9. The Espy data do not list any child offenders executed below the age of 14 in the twentieth century; although Ferguson's execution is listed, his age is not. Amnesty International, "United States of America: The Death Penalty and Juvenile Offenders, AMR 51/23/91," 62.

10. Hale, A Review of Juvenile Executions in America, 99–100.

11. 408 United States 238.

a 17-year-old (executed at age 18), in Texas in 1964 for rape.[12] In the 1976 case *Gregg v. Georgia*,[13] the Supreme Court found the death penalty to be constitutional under the Eighth and Fourteenth amendments—as amended by the requirements of the *Furman* ruling. Even after the *de facto* moratorium on the penalty ended in 1977, US states were still reluctant to execute child offenders. There were no executions of child offenders in the United States between 1965 and 1985.[14] It took eight years and the state of Texas to resume these executions. Texas executed child offenders in 1985 and 1986. South Carolina also executed a child offender in 1986. All together, twenty-two executions of child offenders took place between 1985 and 2005, when the United States abolished the child death penalty; all of those executed were male and 17 years old at the time of their crime except for one 16-year-old.[15] Nine of these executions occurred between 2000 and 2003.

Death sentences for child offenders remained low in the post-*Furman* years (after 1972). Jeffrey Fagan and Valerie West argue that after 1994, these death sentences significantly declined, after controlling for murder rates and rates of child offender homicide.[16] The rate of death sentences per homicide for child offenders declined almost 73 percent between 1994 and 2002.[17] Before 1999, child offender and adult death sentences moved almost in "lockstep," rising and falling together.[18] After 1999, however, the rate of decline in child death sentences was more than 87 percent, while the rate of decline in adult death sentences was less than 36 percent.[19] Fagan and West conclude that the decline in child death sentences since 1989 offered evidence of an emergent norm against these sentences.[20]

Although the age of eligibility for the death penalty has historically varied, the minimum age derived from English law was seven. Children under the age of 14 could legally be executed if intent (*mens rea*) could

---

12. Amnesty International, "United States of America," 62.

13. 428 U.S. 153.

14. Streib, "The Child Death Penalty Today, January 1, 1973–December 31, 2004," 4. Opinion Justice Stevens, *Thompson v. Oklahoma* 487 U.S. 815 (U.S. Supreme Court, 1988).

15. Streib, "The Child Death Penalty Today, January 1, 1973–December 31, 2004," 3, 5. Sean Sellers was 16 when he committed his crime. He was executed in Oklahoma in 1999 when he was 20 years old.

16. Jeffrey Fagan and Valerie West, "The Decline of the Juvenile Death Penalty: Scientific Evidence of Evolving Norms," *Journal of Criminal Law and Criminology* 95, no. 2 (2004): 429–430.

17. Ibid., 466.

18. Ibid., 472.

19. Ibid.

20. Ibid., 494.

be proved. Even as late as the 1988 Supreme Court ruling in *Thompson v. Oklahoma*,[21] in which the court ruled that executions of child offenders who committed their crimes when they were under the age of 16 violated the Eighth and Fourteenth amendments, many US states did not have a minimum age of eligibility for the penalty. Thus, as late as 1988, the minimum age for the penalty in these states was 7 or 14 depending on precedent and practice. No US state specifically set its minimum age at 7, although some did set their minimum age below 13; one state, Indiana, even set its minimum age at 10.[22]

A number of studies have looked at the relationship between the American South and the practice of the death penalty. The penalty, in general, is a southern phenomenon, but it was even more so in terms of child executions.[23] Seven US states have executed child offenders since the *Furman* ruling in 1972. These states are: Georgia, Louisiana, Missouri, Oklahoma, South Carolina, Texas, and Virginia, all southern.[24] Globally, the US South carried out a large percentage of all executions of child offenders; five US states put to death two-thirds of all child offenders executed *in the world* between 1993 and the *Roper* decision in 2005.[25] Since 1994, only three US states—Oklahoma, Texas, and Virginia—have executed child offenders.

Of the twenty-two child offenders executed between 1972 and 2005 (between the *Furman* and *Roper* rulings), thirteen were executed in Texas. As a result, Texas had a "distorting effect" on the practice of the child death penalty both in the United States and globally.[26] Texas accounted for 7.4 percent of the total US population in 2000, but for almost 60 percent of child executions in the United States since *Furman*.[27] The child

21. 487 U.S. 815.

22. Arizona, Delaware, Florida (if the defendant had prior convictions), Oklahoma, Pennsylvania, South Carolina, South Dakota, and Washington had no minimum age at the time of the *Thompson* ruling. Indiana's minimum age was 10, Mississippi's was 13, and Montana's was 12. See Amnesty International, "United States of America: The Death Penalty and Juvenile Offenders," 64; and Seligson, "Are They Too Young to Die?" *Parade Magazine*, October 19, 1986, 5. Conflicting sources indicate there was no minimum age by statute for Idaho and Utah in 1994. See Bedau, *The Death Penalty in America*.

23. Zimring and Hawkins, *Capital Punishment and the American Agenda*, 30, 32.

24. By one historical definition, Missouri and Oklahoma would not be considered southern since they were not states in the Confederacy, although both offered some support for the Confederacy.

25. Amnesty International, "United States of America: Indecent and Internationally Illegal: The Death Penalty against Child Offenders, AMR 51/144/2002" (London, UK: Amnesty International, 2002): 9.

26. Ibid., 10.

27. Using population data taken from the 2000 Census by the US Census Bureau. http://www.census.gov/main/www/cen2000.html.

death penalty in the post-*Furman* era can thus be thought of not only as a southern phenomenon, but as a Texas phenomenon.

Importantly, more than two-thirds of child offenders on death row at the time of *Roper* were African American or Latino, a greater percentage than in adult death sentences.[28] There is a great deal of support for arguments that race and geography have a profound impact on severity in sentencing. Ronald Farrell and Victoria Swigart found that the degree of severity in sentencing was highly correlated with a particular type of offender–victim relationship such that perpetrators of low social status who kill victims of higher social status receive the most severe punishments.[29] In their study investigating the relationship between social hierarchy and the death penalty, Michael Mitchell and Jim Sidanius argue that people with high status will support the death penalty *because* it is unequally applied.[30] Their argument may explain why white people on average support the death penalty more than people of color do.[31] Mitchell and Sidanius found that social hierarchy is positively associated with the rate of execution in society; their findings support the theory that execution rates are higher in the South because of the disparities in status for people of different races.[32] Another variable, political conservatism—an ideology that seeks to maintain the status quo and to enforce the existing social structure—was also consistently correlated with death penalty use.[33] Finally, violent crime was sporadically related to death penalty rates in some US states.[34]

According to Hale, racial disparities in the application of the death penalty began to emerge in the early nineteenth century in response to the movement to abolish slavery.[35] The transition to freedom for slaves produced social upheaval in the South, leading to increased violence. Newly freed slaves experienced tremendous poverty, resulting in an increase in crime, especially by children.[36] Yet racial disparities in the application of

28. National Coalition to Abolish the Death Penalty, *Human Rights, Human Wrongs: Sentencing Children to Death* (Washington, DC: National Coalition to Abolish the Death Penalty, 2003): 12.

29. Ronald A. Farrell and Victoria L. Swigert, "Legal Disposition of Inter-Group and Intra-Group Homicides," *The Sociological Quarterly* 19, no. 4 (1978): 565–576.

30. Michael Mitchell and Jim Sidanius, "Social Hierarchy and the Death Penalty: A Social Dominance Perspective," *Political Psychology* 16, no. 3 (1995): 593.

31. Adam Liptak, "Ruling Likely to Spur Convictions in Capital Cases," *The New York Times*, June 9, 2007.

32. Mitchell and Sidanius, "Social Hierarchy and the Death Penalty," 591–2, 600.

33. Ibid., 593, 608.

34. Ibid., 608.

35. Hale, *A Review of Juvenile Executions in America*, 61–62.

36. Ibid., 72, 81.

the child death penalty did not sharply rise until the Progressive Era, a topic discussed later.

The Child and the State

State intervention in families in the United States began in 1675 when the General Court of Massachusetts created a class of officers called the "tithingmen," whose job was to inspect families in the community.[37] Since social ills were blamed on "defects in family government," parents were held responsible for the health of the community.[38] Parents who neglected their children, for example, those who failed to teach them to read or to socialize them properly, were brought before the court. Charges against parents were difficult to enforce, yet there is evidence that some children were removed from unsuitable homes.[39] Over the next two centuries, child offenders were increasingly seen as victims of their environment, and efforts were made to remove them from jails and place them into apprenticeships.[40] Some individual colonies statutorily exempted children from punishments: For example, in Pennsylvania, whipping was reserved for offenders older than 16.[41] Eighteenth-century America had no facilities for child correction or reform, but the growing economic and social independence of children as well as the revolutionary spirit of remedying injustice led to the development of a penal system for child offenders decidedly different from European models.[42]

The United States began to focus more on education in the years before the Civil War. Support for publicly funded education spread throughout the country, and educational systems became increasingly homogenous, with standard curricula, standard class and age separation, and evaluation through grades.[43] Employment restrictions for children, especially children who were not being educated, began in states in the mid-nineteenth century.[44] Massachusetts in 1836 passed a compulsory attendance law

37. Robert H. Bremmer, ed. *Children and Youth in America: A Documentary History*, vol. 1, part 1, 1660–1865 (Cambridge, MA: Harvard University Press, 1970): 28.

38. Ibid., 39.

39. Ibid., 28, 41.

40. Mark Harrison Moore and George L. Kelling, "The Historical Legacy," in *From Children to Citizens: The Mandate for Juvenile Justice*, ed. Mark Harrison Moore, 25–48 (New York: Springer-Verlag, 1987): 32.

41. Bremmer, *Children and Youth in America*, vol. 1, 307.

42. Moore and Kelling, "The Historical Legacy," 32.

43. Ibid., 35–36.

44. Bremmer, *Children and Youth in America*, vol. 1, 621.

that stipulated that children could not be employed if they were under the age of 15 unless they were receiving an education as well.[45]

This period also saw increased concern about juvenile delinquents and correctional facilities. The first House of Refuge, an alternative facility for delinquents, was established in New York City in 1825[46] and quickly followed by the founding of similar institutions in Philadelphia and Boston. By 1867, there were seven reform schools in New York as well as schools in Providence, Cincinnati, Louisville, Baltimore, St. Louis, and Chicago.[47] This early type of alternative institution emerged from the belief that children were not wholly responsible for their crimes and that correctional facilities treated them "cruelly and corrected them unsatisfactorily." [48] The philanthropists that built these institutions—many of them governors, mayors, and congressmen—believed that "childhood diminished responsibility for crime." [49] These philanthropists saw opportunity for delinquents to become "independent moral agents" through religion, hard work, and education.[50] In 1853, the New York Children's Aid Society formed with the goal of preventing rather than correcting juvenile delinquency.[51] The society pioneered a new philosophy toward delinquency that was anti-institutional and focused on rural placement as opposed to placement in correctional or reform facilities. To establish refuges and reformatories, however, the directors needed legal protection against parents, some of whom fought the schools for custody.[52] The decisions by some US states to reject the interests of parents in favor of those of children were some of the earliest instances of *parens patriae*—or the legal idea that the state may assume the role of parent when needed to achieve the best interest of the child.[53]

Like the tithingmen of the colonial era, the final decades of the nineteenth century saw the emergence of "friendly visitors," middle- and upper-class women volunteers who visited poorer families to offer "the elevating influence of a moral superior." Based on a link between poverty and morality, these efforts included instruction in morals, childrearing,

45. Ibid.
46. Bremmer, *Children and Youth in America*, vol. 1, 671.
47. Ibid., 672.
48. Ibid., 671.
49. Ibid.
50. Ibid.
51. Ibid., 672.
52. *United States v. Green*, 26 Fed. Cas. 30 (1824); *State v. Richardson*, 40 N.H. 272 (1860).
53. Bremmer, *Children and Youth in America*, vol. 1, 671.

and cleanliness.[54] Through these visits, elaborate data on individuals and families were collected and the 'problems' of families were 'diagnosed' and 'treated.' After the Civil War, positivist theories that stressed the physiological and psychological causes of crime gained popularity. Psychological explanations for crime gradually became dominant and produced new approaches to penology[55] that emphasized the importance of children's upbringing and environment and advocated for treatment and rehabilitation over retribution. A new emphasis was also placed on the separation of child criminals from adults.[56]

Reformers from England and elsewhere came to America during this period to observe these innovations, just as Charles Dickens, Gustave de Beaumont, and de Tocqueville had once done, forming a network on juvenile justice issues.[57] The English philanthropist and child advocate Mary Carpenter, discussed in chapters 3 and 4, visited US prisons and reformatories in 1873 and criticized them.[58] These visits suggest a great deal of exchange between European and US reformers. Moreover, there is evidence that many English and French reformers as well as the English Parliament looked to the United States for guidance on reforms for child criminals— often remarking on the high quality and progressive character of juvenile justice institutions and approaches in the United States.

Overall, important changes regarding children took place in the last few decades of the nineteenth century. Children now spent more time in school, and in greater numbers. Both the state and private philanthropists went to great lengths to protect children from dangerous and premature labor and from abuse, exploitation, and unsanitary conditions. Education became publicly funded, though the adoption and enforcement of compulsory education laws varied widely across states.[59] The earliest organizations concerned with child abuse and protection came out of humane efforts for animals. The first such organization, founded in 1874, was the New York Society for the Prevention of Cruelty to Children, which was an offshoot of the American Society for the Prevention of Cruelty to Animals.[60]

54. Moore and Kelling, "The Historical Legacy," 37–38.
55. Ibid., 39.
56. Ibid.
57. Bremmer, *Children and Youth in America*, vol. 1, 683–685.
58. Robert H. Bremmer, ed. *Children and Youth in America: A Documentary History*, vol. 2, 1866–1932 (Cambridge, MA: Harvard University Press, 1971): 468–469.
59. Moore and Kelling, "The Historical Legacy," 39.
60. Bremmer, *Children and Youth in America*, vol. 2, 189–191; Mary Renck Jalongo, "The Story of Mary Ellen Wilson: Tracing the Origins of Child Protection in America," *Early Childhood Education Journal* 34, no. 1 (2006): 1.

The child health movement also made strides in the years after the Civil War, continuing prewar efforts at studying disease and hygiene. The first Board of Health was established in New York one year after the war and by 1877, fourteen US states had a health department.[61] The pediatric section of the American Medical Association was founded in 1880, and the first English-language journal on children's health was published in 1884.[62] Beginning in the 1890s, public schools began playing a larger role in detecting and controlling childhood illnesses.[63]

The state's increasing attention to child welfare came at the expense of parental authority. However, parents, manufacturers, and religious groups did not give up their power easily. The state met with concerted opposition from groups that sought to maintain traditional parental authority, and to preserve the economic benefits of child labor.[64] By the 1880s, however, calls for state control of education, even exclusive control of education, became more common.

Innovation in juvenile justice in the United States continued apace in the Progressive Era. Founded on the belief that children's delinquency is caused by their environment and that children are redeemable, the first juvenile court in the United States was established in Illinois in 1899, further enhancing the United States' reputation as a leader in child welfare and protection.[65] Although there are numerous and differing interpretations regarding the motivation for the court's creation, the court's mission was clear: It sought to provide individualized treatment that would ensure an offender's future welfare rather than punish him for crimes committed.[66] The 1899 Illinois court introduced the doctrine of *parens patriae,* which gave the state authority to make decisions for children when parents were deemed incapable for a variety of reasons.[67]

The Progressive Era also saw the advent of the 'child-saving' movement, a moral crusade that was premised on theories of social Darwinism and the innate moral degeneracy of the poor.[68] As with the "friendly visitors" of the preceding period, the child-saving movement was dominated by

---

61. Bremmer, *Children and Youth in America*, vol. 2, 811.
62. Ibid.
63. Ibid., 812.
64. Bremmer, *Children and Youth in America*, vol. 1, 560–572.
65. Moore and Kelling, "The Historical Legacy," 41.
66. Feld, *Bad Kids*, 62.
67. Sol Rubin and Irving J. Sloan, *Juvenile Offenders and the Juvenile Justice System,* Legal Almanac Series 22 (Dobbs Ferry, NY: Oceana, 1986): 39; Mark Harrison Moore et al., "The Contemporary Mandate," in *From Children to Citizens: The Mandate for Juvenile Justice*, ed. Mark Harrison Moore (New York: Springer-Verlag, 1987): 52.
68. Moore and Kelling, "The Historical Legacy," 41.

middle- and upper-class women who sought to foster traditional values. Child-saving efforts included promoting child welfare and universal education, preventing abuse and corruption (broadly defined to include alcohol use and prostitution), restricting labor, and increasing the supervision of children and the efficiency of law enforcement.[69]

Child labor was another major target of reform. Twenty-eight US states had some form of legislation abolishing or limiting child labor by 1899.[70] Most of these laws, however, regulated only the manufacturers and limited employment for children under the age of 12. The ideas that child labor exploited children and that children's protection was necessary for human progress also gained strength during this time.[71] Theodore Roosevelt attacked child labor in 1912, calling for the "conservation of childhood."[72] The movement successfully legislated many of its goals: All child labor was regulated by the 1930s thanks in large part to the efforts of progressives.[73] Additionally, by 1900, every state outside the South had compulsory education, and by 1918, all states had compulsory education.[74]

These child welfare and penal reform initiatives in the late nineteenth and early twentieth centuries shaped the nature of intervention in families. Prior public intervention was commonly informal and passive, usually taking the form of gossip or advice by members of the community.[75] As private organizations grew (especially after the Civil War), intervention became more routine and impersonal. Growing concern for children, especially in terms of abuse, gave the state justification to intervene in families to protect children. As a result, specialized state institutions— schools, child protection societies, and welfare agencies—developed to enable the state to carry out these functions.[76] These institutions eroded parental control over children and changed the perception of children's capacities.[77]

Yet the United States' luster as a world leader in progressive policymaking would dim as the century advanced, its reputational loss captured by the gradual, but increasingly pronounced divergence between its laws and policies regarding children and the laws and policies of other leading

69. Ibid.
70. Bremmer, *Children and Youth in America*, vol. 2, 601.
71. Ibid., 601–602.
72. Ibid., 602.
73. Moore and Kelling, "The Historical Legacy," 41.
74. Hale, *A Review of Juvenile Executions in America*, 88.
75. Moore and Kelling, "The Historical Legacy," 45.
76. Ibid., 27.
77. Ibid., 33.

states—England, for instance. Like the United States, England had initi-ated its own penal reform for children in the nineteenth century; indeed, the two countries often looked to one another for new models of reform. This relationship changed during the twentieth century, when limita-tions on the child death penalty in England logically followed other penal reform measures for children. The same types of reform did not follow in the United States.

Although the establishment of juvenile courts in the United States re-formed the treatment of child offenders in many ways, it did not affect the child death penalty in any significant way. These courts were pre-cluded from giving the death sentence, but child offenders who commit-ted crimes that were death-eligible could be transferred to adult court. In contrast to late twentieth century practice, transfers to adult criminal court in the early years of the juvenile court were rare, about 1 percent of cases per year.[78] In 1938, the Federal Juvenile Delinquency Law defined a juvenile as an individual under the age of 18, in keeping with an emerg-ing, age-based international consensus about children, but in order to be within the jurisdiction of the juvenile court, the offense had to be one that was not punishable by death or life imprisonment.[79]

Legal rulings in the United States in the mid-twentieth century rein-forced a commitment to the *parens patriae* doctrine. *In re Holmes* [80] ex-empted children from civil rights in court proceedings because juvenile courts were not criminal courts. The Standard Juvenile Court Act of 1959 was based on *parens patriae*, and a series of court cases further institu-tionalized the doctrine as the established way to think about children in the United States.[81] These cases included *Kent v. United States*,[82] *In re Gault*,[83] *McKiever v. Pennsylvania*,[84] and *Schall v. Martin*.[85] *Kent* warned against arbitrariness in the granting of waivers from juvenile court so that an offender could be tried in adult criminal court. *Gault* found that constitutional protections that were afforded to adults, such as the right to cross-examination, should also apply to children in juvenile court.[86] In

---

78. Feld, *Bad Kids*, 73.

79. Robert H. Bremmer, ed. *Children and Youth in America: A Documentary History*, vol. 3, 1933–1973 (Cambridge, MA: Harvard University Press, 1974): 1118.

80. 379 Pa. 599; 109 A.2d 523 (Pa. 1954).

81. Rubin and Sloan, *Juvenile Offenders*, 42; The Standard Juvenile Court Act (6th ed. 1959).

82. 383 U.S. 541 (1966).

83. 387 U.S. 1 (1967).

84. 403 U.S. 528 (1971).

85. 467 U.S. 253 (1984).

86. Rubin and Sloan, *Juvenile Offenders*: 18–19.

McKiever, the court found that juries were not constitutionally required in juvenile courts. In *Schall,* the court used the doctrine of *parens patriae* to deny children's liberty interest in favor of the state's interest in protecting both the child and society.[87]

This emerging body of law in the United States based on *parens patriae* coincided with a new global era for children's rights, which were granted in numerous international conventions and declarations, most importantly, the CRC. The drafters of these conventions, as well as many children's advocates, recognized a problem in the understanding of children's rights that complicated efforts toward change: Children are not independent individuals capable of exercising their rights; rather, they are dependent upon adults for the exercise of their rights. Children's rights may also conflict with the rights of parents and with the interests of the state.

Supreme Court jurisprudence on children's issues in the twentieth century suggests that children's rights are derivative of parental rights, and key rulings by the court address the rights of parents vis-à-vis the state. [88] These include *Meyer v. Nebraska,*[89] *Pierre v. Society of Sisters,*[90] *Prince v. Massachusetts,*[91] *In re Gault,*[92] and *Wisconsin v. Yoder.*[93] *Meyer* upheld a Nebraska law allowing the state to establish school curricula. *Pierre* recognized the state's power to regulate school attendance, but found that power to be limited by parental liberty in selecting the nature of instruction for children. In *Prince,* a case about whether selling religious literature constitutes child labor, the court found that the state's authority only trumps parental authority when parents fail to fulfill their obligations to protect their children.[94] *In re Gault* granted due process rights to juveniles, but the ruling also determined that the state may intervene if a child commits a crime, thus essentially equating juvenile crime with the failure of parents to meet their parental obligations.[95] *Yoder* found that Amish children could not be forced to attend school after the eighth grade, on the grounds of religious freedom.

87. Ibid., 21–22.

88. Roger J.R. Levesque, "The Internationalization of Children's Human Rights: Too Radical for American Adolescents?" *Connecticut Journal of International Law* 9, no. 2 (1994): 260.

89. 262 U.S. 390 (1923).

90. 268 U.S. 510 (1925).

91. 321 U.S. 158 (1944).

92. 387 U.S. 1 (1967).

93. 406 U.S. 205 (1972); Levesque, "The Internationalization of Children's Human Rights": 253–261.

94. Levesque, "The Internationalization of Children's Human Rights," 255–256.

95. Ibid., 260.

Other Supreme Court rulings have established some rights for children. *Tinker v. Des Moines Independent Community School District*[96] found a school rule banning the expression of political views by children to be unconstitutional. *Brown v. Board of Education*,[97] the case in which the court declared separate public schools for black and white children to be unequal and unconstitutional, was also the first Supreme Court case to directly examine the rights of children vis-à-vis the state, granting them the right to equal protection.[98]

Thus, insofar as US Supreme Court rulings may accurately capture the overall consensus of US society or articulate a widely held view, children in the United States at the end of the twentieth century were considered to be dependent upon adults for protection and care, less culpable than adults for their behavior, redeemable, and deserving of more lenient punishment. Public policy regarding the child death penalty was difficult to reconcile with these accepted norms about children. The inconsistency between the penalty and established ideas about children is evident in many key markers of the transition from childhood to adulthood in the United States, including voting, alcohol consumption, civic duty (such as jury membership or military service), and labor restrictions.[99] These restrictions assume that children are less mature than adults, that their decision-making ability and cognitive reasoning are less developed, and that protection from larger social harms is needed.

The Supreme Court and the Child Death Penalty

The Supreme Court issued a number of rulings specifically addressing the child death penalty after *Furman* (1972), when the court ruled that the death penalty in general as it was then applied was arbitrary and violated the Eighth and Fourteenth amendments to the Constitution. These rulings include *Eddings v. Oklahoma*,[100] *Thompson v. Oklahoma, Stanford v. Kentucky*, and *Roper v. Simmons*. The first Supreme Court case to consider age as a mitigating factor, or consideration for reducing a sentence, in the

---

96. 393 U.S. 503 (1969).
97. 347 U.S. 483 (1954).
98. Levesque, "The Internationalization of Children's Human Rights," 259.
99. Jenni Gainborough and Elizabeth Lean, "Convention on the Rights of the Child and Juvenile Justice," *The Link: Connecting Juvenile Justice and Child Welfare, Child Welfare League of America* 7, no. 1 (2008): 1; Mirah A. Horowitz, "Kids Who Kill: A Critique of How the American Legal System Deals with Juveniles Who Commit Homicide," *Law and Contemporary Problems* 63, no. 3 (2000): 166.
100. 455 U.S. 104 (1982).

determination of guilt was *Eddings v. Oklahoma* in 1982, a case involving the death sentence of 16-year-old Monty Lee Eddings. The court found in a 5 to 4 decision that the sentence should be vacated because it did not consider mitigating factors as required by the Eighth and Fourteenth amendments. Although the court did not rule on the larger issue of the constitutionality of the death penalty for 16-year-olds, it nonetheless prohibited any barriers to the use of mitigating factors in sentencing.

Not until *Thompson v. Oklahoma* (1988) did the court, in a 5 to 3 decision, rule on the constitutionality of executing child offenders, reserving the penalty for those 16 and older. Before *Thompson*, age limits to the penalty varied widely by state, as discussed earlier. The second case came the following year with a 5 to 4 decision in *Stanford v. Kentucky,* which held that the Eighth Amendment *does not* prohibit the penalty for offenders who committed their crimes at 16 or 17 years old.

Finally, in 2005, the Supreme Court in *Roper v. Simmons* found in a 6 to 3 decision that the death penalty for child offenders under the age of 18 was unconstitutional under the 'evolving standards of decency' of the Eighth Amendment. As discussed in the previous chapter, the court in *Roper* held that a national consensus against the child death penalty had emerged in the sixteen years since the *Stanford* decision. *Roper* commuted the death sentences of seventy-two 17-year-olds around the country and brought the United States into compliance with international law.

As discussed in chapter 5, NGOs like AIUSA, the ACLU, and the American NCADP joined forces to build a national consensus against the child death penalty similar to that recognized in *Atkins v. Virginia*. In *Atkins* in 2002, the court revisited *Penry v. Lynaugh* (1989), in which it had rejected the claim that the Eighth Amendment disallowed death sentences for the "mentally retarded," and found that a national consensus against these executions had emerged in the thirteen years since the 1989 ruling.

The coalition's efforts would prove successful. Although the degree of change was not as great in *Roper* as in *Atkins*, Justice Kennedy in his majority opinion concluded, "We think the same consistency of direction of change has been demonstrated."[101] The states that abolished in

---

101. Amnesty documents and Supreme Court briefs in the *Roper* case argued that no state had lowered age limits for the death penalty, lending support to the "direction of change" cited by Justice Kennedy. Yet Amnesty documents in 1991 and the *Stanford* ruling list New Hampshire as one of the states requiring that defendants be 18 years old to be eligible for death. New Hampshire is not listed, however, in the *Roper* decision. Amnesty International. See "United States of America: The Death Penalty and Juvenile Offenders"; Amnesty International, "United States of America: Indecent and Internationally Illegal."

the post-*Stanford* years were not ones that carried out many executions. Before January 1993, the state of Washington had not put anyone to death in thirty years, and had only executed two child offenders and none since 1932, according to the Espy data.[102] Kansas, South Dakota, and Wyoming had never executed a child offender. The Kansas legislature reinstated the penalty after twenty-two years, after not having executed anyone since 1965.[103] South Dakota had not executed anyone since 1947.[104] Even Missouri and New York, the two states (of the group of eight states) that had carried out the most executions of child offenders, had only put to death nine child offenders altogether, according to the Espy data, and only one (Missouri in 1993) after *Furman*. New York had not executed anyone since the 1960s.[105] Nonetheless, the policy shift in these states was meaningful, according to the majority in *Roper*. As discussed earlier, before the *Thompson* ruling, two of the eight states had a minimum age lower than fourteen (Indiana and Montana), and two others had no age limit at all (South Dakota and Washington). Additionally, Missouri, Indiana, and Washington had collectively sentenced a total of eight child offenders to death since *Furman*.[106] Appendix B provides specific information on legislation in each state.

Moreover, the federal government had not executed a child offender since 1874, according to the Espy file. There was even more reason to believe that the practice was a thing of the past when the federal death penalty was reinstated in 1988 by President Ronald Reagan in the Anti-Drug Abuse Act. The Act provided for death sentences for murders related to

102. James Wallace, "Appeal Fails; Dodd Hanged; Killer of 3 Boys Is First Felon Executed in State in 30 Years," *Seattle Post-Intelligencer*, January 5, 1993, A1.

103. John Dvorak, "Kansas Approved Death Penalty after 22 Years; Governor Says She Won't Fight Law," *Kansas City Star*, April 9, 1994.

104. Karen Ducheneaux, "Governor Signs Bill to Ban Execution of Juveniles," *Associated Press*, March 4, 2004.

105. New York was ranked second in the number of official executions before *Furman*. See James M. Galliher and John F. Galliher, "A 'Commonsense' Theory of Deterrence and the 'Ideology' of Science: The New York State Death Penalty Debate," *Journal of Criminal Law and Criminology* 92, no. 1–2 (2001–2002): 308. The child death penalty was first taken up in New York in 1948, when Governor Thomas Dewey raised the age of eligibility from 7 to 15. A revision of the penal code in 1963 further raised the age to 18, which was reaffirmed in the 1965 revised penal code. The 1963 decision was largely influenced by the Model Penal Code developed by the American Law Institute, which recommended the death penalty be reserved for offenders over the age of 18. Additionally, a court case in 1973, *People v. Fitzpatrick*, repealed the state's death penalty. See Salvatore J. Modica, "New York's Death Penalty: The Age Requirement," *Journal of Civil Rights and Economic Development* 13, no. 3 (1998–1999): 586–587, 594–584.

106. Bedau, *The Death Penalty in America*, 67.

traffic in illegal drugs, but excluded offenders under the age of 18.[107] In 1994, President Bill Clinton signed the Federal Death Penalty Act, which expanded the penalty from the narrow statute of the 1988 law to include more than fifty offenses.[108] Yet even though the country was in the midst of a juvenile crime wave, the 1994 Act also excluded offenders who committed their crimes when they were younger than 18. The federal government's reaffirmation of the age 18 as the eligibility age for the penalty contributed to the court's perception in *Roper* of a national consensus.

International Law in Supreme Court Decision Making

The United States has a long history of referencing international and foreign law in its opinions.[109] The Eighth Amendment, especially, has resulted in multiple Supreme Court rulings that have attempted to define 'cruel and unusual punishment' according to both foreign and national standards. In *Weems v. United States* (1910), the court found that the meaning of the clause was not static.[110] Justice Joseph McKenna stated in his majority opinion:

> The clause of the Constitution, in the opinion of the learned commentators, may be therefore progressive, and is not fastened to the obsolete, but may acquire meaning as public opinion becomes enlightened by a humane justice.

In 1958, the court in *Trop v. Dulles* [111] held in a 5 to 4 decision that loss of citizenship as a form of punishment by the United States was unconstitutional under the Eighth Amendment. The ruling interpreted the Amendment as drawing "its meaning from the evolving standards of decency that mark the progress of a maturing society." In effect, *Trop* opened the door for consideration of international standards in the interpretation of the Eighth Amendment. Referencing UN surveys of domestic law in eighty-four countries, the court in *Trop* found the practices of other

107. Amnesty International, "United States of America: Indecent and Internationally Illegal," 6.

108. Ibid., 5–6.

109. *Kennedy v. Mendoza-Martinez*, 372 U.S. 144 (1963); *Miranda v. Arizona*, 384 U.S. 436, 488 (1966); *Lackey v. Texas*, 514 U.S. 1045 (1995); *Knight v. Florida*, 120 S. Ct. 459 (1999); *Atkins v. Virginia*, 536 U.S. 304 (2002); *Lawrence v. Texas*, 539 U.S. 558 (2003); *Grutter v. Bollinger*, 539 U.S. 306, 344 (2003).

110. 217 U.S. 349 (1910).

111. 356 U.S. 86 (1958).

nations to be relevant to their interpretation of 'cruel and unusual.'[112] In the *Furman* decision, the court cited abolitionist trends around the world. In *Coker v. Georgia* (1977),[113] the court, addressing the constitutionality of the death penalty for rape, held that the majority in *Trop:*

> took pains to note the climate of international opinion concerning the accept-ability of a particular punishment. It is thus not irrelevant here that out of sixty major nations in the world surveyed in 1965, only three retained the death penalty for rape where death did not ensue.

The decision drew from UN reports to establish international opinion.[114] Similar references are found in the court's ruling in *Enmund v. Florida* (1982), which considered the constitutionality of the death penalty for felony murder.[115]

Moreover, the use of foreign law in Supreme Court oral arguments has increased over time. In a study of the use of foreign law in litigant briefs submitted to the court in 2002 and 2003, Jerry Goldman and Timothy Johnson found that a significant minority of cases cited foreign law, thus indicating that attorneys believed the citations might influence the justices.[116] Although a number of important cases skewed the data,[117] the sources of the foreign law cited were predominantly international law (40 percent), followed by English law (25 percent), and small percentages of European Community law and Austrian law (7 and 4 percent, respectively).[118] Goldman and Johnson found that the "vast majority" of references to foreign law in justices' decisions were in cases involving the death penalty.[119]

The debate about the role of international and foreign law in US rulings has been particularly contentious in cases involving the death penalty for child offenders. In his majority opinion in *Thompson*, Justice John Paul

112. Weissbrodt, Fitzpatrick, and Newman, *Human Rights: Law, Policy and Process,* 740.

113. 433 U.S. 584, 596 (1977).

114. Weissbrodt, Fitzpatrick, and Newman, *Human Rights: Law, Policy, and Process,* 741.

115. 458 U.S. 782, 788–789.

116. Jerry Goldman and Timothy R. Johnson, "Exploring the Use of Foreign Law and Foreign Sources in the United States Supreme Court's Decision Making Process," (Paper presented at the 2005 annual meeting of the American Political Science Association conference, Washington, DC, September 1–4, 2005): 10.

117. Ibid. Goldman and Johnson found significant references to foreign law in two cases: *Rasul v. Bush* (2004) and *Hamdan v. Rumsfeld* (2004).

118. Ibid., 10–11.

119. Ibid., 15.

Stevens wrote that the execution of child offenders under the age of 15 offended "civilized standards of decency," and went on to detail the national practices of numerous countries regarding the child death penalty.[120] Moreover, Justice Stevens cited the ICCPR, the American Convention on Human Rights, and the Fourth Geneva Convention. In response, Justice Antonin Scalia argued that the reliance by the majority on "civilized standards of decency in other countries [. . .] is totally inappropriate as a means of establishing the fundamental beliefs of this nation."[121]

In the 2005 *Roper* ruling, Justice Kennedy extensively cited international law, arguing that the court has referenced international law in other key decisions since *Trop*. Justice Kennedy demonstrated the international consensus on the abolition of the child death penalty by citing the CRC, the ICCPR, the American Convention on Human Rights, and the African Charter, as well as national practices around the world. He stated:

> It is proper that we acknowledge the overwhelming weight of international opinion against the child death penalty, resting in large part on the understanding that the instability and emotional imbalance of young people may often be a factor in the crime [. . .] The opinion of the world community, while not controlling our outcome, does provide respected and significant confirmation for our own conclusions.

Justice Scalia's dissent continued his long-standing position against the relevance of international law to Supreme Court decision making.

The US Puzzle

Before the Supreme Court decision in *Roper*, the practice of the child death penalty put the United States on a collision course with the international children's rights regime. This conflict came to a head in two events in the 1990s: the US ratification of the ICCPR in 1992, and its failure to ratify the 1990 CRC. The United States' noncompliance with international standards of juvenile justice marked a dramatic departure from its earlier leadership in this area. The United States participated in and even helped to shape many of the norms that would later be adopted by the international

---

120. Justice John Paul Stevens. Judgment of the Court, *Thompson v. Oklahoma* (487 U.S. 815). *Supreme Court of the United States* (1988).

121. Justice Antonin Scalia. Dissenting Opinion, *Thompson v. Oklahoma* (487 U.S. 815). *Supreme Court of the United States* (1988).

community. Indeed, child welfare initiatives in the United States in the nineteenth and early twentieth centuries, including juvenile justice reform, served as a model for many countries, which drew on American institutions and philosophies about children in establishing their own systems of protection for child offenders.[122]

How did the United States go from leader to laggard in the areas of child welfare and juvenile justice? A diffusion study of the US case for this norm must account not only for why and how the norm diffused through law in the United States, but also for *why it did not diffuse earlier.* There were two main reasons for the persistence of the child death penalty in the United States after most countries had ended the penalty altogether or restricted it to offenders who commit their crimes when they are 18 or older: the US federal system that allowed individual states to set their own death penalty policy and, where applicable, to establish their own age restrictions (until the *Thompson* decision in 1988); and the role of racial subordination in the practice of the child death penalty.

Federalism and the Prohibition of the Child Death Penalty

The US federal system of government is a relatively uncommon method of organizing state authority, whereby the federal government and individual states share legal sovereignty over US territory. The United States responded to the international rebuke over the child death penalty by defending its federal structure and the right of individual states to determine the penalties associated with particular crimes within their jurisdiction, given constitutional limitations. When the United States ratified the ICCPR in 1992, it modified the terms of the treaty by submitting an understanding addressing US federalism in addition to its specific reservation on the child death penalty. This understanding, quoted below, was similar to a reservation submitted by the United States when it ratified the 1987 Convention Against Torture and other Cruel, Inhuman, or Degrading Treatment or Punishment (Reservation II.5) and the Convention on the

---

122. Josine Junger-Tas, "Trends in International Juvenile Justice: What Conclusions Can Be Drawn?" in *International Handbook of Juvenile Justice*, eds. Josine Junger-Tas and Scott H. Decker (New York: Springer, 2006): 507; Adolphe Prins and Ugo Conti, "Some European Comments on the American Prison System," *Journal of the American Institute of Criminal Law and Criminology* 2, no. 2 (1911): 207; Sen, *Colonial Childhoods,* 62; David Tanenhaus and Steven Drizin, "Owing to the Extreme Youth of the Accused: The Changing Legal Response to Juvenile Homicide," *The Journal of Criminal Law and Criminology* 92, no. 3–4 (2002): 646.

Elimination of All Forms of Racial Discrimination (Reservation II), both ratified in 1994. The US memorandum of understanding regarding the ICCPR stated:

> That the US understands that this Covenant shall be implemented by the Federal Government to the extent that it exercises legislative and judicial jurisdiction over the matters covered therein, and otherwise by the state and local governments; to the extent that state and local governments exercise jurisdiction over such matters, the Federal Government shall take measures appropriate to the Federal system to the end that the competent authorities of the state or local governments may take appropriate measures for the fulfillment of the Covenant (United States understanding No. 5 submitted upon ratification to the ICCPR).

By submitting its reservation, the United States sought to limit the treaty's application by defending its right to impose the child death penalty based on two criteria: First, the US Constitution did not prohibit the penalty for children; and second, the US federal system allows individual states to make decisions about penalties for crimes within state jurisdiction.

Additionally, the United States' poor record on ratification of human rights treaties can be partly explained by the peculiarity of the American political system and its treaty ratification process. It should be remembered that the United States has one of the most difficult treaty ratification processes in the world, requiring approval of two-thirds of the Senate. The process of ratification in the United States is therefore far more onerous than the majority requirement in a parliamentary system. Additionally, many international human rights treaties in the United States are non-self-executing, requiring additional legislation for domestic implementation. This two-part process ensures the participation of the legislative branch in both stages, first in initial consent and then in enacting and implementing further legislation, slowing the diffusion of international human rights law both nationally and subnationally. The United States declared the ICCPR non-self-executing in Declaration No.1, thus complicating debates about the applicability of the ban on the child death penalty to domestic law and hindering its application.

Racial Disparities in the US Practice of the Child Death Penalty

Race was the second reason that US policy toward children convicted of serious crimes became increasingly punitive. African American male child offenders faced the death penalty much more often than white male child offenders. This pattern was consistent throughout the twentieth century; it clearly indicates that race was a key factor in determining which children would fall under the protective umbrella of children's rights. A number of studies have looked at the overrepresentation of people of color in US executions.[123] The purpose here is not to review this literature, but rather to consider the child death penalty in light of what is already known about race and the death penalty overall and to examine why US death penalty practice diverged so markedly from international norms about children and juvenile justice. Racial disparities in executions were in fact even greater among children than adults. Furthermore, as with adult offenders, the evidence suggests that crimes with a particular offender–victim relationship were more likely to incur the death penalty in the post-*Furman* period (after 1972), especially the combination of an African American male offender and a white female victim.[124]

Of the 183 child offenders known to have been executed in the United States between 1642 and 2003, 136 are known to have been children of color.[125] Table 6.1 demonstrates the overrepresentation of nonwhite offenders executed for crimes committed as children, according to the Espy file.

As the table shows, the disparity in executions between white and nonwhite child offenders increased from the seventeenth to the twentieth century and dramatically spiked in the twentieth century as the penalty came to be reserved exclusively for nonwhite offenders (in the decades before *Furman*). Again, these are known executions, and they do not include non-state-sanctioned executions, such as lynching.

Figure 6.2 charts the number of executions of white and nonwhite child offenders by year from the seventeenth to the twentieth centuries, according to the Espy data.

123. Howard H. Allen, Jerome M. Clubb, and Vincent A. Lacey, *Race, Class, and the Death Penalty: Capital Punishment in American History* (Albany, NY: State University of New York Press, 2008); Amnesty International USA, *Killing with Prejudice*; Bedau, *The Death Penalty in America*; David Dow and Mark Dow, *Machinery of Death: The Reality of America's Death Penalty Regime* (New York: Routledge, 2002); Jackson, Jackson, and Shapiro, *Legal Lynching*; Gary Kleck, "Racial Discrimination in Criminal Sentencing: A Critical Evaluation of the Evidence with Additional Evidence on the Death Penalty," *American Sociological Review* 46, no. 6 (1981): 783–805; Michael Mitchell and Jim Sidanius, "Social Hierarchy and the Death Penalty"; Ogletree and Sarat, *From Lynch Mobs to the Killing State*.

124. Farrell and Swigert, "Legal Disposition of Inter-Group and Intra-Group Homicides"; Streib, "The Juvenile Death Penalty Today, January 1, 1973–February 28, 2005," 5.

125. The race of some child offenders is unknown.

Table 6.1 PERCENTAGE OF KNOWN NONWHITE CHILD
OFFENDERS EXECUTED IN THE UNITED STATES, BY CENTURY.

Century	Percentage of Known Nonwhite Child Offenders Executed
17th	0
18th	62.5
19th	68
20th	88.5

Espy and Smykla, "Executions in the US." Table reproduction courtesy of Brill Publishing.

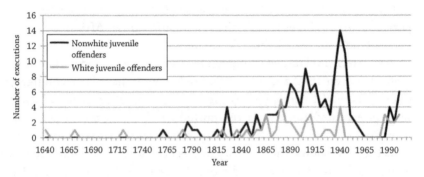

Figure 6.2 Number of White and Nonwhite Child Offender Executions, by Year.
Illustration reproduction courtesy of Brill Publishing.

According to Figure 6.2, executions of nonwhite child offenders reached their highest point in the 1940s, as the punishment was increasingly and then exclusively reserved for nonwhite offenders. The period after 1972 shows more parity in executions between white and nonwhite child offenders, although nonwhite child offenders are still overrepresented relative to their percentage of the US population. Importantly, African Americans made up the overwhelming majority of nonwhite child offenders who were executed in the United States. See Figure 6.3.

The data reveal that African Americans made up 92 percent of all nonwhite child offenders executed in US history. The overrepresentation of African American children in US executions continually increased over the course of the last four centuries, from 0 percent in the seventeenth century, to 50 percent in the eighteenth century, to 57 percent in the nineteenth century and 79 percent in the twentieth century.

Not only did African Americans comprise an increasing and disproportionate number of child offenders executed, but the nature of their crimes, which excluded them from the protection of reform measures,

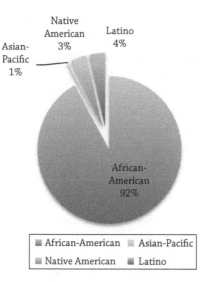

Figure 6.3 Racial Composition of Nonwhite Child Offenders Executed in the United States from 1642–2003.
Illustration reproduction courtesy of Brill Publishing.

is likewise revealing of systemic racial subordination in the United States. Only African Americans were executed for the crimes of rape (27), attempted rape (2), robbery (1), and attempted murder (1), according to the Espy file. There were no white children executed for rape alone in the United States. In addition, of the seven girls whose executions were recorded in the Espy data, none were white. Other sources suggest that as many as ten girls, all of color, have been executed in the United States.[126] Moreover, of the forty-one child offenders executed for crimes other than murder from the seventeenth to the twentieth centuries, thirty-six were African American. In fact, no child offender of any other minority group has ever been executed in the United States for a nonlethal crime. The data reveal that the last white person under the age of 18 to be executed for a crime other than murder was during the Civil War for espionage. The last African American child offender executed for a nonlethal crime was in 1954, when a 17-year-old was executed for rape. At the time of *Roper* (2005), all child offenders on death row were convicted of murder.

Death penalty scholarship has already established that the penalty in general in the United States has increasingly been a southern

126. National Coalition to Abolish the Death Penalty, "Human Rights, Human Wrongs," 12.

phenomenon.[127] This regionalism is even more pronounced for the child death penalty. Seventy-two percent of all child offender executions since the seventeenth century took place in the South. Ninety-one percent of all executions of African American child offenders in the United States took place in the South. Moreover, no child executions have taken place outside the South since before the 1972 *Furman* ruling. A total of twelve white child offenders were executed in the South during the entire twentieth century, only two of whom were executed before *Furman*.

The highest period of disparity in the executions of white and nonwhite child offenders was in the pre-*Furman* period, when, for the years between 1944 and 1965, *the only recorded child executions were of African American males*. During the post-*Furman* period, from 1973 until 2003, this racial disparity decreased, as 54.5 percent of child offenders executed were non-white, although almost 92 percent of these were African American. The disparity is still large, however, considering African Americans' overall percentage of the US population, between 11 and 12 percent in the 1980s and 1990s.[128] The data therefore support the finding that in the twentieth century, the child offenders most likely to be denied children's rights, as defined by international law, were murderers or rapists (or both), and that the overwhelming majority of these were African American males who committed their crimes in the US South.

Nor is the child death penalty the only area of children's rights affected by race in the United States. Children of color tend to have higher rates of poverty and infant mortality, and they experience differential treatment in sentencing.[129] Moreover, race appears to have an impact on death penalty practice at the international level. Carsten Anckar has found a statistically significant correlation between states that abolished slavery relatively late, after 1879, and those that exhibit "a more positive attitude" toward the penalty as compared with states that abolished slavery earlier.[130] Because of the links between slavery and racial subordination, this

127. Zimring and Hawkins, *Capital Punishment and the American Agenda*, 46–47.

128. Campbell Gibson and Kay Jung. "Historical Census Statistics on Population Totals by Race, 1790 to 1990, and by Hispanic Origin, 1970 to 1990, for the United States, Regions, Divisions, and States," Working Paper Series No. 56. P. Division, U.S. Census Bureau (2002).

129. Feld, *Bad Kids*, 73; Vicky MacLean, "Social Inequalities in Access to Health Care Among African-Americans, Latinos, and Caucasians," *American Sociological Association*, San Francisco (2008); David Williams and Chiquita Collins, "US Socioeconomic and Racial Differences in Health: Patterns and Explanations," *Annual Review of Sociology* 21, no. 1 (1995): 349–386.

130. Carsten Anckar, *Determinants of the Death Penalty: A Comparative Study of the World*, Routledge Research in Comparative Politics 8 (New York: Routledge, 2004): 88.

finding indicates that race may be a factor in the use of the penalty outside the United States as well. Additionally, Anckar has argued that the higher the degree of religious, ethnic, or linguistic fragmentation in a state (differences that may include racial cleavages), the greater the inclination to use the penalty.[131]

Although the history of juvenile justice in the United States in the twentieth century shows a gradual shift from the goal of rehabilitation to more retaliatory and punitive measures, that shift accelerated in the 1960s and 1970s as juvenile crime began to increase.[132] By the 1980s, the large number of homicides by juveniles led some scholars and reporters to argue that a new breed of young offender had emerged, the superpredator, who was becoming increasingly violent with each additional child cohort.[133] In 1993, the age group 15–19 had the second highest number of individuals arrested for criminal homicide, only slightly behind the 20–24 age group. Those 19 and under made up almost 31 percent of those arrested in 1993 for criminal homicide.[134] Gang killings almost quadrupled between 1989 and 1991, while juvenile gang killings increased by more than 1.5 times in the same period.[135] By 1993, the rate of juvenile gang killings in the United States was more than double that of 1989, with 1,147 in 1993.[136] Violent juvenile crime corresponded with high death penalty rates, with the South having both a high death penalty rate for child offenders and some of the highest juvenile crime rates in the country.[137]

Yet it was not so much the number of criminals that received attention in the media, but the type of crime and the race of the offender. In the 1980s, African American juveniles were arrested for homicide at more than seven times the rate of white juveniles.[138] The superpredator whose depiction saturated the American media was young, male, urban, and typically of color.[139] Violent crimes dominated the local and national news

131. Ibid., 38.

132. Feld, *Bad Kids*, 5; Gainborough and Lean, "Convention on the Rights of the Child"; Horowitz, "Kids Who Kill," 141.

133. William Bennett and John J. DiIulio, et al., *Body Count: Moral Poverty—and How to Win America's War against Crime and Drugs* (New York: Simon & Schuster, 1996); Tanenhaus and Drizin, "'Owing to the Extreme Youth of the Accused,'" 642.

134. Bedau, *The Death Penalty in America*, 61.

135. Bedau, *The Death Penalty in America*, 64.

136. Ibid.

137. Peter Elikann, *Superpredators: The Demonization of Our Children by the Law* (New York: Insight, 1999): 152.

138. Feld, *Bad Kids*, 203.

139. See Richard Lacayo and Richard Behar, "When Kids Go Bad," *Time*, September 19, 1994; Paul Kaihla, "Kids Who Kill," *Maclean's*, August 15, 1994; Gordon Witkin and S.J. Hedges, "Kids Who Kill," *U.S. News & World Report*, April 8, 1991; Alexandra Marks, "Unusual Unity on Youth Crime," *Christian Science Monitor*, February 20, 1997.

and were portrayed as the random crimes of strangers. The response by legislators was to appear tough by introducing the 'war on crime' and the 'war against drugs' into the American lexicon. Public discourse was peppered with references to gang killings, drug offenses, and random violent crimes such as carjacking, crimes that typically invoked images of African Americans.

The superpredator myth was eventually discredited as the causes of the juvenile crime wave were found to be predominantly environmental (access to guns, marketing of crack cocaine) and demographic (an overall increase in the youth population), not the emergence of an especially violent cohort of offenders.[140] Nonetheless, states responded forcefully to the myth. Officials cited the viciousness of child offenders, claiming that they should be excluded from protective institutions, like youth detention centers, based on their deeds. Transfers from juvenile court to adult court became commonplace in the 1990s, and states increased the number of children housed with adults in prison.[141] Nonwhite children suffered the most from these measures.[142] One study in the 1990s found that 57 percent of all child offenders transferred to adult court for violent crimes were African American.[143] Individual state statistics are more disturbing: In California, studies found that possibly as many as 70 percent of transfers of children to adult criminal court were for nonwhite offenders, while in Illinois, the number was 90 percent.[144] As children were increasingly transferred to adult criminal court, their rehabilitation, a founding principle of the first juvenile court in 1899, was abandoned.[145]

Barry Feld argues that the shift from rehabilitation to a more punitive model was the result of socioeconomic and environmental changes that produced a "very visible escalation" in juvenile homicide and gun violence among African Americans.[146] Feld contends that African Americans' migration to the North and increased urbanization around mid-century focused national attention on issues of racial inequality, especially on procedural issues in the criminal justice system.

---

140. Philip Cook and John H. Laub, "The Unprecedented Epidemic in Youth Violence," *Crime and Justice* 24 (1998): 53, 58; Feld, *Bad Kids*, 11.

141. Tanenhaus and Drizin, "Owing to the Extreme Youth of the Accused," 643.

142. Ibid., 666–667; Gainborough and Lean, "Convention on the Rights of the Child," 11.

143. Tanenhaus and Drizin, "Owing to the Extreme Youth of the Accused," 667.

144. Gainborough and Lean, "Convention on the Rights of the Child," 11.

145. Ibid.; Horowitz, "Kids Who Kill," 142; Tanenhaus and Drizin, "Owing to the Extreme Youth of the Accused," 665.

146. Feld, *Bad Kids*, 14.

The Supreme Court responded to calls for racial equality by examining procedural rights in juvenile and adult criminal courts, but its focus on due process concerns came at a cost. The procedural safeguards that resulted from *Gault* (1967) and other cases "legitimated the imposition of punitive sentences" that primarily affected child offenders of color.[147] In other words, concerns about racial inequality effectively conferred legitimacy on a system that was by then widely understood to be prejudicial against African American child offenders.

The child death penalty thus served to reproduce the racial polity in the United States. Its selective application suggested that young, black males, unlike their white counterparts, were only to be afforded the protections of childhood on a conditional basis. Their legal status as children was contingent upon a state that could—and frequently did—revoke it. The child sentenced to death is a legal child in a host of ways, but none of these limitations or protections are useful on death row.[148] The child offender on death row has been denied children's rights recognized and codified in international law. He (most commonly) has lost his legal status as a child in precisely that context where the rights afforded children are most needed.

In many ways, the greater fairness in the penalty's application in the post-*Furman* period reflected an emerging consensus that racial discrimination was illegitimate, or at least, that the perception of racial discrimination in the application of death sentences reflected badly on US public policy. The systematic exclusion of African American young men from the category 'child' and the denial of protections to them was a point of conflict with the emerging children's rights regime that insisted upon racial equality and uniform standards of juvenile justice. These tensions—between liberal protections for children *and* capital punishment that was applied disproportionately to African American boys—resulted in the continuation of the penalty into the twenty-first century as well as its more just application, though racial disparity persisted.

In sum, the US case shows how the US federal system allowed the penalty to persist in some states, particularly those in the South. Issues of racial subordination, more visible in the South, resulted in the extreme overrepresentation of African Americans among child offenders who were put to death, especially in the pre-*Furman* period, before 1972. As rights for children expanded in the last half of the century, African American children were increasingly transferred out of protective institutions like

---

147. Ibid., 80–81.
148. Gainborough and Lean, "Convention on the Rights of the Child," 11; Horowitz, "Kids Who Kill," 166.

juvenile courts and youth detention centers. The penalty continued to be applied throughout the twentieth century, despite international condemnation, because of the US federal system, its onerous treaty ratification process, and the racial subordination endemic to its juvenile and criminal justice systems.

CHINA CASE STUDY

Current death penalty policy in China must be understood in the context of crime trends in the tumultuous post-Mao era. Juvenile delinquency contributed to a crime wave in the 1980s, with the rate of delinquency increasing from 1.4 percent of total crime in 1977 to 23.8 percent by 1989.[149] In response, a campaign known as "severe blows" or *yanda*, a harsh attempt to rid society of criminals and to deter crime by applying severe penalties, was launched in 1983.[150] The death penalty was widely used during the campaign.[151] The theory behind *yanda* was that "bringing evil to justice for all to see . . . will lead to a decrease in crime," which meant that executions were extensively publicized.[152] In 1985, the age of criminal responsibility was lowered so that 14- and 16-year-olds could be held responsible for their crimes.[153] The National People's Congress in 1991 passed the Juvenile Protection Law, and efforts were made to standardize the juvenile justice system, especially the Criminal Procedure Code (1996) and the Criminal Law (1997), which outlawed the child death penalty.[154] The 1991 Juvenile Protection Law defined a juvenile as an individual younger than 18.[155] In 1999, the Tenth Standing Committee Conference of the Ninth National People's Congress passed the Juvenile Delinquency Prevention Law, emphasizing ways of preventing delinquency through education as opposed to punishment.[156] The shift from the policies of *yanda* to the 1999 law in less than two decades is extraordinary.

149. Borge Bakken, "Crime, Juvenile Delinquency, and Deterrence Policy in China," *The Australian Journal of Chinese Affairs* 30 (1993): 31, 36, 38–39.

150. Ibid., 31, 50.

151. Ibid., 31.

152. Ibid., 50.

153. Ibid., 52.

154. Zhang Lening and Jianhong Liu, "China's Juvenile Delinquency Prevention Law: The Law and the Philosophy," *International Journal of Offender Therapy and Comparative Criminology* 51, no. 5 (2007): 544.

155. Ibid., 544.

156. Ibid., 541–546.

Although the 1997 Criminal Law (Article 44) ended the legal execution of child offenders, China has struggled to accurately determine the age of some criminal defendants. This is a common problem in states that did not precede death penalty restrictions with extensive and effective birth registration. Prior to the abolition of the child death penalty *in law*, Chinese criminal law allowed the penalty to be imposed on offenders who commit their crimes when they are between the ages of 16 and 18, but with a two-year suspension.[157] Further complicating matters, China's justice system is decentralized, highly political, and poorly funded.[158] These challenges are compounded for international human rights researchers, such as those in Amnesty, because of the lack of candor and transparency on the part of the Chinese government regarding the penalty. Reliable national statistics on the penalty's application in China are difficult to come by, often forcing researchers to rely on local newspapers for announcements.[159]

Human Rights Watch reports that China continued to execute child offenders after 1997 because of insufficient efforts to verify the age of offenders.[160] Two child offenders have been executed since 2003, according to Human Rights Watch: Zhao Lin, who was found guilty of murder in 2000 when he was 16 and executed in 2003; and Gao Pan, executed for murder and robbery committed when he was under 18.[161] In 2004, China denied in a response to the UN Commission on Human Rights that it executed offenders who commit their crimes when they are under 18.[162] Thus, although China is in compliance with the norm against the child

157. Bakken, "Crime, Juvenile Delinquency," 52.

158. Amnesty International, "People's Republic of China: Executed 'According to the Law?' The Death Penalty in China" (2004): 53. Murray Scot Tanner and Eric Green, "Principals and Secret Agents: Central Versus Local Control over Policing and Obstacles to 'Rule of Law' in China," *The China Quarterly*, vol. 191 (2007): 644–670; Oliver Melton, "China's Five-Year Planning System: Implications for the Reform Agenda," Testimony for the U.S.–China Economic and Security Review Commission, April 22, 2015, 6. Yuhua Wang, "Judicial Hierarchy and Judicial Outcomes: Evidence from a Natural Experiment in China," Working Paper, Harvard University, May 11, 2015, 2.

159. Amnesty International, "People's Republic of China," 6.

160. Human Rights Watch, "Enforcing the International Prohibition on the Juvenile Death Penalty," May 30, 2008.

161. Ibid.

162. United Nations Economic and Social Council, "Civil and Political Rights, Including the Question of Disappearances and Summary Executions: Extrajudicial, Summary or Arbitrary Executions: Report of the Special Rapporteur, Philip Alston: Addendum: Summary of Cases Transmitted to Governments and Replies Received" (Commission on Human Rights, 2005): 41.

death penalty *in law,* it has not effectively implemented its national ban. Without a vibrant and empowered civil society, there is no domestic-level force for compliance. That being said, there have been no reported executions of child offenders in China since 2004, although government secrecy on the issue cautions against any firm conclusion about the use of the penalty.

PAKISTAN CASE STUDY

In 2000, Pakistan passed the Juvenile Justice System Ordinance that banned the death penalty for child offenders under the age of 18 at the time of their crime, but protections for children were implemented considerably earlier. As part of the former British Empire, the age of majority was established in colonial law at 18 in the Majority Act of 1876.[163] With the introduction of *sharia* law by President Zia-ul-haq in the late 1970s, the Pakistan Penal Code was made compliant with Islamic law, as interpreted by the new regime.[164] Puberty was established as the new age of majority.[165] Individual provinces established a higher age of eligibility for the death penalty, 16 in Sindh Province[166] and 15 in Punjab.[167] During this period, the use of the penalty was remarkably high: About eight hundred individuals were hanged in 1979, according to the government's count, the highest number in Asia for that year.[168] In the 1980s, a National Commission for Child Welfare and Development was established to coordinate protections for children, focusing in particular on children in conflict with the law.[169]

Following Pakistan's ratification of the CRC in 1990, the United Nations began to apply pressure to raise the age of eligibility for the death penalty. UNICEF helped to draft a juvenile justice act that raised the minimum age

163. Andrea Geiger, "International Law–Juvenile Justice in Pakistan; Notes," *Suffolk Transnational Law Review* 23 (1999–2000): 726–727.

164. Ibid., 726.

165. Amnesty International, "Pakistan: Death Penalty for Juveniles," AI Index: ASA 33/07/95 (1995): 6.

166. Sindh Children Act of 1955, section 68 (1).

167. Punjab Youthful Offenders Ordinance of 1983, section 45 (1); Amnesty International, "Pakistan: Death Penalty for Juveniles," 6.

168. Amnesty International USA, "The Pakistan Campaign 1981" (University of Colorado at Boulder AIUSA Archives, 1981): 2.

169. UNICEF Regional Office South Asia, "Juvenile Justice in South Asia: Improving Protection for Children in Conflict with the Law" (Kathmandu, 2006): 100.

but, as will be seen, the legal system in Pakistan was plagued by contradiction between federal and provincial laws and the varying interpretations and legal practices of courts at different levels and in diverse locations.[170]

Death sentences for child offenders (those not covered by the 2000 ordinance) were commuted by President Pervez Musharraf in 2001 in the Presidential Commutation Order, but this order excluded child offenders given the penalty for *qisas*, retaliatory or corrective law, or *hadd* crimes, severe crimes with punishments prescribed in the Koran.[171] Musharraf passed the ordinance only after a meeting with Amnesty's Secretary General, Irene Khan, in which Khan encouraged the commutations.[172] The Juvenile Justice System Ordinance was also not applicable to tribal areas located in the north and west of the state, however, and in 2001, a child offender was executed for a crime he committed at age 13.[173] In 2004, the ordinance was extended to the tribal areas, but the Federally Administered Northern Areas and Azad Jammu and Kashmir remained outside its authority.[174] Even British colonial law, the 1860 Penal Code for example, did not always extend to tribal areas.[175] This is one reason why parts of Pakistan never internalized the norm against the child death penalty while under British control.

As in China, incomplete birth registration records and an ineffective birth registration system hinder Pakistan's efforts to enforce death penalty restrictions.[176] With only 29.5 percent of births registered, child offenders face great difficulty in proving they were children at the time of their crime.[177] Moreover, much of the legal infrastructure necessary for the implementation of the Juvenile Justice System Ordinance is not in place.[178] The promised commutation by presidential order was especially difficult to implement given the inability to determine the age of offenders.[179]

---

170. Amnesty International, "Pakistan: Death Penalty for Juveniles," 5.

171. Human Rights Watch, "The Last Holdouts: Ending the Child Death Penalty in Iran, Saudi Arabia, Sudan, Pakistan, and Yemen" (New York: Human Rights Watch, 2008): 14. M. Mukarram Ahmed and Muzaffar Husain Syed, *Encyclopaedia of Islam*, 25 vols. (New Delhi: Anmoi, 2005): 303.

172. Amnesty International, "Pakistan: Death Penalty for Juveniles Reintroduced," AI Index: ASA 33/025/2004 (2004).

173. Ibid.

174. Ibid.

175. Amnesty International, "Pakistan: Death Penalty for Juveniles," 5.

176. Human Rights Watch, "The Last Holdouts," 10.

177. Ibid.

178. Ibid.

179. Amnesty International, "Pakistan: Death Penalty for Juveniles Reintroduced."

In 2004, the Lahore High Court declared the Juvenile Justice System Ordinance to be "unreasonable, unconstitutional, and impractical," and revoked the ordinance.[180] The High Court ruled that the use of age limits, specifically, the age of 18, to assess the culpability of child offenders was "arbitrary."[181] Citing social, economic, climatic, and even dietary factors, the court found that children in Pakistan matured at an accelerated rate compared with Western children:[182]

> We have every reason to understand that a child [in Pakistan] starts under-
> standing the nature and consequences of his conduct sooner than a child in
> the West. Growing up in close proximity and interaction with adults due to
> social and economic conditions, doing odd jobs, and getting employed at a rel-
> atively young age ... hot climate and exotic and spicy food all contribute to-
> wards a speedy physical growth and an accelerated maturity of understanding
> of a child in our society.[183]

The court also ruled that Islamic law sets the age of majority at puberty, and that differential treatment of offenders by age violated constitutional guarantees of equality before the law.[184] The similarities between the Lahore court's claims about the nature of children and those made by British colonialists (discussed in chapter 4) are notable. In effect, the argument affiliates children's "nature" with their race, assigning a greater degree of culpability (even cunning) to non-Western children.

An appeal of the Lahore ruling was filed by the federal government and the children's rights NGO, SPARC (Society for the Protection of the Rights of the Child), and the Supreme Court of Pakistan temporarily reinstated the ordinance until a decision was made.[185] The court has yet to issue a ruling.[186] Child offenders continued to be sentenced to death during this period. In 2006, Mutaber Khan, allegedly 16 at the time of his crime,

---

180. International Federation for Human Rights and Human Rights Commission for Pakistan, "Slow March to the Gallows: Death Penalty in Pakistan" (Paris, January 2007): 38.

181. Amnesty International, "Pakistan: Death Penalty for Juveniles Reintroduced."

182. Ibid.

183. Khabir Ahmad, "The Battle for Children's Rights in Pakistan," *The Lancet* 365, no. 9468 (2005).

184. Amnesty International, "Pakistan: Death Penalty for Juveniles Reintroduced."

185. International Federation for Human Rights and Human Rights Commission for Pakistan, "Slow March to the Gallows: Death Penalty in Pakistan," 38.

186. Abdullah Khoso, "Detention of Juveniles in Pakistan," *Chronicle*, International Association of Youth and Family Judges and Magistrates, January 2012 edition, 40.

was executed for murders in the Swat province.[187] As stated, the practice of juvenile justice remains problematic, as birth registration issues cloud determinations of age. Twelve child offenders remained on death row in Pakistan in 2008, when a moratorium on the death penalty for all crimes and all offenders began.[188] The execution of an adult offender took place in 2012 despite the moratorium.[189] Pakistan ended its moratorium in 2014 and resumed executions, but only for those sentenced by the Anti-Terrorism Court (ATC) or convicted of terrorism-related charges.[190] Pakistan resumed child executions in 2015 when it put to death a 16-year-old, Muhammad Afzal, who played no role in terrorism and was not convicted by the ATC.[191]

This circuitous path toward compliance could not have been possible without a vibrant civil society. Children's rights NGOs in Pakistan proliferated in the 1990s and now form an important part of civil society. Global Juvenile Justice Indicators, designed by the United Nations (including UNICEF), have been used as a guide by IGOs and domestic NGOs to measure Pakistan against international legal standards.[192] District-based monitoring systems are being established all over the country, and the National Commission on Child Welfare and Development has been tasked with identifying appropriate indicators of child protection.[193]

SPARC remains a leader in juvenile justice and publishes a yearly report on the *State of Pakistan's Children*. Begun in 1992, SPARC draws its inspiration from the CRC. The organization sent an alternative report to the UN Committee on the Rights of the Child in 2003 while the committee was reviewing Pakistan's Second Report. It also worked to enact the Juvenile Justice System Ordinance, and has established children's rights committees to monitor and publicize children's rights in more than forty districts throughout the country. A key actor in Pakistan's civil society, SPARC is critical to the diffusion of international human

187. International Federation for Human Rights and Human Rights Commission for Pakistan, "Slow March to the Gallows: Death Penalty in Pakistan," 38.

188. Akhtar Amin, "Following in Footsteps of Other Nations: Rights Groups Want End to the Death Penalty," *Daily Times*, October 11, 2008.

189. Amnesty International, *Death Sentences and Executions in 2012*, ACT 50/001/2013, April 10, 2013.

190. Amnesty International, "Death Sentences and Executions in 2014," ACT 50/0001/2015, March 31, 2015.

191. Amnesty International, "Juveniles Amongst 12 Prisoners Executed Overnight in Pakistan," March 17, 2015.

192. UNICEF Regional Office South Asia, "Juvenile Justice in South Asia: Improving Protection for Children in Conflict with the Law," 100.

193. Ibid., 100.

rights norms about children, including the norm against the child death penalty. Along with SPARC, Amnesty, and UNICEF, other organizations have pressured Pakistan's government for juvenile justice reform. These include AMAL, a youth-focused organization that works on HIV/AIDS prevention and has partnered with the Consortium for Street Children, Save the Children, Lawyers for Human Rights and Legal Aid, and AGHS Legal Aid Cell. These latter two groups have provided legal counsel for child offenders.[194]

LAGGARDS

This section explores the theoretical issues regarding normative laggards in the diffusion of the norm against the child death penalty. It will address the characteristics and theory relating to laggards in general before focusing on hegemonic laggards in particular. Next, it will consider the roles of the state, science, and regime type (specifically federal systems) in laggard states as well as the role of race in countries that did not abolish the child death penalty until after the cascades or that have yet to abolish the penalty. Finally, I examine the process of socialization and the effect of the model of a globalized childhood on laggard states.

Laggards are states that did not abolish the child death penalty during either the early period or the cascades, or before 2005. The presence of laggards in normative diffusion is partly explained by theories of sociological institutionalism, which expect some states to seek the reputational benefits of compliance with international law as opposed to actually complying with it.[195] States also wish to avoid becoming laggards because they do not want the exposure and scrutiny that come with being one of just a few transgressors. Simmons argues that laggards are the easiest targets of noncompliance, which is why there is a stronger impetus to ratify when neighboring states have previously ratified.[196] Given this phenomenon, the cases of China and Pakistan make sense. Both states ratified international law governing the treatment of children and brought their domestic criminal codes into compliance with international law.[197] However, at

194. UNICEF Regional Office South Asia, "Juvenile Justice in South Asia: Improving Protection for Children in Conflict with the Law," 101.

195. Meyer, "Globalization: Theory and Trends," 264.

196. Beth A. Simmons, *Mobilizing for Human Rights, International Law in Domestic Politics* (New York: Cambridge University Press, 2009): 355.

197. As noted earlier, Pakistan resumed execution of child offenders in 2015 when it put to death a 16-year-old.

least in China, the law's implementation is incomplete because its legal system remains decentralized and its system of birth registration inadequate, making it difficult to determine the actual age of offenders.[198] From earlier chapters, it is clear that as legal protections for children diffused through the West in the late nineteenth century, birth and death registrations were an important tool for scientists and the government, and their widespread introduction coincided with and facilitated legal protections for children. Moreover, the United Kingdom and France sought to implement mandatory birth and death registration in colonies as part of their intervention in family law (see chapter 4). There is, of course, also the issue of political will. In most cases, the procedural roadblocks to commuting the death sentences of offenders whose age is contested (the majority of cases in China and Pakistan) are few. If international law and the reputational benefits of compliance with international law influenced the decisions of China and Pakistan to abolish the child death penalty, then the refusal of these states to commute the sentences of those whose age is contested suggests limits to the power of international law.

As stated, laggard states are those that were able to resist the pressure of the cascades and to reject or contest the link between child protection and state legitimacy. Both constructivists and sociological institutionalists have difficulty explaining why norms (and scripts) are powerful enough to garner *almost* universal support, but not to bring the last holdouts into compliance. One would think that as the global model of childhood became ever more entrenched and as the norm against the child death penalty became firmly institutionalized, states would find it increasingly difficult to thwart international expectations. States like Iran, Saudi Arabia, and Sudan, which unapologetically continue to execute child offenders, therefore present a challenge to normative theorists.

For sociological institutionalism, as well as realism in international relations, hegemonic laggards such as the United States present an even greater challenge to their core theories. These theorists expect powerful Western states to create and diffuse norms. In the case of the British and French empires, this pattern is evident. The United States, however, presents a paradox in the context of rights for children. At the turn of the

198. Amnesty International, "People's Republic of China: Executed 'According to the Law?' The Death Penalty in China," 53; Tanner and Green, "Principals and Secret Agents: Central Versus Local Control over Policing and Obstacles to 'Rule of Law' in China," 644–670; Melton, "China's Five-year Planning System: Implications for the Reform Agenda," 6; Wang, "Judicial Hierarchy and Judicial Outcomes: Evidence from a Natural Experiment in China," 2.

twentieth century, the United States was an international leader in child protection, especially in juvenile justice. With the founding of the first juvenile court and the implementation of numerous other reform measures, child offenders in the United States enjoyed protections far superior to child offenders in most other countries. Yet by the start of the twenty-first century, the United States had fallen out of step with the rest of the world, and its juvenile justice system was widely seen as archaic and draconian; nothing illustrated this disconnect more clearly than the ongoing practice of the child death penalty. Given the United States' early leadership on juvenile justice issues, it is contradictory for sociological institutionalists to expect both hegemonic *leaders* and hegemonic *laggards*. If scripts and models emerge from the West and are diffused and promoted by the West, how can the hegemon reject a defining norm of these scripts and models? Realism struggles with a similar issue. Realism expects the dominant norms in society to be advanced by and for the hegemon. Yet the success of the norm against the child death penalty, despite the United States' lack of support—and at times, its direct opposition—demonstrates the inadequacy of these theories.

Causes of Noncompliance: Race, Federalism, and Region

Despite the two countries' subsequently divergent paths, abolition of the child death penalty in the United States began similarly to abolition in England. A father's power over his children was greatly diminished in the United States in the nineteenth century. As concerns about child labor, neglect, exploitation, and health increased, a growing number of institutions developed to study, protect, and monitor childhood. The state began to take control of these institutions toward the end of the nineteenth century until, by the mid-twentieth century, the state regulated nearly every aspect of children's lives.

Yet twentieth century protections for children in the United States— unlike in the United Kingdom and France—were limited by their crimes. A child in the United States who committed particular crimes such as rape and murder could be divested of the protections afforded children and treated as an adult by the state, and could thus be eligible for adult penalties, including death.[199] That this conditional understanding of childhood

---

199. Even after *Roper*, children that commit particular crimes can be tried in adult courts and imprisoned in adult facilities, but they cannot be given the death penalty.

lasted as long as it did, more than 105 years after the establishment of the first juvenile court, is as puzzling as why it ended in 2005.

Domestic factors explain why the United States did *not* comply with international law *until* 2005 and partly explain why the United States came to comply with international law in 2005. Some evident causes have been addressed here: NGO pressure, racial issues, a fear of child criminals, the US federal system, and regional practices. Domestic factors also explain why China and Pakistan have failed to comply with the norm against the child death penalty. A poor system of birth registration (in both China and Pakistan), a juvenile justice system that is dysfunctional (Pakistan), a lack of control over large regions of the state (Pakistan), terrorism and security issues (in both states), and an anemic civil society (China), combine to result in a contradictory approach to juvenile justice. While both states have accepted the norm's legitimacy through the ratification of international treaties and the passage of national legislation, domestic factors hinder full compliance.

Evidence from the US case points to five factors that contributed to the failure to abolish the child death penalty prior to 2005. Some of these also apply to China and Pakistan: First, norm entrepreneurs such as AIUSA did not begin their campaigns against the child death penalty until 1987, and the coalition of NGOs and philanthropies that influenced the *Roper* court in 2005 did not form until 2002. Amnesty, AIUSA, UNICEF, and local-level NGOs (in the United States and Pakistan) joined forces to bring these countries into compliance. Although the campaign by Amnesty and AIUSA focused its efforts on the United States, other campaigns targeted China and Pakistan as well.

Second, race matters. An offender in the United States is more likely to be sentenced to death if *he* is of color and if his victim is white and female than with any other victim–offender combination.[200] Espy data on children executed in the United States demonstrate the extreme racial disparities in executions and sentencing for death-eligible crimes. The Lahore court in Pakistan threw out the legislation abolishing the child death penalty, in part because the court considered Pakistani children to be more mature at a younger age than Western children. This argument is familiar to students of colonialism, as it was the justification for differential treatment of native children by the British colonialists. This view of Pakistani children by the Lahore court requires further analysis.

---

200. Farrell and Swigert, "Legal Disposition of Inter-Group and Intra-Group Homicides."

Third, a collective panic over child criminals swept the United States in the late 1980s and early 1990s. The country experienced a juvenile crime wave that was exploited by the media through the dissemination of images of young, male, urban, African American 'superpredators' committing stranger-on-stranger violence. As a result, child offenders who committed violent crimes received little sympathy from the American public. Politicians pandered to these fears by adopting policies that were tough on crime and criminals. China similarly cracked down on crime in the 1980s with the *yanda* measures, which made the global model of the vulnerable and less culpable child a harder sell to the Chinese public and policymakers.

Fourth, the US federal system hindered compliance with international law in three ways: First, the Supreme Court is the branch of government least affected by international pressure, as the court's justices are appointed for life. The Supreme Court's decision in the *Furman* case in 1972 was very narrow, and its rejection of the norm against executing child offenders under the age of 18 in *Stanford* in 1989 was a setback to the domestic abolitionist movement. Second, the *Furman* ruling fueled calls for US states' rights. Although Franklin Zimring argues that there was no actual backlash against the ruling since only one state reinstated the death penalty after *Furman*, the decision nonetheless motivated supporters of the penalty and contributed to the issue's politicization in the 1970s.[201] If the *Furman* decision had been less narrow, the United States might have abolished the death penalty in 1972 during the first cascade. If the US government had jurisdiction to set death penalty policy for the entire country, as is the case in most nonfederal systems, child offenders would have been excluded from the death penalty in 1994. Third, the peculiarity of the US legal system, which has both monist and dualist aspects to its treatment of international law and its system of treaty ratification, makes ratification more difficult in the United States than in other states that adopt a purely monist approach. The difficulty is exacerbated by the strict ratification rules for international treaties, which require approval by two-thirds of the Senate. As seen in the Pakistan case, federalism is a key reason for noncompliance with the norm, as the central government has incomplete authority.

Finally, region trumps all. Were it not for a handful of US states, most of them in the South, the child death penalty would have ended in the mid-twentieth century, early enough in the norm lifecycle for the United

---

201. Zimring and Hawkins, *Capital Punishment and the American Agenda*, 43.

States to have been considered an early adopter. Texas alone led the trend, not just nationally but internationally as well. Furthermore, in the United States, racism (especially in sentencing) is closely linked to region. Noncompliance in Pakistan is also due to region. With the exception of the most recent execution in spring 2015, the child death penalty has only been carried out in the SWAT district of Pakistan where the government holds little, if any, sway.

Causes of Compliance: The Process of International Socialization

If domestic factors alone could explain why the United States, China, and Pakistan abolished the child death penalty (in law), it would suggest that actors within these countries agitated for reform based on the content of the norm against the penalty. In other words, the norm's content, and specifically, its rejection of the penalty for child offenders as regressive, inhumane, and barbaric, persuaded local actors to change domestic policy. Indeed, while international law in the ICCPR and later in the CRC might have established the scope of human rights activism, norm entrepreneurs in the 1980s set the agenda. In the United States, norm entrepreneurs, such as Amnesty and AIUSA, recognized the child death penalty as one of the few areas in which death penalty reform could be achieved. Moreover, abolitionists, child advocates, diplomats, NGOs, and foundations concerned with juvenile justice diligently worked in the period between the *Stanford* and *Roper* rulings (between 1989 and 2005) to solidify the national consensus; isolate those states that continued to execute child offenders; employ international legal instruments in national and international cases; petition international institutions; and mobilize opposition to the penalty.

I suggest, however, that what resonated with the American public, as suggested by the widespread opposition to the child death penalty noted in the 1986 AIUSA study, was the inconsistency between executing children and the globalized model of childhood developed, in part, in the United States. The inconsistency is evident in many markers of the transition from childhood to adulthood: Child offenders who could be executed in the United States were, depending on the jurisdiction, unable to vote, serve on a jury, marry, or consent to sex. They could not work in hazardous occupations, buy alcohol or cigarettes, or go to war.

Exempting children from the death penalty had a compliance pull all its own, because it nested within other ideas about children already accepted in American society. Abolition for child offenders fit within the American model of childhood: The contradiction between the greater vulnerability and reduced culpability ascribed to children *and* law and policy that permit their execution was irreconcilable. Evidence of this conflict is found in the rarity of the practice and in the inequality endemic to the penalty's application. Evidence from the US case suggests that although domestic factors account for the trajectory of the US movement for abolition, they do not alone explain why the United States abolished the penalty in 2005.

If international factors alone could explain why the United States abolished the penalty in 2005, it would mean that the United States accepted its obligation to obey international law and norms, regardless of their content. If this were the case, the United States should have abolished when the norm first became binding law in the 1976 ICCPR or when the consensus was first expressed during the drafting process. Instead, the US rejection of the specific article in the ICCPR prohibiting child executions demonstrates that the United States interpreted the norm as contested, or, at least, as contestable. In other words, the United States recognized both the authority of customary law and the binding obligation of the ICCPR, but proceeded as though these sources of authority did not trump its own.

The US case bears greater resemblance to the Pakistan case than to the China case. China abolished the child death penalty in law during a period of deep concern about child criminals. Its ban on the penalty went against the very grain of the *yanda* measures, premised on the notion of punishment as deterrence. There appears to have been no domestic movement to end the penalty. Since China's reforms to its juvenile justice system enshrined protections found in the CRC and were mostly adopted after the CRC came into effect, it is likely that international considerations, such as reputational concerns, influenced China's decision to abolish the penalty.

In Pakistan, human rights NGOs sought to expand legal protections for children, but these NGOs were assisted by important international actors like Irene Khan of Amnesty, who made personal appeals to President Musharraf to bring the state into compliance with international law. The case demonstrates the necessity of both domestic and international sources of pressure, even though the NGO presence in Pakistan is not as robust as that found in the United States in the transnational collaboration that sought a Supreme Court ruling in *Roper*.

All three states were persuaded to comply with international norms of child protection partly through four related socializing processes, at times occurring simultaneously. These four processes were: the adoption of the global model of childhood; publication of the model and its principles;

monitoring of compliance with international standards of juvenile justice and child welfare; and rebuke by the international community for noncompliance.

Adoption of the Model of Childhood

International human rights law establishes both rights and protections for children, including protection from the death penalty. This prohibition was part of the model of childhood formed in Western countries and diffused throughout the world in the nineteenth and twentieth centuries. Sociological institutionalists have argued that as ideas about children and childhood developed and came to include notions such as reduced culpability, state institutions including the juvenile justice system developed to monitor compliance with the evolving standards. The state thus grew in tandem with an increasingly complex model of childhood. Similarly, as children's rights became international law, international institutions like UNICEF monitored implementation within states. These institutions grew and developed as the model of childhood grew and developed.

Today, the model of childhood—never static and now global—includes more or less uniform and ever more exacting and ambitious standards of child welfare and protection, as measured by a range of global indices and indicators of child well-being. When states adopt the global model of childhood as codified in international legal instruments like the CRC, they are in effect signing up for a program of systematic external monitoring and (noncoercive) intervention by global institutions. Through these means, international law and institutions shape state-level policies on children, without the use of force. Through this ongoing socializing process, states are acclimated to the content of the model of childhood, to the idea of a protective relationship between the state and the child, and to the international community's commitment to that protection.

International and Domestic Publication of the Model

Global institutions, and NGOs particularly, publicized the model of childhood and sought to use international law to leverage state action. Tools for promoting the model included reports and press statements by NGOs like AIUSA; grassroots advocacy; lobbying; legal action through the drafting and submission of legal briefs; and the initiation of lawsuits. Yet these tools have served different purposes at different stages of the model's lifecycle. During the cascades of the norm against the child death penalty, as the model of childhood was fast diffusing, NGO campaign materials were means of persuasion, designed to exert pressure on states to adopt the model and the norms it contained. Post-adoption, they strengthen and reinforce the model, socializing states to the expectation of accountability in meeting international standards of child welfare and protection.

Monitoring

Benchmarks of childhood (in areas including health, well-being, education, etc.) are quantified, and countries are measured against these uniform standards in publications by international and domestic agents, such as by UNICEF in the *State of the World's Children* or in AIUSA's multiple reports about the child death penalty. AIUSA routinely published the list of child executions since 1990. In Pakistan, SPARC has instituted a complex system of monitoring, reported violations of the CRC, and published a yearly report on the state of Pakistan's children, while government agencies employ UN indicators to monitor the rights of child offenders throughout the country. These monitoring systems and the well-publicized reports and publications they produce are important means of accountability and compliance. They aim to shore up global standards of child protection and to shame the dwindling number of recalcitrant states by linking compliance with legitimacy and characterizing noncompliance as backward and uncivilized.

Rebuke and Stigma

Rebuke of states that continued to execute child offenders by Amnesty, AIUSA, other NGOs, the United Nations, other IGOs, and states began early, although rebuke was by no means directed equally at noncompliant states. A series of UN General Assembly resolutions, beginning in 1980, affirmed the norm's widespread acceptance and *opinio juris*, or the legal obligation to obey the norm.[202] The UN Economic and Social Council adopted the 1984 Safeguards Guaranteeing Protection of the Rights of

202. Weissbrodt, Fitzpatrick, and Newman, *Human Rights: Law, Policy, and* Process, 714–717. See resolutions U.N. Doc A/RES/35/172 (1980), A/RES/36/22 (1981), A/RES/38/96 (1983), A/RES/51/92 (1996), A/RES/53/147 (1998), A/RES/55/111 (2000), A/40/3 (1985).

Those Facing the Death Penalty (E/1984/84), reaffirming a global prohibition of the practice, and the UN Commission on Human Rights issued several other resolutions over the course of two decades.[203]

Additionally, the reservation by the United States to Article 6§5 of the ICCPR elicited vehement rebuke from states in Europe. The European Union urged the United States to withdraw the reservation immediately.[204] Belgium, Denmark, Finland, France, Germany, Italy, the Netherlands, Norway, Portugal, Spain, and Sweden made individual declarations criticizing the United States' reservation. The UN Human Rights Committee, which monitors implementation of the ICCPR, found that the reservation offended the "object and purpose of the treaty."[205]

By the time the United States abolished the child death penalty in 2005, the norm against executing child offenders had gained such widespread acceptance that it was considered customary law. Customary law can be defined as the customs and practices of nations that are "widespread, rather than unanimous," and, as such, are a "source of international law."[206] All governments are bound to customary law regardless of their recognition of a given norm (even in treaties or national legislation) unless they have persistently objected to it during its development.[207] Although the US Supreme Court first declared in 1900 that customary law is part of national law and is considered on par with other sources of

---

203. E/CN.4/RES/1997/12 (1997), E/CN.4/RES/1998, E/CN.4/RES/1999/61, E/CN.4/RES/2000/65, E/CN.4/RES/2001/68, E/CN.4/RES/2001/75. /8, E/CN.4/RES/2002/77, E/CN.4/RES/2003/67.
The UN Sub-Commission on the Promotion and Protection of Human Rights adopted resolutions E/CN.4/SUB.2/RES/1999/4 and E/CN.4/SUB.2/RES/2000/17, reaffirming the international legal ban on the practice. Additionally, the UN Special Rapporteur on Extrajudicial, Summary, and Arbitrary Executions criticized the United States in E/CN.41993/46 (1992), E/CN.4/1994/7 (1993), E/CN.4/1995/61 (1994), A/51/457 (1996), E/CN.4/1997/60 (1996), E/CN.4/1998/68 (1997), E/CN.4/1999/39 (1999), E/CN.4/2000/3 (2000), E/CN.4/2001/9 (2001), E/CN.4/2002/74 (2002), E/CN.4/2004/7 (2004). See also Former US Diplomats Morton Abramowitz et al. as *Amici Curiae* 7. *Roper v. Simmons* No. 03-633. 543 U.S. 551 (2005).
204. Weissbrodt, Fitzpatrick, and Newman, *Human Rights: Law, Policy, and Process,* 717.
205. United Nations Human Rights Committee, "Consideration of Reports Submitted by States Parties under Article 40 of the Covenant: Comments of Human Rights Committee 53d Sess., 1413th Mtg. Para. 14, at 4 UN Doc. CCPR/C/79/Add.50 (1995)" (1995); UN Human Rights Committee, General Comment 24, UN Doc CCPR/C/21/Rev 1/Add 6 para 10 (1994).
206. Weissbrodt, Fitzpatrick, and Newman, *Human Rights: Law, Policy, and Process,* 22.
207. Ibid.

international law, such as treaty law,[208] customary law has been most successfully employed in US courts when it affirms a national consensus regarding standard practices. The opinion in *Roper* demonstrates this. Both domestic and international NGOs, such as Amnesty and AIUSA, among others, pressured the United States and other states that had continued to violate the norm against executing child offenders since the 1980s, and, in the US case, these organizations helped to shape a national consensus against the practice.

Pressure by NGOs forced the United States to enter into a twenty-year debate with opponents of the child death penalty, including the United Nations, domestic and international human rights groups, and diplomats. This debate had two stages: First, during the 1980s and early 1990s, the United States denied there was an international consensus in the form of customary law. The most important part of this denial is what the United States did *not* say: The United States did not say that customary law did not exist, that it did not apply to states, and that it did not apply to the hegemon. Rather, the United States said that an international consensus about the child death penalty had not yet formed. Its line of argument thus suggested that customary law was indeed legitimate law, with application to the United States, but in this particular case, there was no customary law to apply.

Second, the United States denied the norm's applicability to itself. In the 1990s, the United States began to argue that even if there were customary law against executing child offenders, it had been a persistent objector to the law and was thus exempt from compliance. Although one regional court found the US claim of persistent objector status plausible,[209] the claim was nonetheless difficult to support given that the United States did not object to the norm during the drafting of the 1949 Fourth Geneva Convention (Article 68),[210] was not present during the debates over Article 6 of the ICCPR, did not cite the provisions of Article 6 in its later list of

208. U.S Supreme Court, *The Paquette Habana*, 175 U.S. 677, 700 (1900); 1 Restatement (Third) of the Foreign Relations Law of the United States § 111 (1987).

209. Inter-American Commission on Human Rights, "Pinkerton and Roach v. United States, Res 3-87, Case 9467, Annual Report of the Inter-American Commission on Human Rights, 147, OEA/Ser.L/V/II.71, Doc. 9, Rev. 1, Para. 56," (1986–1987). The Inter-American Commission, however, found that although a customary norm had yet to be established, there was a norm of *jus cogens* within the Organization of American States. An agreed-upon age limit for eligibility for the death penalty, however, had yet to be determined.

210. Although it did suggest that "careful consideration" be given the age limit of 18. See Weissbrodt, Fitzpatrick, and Newman, *Human Rights: Law, Policy, and Process*, 722.

articles of concern,[211] and did not register an official reservation either to Article 4 (prohibiting the execution of children under the age of 18) of the American Convention on Human Rights or to Article 37 of the CRC (because it was never ratified).

The point bears repeating: The important part of the debate was what the United States did *not* say. The United States, in this second stage, did not say that it was not subject to customary law. Rather, the United States said that in customary law, a loophole existed whereby it could claim exemption. The exemption was not based on hegemony or on a rejection of the legitimacy of international law by the United States, but rather on the rules of international law itself. Its rejection of international customary law, the United States argued, was in fact legal within international law. Essentially, the second stage of this denial reaffirmed the legitimacy and relevance of customary law in general and further acknowledged that customary law against the child death penalty existed and applied to states. It is important to note that at the time that the United States was claiming its exemption, some legal theorists had suggested that the norm against executing child offenders had already achieved the status of *jus cogens*,[212] making it binding upon the United States regardless of its claim of persistent objector status.[213]

The coalition against the child death penalty, discussed in chapter 5, organized in response to the pending *Roper* case and encouraged the drafting of multiple *amici* briefs in support of abolition. Former US diplomats with expertise on the impact of US domestic policy on foreign relations petitioned the federal government about the international effects of the child death penalty in the United States. They argued that the continued practice of executing children hindered diplomats in their efforts to promote US values and policies abroad.[214] Other communities of critics also developed, including Nobel Peace Prize winners and child advocates and agencies. NGOS, especially AIUSA, elicited the help of foreign governments and individuals to write to states with child offenders on death row. Lawyers, some associated with prominent NGOs, took on the cases of child offenders, almost always *pro bono*, and used the international condemnation of the practice in their defense strategy.

211. Although it did reserve on that article when it ratified the ICCPR in 1992.
212. De la Vega and Fiore, "The Supreme Court of the United States"; Sawyer, "Comment: The Death Penalty Is Dead Wrong."
213. Vienna Convention on the Law of Treaties, "115 U.N.T.S. 331, 8 I.L.M. 679, Articles 53 and 64" (1980).
214. Former U.S. Diplomats Morton Abramowitz et al.; Richard Gibson, "Europeans Criticize America for Putting Minors to Death," *The Blade*, September 27, 1987.

These critics focused on the child death penalty's cost to the United States in terms of diminished legitimacy and moral authority. They underscored US deviance from the now established global model of childhood. They drew similarities between the United States and other states widely considered to be rogue nations, and they cited the differences between the United States and more 'civilized' states. It was an effective strategy. By engaging the United States through UN agencies, diplomats, NGOs, and nation-to-nation rebuke, the United States was forced to continually interact with critics who opposed its policies and practices and who obliged it to acknowledge the international consensus against the child death penalty. The results of international rebuke were clear: The imposition of child death sentences began to decline by 1999, and by the time of *Roper*, death penalty rates for child offenders were at their lowest in fifteen years.[215] The number of US states executing children had also declined to three by the time of *Roper*. The United States was increasingly defensive when forced to address the issue in international forums and changed its argument for contesting the norm (as described). By the time the Supreme Court heard *Roper*, both the justices and the states that continued to execute child offenders already felt the weight of international opinion.

As the consensus against the child death penalty solidified, individual US states voluntarily adopted laws prohibiting the penalty. Even states that maintained the penalty in law drastically reduced the practice. This trend indicates that the process of socialization that shaped US federal policy had an equal, and arguably even more powerful, effect at the state level. The national consensus recognized in *Roper* reflected this state-level process of socialization.

China and Pakistan brought their death penalty laws into compliance with the CRC before the United States did, in 1997 and 2001, respectively. In Pakistan's case, there was strong pressure from civil society to end the penalty for child offenders, but these activists were assisted by international organizations, especially by UNICEF and Amnesty. As demonstrated in both the Pakistan and US cases, there is evidence that in addition to the late period mechanisms of international pressure and a globalized childhood, principled activism was critical to changing law and policy in these countries. There is no evidence in the China case to suggest domestic pressure to abolish the penalty.

---

215. Streib, "The Juvenile Death Penalty Today, January 1, 1973–December 31, 2004," 3.

CONCLUSION

The adoption of the global model of childhood by the United States, China, and Pakistan, one that limited state practice in accordance with international law and norms, left these states vulnerable to international pressure. In the United States, the increased citation of international law in Supreme Court decisions further ratcheted up the pressure, as did the sharp rebuke by UN agencies, diplomats, and other nations and the NGO campaigns that helped to shape the national consensus against the penalty. The United States could not simultaneously accept the global model of childhood and reject the moral authority of international law protecting children. China and Pakistan likely felt similar pressure following their ratification of the CRC.

Change in the United States came first in the form of legal prohibitions by individual states that were reluctant to maintain a penalty at odds with international opinion, second in the prohibition by the federal government for crimes that are within federal jurisdiction, and finally, with the Supreme Court ruling that recognized the "unusual" nature of the penalty, both at home and abroad. A very different pattern of diffusion appears to have taken place in Pakistan, as the initial decision to abolish the penalty was made at the national level, with some districts resisting the norm.

The publication of the model of childhood, the monitoring of state practice, and the rebuke of states that fail to comply with accepted standards were all important aspects of international change. However, the globalization of the model—a phenomenon that made state treatment of children an international concern—was *the* primary mechanism of influence in the eventual compliance of laggard states with international law prohibiting the death penalty for child offenders. Finally, principled activism was essential to the norm's diffusion, especially in the United States. Without the campaigns by AIUSA and Amnesty and concerted action by a formidable coalition of NGOs, domestic nonprofits, professional organizations, and foundations, the ruling in favor of abolition might not have happened. Death penalty opponents and child advocates in the late period were able to use the chorus of condemnation by the international community to win compliance with international law and norms of child protection. Their tactics suggest that theories of socialization, especially constructivist theories of persuasion and argumentation, best explain the path to abolition in the United States.

CHAPTER 7

ᴄ∿ᴏ

Conclusion

INTRODUCTION

This book examines how an idea that begins in one part of the world becomes a global norm that almost all states in the international system obey. The development of the norm of abolition of the death penalty for child offenders under the age of 18 presented several puzzles: First, how did the construction of childhood that prevailed in the late twentieth century come about? Why, for example, was childhood defined by age rather than by behavioral or intellectual markers? Why did children come to be viewed as less culpable for their crimes and thus ineligible for adult penalties such as death? Second, how did this particular construction of childhood, one characterized by the immaturity, heightened vulnerability, and lesser culpability of children, diffuse throughout the world? How did the model of childhood—the childhood that parents aim to provide and that governments seek to ensure for children—come to look the same in almost every country? Third, how did this happen given that the ban on the child death penalty had the distinction of being opposed by the United States throughout its development? How did the norm diffuse despite opposition from the hegemon?

By considering how states incorporate a specific norm into their domestic value system and legal framework, I have sought to understand how such factors as state structure, international pressure, nonstate actors, and law produce human rights change and catalyze international transformation. This study has revealed clear diffusion patterns, suggesting that the international spread of ideas may be an important explanation for the global trend toward isomorphism among domestic legal systems and the increasing alignment of these domestic frameworks with international law and norms.

The norm against the child death penalty has several important features: First, it grew out of a specific Western construction of childhood, developed over the course of centuries, as a distinct period of human life separate from adulthood (denoted by age), a period of increased vulnerability and reduced culpability for one's actions. By the early twentieth century, norms of child protection by the state prevailed in many Western countries, including England, France, and the United States. England and France abolished the death penalty for child offenders under the age of 18 early in the century, consistent with other norms about children in these states. England and France then spread this construction of childhood, including the norm against the child death penalty, to their colonies—first, through coercive measures that established a state order and a legal system based on their own objectives, and second, through the legal acculturation by which these states were socialized to norms of state protection for children. The coercive socialization that took place in British and French colonies greatly shaped law and policy regarding children after these colonies won independence.

Second, the boundaries of the norm against the child death penalty have shifted considerably over time. The norm first emerged in more radical form in the nineteenth century, as part of the emerging trend of general abolition for all crimes and all offenders, including children. It then lost its radicalism as the trend toward general abolition waned over the twentieth century and was overtaken by a more modest, conservative trend of abolition for certain classes of people only, child offenders among them. By the 1990s, the norm regained its radicalism, as most states again abolished the penalty for all crimes and all offenders, including child offenders.

The norm has other distinct characteristics as well. The earliest states to abolish the penalty were predominantly in the Global South. Venezuela, Costa Rica, and Brazil abolished the penalty for all crimes and all offenders beginning in 1863. Realists and sociological institutionalists expect global norms to emerge from powerful actors, not from states in the periphery of the international system. It is also noteworthy that in contrast to other human rights norms, the norm against the child death penalty had two distinct cascades, rather than just one. The first began in the 1960s and ended in 1981; the second cascade started in 1985 and ended in 2005 with abolition by the United States.

Yet the abolition of the child death penalty also likely has much in common with other successful human rights norms, including the use of the rhetoric of civilization to produce change. After World War II, children became part of the civilizing rhetoric of newly minted international institutions like UNICEF, whose relief work and development programs, concurrent with global trends toward democratization and decolonization, set uniform standards of child welfare and diffused protections for children. An international children's rights regime began modestly with the ICCPR in the 1960s and 1970s and then strengthened and broadened in scope with the ratification of the CRC in the 1990s.

The development of rights and protections for children in international law meant that states no longer had complete control over the way children were treated. *Childhood was now an international idea.* In important ways, the state was dispossessed of full authority over its children because its policies and practices were now a legitimate international concern. As discussed in chapter 1, the shift in authority over children from the state to the international community in fact marked the completion of a greater and more gradual pattern of divestment from the father, who was sovereign of the family, to the state, and finally from the state to the international community.

Moreover, the international community's control over childhood was (and is) ideological. In setting global standards of childhood, the international community in effect defines childhood. Taking on both watchdog and judicial functions, the international community identifies areas and the scope of protection; patrols childhood's boundaries; cites violations of those protections; and calls out violators. This assumption of ideological authority and its enshrinement in international law helped to diffuse several human rights norms in the postwar era, including the norm against the child death penalty.

KEY FINDINGS

Although a number of legal and international relations studies have focused on compliance with human rights norms once they are codified in international law, few studies to date have shed light on the origins of specific rights and their evolution toward global acceptance. This book makes several contributions to the international relations literature on norms, international and comparative law, diffusion theory, and human rights. It expands on previous work on the international spread of norms by illuminating micro-level processes of legal diffusion and political change, and it makes seven key theoretical contributions. First, while political scientists, legal theorists, and sociologists have distinguished between early adopters and other states, they have not paid sufficient attention to the phenomenon of late adopters. The literature often assumes that the same mechanics and processes of diffusion apply whether states adopt norms during cascades or whether they adopt norms as laggards, after they have been institutionalized. Yet in my research, I found a distinct logic or pattern of late adoption whereby some late adopters of the norm against the child death penalty (specifically, two of the cases of chapter 6, the United States and Pakistan) were moved toward compliance through a combination of domestic-level principled activism *and* international systemic-level pressure to meet the demands of the now global model of childhood.

In effect, this pattern of late adoption combines the bottom-up force of early-period diffusion with the international pressure of the cascade. Although the principled activism of the late period differs from the principled activism of the early period in that it draws on international law and norms found in global civil society, it nonetheless has much in common with its predecessor. Most importantly, the rhetoric of civilization was successfully employed in both periods of domestic activism, and was used to claim that child protection was a moral imperative for civilized people and states.

Second, in contrast to the expectations of realists, the norm against the child death penalty had a hegemonic laggard. Beginning in 1985, with the post-*Furman* executions of child criminals, the United States—once a key innovator of protections for children—not only opposed the norm of abolition of the child death penalty, but further sought to justify its opposition in international and national forums. Further investigation of the US case, however, revealed that federal courts had been in compliance with the norm possibly as early as 1875, the year after the last federal execution of a child offender, according to the Espy data, even though the practice was not prohibited in law in federal jurisdiction until 1994. If it had not been for states like Texas and Oklahoma that supported the child death penalty and carried out child executions, the United States might have abolished much earlier than it did. The case therefore suggests that it was the federal system of government, one that allows for great variation in US state practice, along with institutional racism that has historically excluded African American boys from the protections afforded other children, which contributed to the late adoption of the norm in the United States.

Additionally, the United States was a laggard because of the timing of its opposition to the norm. The United States initially went along with global trends in death penalty practice, with US states abiding by a self-imposed moratorium on the penalty in the late 1960s and early 1970s as the Supreme Court weighed its constitutionality (resulting in the *Furman* decision in 1972). By the time the United States began to challenge the norm in the late 1970s (with the *Gregg* ruling), reintroduce the practice of executing child offenders in the mid-1980s, and vociferously oppose the norm in the 1990s (through reservations to the ICCPR and a refusal to ratify the CRC), the first cascade had already ended and the second cascade was well under way. The lag in the United States' opposition thus allowed the norm to be enshrined in international law and adopted by a majority of countries without the hegemon's support. The timing of US opposition to the norm was thus critical. Had US opposition been voiced earlier, such as during the drafting of the ICCPR, the pattern of diffusion could very well have been different.

Third, in contrast to realist notions of power, the coercive spread of the norm against the child death penalty socialized developing countries to Western ideas of childhood and state responsibility for children. While sociological institutionalism downplays the role of colonialism in this process, I found that British and French colonialism were crucial to the diffusion of the norm to large parts of the world. These colonial powers used the death penalty in their colonies to maintain order, but also *diffused abolition of the child death penalty* during the twentieth century. This process of coercive socialization introduced the colonies of Britain and France to a Western construction of childhood and acculturated them to Western legal traditions by making the state the central authority in setting standards of child welfare and protection and enforcing compliance with those standards. This differed from the pattern in Latin America, where former colonies abolished the death penalty (including for child offenders) decades before Portugal, Spain, and Belgium, their former colonial powers. My study thus identifies a pattern of diffusion through coercive socialization that was unique to the British and French colonial powers. Colonialism was vital to the spread of the norm against the child death penalty, but only a certain type of colonialism had a part—that of the British and the French (and Soviet imperialism, to a lesser extent).

Fourth, international law has many mechanisms in common with domestic law. In the US case, I found that domestic laws requiring compulsory education in US states in the nineteenth and twentieth centuries were effective in securing compliance sometimes fifty years before the government was willing to enforce these laws. This finding undermines arguments by realists and legal positivists that law needs teeth to be effective. International law about children's rights now often serves as the sole justification of principled actors who seek to bring states into compliance with the global model of childhood.

Fifth, the emergence, development, and promotion of a global model of childhood after World War II was itself a key mechanism of normative spread and state compliance. As an important part of the liberal state model in the second half of the twentieth century, law and norms protecting children and ensuring a standardized childhood became necessary for international legitimacy and membership in a community of equal states. In the decades after the war, the meaning of an acceptable childhood continued to develop, and the state's responsibility for ensuring that childhood continued to grow. This phenomenon was similar to the pattern seen in the nineteenth century in England, France, Japan, and the United States, where the model of childhood came to encompass nearly all aspects of children's lives and where state institutions developed to assess compliance and punish those families that did not meet their obligations.

As the international community adopted the model of childhood, international, transnational, and national institutions, along with NGOs, emerged to monitor and regulate children's lives everywhere. This is akin to the process at the state level, where ideas about childhood and its need for regulation shaped state bureaucracy; state bureaucracy, in turn, validated itself by continuing to develop the model of childhood and the state's role in its oversight and protection. At the international level, the model of the global child and the need to ensure state compliance with the model justified the founding, growth, and consolidation of international organizations devoted to children's issues, which in turn, shaped the content of the global model and further increased its need for regulation. UNICEF and Amnesty, for example, used their moral authority to incorporate children's issues into the canon of liberal protections: UNICEF, by expanding the idea of children's welfare from one of basic material needs to a "whole child" approach that touched on all areas of children's lives, and Amnesty and AIUSA, by selecting the child death penalty as an important human rights issue.

Sixth, this study identifies legal diffusion as an *independent* variable that explains the similarity in state institutions and norms of childhood across the international system. Other approaches to the diffusion of norms of childhood, such as sociological institutionalism, have neglected the role of law in the spread of global cultural models. For these theorists, law and national policy are seen as the dependent variable, as evidence of the isomorphism of state models.[1] Yet the case studies in this book demonstrate that legal diffusion is in fact a primary *method* of norm diffusion that should be recognized as an independent variable that can explain isomorphism both in state organization and in the values of newly independent states.

Finally, a combination of sociological institutionalism and agentic constructivism best explains the norm's diffusion. Sociological institutionalists can account for the pull of cultural scripts and the power of these scripts or models to cause or induce states to emulate global normative frameworks. Constructivists can account for the role of principled actors and NGOs and IGOs, whose initiatives and campaigns create and advance norms, thereby shaping both the content of the global model of childhood and its application. Once a global model of childhood existed, it exerted a powerful pull on states to adopt policies guaranteeing the rights of children. Domestic actors of other states were then socialized to the rapidly globalizing model through legal acculturation to a Western system of rights and liberties. This process is not, strictly speaking, external and purely coercive; nor is it mere emulation. Rather, it is a combination of brute force (realism), socialization through law (constructivism), and the pull of an increasingly international model of legitimate statehood (sociological institutionalism and international legal theory). Taken together, these schools of thought explain the push of agency and structural pull of norms.

Network theory is also useful here. We can view the diffusion of the norm prohibiting the child death penalty as the product of a young network of principled actors that matured and grew into the elaborate complex of actors and institutions that today monitor, regulate, govern, implement, and enforce now global norms regarding children and childhood. In this vein, the relationship between agency and structure is played out in an intricate web of states, IGOs, NGOs, regional coalitions, individuals, national policy and practice, and bodies of law. Network theory straddles sociological institutionalist and constructivist approaches and provides insight into the way the story of the abolition of the child death penalty is about more than the spread of a single human rights norm. It is also about the diffusion of a type of organization, a particular form of international order, whereby the state, and more than ever, the international community, serves as the final arbiter of how childhood is defined and of how children are treated, protected, and empowered.

1. Meyer, "Globalization: Theory and Trends"; John Meyer et al., "World Society."

AUTHORITY

As the book has shown, authority over children has shifted in the last two to three centuries from the father, who was sovereign of the family, to the state.[2] The last half of the twentieth century witnessed a second shift of authority from the state to the international community. This second shift was not coercive in that there was no enforcement of children's rights at the international level. Rather, the authority of the international community is ideological. Ideological authority over childhood can be understood as the authority to determine what childhood means, to decide its core characteristics and, relatedly, when it begins and ends; what specific responsibilities it demands of adults; what special protections it affords; and the nature and adjudication of violations. The ability to define the problem and the solution, qualities of ideational power, is an important organizing principle in international relations. Material authority over childhood is the ability to control children's actions and environment. Parents continue to have primary material authority over children, determining to a large degree the content of their days; what they eat and wear; where they live; how and where they are educated; and whether they work. If parents fail to meet their obligations according to the model of childhood (as defined by the state, and, more than ever, by the international community), then parents' material authority over children can in many societies be transferred to the state.

Michel Foucault has theorized the transition of the state from a monarchy to a new form of "governmentality" that required the creation of new forms of expertise and legitimacy to "categorize, differentiate, and normalize populations."[3] State authority began to usurp paternal authority because state institutions were seen as more efficient and reliable

2. As discussed in chapter 3, Holly Brewer has argued that parental authority, eroded by the state over the course of the nineteenth and twentieth centuries, had only recently been granted. See Holly Brewer, *By Birth or Consent: Children, Law, and the Anglo-American Revolution in Authority* (Chapel Hill, NC: University of North Carolina Press, 2005). This may indicate that the granting of parental authority itself was one of the first efforts to improve child welfare.

3. Bloch, *Governing Children*; Jacques Donzelot and Robert Hurley, *The Policing of Families* (Baltimore: Johns Hopkins University Press, 1997); Michel Foucault, *Madness and Civilization; A History of Insanity in the Age of Reason* (New York: Pantheon, 1965); Foucault, *The History of Sexuality*, vol. 1; Michel Foucault, "Governmentality," in *The Foucault Effect: Studies in Governmentality*, eds. Graham Burchell, Colin Gordon, and Peter Miller, (Chicago: University of Chicago Press, 1991): 87–104; Michel Foucault, *Discipline and Punish: The Birth of the Prison*, 2nd ed. (New York: Vintage, 1995).

monitors of childhood. As the US, English, and French cases demonstrate, parents came to be perceived as untrustworthy, ill-suited guardians of children, as the burgeoning field of social scientific studies indicated that the greatest source of abuse and neglect was the home and as children came to be seen as the future of the nation. The state stepped in to monitor the material aspect of childhood as it sought to ensure that children were given proper nutrition, an education, protection from unsuitable or excessive labor, and were free from abuse. The model of childhood grew more multifaceted under state authority, and state bureaucracies expanded accordingly to accommodate it. The growing attention in the West in the nineteenth century to issues of child nutrition, hygiene, welfare, and psychological well-being, as well as the bureaucratic growth that served this heightened interest, suggests a co-constitutive relationship between the state and the child. Yet the state was (and still is) challenged from all sides. The US case, for example, indicates that state authority over children has, at times, been affirmed by some US courts while undermined by others.

The greatest threat to state authority over childhood is the international community, which, as discussed, now wields ideological power over childhood. Through instruments such as the *State of the World's Children*, a yearly UNICEF publication, and international declarations and conventions, the ideological authority of the international community commands the attention and respect of sovereign states. *The State of the World's Children* cites the current goals of international institutions (such as the UN Millennium Development Goals), and offers a detailed report on the performance of each country as measured against both the global model of childhood and its established benchmarks and criteria. Likewise, the UN Committee on the Rights of the Child monitors compliance with the CRC by all signatory states.

CRITIQUES OF THE GLOBAL MODEL OF CHILDHOOD

The most persuasive critiques of the global model of childhood follow: First, the model is treated as if it is ahistorical, or as though the childhood that we recognize and aspire to provide for children has always existed in the same form. This, as will be argued, conceals a violent history of state and international consolidation and of shifting authority over children. Second, the global model of childhood has been imperfectly realized in practice. It has failed to protect children from war, torture, exploitation, and other forms of abuse. Third, the global model of childhood has become part of a new moral imperialism, according to which norms about childhood and children are used by powerful states and international institutions to justify intervention in weak states.

The Limitations of an "Ahistorical" Model

In the preceding chapters, I have presented a historical narrative describing how a single model of childhood emerged in the West, was diffused by a few Western states, and became prevalent throughout the world. According to this model, childhood has come to be defined by a single measurement: age. The construction of childhood cannot be understood apart from the creation and development of the modern bureaucratic state, whose mission to ensure the progress and well-being of its citizens and society required "objective" measurements that could be applied across class, gender, race, language, and ethnicity.

Science, both natural and social, and law gave these concurrent and connected processes—state consolidation and the construction of childhood—legitimacy by presenting the seemingly objective measurements of childhood as fair, impartial, and True. This stamp of approval from emerging fields like pediatrics and the passage of law and policy (guided and informed by science) setting new standards of child welfare and protection advanced the humanitarian ideas of child advocates and led to a new orthodoxy or received view of childhood. According to this view, all children experience similar paths to adulthood, marked by "normal" progress in intellect, emotional maturity, and physical development.

This construction of childhood as universal and, notably, as ahistorical clearly simplifies the maturation process. One would be hard-pressed to argue that a child, on reaching the age of 18, makes a sudden cognitive and emotional leap into mature adulthood. The use of the age 18 as a demarcation or threshold point between childhood and adulthood is therefore an arbitrary marker and a legal contrivance, a means for the imposition of social order and a tool of governance. Through its institutions and bureaucracy, the state can continually identify, develop, measure, and regulate new, scientifically supported, areas or aspects of childhood. The child thus justifies the expansion of the state through its need for regulation and oversight, a need built in to the steadily expanding definition of what it means to be a child.

The related ideas that children are the future of the nation and that the state ensures its future through their protection have also acquired the gloss of ahistorical truth. Yet the increasing distrust of the child's caregivers through the last two centuries mirrors the distrust of non-Western variations of childhood in national laws. At the international level, the construction of a single, legal model of childhood against which the performance of all states is measured was borne out of a distrust of the unregulated childhood and the savage and uncivilized father. The shift in authority over children from the father to the state to the international community, detailed in this book, came at the expense of families and local communities. The seemingly ahistorical nature of childhood conceals the violence and coercion that often accompanied this power shift, which enabled the process of state-building and the development of international order.

An Imperfect Model

As child advocates and scholars who study childhood know only too well, protection for children around the world is grossly imperfect. Child labor is still problematic in many parts of the world, with 150 million children employed as laborers.[4] Globally, children make up one third of all detected trafficking victims; two-thirds of these victims are girls, according to the United Nations.[5] Previous chapters have already documented the continued use of the child death penalty in Iran and elsewhere. These facts pose the question: How can a model of childhood powerful enough to shape both national and international law not be powerful enough to compel compliance with the norms and standards of child welfare that comprise the model? How can the international community wield ideological authority over children's lives and yet be unable to end some of the most egregious violations of their human rights? How does a globalized model of childhood coexist with child abuse, prostitution, trafficking, torture, and execution?

I would first argue that the apparent limitations of the model of childhood in the face of continued violations of children's rights do not reflect

---

4. UNICEF, *Child Protection: Current Status and Progress*, http://data.unicef.org/child-protection/overview.html.

5. United Nations Office on Drugs and Crime, "Global Report on Trafficking in Persons," 2014, https://www.unodc.org/documents/data-and-analysis/glotip/GLOTIP_2014_full_report.pdf.

weakness in the model *per se*, but rather speak more to the nature of human rights change through law in general. Norms need not be perfectly applied to advance global change; on the contrary, change in human rights, as this study and many others attest, is incremental. Moreover, deviations from a norm should not be taken to mean that a norm is not widespread or powerful or that it does not work to shape human rights practice. We would never say, for example, that there is no norm against chemical weapons simply because the Assad regime in Syria used them. Rather, we emphatically affirm the norm against chemical weapons through international public outcry over their use. Likewise, the prevalence of child soldiers in certain parts of the world and the continued executions of a handful of child offenders worldwide do not dilute the power of these norms.

That being said, all norms within the global model of childhood are not created equal. The variation in norm compliance within the children's rights regime is the result of a number of factors, including the content of norms and their compatibility with other prevailing norms in a given culture or society, as well as the ease of implementation and the centrality of decision making. First, the content of norms about children matters, and the class of children most likely to benefit from protections may affect compliance. The norm against the child death penalty demands protection for the least sympathetic children—usually those that commit rape and murder—society's hardest cases. By contrast, norms against child abuse are directed at far more sympathetic children, resulting in an easier path to legalization and state compliance. Chapters 3 and 6 document this process in England, France, and the United States.

State resources and infrastructure are also important. The child death penalty is actually one of the easiest prohibitions materially to implement. Ending the penalty itself requires no additional infrastructure, as prisons and other facilities to house criminals already exist. Compared with norms that require free, universal primary school—a huge financial burden on poor countries—the abolition of the child death penalty is practically without cost. No state executes enough child offenders to argue that the cost of their imprisonment in terms of food, shelter, and facilities imposes too great a financial burden on the state.

The centrality of decision making also affects compliance with norms of child protection. Campaigns against child labor and child soldiers, for example, must address the practices of numerous nonstate actors. By contrast, campaigns to end the child death penalty target a single actor: the state. Although the level of centralization varies somewhat (chapter 6 details the regional challenges to state authority in Pakistan and the difficulties inherent in the US federal system), the norm against the child death penalty, being state- and policy-specific, is generally far more centralized than other issues and areas of child protection. More centralized norms, *ceteris paribus*, should lend themselves to greater compliance with less effort.

Finally, the global model of childhood exerts an ideological pull. It does not, as chapter 1 makes clear, wield material authority over childhood; it cannot back most of its principles with coercion. As a result, the model of childhood coexists with egregious violations of that model. Nonetheless, ideological models—especially those supported by international law, national practice, and a global consensus—are powerful vehicles of change in the international system. Remarkable change in the lives of children has occurred in the last few centuries. Yet the quality of that change continues to stoke debate, as the next section makes clear.

The New Moral 'Imperialism'

There have been two major critiques of the international human rights regime in the international relations literature: its presumed Western origins; and the inability of developing states in the Global South to shape human rights norms themselves, thus denying or calling into question a truly global consensus. The norm against the child death penalty helps to unpack these critiques. First, it is uncertain where the idea of childhood first emerged, when children began to be treated differently from adults, and when special consideration was first given in judging their actions. According to my research, however, it is clear that an age-based understanding of childhood, marked by the parameters of birth (or conception) to age 18, spread throughout the world because some Western states adopted it and because the British and French advanced it in their colonies and promoted its acceptance by the international community after World War II.

As such, the West did not *create* childhood. Rather, a particular construct or model of childhood emerged in some Western states—a childhood based on age rather than on rite or ritual, ability, responsibility, or circumstance— that was consistent with other ideas of Western political order, including democracy and individual rights. Age as a marker of childhood became a tool of states that required uniform standards to regulate the treatment and welfare of children, standards that could be consistently applied by multiple bureaucracies. The size and complexity of the state as a regulatory power required a clear and simple classification of childhood, a system not subject to the arbitrary discretion of untold numbers of state employees and disparate agencies individually determining if certain rites had occurred or if a degree of mental maturity or intellectual acumen had been reached. The British and French in their colonies and, later, the international community, needed the same large-scale classification system; an age-based definition of childhood met these objectives. The key distinction here is between the origins of child protection *in general* and the origin of a particular type of child protection that was age based. There is no evidence to suggest that the former had its origins in the West, while the latter was likely a unique Western construct in societies that required the establishment of common standards to facilitate state regulation. It is evident from my research that the West interpreted child protection in a way that would become dominant throughout the world by the end of the twentieth century.

The diffusion of the norm against the child death penalty also suggests a nuanced understanding of the agency of the Global South. When norms of childhood, including the ban on the child death penalty, were first adopted in international law (such as in the ICCPR), newly independent states like Algeria and Kenya were not in a position to influence the norms' content to any meaningful degree. Just as the United States was at a disadvantage in the timing of its opposition to the norm against the child death penalty, former colonies were similarly disadvantaged in the timing of the human rights regime in general. The regime began in the decades after World War II, at a time when many states in the Global South were in their formative years and unable to shape emerging norms. As a result, many norms became embedded in the international system before a great many states gained a voice in the international arena.

The CRC, however, is a postcolonial treaty, one that arguably enjoys a high level of support and consensus within the international community. Yet Maria Grahn-Farley has argued that even the CRC, the most widely ratified human rights convention, possesses a "colonial dynamic" that is exposed when you examine the response by Western states to reservations made to the treaty by former colonies.[6] Grahn-Farley states, "international law is colonial within the legal method itself. Even when both the substance of the law and the procedural rules can be seen as neutral, a deep colonial structure remains."[7] Studies like these call upon us to look beyond the neutrality and objectivity of the content of the law itself, and to cast a critical eye on the processes of drafting, argumentation, and consensus-building that create international law. Nonetheless, norms are

6. Maria Grahn-Farley, "Neutral Law and Eurocentric Lawmaking: A Postcolonial Analysis of the UN Convention on the Rights of the Child," *Brooklyn Journal of International Law* 34, no. 1 (2009): 3.

7. Ibid., 4.

emerging from the Global South in other ways. Constructivists (and now sociological institutionalists) suggest that some norms from the South may be publicized and diffused by a new kind of agency: NGOs (many from the South) may be able to effectively navigate the human rights regime and to shape norms and institutions that were previously the domain of just a few powerful actors.

References to civilization were characteristic of all three mechanisms of diffusion and every temporal period of normative spread. Early principled activists relied on the language of humanitarianism and a civilized social order in their efforts to enact domestic-level change. Later principled activists made provocative comparisons between countries like the United States for its practice of the child death penalty and states not considered part of international society, such as Iran, Nigeria, and the DRC. British and French colonialists premised the colonial mission in part upon the dubious idea of bringing the benefits of civilization to the colonies.

The successful use of civilizing rhetoric as part of all mechanisms of diffusion and temporal periods reviewed in this book indicates that the discourse of civilization may be instrumental to the diffusion of human rights ideas and norms generally. It is principally on this basis that critical theorists raise concerns about the "new moral imperialism of childhood," and about the homogenization or uniform conception of children's nature and abilities and the standardization of children's lives throughout the world.[8] These theorists suggest that children have become part of the civilizing mission of the international community, and that an inability to meet norms and standards of childhood advanced by the international community makes states vulnerable to intervention.[9] Indeed, states in the Global South that fail to meet human rights standards increase their risk of intervention, a risk already high due to weak international standing. Not surprisingly, children have been part of intervention rhetoric in many recent conflicts—in Afghanistan, Sudan, and most recently, Syria.

8. Pupavac, "Misanthropy without Borders"; Karen Valenin and Lotte Meinert, "The Adult North and the Young South: Reflections on the Civilizing Mission of Children's Rights," *Anthropology Today* 25, no. 3 (2009): 23–28; Watson, "Children and International Relations"; Alison Watson, "Saving More Than the Children: The Role of Child-Focused NGOs in the Creation of Southern Security Norms," *Third World Quarterly* 27, no. 2 (2006): 227–237; Jo Boyden, "Childhood and the Policy Makers: A Comparative Perspective on the Globalization of Childhood," in *Constructing and Reconstructing Childhood: Contemporary Issues in the Sociological Study of Childhood*, eds. Allison James and Alan Prout (New York: Falmer, 1990): 187–210; Bloch, *Governing Children*; Bloch, "The Child in the World."

9. Pupavac, "Misanthropy without Borders"; Lewis, "Human Rights"; Watson, "Children and International Relations."

Finally, as this book has shown, the liberal state model with its monopoly on legitimacy requires that states protect children in accordance with the global model of childhood. Membership in the international community of states and global society is the ultimate badge of civilization, denoting a shared set of values, including a commitment to humanitarianism, and to the common goals of progress and justice.

CONCLUSION

The story of the norm against the death penalty for child offenders is a story about social change. This study has demonstrated that remarkable social change can begin with the ideas and convictions of individuals. Moreover, it has shown that principled activism is not an obsolete notion in international affairs. Principled actors continue to shape and reshape our very conception of the possible in terms of human rights and a just society.

Nonetheless, the successful diffusion of the norm against the child death penalty and the elevation of children in the international sphere obscures the violence of this history. As the state and the international community developed by defining and regulating progress and justice, childhood was a key site of intervention. As children's competence, and thus culpability, waned over time, children needed the state and, eventually, the international community, to protect and empower them. As symbols of progress and justice, children feature prominently in the established narrative of a global people escaping the barbarism and chaos of the past and embracing an international order that is comforting in its normative homogeneity.

APPENDIX A

Documented Executions of Children in England in the Nineteenth Century

Year	Location of Execution (if Known)	Name (Age) and Crime (if Known)
1800		Boy (10), for "secreting notes at the Chelmsford Post Office"[1]
1801		Andrew Brenning, boy (13), for stealing a spoon,[2] possibly commuted[3]
1808	Lynn	Girl (7)[4]
1808	Lynn	Michael Hamond (7) and sister (11), for felony[5]
1814	Old Bailey	Four boys: Morris (8), Solomons (9), Fusler (12), and Wolfe (12),[6] for burglary[7]
1814		Burrel, boy (11), for stealing a pair of shoes[8]
1831	Chelmsford	Boy (9), for setting a house on fire[9]
1831	Maidstone	John Any Bird Bell, boy (13), for murder[10]
1833		Nicholas White, boy (9), for pushing a stick through a window and stealing, likely reprieved[11]
1887		Boy (14), for stealing[12]
1887		Joseph Morely (17), for murder[13]

1. Koestler, *Reflections on Hanging*, 20.
2. Ibid., 21. Christoph, *Capital Punishment and British Politics*, 15.
3. Harry Potter, *Hanging in Judgment* (London: SCM, 1993): 7.
4. Christoph, *Capital Punishment and British Politics*, 15.
5. Pritchard, *A History of Capital Punishment*, 18.
6. Pinchbeck and Hewitt, *Children in English Society*, 352.
7. Teeters, Hang by the Neck, 319.
8. Ibid.
9. Teeters places this execution in Plemscourt. See also Christoph, *Capital Punishment and British Politics*, 15; Koestler, *Reflections on Hanging*, 21; Pritchard, *A History of Capital Punishment*, 18; Teeters, Hang by the Neck, 13.
10. Koestler, *Reflections on Hanging*, 21.
11. Ibid.
12. Potter, "Hanging in Judgment," 7.
13. Radzinowicz and Hood, *A History of English Criminal Law*, 679.

APPENDIX B

————— ⌁ —————

Jurisdictions that Abolished the Death Penalty for Child Offenders under the Age of 18 Prior to *Roper v. Simmons*

California
   Cal. Penal Code Ann. §190.5 (West 1988)
Colorado
   Colo. Rev. Stat. §1611-103(1)(a) (1986)
Connecticut
   Conn. Gen. Stat. §53a-46a(g)(1) (1989)
Illinois
   Ill. Comp. Stat. Ann. ch. 720, § 5/9-1(b) (West 1992)
Indiana
   Ind. Code Ann. §35-50-2-3 (1993)
Kansas
   Kan. Stat. Ann. §21-4622 (1995)
Maryland
   Md. Ann. Code, Art. 27, § 412(f) (Supp. 1988)
Montana
   Mont. Code Ann. §45-5-102 (2003)
Nebraska
   Neb. Rev. Stat. §28-105.01 (1985)
New Jersey
   N.J. Stat. Ann. §2A:4A-22(a) (West 1987) and N.J. Stat. Ann. §2C:11-3(g) (West Supp. 1988)

New Mexico

N.M. Stat. Ann. §§ 28-6-1(A), 31-18-14(A) (1987)

New York

N.Y. Penal Law Ann. §125.27 (West 2004)

Ohio

Ohio Rev. Code Ann. §2929.02(A) (1987)

Oregon

Or. Rev. Stat. §§161.620 and Or. Rev. Stat. 419.476(1) (1987)

South Dakota

2004 S.D. Laws ch. 166 to be codified in S.D. Codified Laws §23A—27A—42

Tennessee

Tenn. Code Ann. §§37-1-102(3), 37-1-102(4), 37-1103, 37-1-134(a)(1) (1984 and Supp. 1988)

Washington

Minimum age of 18 established by judicial decision. *State v. Furman*, 122 Wash. 2d 440, 858 P.2d 1092 (1993)

Wyoming

Wyo. Stat. §6-2-101(b)

Federal

18 United States Code § 3591(a)(2)(D), 18 United States Code § 3591 (b)(2) (1994)

BIBLIOGRAPHY

Achvarina, Vera, and Simon F. Reich. "No Place to Hide: Refugees, Displaced Persons, and the Recruitment of Child Soldiers." *International Security* 31, no. 1 (2006): 127–164.

Aderinto, Saheed. "'The Girls in Moral Danger': Child Prostitution and Sexuality in Colonial Lagos, Nigeria, 1930s to 1950." *Journal of Humanities and Social Science* 1, no. 2 (2007): 1–22.

Adler, Emanuel. "Constructivism and International Relations." In *Handbook of International Relations*, edited by Walter Carlsnaes, Thomas Risse-Kappen, and Beth Simmons, 112–145. London: Sage, 2002.

African Commission on Human and Peoples' Rights, The Working Group on the Death Penalty in Africa. "Study on the Question of the Death Penalty in Africa," adopted at the 50th Ordinary Session (24 October–7 November 2011), Banjul, The Gambia.

Agozino, Biko. "Crisis of Authoritarianism in the Legal Institutions." *Journal of Contemporary Criminal Justice* 19, no. 3 (2003): 315–329.

Aguilar, Mario I. *Rethinking Age in Africa: Colonial, Post-Colonial, and Contemporary Interpretations of Cultural Representations.* Trenton, NJ: Africa World, 2007.

Ahlberg, Beth Maina. *Women, Sexuality and the Changing Social Order.* Philadelphia: Gordon and Breach, 1991.

Ahmad, Khabir. "The Battle for Children's Rights in Pakistan." *The Lancet* 365, no. 9468 (2005): 1376–1377.

Allen, Howard W., Jerome M. Clubb, and Vincent A. Lacey. *Race, Class, and the Death Penalty: Capital Punishment in American History.* Albany, NY: State University of New York Press, 2008.

Alston, Philip, and John Tobin. *"Laying the Foundation for Children's Rights."* UNICEF Innocenti Research Centre. Florence, Italy: UNICEF, 2005.

Amin, Akhtar. "Following in Footsteps of Other Nations: Rights Groups Want End to Death Penalty." *Daily Times*, October 11, 2008.

Amnesty International. "1989 Campaign against the Death Penalty: Country Appeals Series, Circular No. 17f: Recommended Actions and Addresses on USA, AMR 51/09/89." University of Minnesota Law School: Private Archives of David Weissbrodt, March 1, 1989.

Amnesty International. "Children and the Death Penalty: Executions Worldwide since 1990, ACT 50/007/2002." 2002.

Amnesty International. "Country: United States of America: Subect Title: The Death Penalty: Developments in 1987 Amr 51/01/88." University of Minnesota: Private Archives of David Weissbrodt, 1988.

Amnesty International. "Death Sentences and Executions in 2012." ACT 50/001/ 2013, April 10, 2013.

Amnesty International. "Death Sentences and Executions in 2014." ACT 50/0001/ 2015, March 31, 2015. https://www.amnesty.org/en/documents/act50/0001/ 2015/en/.

Amnesty International. "Executions of Juveniles since 1990." http://www.amnesty. org/en/death-penalty/executions-of-child-offenders-since-1990.

Amnesty International. "The Exclusion of Child Offenders from the Death Penalty under General International Law, Act 50/004/2003." July 17, 2003.

Amnesty International. "Facts and Figures on the Death Penalty." Amnesty International, 2005.

Amnesty International. "Juveniles Amongst 12 Prisoners Executed Overnight in Pakistan." March 17, 2015. http://www.amnestyusa.org/news/news-item/ juveniles-amongst-12-prisoners-executed-overnight-in-pakistan.

Amnesty International. "Pakistan: Death Penalty for Juveniles." AI Index: ASA 33/ 07/95. 1995.

Amnesty International. "Pakistan: Death Penalty for Juveniles Reintroduced." AI Index: ASA 33/025/2004. 2004.

Amnesty International. "People's Republic of China: Executed 'According to the Law?' The Death Penalty in China." March 17, 2004. http://www.refworld.org/ docid/4129cf224.html.

Amnesty International. "People's Republic of China: The Olympics Countdown– Broken Promises." 2008.

Amnesty International. "Report of the International Meeting on the Death Penalty 27–29 March 1987, ACT 05/24/87." University of Minnesota Law School: Private Archives of David Weissbrodt, 1987.

Amnesty International. "Stop Child Executions!" New York, 2006. www.ac-t500022004en.pdf.

Amnesty International. *United States of America: Indecent and Internationally Illegal: The Death Penalty against Child Offenders.* AMR 51/144/2002. London, UK: Amnesty International, 2002.

Amnesty International. "United States of America: The Death Penalty and Juvenile Offenders," AMR 51/23/91, 1991.

Amnesty International. "USA: Supreme Court Outlaws Executions of Child Offenders." New York, 2005.

Amnesty International, International Council, and Working Party B. "Pre-Council Meeting on Death Penalty Held on Thursday 15 September." University of Minnesota Law School: Private Archives of David Weissbrodt, 1977.

Amnesty International, and International Secretariat. "Death Penalty Handbook: External, Part 2: International Legal Standards on the Death Penalty, ACT 05/ 17/82." University of Minnesota: Private Archives of David Weissbrodt, 1982.

Amnesty International USA. *Killing with Prejudice: Race and the Death Penalty.* New York: Amnesty International USA, 1999.

Amnesty International USA. "The Pakistan Campaign 1981." University of Colorado Boulder, AIUSA Archives, 1981.

Amnesty International USA, and A. Whitney Ellsworth. "Background Paper for AIUSA AGM Working Party on Death Penalty." University of Minnesota: Private Archives of David Weissbrodt, Unknown year.

Anckar, Carsten. *Determinants of the Death Penalty: A Comparative Study of the World.* Routledge Research in Comparative Politics 8. New York: Routledge, 2004.

Anderson, David. *Histories of the Hanged: The Dirty War in Kenya and the End of Empire.* New York: W.W. Norton, 2005.

Anderson, J.N.D. *Islamic Law in Africa.* London: Colonial Research Publication, Her Majesty's Stationery Office, 1954.

Ariès, Phillipe. *Centuries of Childhood.* New York: Knopf, 1962.

Armstrong, David. "The Invention of Infant Mortality." *Sociology of Health and Illness* 8, no. 3 (1986): 211–232.

Armstrong, David. *Political Anatomy of the Body: Medical Knowledge in Britain in the Twentieth Century.* Cambridge, UK: Cambridge University Press, 1983.

Ashurst, Francesca, and Couze Venn. *Inequality, Poverty and Education: A Political Economy of School Exclusion.* New York: Palgrave Macmillan, 2014.

Austin, John, and Sarah Austin. *The Province of Jurisprudence Determined.* 2nd ed. London: J. Murray, 1861–1863.

Austin, John, Robert Campbell, and Sarah Austin. *Lectures on Jurisprudence, or, the Philosophy of Positive Law.* 3rd ed. London: J. Murray, 1869.

Austin, John, and Wilfrid E. Rumble. *The Province of Jurisprudence Determined.* Cambridge Texts in the History of Political Thought. New York and Cambridge: Cambridge University Press, 1995.

Bae, Sangmin. "The Death Penalty and the Peculiarity of American Political Institutions." *Human Rights Review* 9, no. 2 (2008): 233–240.

Bae, Sangmin. "The Right to Life vs. the State's Ultimate Sanction: Abolition of Capital Punishment in Post-Apartheid South Africa." *International Journal of Human Rights* 9, no. 1 (2005): 49–68.

Bae, Sangmin. *When the State No Longer Kills: International Human Rights Norms and Abolition of Capital Punishment.* SUNY Series in Human Rights. Albany, NY: State University of New York Press, 2007.

Bailey, Martin. *The Union of Tanganyika and Zanzibar: A Study in Political Integration.* Syracuse, NY: Syracuse University, 1973.

Bailey, Victor. *Delinquency and Citizenship: Reclaiming the Young Offender, 1914–1948.* Oxford: Oxford University Press, 1987.

Baistow, Karen. "From Sickly Survival to the Realisation of Potential: Child Health as a Social Project in Twentieth Century England." *Children & Society* 9, no. 1 (1995): 20–35.

Bakken, Borge. "Crime, Juvenile Delinquency, and Deterrence Policy in China." *The Australian Journal of Chinese Affairs* 30 (1993): 29–58.

Barkan, Joel D. "Comparing Politics and Public Policy in Kenya and Tanzania." In *Politics and Public Policy in Kenya and Tanzania*, edited by Joel D. Barkan and John J. Okumu, 3–40. New York: Praeger, 1979.

Barnett, Michael. "Social Constructivism." In *The Globalization of World Politics*, edited by John Baylis and Steve Smith, 148–166. New York: Oxford University Press, 2005.

Barnett, Michael, and Raymond Duvall. "Power in International Politics." *International Organization* 59, No. 1 (2005): 39–75.

Bartholet, Elizabeth. "Ratification by the United States of the Convention on the Rights of the Child: Pros and Cons from a Child's Rights Perspective." *The Annals of the American Academy of Political and Social Science* 633 (2011): 80–101.

Baumgartner, Frank R., Suzanna De Boef, and Amber E. Boydstun. *The Decline of the Death Penalty and the Discovery of Innocence.* Cambridge and New York: Cambridge University Press, 2008.

Beckstrom, John H. "Transplantation of Legal Systems: An Early Report on the Reception of Western Laws in Ethiopia." *The American Journal of Comparative Law* 21, no. 3 (1973): 557–583.

Bedau, Hugo Adam, ed. *The Death Penalty in America: Current Controversies*. New York: Oxford University Press, 1997.

Ben-Arieh, Asher, and Robert Goerge. "Beyond the Numbers: How Do We Monitor the State of Our Children?" *Children and Youth Services Review* 23, no. 8 (2001): 603–631.

Bennett, William J., John J. Dilulio, et al. *Body Count: Moral Poverty—and How to Win America's War against Crime and Drugs*. New York: Simon & Schuster, 1996.

Benoit, Ellen. "Not Just a Matter of Criminal Justice: States, Institutions, and North American Drug Policy." *Sociological Forum* 18, no. 2 (2003): 269–294.

Benton, Lauren. *Law and Colonial Cultures: Legal Regimes in World History, 1400–1900*. Cambridge, UK: Cambridge University Press, 2002.

Black, Maggie. *Children First: The Story of UNICEF, Past and Present*. New York: Oxford University Press, 1996.

Blacker, John. "The Demography of Mau Mau: Fertility and Mortality in Kenya in the 1950s: A Demographer's Viewpoint." *African Affairs* 106, no. 423 (2007): 205–227.

Bloch, Marianne N. *Governing Children, Families, and Education: Restructuring the Welfare State*. New York: Palgrave Macmillan, 2003.

Bloch, Marianne N., Devorah Kennedy, Theodora Lightfoot, and Dar Weyenberg, *The Child in the World/The World in the Child: Education and the Configuration of a Universal, Modern, and Globalized Childhood*. Basingstoke, UK: Palgrave Macmillan, 2006.

Bob, Clifford. *The Marketing of Rebellion: Insurgents, Media, and International Activism*. Cambridge, UK: Cambridge University Press, 2004.

Bohman, James. "Children and the Rights of Citizens: Nondomination and Intergenerational Justice." *The Annals of the American Academy of Political and Social Science* 633 (2011): 128–140.

Boli, John, and George M. Thomas. *Constructing World Culture: International Nongovernmental Organizations since 1875*. Stanford, CA: Stanford University Press, 1999.

Boli-Bennett, John, and John W. Meyer. "The Ideology of Childhood and the State: Rules Distinguishing Children in National Constitutions, 1870–1970." *American Sociological Review* 43, no. 6 (1978): 797–812.

Borchenek, Michael. Human Rights Watch. "Dispatches: Executions Down, But Not for Juvenile Offenders." April 1, 2015. https://www.hrw.org/news/2015/04/01/dispatches-executions-down-not-juvenile-offenders.

Boyden, Jo. "Childhood and the Policy Makers: A Comparative Perspective on the Globalization of Childhood." In *Constructing and Reconstructing Childhood: Contemporary Issues in the Sociological Study of Childhood*, edited by Allison James and Alan Prout, 184–215. New York: Falmer, 1990.

Boyea, Brent D. "Linking Judicial Selection to Consensus." *American Politics Research* 35, no. 5 (2007): 643–670.

Brace, Paul, and Brent D. Boyea. "State Public Opinion, the Death Penalty, and the Practice of Electing Judges." *American Journal of Political Science* 52, no. 2 (2008): 360–372.

Bradley, Curtis A. "The Juvenile Death Penalty and International Law." *Duke Law Journal* 52, no. 3 (2002): 485–557.

Bremmer, Robert H., ed. *Children and Youth in America: A Documentary History*. Vol. 1, Part 1, 1660–1865. Cambridge, MA: Harvard University Press, 1970.

Bremmer, Robert H., ed. *Children and Youth in America: A Documentary History*. Vol. 2, 1866–1932. Cambridge, MA: Harvard University Press, 1971.

Bremmer, Robert H., ed. *Children and Youth in America: A Documentary History*. Vol. 3, 1933–1973. Cambridge, MA: Harvard University Press, 1974.

Brewer, Holly. *By Birth or Consent: Children, Law, & the Anglo-American Revolution in Authority*. Chapel Hill, NC: The University of North Carolina Press, 2005.

Brocklehurst, Helen. *Who's Afraid of Children: Children, Conflict, and International Relations*. Surrey, UK: Ashgate, 2006.

Burke-White, William. "International Legal Pluralism." *Michigan Journal of International Law* 25, no. 963 (2004): 963–979.

Burman, Erica. "Developing Differences: Gender, Childhood and Economic Development." *Children & Society* 9, no. 3 (1995): 121–142.

Burton, Antoinette. "From Child Bride to 'Hindoo Lady': Rukhmabai and the Debate on Sexual Respectability in Imperial Britain." *The American Historical Review* 103, no. 4 (1998): 1119–1146.

Cahill, Mia. "The Legal Problem of Sexual Harassment and Its International Diffusion." In *How Claims Spread: Cross-National Diffusion of Social Problems*, edited by Joel Best, 243–265. New York: Walter De Gruyter, 2001.

Calder, Ritchie. *Growing up with UNICEF*. Public Affairs Pamphlet No. 330. New York: Public Affairs Pamphlets, 1962.

Cambridge Survey Research and Amnesty International. "An Analysis of Political Attitudes Towards the Death Penalty in the State of Florida." Washington, DC: Cambridge Survey Research, 1986. http://www.worldcat.org/title/analysis-of-political-attitudes-towards-the-death-penalty-in-the-state-of-florida-executive-summary/oclc/22528994.

Campbell, Chloe. "Juvenile Delinquency in Colonial Kenya, 1900–1939." *The Historical Journal* 45, no. 1 (2002): 129–151.

Canagarajah, Sudharshan, and Helena Skyt Nielson. "Child Labor in Africa: A Comparative Study." *Annals of the American Academy of Political and Social Science* 575 (2001): 71–91.

Carpenter, R. Charli. "Surfacing Children: Limitations of Genocidal Rape Discourse." *Human Rights Quarterly* 22, no. 2 (2000): 428–477.

Carpenter, R. Charli. "Setting the Advocacy Agenda: Theorizing Issue Emergence and Nonemergence in Transnational Advocacy Networks." *International Studies Quarterly* 51, no. 1 (2007): 99–120.

Carpenter, R. Charli. "Studying Issue (Non)-Adoption in Transnational Advocacy Networks." *International Organization* 61, no. 3 (2007): 643–667.

Case of Pinkerton v. Roach, 9647, OEA/Ser.L/V/II.71, doc. 9 rev. 1 (1987). Inter-American Commission on Human Rights, Report No. 25/05.

Chanock, Martin. "The Law Market: The Legal Encounter in British East and Central Africa." In *European Expansion and Law: The Encounter of European and Indigenous Law in 19th- and 20th-Century Africa and Asia*, edited by W.J. Mommsen and J.A. De Moor, 279–305. New York: Berg, 1992.

Charrad, Mounira M. *States and Women's Rights: The Making of Postcolonial Tunisia, Algeria, and Morocco*. Berkeley, CA: University of California Press, 2001.

Chayes, Abram, and Antonia Handler Chayes. "On Compliance." *International Organization* 47, no. 2 (1993): 175–205.

Checkel, Jeffrey. "Norms, Institutions, and National Identity in Contemporary Europe." *International Studies Quarterly* 43, no. 1 (1999): 83–114.

Chen, Weixia. "The Death Penalty in Japan and China: A Comparative Study." MA thesis, University of California, 2003.

Chiba, Masaji. *Legal Pluralism: Toward a General Theory through Japanese Legal Culture.* Tokyo: Tokai University Press, 1989.

Chowdhry, Geeta, and Mark Beeman. "Challenging Child Labor: Transnational Activism and India's Carpet Industry." *Annals of the American Academy of Political and Social Science* 575 (2001): 158–175.

Christoph, James B. *Capital Punishment and British Politics: The British Movement to Abolish the Death Penalty, 1945–57.* Chicago: University of Chicago Press, 1962.

Clancy-Smith, Julia Ann, and Frances Gouda. *Domesticating the Empire: Race, Gender, and Family Life in French and Dutch Colonialism.* Charlottesville, VA: University of Virginia Press, 1998.

Clark, Ann Marie. *Diplomacy of Conscience: Amnesty International and Changing Human Rights Norms.* Princeton, NJ: Princeton University Press, 2001.

Clark, Anthony Arend, Robert J. Beck, and Robert van der Lugt, eds. *International Rules: Approaches from International Law and International Relations.* Oxford: Oxford University Press, 1996.

Clark, Ian. *International Legitimacy and World Society.* New York: Oxford University Press, 2007.

Cole, Wade M. "Sovereignty Relinquished? Explaining Commitment to the International Human Rights Covenants, 1966–1999." *American Sociological Review* 70, no. 3 (2005): 472–495.

Collingwood, J.J.R. *Criminal Law of East and Central Africa.* London: Sweet & Maxwell, 1967.

Committee on the Rights of the Child. "Second Periodic Report: Algeria Crc/C/93/Add.7." 2003.

Committee on the Rights of the Child. "Second Periodic Report: Tunisia Crc/C/83/Add.1." 2001.

Conner, Adam, and Betsy William. "Banning the Juvenile Death Penalty: Success through Funding of Nonprofit Advocacy and Coalition Work." *Responsive Philanthropy: The NCRP Quarterly.* 2005. https://ncrp.org/files/rp-articles/PDF/RP-Summer-2005-Banning_the_Juvenile_Death_Penalty.pdf.

Cook, Philip J., and John H. Laub. "The Unprecedented Epidemic in Youth Violence." *Crime and Justice* 24 (1998): 27–64.

Cunningham, Hugh. *Children and Childhood in Western Society since 1500.* New York: Longman, 1995.

Dalberg-Larsen, Jørgen. *The Unity of Law, an Illusion?: On the Legal Pluralism in Theory and Practice,* Mobility and Norm Change 2. Glienicke/Berlin and Cambridge, MA: Galda + Wilch, 2000.

Daston, Lorraine, and Peter Galison. "The Image of Objectivity." In Special Issue: *Seeing Science. Representations* 40 (1992): 81–128.

de Berry, Jo. "Child Soldiers and the Convention on the Rights of the Child." *Annals of the American Academy of Political and Social Science* no. 575 (2001): 92–105.

de la Vega, Connie, and Jennifer Fiore. "The Supreme Court of the United States Has Been Called Upon to Determine the Legality of the Juvenile Death Penalty in *Michael Domingues v. State of Nevada.*" *Whittier L.Rev* 215 (1999): 225–226.

de Mause, Lloyd, ed. *The History of Childhood.* New York: The Psychohistory Press, 1974.

Donnelly, Jack. *Universal Human Rights in Theory and Practice.* 2nd ed. Ithaca, NY: Cornell University Press, 2003.

Donzelot, Jacques, and Robert Hurley. *The Policing of Families*. Baltimore: Johns Hopkins University Press, 1997.

Dow, David, and Mark Dow. *Machinery of Death: The Reality of America's Death Penalty Regime*. New York: Routledge, 2002.

Downs, George W., David M. Rocke, and Peter N. Barsoom. "Is the Good News About Compliance Good News About Cooperation." *International Organization* 50, no. 3 (1996): 379–406.

Ducheneaux, Karen. "Governor Signs Bill to Ban Execution of Juveniles." *Associated Press* and *Rapid City Journal*, March 4, 2004.

Duke, Emma. "Infant Mortality; Results of a Field Study in Johnstown, Pa, Publication No. 9." Washington, DC: United States Children's Bureau, 1915, reprint.

Dupret, Baudouin, Maurits Berger, and Laila Al-Zwaini. *Legal Pluralism in the Arab World*. Arab and Islamic Laws Series 18. Boston: Kluwer Law International, 1999.

Dvorak, John. "Kansas Approved Death Penalty after 22 Years; Governor Says She Won't Fight Law." *Kansas City Star*, April 9, 1994.

Earls, Felton. "Children: From Rights to Citizenship." *The Annals of the American Academy of Political and Social Science* 633, no. 1 (2011): 6–16.

Elias, Norbert. *The Civilizing Process*. Vol. 1, *The History of Manners*. New York: Urizen Books, 1978.

Elias, T. Olawale. *British Colonial Law: A Comparative Study of the Interaction between English and Local Laws in British Dependencies*. London: Stevens & Sons, 1962.

Elikann, Peter. *Superpredators: The Demonization of Our Children by the Law*. New York: Insight, 1999.

Elkins, Zachary, and Beth Simmons. "On Waves, Clusters, and Diffusion: A Conceptual Framework." *The Annals of the American Academy of Political and Social Science* 598, no. 1 (2005): 33–51.

Entelis, John P. *Algeria: The Revolution Institutionalized*. Boulder, CO: Westview, 1986.

European Union, Council of the European Union, *Guidelines to European Policy Towards Third Countries on the Death Penalty*, 29 June, 1998. http://www.consilium.europa.eu/uedocs/cmsUpload/Guidelines%20DeathPenalty.pdf.

Espy, M. Watt, and John Ortiz Smykla. "Executions in the U.S. 1608–2002: The Espy File [Computer File]." Interuniversity Consortium for Political and Social Research, 2002.

Fagan, Jeffrey, and Valerie West. "The Decline of the Juvenile Death Penalty: Scientific Evidence of Evolving Norms." *Journal of Criminal Law and Criminology* 95, no. 2 (2005): 427–497.

Farrell, Ronald A., and Victoria L. Swigert. "Legal Disposition of Inter-Group and Intra-Group Homicides." *The Sociological Quarterly* 19, no. 4 (1978): 565–576.

Fass, Paula S. "A Historical Context for the United Nations Convention on the Rights of the Child." *The Annals of the American Academy of Political and Social Science* 633 (2011): 17–29.

Faulkner, Frank. "Kindergarten Killers: Morality, Murder and the Child Soldier Problem." *Third World Quarterly* 22, no. 4 (2001): 491–504.

Feld, Barry C. *Bad Kids: Race and the Transformation of the Juvenile Court*, Studies in Crime and Public Policy. New York: Oxford University Press, 1999.

Finnemore, Martha. "Norms, Culture, and World Politics: Insights from Sociology's Institutionalism." *International Organization* 50, no. 2 (1996): 325–347.

Finnemore, Martha, and Kathryn Sikkink. "International Norm Dynamics and Political Change." In *Exploration and Contestation in the Study of World Politics*, edited by Peter J. Katzenstein, Robert O. Keohane, and Stephen D. Krasner, 247–279. Cambridge, MA: MIT Press, 1999.

Finnemore, Martha, and Stephen J. Toope. "Alternatives to 'Legalization': Richer Views of Law and Politics." *International Organization* 55, no. 3 (2001): 743–758.

Fisher, Stanley Z. *Ethiopian Criminal Procedure: A Sourcebook*. Addis Ababa, Ethiopia: Haile Selassie University, 1969.

Fisher, Stanley Z. "Traditional Criminal Procedure in Ethiopia." *The American Journal of Comparative Law* 19, no. 4 (1971): 709–746.

Fishman, Sarah. *The Battle for Children: World War II, Youth Crime, and Juvenile Justice in Twentieth-Century France*. Cambridge, MA: Harvard University Press, 2002.

Fishman, Sarah. Personal correspondence. July 9, 2008.

Florini, Ann. *The Third Force: The Rise of Transnational Civil Society*. Tokyo and Washington: Carnegie Endowment for International Peace, 2000.

Foreign Area Studies at the American University, and Harold D. Nelson, eds. *Tunisia: A Country Study*. Washington, DC: Supt. Of Docs, United States Government, 1986.

Foreign Area Studies at the American University, and Irving Kaplan. *Tanzania: A Country Study*. Washington, DC: American University, 1978.

Former U.S. Diplomats Morton Abramowitz et al. as *Amici Curiae* 7. *Roper v. Simmons* No. 03-633. 543 U.S. 551 (2005).

Foucault, Michel. *The Birth of the Clinic: An Archeology of Medical Perception*. London: Tavistock, 1963.

Foucault, Michel. *Discipline and Punish: The Birth of the Prison*. 2nd ed. New York: Vintage Books, 1995.

Foucault, Michel. "Governmentality." In *The Foucault Effect: Studies in Governmentality*, edited by Graham Burchell, Colin Gordon, and Peter Miller, 87–105. Chicago: University of Chicago Press, 1991.

Foucault, Michel. *The History of Sexuality*. Vol. 1: *An Introduction*. Translated by Robert Hurley. New York: Vintage, 1981.

Foucault, Michel. *Madness and Civilization: A History of Insanity in the Age of Reason*. New York: Pantheon, 1965.

Fourchard, Laurent. "Lagos and the Invention of Juvenile Delinquency in Nigeria." *Journal of African History* 46 (2006): 115–137.

Fox, Jonathan. "Religion as an Overlooked Element in International Relations." *International Studies Review* 3, no. 3 (2001): 53–73.

Franck, Thomas M. *Fairness in International Law and Institutions*. New York: Oxford University Press, 1995.

Franck, Thomas M. "Legitimacy in the International System." *The American Journal of International Law* 82, no. 4 (1988): 705–759.

Frey, Barbara, and Mike Brehm. "20 Years Later: An Assessment of the Continuing Reticence of the United States to Ratify the United Nations Convention on the Rights of the Child." Working paper, 2010.

Frost, Nick, and Mike Stein. *The Politics of Child Welfare: Inequality, Power and Change*. New York: Harvester Wheatsheaf, 1989.

Fuchs, Rachel Ginnis. *Abandoned Children: Foundlings and Child Welfare in Nineteenth-Century France*. SUNY Series in Modern European Social History. Albany, NY: State University of New York Press, 1984.

Fuller, Edward. *An International Yearbook of Child Care and Protection.* London: Longman, 1925.

Fuller, Edward. *The International Yearbook of Child Care and Protection.* Vol. 2. London: Longman, 1925.

Fuller, Edward. *The International Handbook of Child Care and Protection.* Vol. 3. London: Save the Children Fund, 1928.

Fuller, Edward. *The Right of the Child: A Chapter in Social History.* London: Victor Gollancz, 1951.

Fulwood, Charles. Campaign Against the Death Penalty, and Amnesty International USA. "Strategy against the Death Penalty, Approved by the Board of Directors." University of Minnesota Law School: Private Archives of David Weissbrodt, November 18, 1984.

Gainborough, Jenni, and Elizabeth Lean. "Convention on the Rights of the Child and Juvenile Justice." *The Link: Connecting Juvenile Justice and Child Welfare, Child Welfare League of America* 7, no. 1 (2008): 1–14.

Galliher, James M., and John F. Galliher. "A 'Commonsense' Theory of Deterrence and the 'Ideology' of Science: The New York State Death Penalty Debate." *Journal of Criminal Law and Criminology* 92, no. 1/2 (2001–2002): 307–334.

Garrison, Fielding H, and Arthur Fredrick Abt. *History of Pediatrics*, Philadelphia: W. B. Saunders, 1965.

Garvey, Stephen. *Beyond Repair? America's Death Penalty.* Durham, NC: Duke University Press, 2003.

Gatrell, V.A.C. *The Hanging Tree: Execution and the English People, 1770–1868.* Oxford: Oxford University Press, 1994.

Geiger, Andrea. "International Law--Juvenile Justice in Pakistan; Notes." *Suffolk Transnational Law Review* 23 (1999–2000): 713–746.

Gibson, Campbell, and Kay Jung. "Historical Census Statistics on Population Totals by Race, 1790 to 1990, and by Hispanic Origin, 1970 to 1990, for the United States, Regions, Divisions and States." *Working Paper Series No. 56. P. Division, U.S. Census Bureau* (2002). http://mapmaker.rutgers.edu/REFERENCE/Hist_Pop_stats.pdf.

Gibson, Richard. "Europeans Criticize America for Putting Minors to Death." *The Blade*, September 27, 1987, Section B, p. 1.

Gnaerig, Burkhard. "The Challenges of Globalization: Save the Children." *Nonprofit and Voluntary Sector Quarterly* 28, no. 1 (1999): 140–146.

Goldman, Jerry, and Timothy R. Johnson. "Exploring the Use of Foreign Law and Foreign Sources in the United States Supreme Court's Decision Making Process." Paper presented at the 2005 annual meeting of the American Political Science Association, Washington, DC, September 1–4, 2005.

Goldsmith, Jack L., and Eric A. Posner. "A Theory of Customary International Law." *University of Chicago Law Review* 66, no. 1113 (1999): 1113–1177.

Goldstein, Judith, Robert O. Keohane, and Social Science Research Council (US). Committee on Foreign Policy. *Ideas and Foreign Policy: Beliefs, Institutions, and Political Change*, Cornell Studies in Political Economy. Ithaca, NY: Cornell University Press, 1993.

Grahn-Farley, Maria. "Neutral Law and Eurocentric Lawmaking: A Postcolonial Analysis of the UN Convention on the Rights of the Child." *Brooklyn Journal of International Law* 34, no. 1 (2009): 1–266.

Greenberg, David F., and Valerie West. "Siting the Death Penalty Internationally." *Law & Social Inquiry* 33, no. 2 (2008): 295–343.

Grier, Beverly. "Invisible Hands: The Political Economy of Child Labour in Colonial Zimbabwe, 1890–1930." *Journal of Southern African Studies* 20, no. 1 (1994): 27–52.

Griffiths, John. "What Is Legal Pluralism?" *Journal of Legal Pluralism and Unofficial Law* 24, no. 1 (1986): 1–55.

Hafner-Burton, Emilie, and Kiyoteru Tsusui. "Human Rights in a Globalizing World: The Paradox of Empty Promises." *American Journal of Sociology* 110, no. 5 (2005): 1373–1411.

Hale, Robert L. *A Review of Juvenile Executions in America.* Criminology Studies 3. Lewiston, NY: Edwin Mellen, 1997.

Hall, Rodney Bruce. "Moral Authority as a Power Resource." *International Organization* 51, no. 4 (1997): 591–622.

Halls, W.D. *The Youth of Vichy France.* New York and Oxford: Oxford University Press, 1981.

Hands Off Cain. "The 2005 Report." 2005. http://www.handsoffcain.info/bancadati/index.php?tipotema=arg&idtema=6000633.

Harmen, Zena. "UNICEF: Achievement and Challenge." In *Nobel Lectures, Peace 1951–1970*, edited by Frederick W. Haberman. Amsterdam: Elsevier, 1972. http://www.nobelprize.org/nobel_prizes/peace/laureates/1965/unicef-lecture.html.

Hasenclever, Andreas, Peter Mayer, and Volker Rittberger. *Theories of International Regimes.* Vol. 55. Cambridge Studies in International Relations. Cambridge, UK: Cambridge University Press, 1997.

Hathaway, Oona A. "Why Do Countries Commit to Human Rights Treaties?" *Journal of Conflict Resolution* 51, no. 4 (2007): 588–621.

Hazlehurst, Kayleen M. *Legal Pluralism and the Colonial Legacy: Indigenous Experiences of Justice in Canada, Australia, and New Zealand.* Aldershot, UK: Avebury, 1995.

Healey, John G., and Amnesty International USA. "Memorandum: 1984–1985 Death Penalty Report, To: AIUSA Board of Directors." Archives of the University of Colorado at Boulder Libraries, AIUSA NY 378-17, 1985.

Heilbroner, Robert L. *Mankind's Children: The Story of UNICEF.* New York: The Public Affairs Committee, 1959.

Hendrick, Harry. *Children, Childhood, and English Society, 1880–1990.* Cambridge, UK: Cambridge University Press, 1997.

Henkin, Louis. *How Nations Behave; Law and Foreign Policy.* New York: F.A. Praeger, 1968.

Heywood, Colin. *Childhood in Nineteenth-Century France: Work, Health, and Education among the 'Classes Populaires.'* New York: Cambridge University Press, 1988.

Heywood, Jean S. *Children in Care: The Development of the Service for the Deprived Child.* 2nd ed. London: Routledge & Kegan Paul, 1965.

Hicks, Steve. "The Political Economy of War-Affected Children." *Annals of the American Academy of Political and Social Science* 575 (2001): 106–121.

Hirsch, David. *Law against Genocide: Cosmopolitan Trials.* Portland, OR: Glasshouse, 2003.

Holloway, Sarah, and Gill Valentine. *Children's Geographies: Playing, Living, Learning,* Critical Geographies 8. London and New York: Routledge, 2000.

Holzscheiter, Anna. *Children's Rights in International Politics.* New York: Palgrave Macmillan, 2010.

Hood, Roger. *The Death Penalty: A Worldwide Perspective.* Oxford: Oxford University Press, 2002.

Hooker, M.B. *Legal Pluralism: An Introduction to Colonial and Neo-Colonial Laws.* Oxford: Clarendon, 1975.

Hopf, Ted. "The Promise of Constructivism in International Relations Theory." *International Security* 23 (1998): 171–200.

Hopgood, Stephen. *Keepers of the Flame: Understanding Amnesty International.* Ithaca, NY: Cornell University Press, 2006.

Horowitz, Mirah A. "Kids Who Kill: A Critique of How the American Legal System Deals with Juveniles Who Commit Homicide." *Law and Contemporary Problems* 63, no. 3 (2000): 133–177.

Human Rights Watch. "Enforcing the International Prohibition on the Juvenile Death Penalty," May 30, 2008.

Human Rights Watch. "Iran Leads the World in Executing Children." June 19, 2007.

Human Rights Watch. "Iran, Saudi Arabia, Sudan: End Juvenile Death Penalty." October 8, 2010.

Human Rights Watch. "The Last Holdouts: Ending the Juvenile Death Penalty in Iran, Saudi Arabia, Sudan, Pakistan and Yemen." New York: 2008. https://www.hrw.org/reports/2008/crd0908/.

Humbaraci, Arslan. *Algeria: A Revolution That Failed; A Political History since 1954.* London: Pall Mall, 1966.

Hunt, Lynn. *Inventing Human Rights: A History.* New York: W.W. Norton, 2007.

Huntington, Samuel P. *The Third Wave: Democratization in the Late Twentieth Century.* Norman, OK: University of Oklahoma Press, 1991.

Hurd, Ian. "Legitimacy and Authority in International Politics." *International Organization* 53, no. 2 (1999): 379–408.

Hynd, Stacey. "Killing the Condemned: The Practice and Process of Capital Punishment in British Africa: 1900–1950s." *Journal of African History* 49, no. 3 (2008): 403–418.

Iliffe, John. *The African Poor: A History.* Cambridge, UK: Cambridge University Press, 1987.

Inter-American Commission on Human Rights. "*Pinkerton and Roach v. United States*," Annual Report of the Inter-American Commission on Human Rights, 147, Oea/Ser.L/V/Ii/71, Doc. 9, Rev. 1, Para. 56." 1986–1987.

International Federation for Human Rights, and Human Rights Commission for Pakistan. "Slow March to the Gallows: Death Penalty in Pakistan." Paris, January 2007. https://www.fidh.org/IMG/pdf/Pakistan464angconjointpdm.pdf.

Jackson, Jesse, Jesse Jackson, Jr., and Bruce Shapiro. *Legal Lynching: The Death Penalty and America's Future.* New York: New Press, 2001.

Jackson, Louise A. *Child Sexual Abuse in Victorian England.* New York: Routledge, 2000.

Jackson, Tudor. *The Law of Kenya; an Introduction.* Nairobi, Kenya: East African Literature Bureau, 1970.

Jacobs, David, and Jason T. Carmichael. "The Political Sociology of the Death Penalty: A Pooled Time-Series Analysis." *American Sociological Review* 67, no. 1 (2002): 109–131.

Jacobs, David, and Stephanie L. Kent. "The Determinants of Executions since 1951: How Politics, Protests, Public Opinion, and Social Divisions Shape Capital Punishment." *Social Problems* 54, no. 3 (2007): 297–318.

Jalongo, Mary Renck. "The Story of Mary Ellen Wilson: Tracing the Origins of Child Protection in America." *Early Childhood Education Journal* 34, no. 1 (2006): 1–4.

James, Allison. "To Be(Come) or Not to Be(Come): Understanding Children's Citizenship." *The Annals of the American Academy of Political and Social Science* 633 (2011): 167–179.

Jessica, Neuwirth, and Amnesty International USA. "Memo To: Paul Hoffman, Jane?, David Weissbrodt, Mary Mcclymont, Joan Hartman Fitzpatrick, Re: Meeting with Jack Boger." New York: University of Minnesota Law School: Private Archives of David Weissbrodt, 1986.

Junger-Tas, Josine. "Trends in International Juvenile Justice: What Conclusions Can Be Drawn?" In *International Handbook of Juvenile Justice*, edited by Josine Junger-Tas and Scott H. Decker, 503–533. New York: Springer, 2006.

Kaihla, Paul. "Kids Who Kill." *Maclean's*, August 15, 1994: 32–39.

Kaniki, M.H.Y. "The End of the Colonial Era." In *Tanzania under Colonial Rule*, edited by M.H.Y. Kaniki, 344–387. London: Longman, 1978.

Kaufman-Osborn, Timothy V. "Capital Punishment as Legal Lynching?" In *From Lynch Mobs to the Killing State: Race and the Death Penalty in America*, edited by Charles Ogletree, Jr. and Austin Sarat, 21–54. New York: New York University Press, 2006.

Kean, A.W.G. "The History of the Criminal Liability of Children." *The Law Quarterly Review* 53 (1937): 364–370.

Keck, Margaret E., and Kathryn Sikkink. *Activists Beyond Borders*. Ithaca, NY: Cornell University Press, 1998.

Kedourie, Elie. *Nationalism in Asia and Africa*. New York: World, 1970.

Keeney, James D. "Review: Report of the Kenya Commission on the Law of Succession." *University of Pennsylvania Law Review* 119, no. 6 (1971): 1071–1075.

Keohane, Robert O. *After Hegemony: Cooperation and Discord in the World Political Economy*. Princeton, NJ: Princeton University Press, 1984.

Khoso, Abdullah. "Detention of Juveniles in Pakistan." *Chronicle*, International Association of Youth and Family Judges and Magistrates, January 2012 edition: 40–43. http://www.aimjf.org/download/Chronicle/English/The_ Chronicle/ Chronicle_Jan_2012_EN.pdf.

Kidder, Robert L. "Toward an Integrated Theory of Imposed Law." In *The Imposition of Law*, edited by Sandra B. Burman and Barbara E. Harrell-Bond, 289–305. New York: Academic Press, 1979.

Kille, Kent J., ed. *The UN Secretary-General and Moral Authority*. Washington, DC: Georgetown University Press, 2007.

Kingdon, John W. *Agendas, Alternatives, and Public Policies*. New York: HarperCollins, 1984.

Kingsbury, Benedict. "The Concept of Compliance as a Function of Competing Conceptions of International Law." *Michigan Journal of International Law* 19 (1998): 345–372.

Kirby, Peter. "The Historic Viability of Child Labour and the Mines Act of 1842." In *A Thing of the Past? Child Labour in Britain in the Nineteenth and Twentieth Centuries*, edited by Michael Lavalette, 101–118. New York: St. Martin's Press, 1999.

Kleck, Gary. "Racial Discrimination in Criminal Sentencing: A Critical Evaluation of the Evidence with Additional Evidence on the Death Penalty." *American Sociological Review* 46, no. 6 (1981): 783–805.

Knell, B.E.F. "Capital Punishment: Its Administration in Relation to Juvenile Offenders in the Nineteenth Century and Its Possible Administration in the Eighteenth." *British Journal of Criminology* 5, no. 2 (1965): 198–207.

Koestler, Arthur. *Reflections on Hanging*. London: Victor Gollancz, 1956.

Koh, Harold. "How Is International Human Rights Law Enforced?" *Indiana Law Journal* 74, no. 4 (1999): 1397–1417.

Koh, Harold. "Review Essay: Why Do Nations Obey International Law?" *Yale Law Journal* 106, no. 8 (1997): 2599–2659.

Krasner, Stephen D. "Sovereignty, Regimes, and Human Rights." In *Regime Theory and International Relations*, edited by Volker Rittberger, 139–167. Oxford: Clarendon, 1993.

Krisch, Nico. "The Pluralism of Global Administrative Law." *European Journal of International Law* 17, no. 1 (2006): 247–278.

Lacayo, Richard, and Richard Behar. "When Kids Go Bad." *Time*, September 19, 1994.

Lake, David, and Wendy Wong. "The Politics of Networks: Interests, Power, and Human Rights Norms." In *Networked Politics: Agency, Power, and Governance*, edited by Miles Kahler, 127–151. Ithaca, NY: Cornell University Press, 2009.

Lapid, Yosef, and Friedrich V. Kratochwil. *The Return of Culture and Identity in IR Theory*. Boulder, CO: Lynne Rienner, 1996.

Lavalette, Michael. "The Changing Form of Child Labour *Circa* 1880–1918: The Growth of 'Out of School Work.'" In *A Thing of the Past? Child Labour in Britain in the Nineteenth and Twentieth Centuries*, edited by Michael Lavalette, 118–139. New York: St. Martin's, 1999.

League of Nations. "Statistical Yearbook of the League of Nations." Edited by the Economic and Financial Section. Geneva: League of Nations, 1927–1945.

Lechner, Frank J., and John Boli. *World Culture: Origin and Consequences*. Malden, MA: Blackwell, 2005.

Ledger, Sally, and Holly Furneaux. *Charles Dickens in Context*. New York and Cambridge: Cambridge University Press, 2013.

Lee, Katie. "China and the International Covenant on Civil and Political Rights: Prospects and Challenges." *Chinese Journal of International Law* 6, no. 2 (2007): 445–474.

Lening, Zhang, and Jianhong Liu. "China's Juvenile Delinquency Prevention Law: The Law and the Philosophy." *International Journal of Offender Therapy and Comparative Criminology* 51, no. 5 (2007): 541–554.

Lerch, Marika, and Guido Schwellnus. "Normative by Nature? The Role of Coherence in Justifying the EU's External Human Rights Policy." *Journal of European Public Policy* 13, no. 2 (2006): 304–321.

Lessard, Micheline R. "Civilizing Women: French Colonial Perceptions of Vietnamese Womanhood and Motherhood." In *Women and the Colonial Gaze*, edited by Tamara L. Hunt and Micheline R. Lessard, 148–161. New York: New York University Press, 2002.

Levesque, Roger J.R. "The Internationalization of Children's Human Rights: Too Radical for American Adolescents?" *Connecticut Journal of International Law* 9, no. 2 (1994): 237–293.

Lewis, Joanna. "Nasty, Brutish and in Shorts? British Colonial Rule, Violence and the Historians of Mau Mau." *The Round Table* 96, no. 389 (2007): 201–223.

Lewis, Norman. "Human Rights, Law and Democracy in an Unfree World." In *Human Rights Fifty Years On: A Reappraisal*, edited by Tony Evans. Manchester, UK: Manchester University Press, 1998.

Linde, Robyn. "From Rapists to Superpredators: What the Practice of Capital Punishment Says about Race, Rights, and the American Child." *International Journal of Children's Rights* 19, no. 1 (2011): 127–150.

Liptak, Adam. "Ruling Likely to Spur Convictions in Capital Cases." *The New York Times*, June 9, 2007.

London Times. "Execution of John Any Bird Bell, for Murder." August 2, 1831: 14(606), 4a. *London Times.* "Summer Assizes." July 30, 1831: 14(604).

Lowenstein, Steven. "Ethiopia." In *African Penal Systems*, edited by Alan Milner. New York: Praeger, 1969: 35–57.

Lowenstein, Steven. *Materials on Comparative Criminal Law as Based Upon the Penal Code of Ethiopia and Switzerland.* Addis Ababa, Ethiopia: Haile Selassie University, 1965.

Lynn, Steven. "Locke and Beccaria: Faculty Psychology and Capital Punishment." In *Executions and the British Experience from the 17th Century: A Collection of Essays*, edited by William B. Thesing. Jefferson, NC: McFarland, 1990: 29–44.

MacLean, Vicky M. "Social Inequalities in Access to Health Care Among African Americans, Latinos, and Caucasians." *American Sociological Association*, San Francisco (2008).

Maddison, Angus. *Statistics on World Population, GDP and Per Capita GDP, 1-2008 AD.* University of Groningen (2010).

Makaramba, Robert V. *Children Rights in Tanzania.* Dar es Salaam, Tanzania: Friedrich Ebert Stiftung, 1998.

Marks, Alexandra. "Unusual Unity on Youth Crime." *Christian Science Monitor.* February 20, 1997. http://www.csmonitor.com/1997/0220/022097.us.us.3.html.

Marshall, Monty G., Ted Robert Gurr, and Keith Jaggers. "Polity IV Project: Political Regime Characteristics and Transitions, 1800–2013." Center for Systemic Peace (2013). http://www.systemicpeace.org/polity/polity4.htm.

McClymont, Mary E. "Personal Letter to David Weissbrodt." Washington, DC: University of Minnesota Law School: Private Archives of David Weissbrodt, September 19, 1985.

McEvoy-Levy, Siobhan, ed. *Troublemakers or Peacemakers? Youth and Post-Accord Peacebuilding.* Notre Dame, IN: University of Notre Dame Press, 2006.

Melton, Oliver. "China's Five-Year Planning System: Implications for the Reform Agenda." Testimony for the U.S.-China Economic and Security Review Commission, April 22, 2015: 6. http://www.uscc.gov/sites/default/files/Melton%20-%20Written%20Testimony.pdf.

Menski, Werner. *Comparative Law in a Global Context.* Cambridge, UK: Cambridge University Press, 2006.

Merry, Sally Engle. "Legal Pluralism." *Law and Society Review* 22, no. 5 (1988): 869–896.

Meyer, John W. "Globalization: Theory and Trends." *International Journal of Comparative Sociology* 48, no. 4 (2007): 261–273.

Meyer, John W. "The Nation as Babbitt: How Countries Conform." *Contexts* 3, no. 3 (2004): 42–47.

Meyer, John W., John Boli, George M. Thomas, and Francisco O. Ramirez. "World Society and the Nation-State." *The American Journal of Sociology* 103, no. 1 (1997): 144–181.

Meyer, Philippe. *The Child and the State: The Intervention of the State in Family Life.* New York: Cambridge University Press, 1983.

Miege, J.L. "Legal Developments in the Maghrib: 1830–1930." In *European Expansion and Law: The Encounter of European and Indigenous Law in the 19th- and 20th-Century Africa and Asia*, edited by W.J. Mommsen and J.A. De Moor. New York: Berg, 1992: 101–109.

Miller, Alice, and Joan Fitzpatrick. "International Standards of the Death Penalty: Shifting Discourse." *Brooklyn Journal of International Law* 19, no. 2 (1993): 273–366.

Mitchell, Michael, and Jim Sidanius. "Social Hierarchy and the Death Penalty: A Social Dominance Perspective." *Political Psychology* 16, no. 3 (1995): 591–619.

Modica, Salvatore J. "New York's Death Penalty: The Age Requirement." *Journal of Civil Rights and Economic Development* 13, no. 3 (1998–1999): 585–612.

Mommsen, W.J. "Introduction." In *European Expansion and Law: The Encounter of European and Indigenous Law in 19th- and 20th-Century Africa and Asia*, edited by W.J. Mommsen and J.A. De Moor. New York: Berg, 1992: 1–14.

Moore, Mark Harrison, and George L. Kelling. "The Historical Legacy." In *From Children to Citizens: The Mandate for Juvenile Justice*, edited by Mark Harrison Moore, 25–48. New York: Springer-Verlag, 1987.

Moore, Sally Falk. "Law and Social Change: The Semi-Autonomous Social Field as an Appropriate Subject of Study." *Law and Society Review* 7, no. 4 (1973): 719–746.

Moore, Sally Falk. "Legal Systems of the World." In *Law and the Social Science*, edited by Leon Lipson and Stanton Wheeler, 11–62. New York: Russell Sage Foundation, 1986.

Moravcsik, Andrew. "The Origins of Human Rights Regimes: Democratic Delegation in Postwar Europe." *International Organization* 54, no. 2 (2000): 217–252.

Morris, H.F. "A History of the Adoption of Codes of Criminal Law and Procedure in British Colonial Africa, 1876–1935." *Journal of African Law* 18, no. 1 (1974): 6–23.

Mount, Ferdinand. *The Subversive Family: An Alternate History to Love and Family.* New York: Free Press, 1982.

Mukarram Ahmed, M., and Muzaffar Husain Syed. *Encyclopaedia of Islam.* 25 vols. New Delhi: Anmoi, 2005.

Mwalimu, Charles. *The Kenyan Legal System: An Overview.* Washington, DC: Law Library of Congress, 1988.

Myers, William E. "The Right Rights? Child Labor in a Globalizing World." *Annals of the American Academy of Political and Social Science* 575 (2001): 38–55.

National Coalition to Abolish the Death Penalty. *Human Rights, Human Wrongs: Sentencing Children to Death.* Washington, DC: National Coalition to Abolish the Death Penalty, 2003.

Neumayer, Eric. "Death Penalty Abolition and the Ratification of the Second Optional Protocol." *International Journal of Human Rights* 12, no. 1 (2008): 3–21.

Neumayer, Eric. "Death Penalty: The Political Foundations of the Global Trend Towards Abolition." *Human Rights Review* 9, no. 2 (2008): 241–268.

Noonan, Rita K. "Women against the State: Political Opportunities and Collective Action Frames in Chile's Transition to Democracy." *Sociological Forum* 10, no. 1 (1995): 81–111.

Normandeau, Andre. "Pioneers in Criminology: Charles Lucas—Opponent of Capital Punishment." *Journal of Criminal Law and Criminology* 61, no. 2 (1970): 218–228.

Ochieng, W.R. *A Modern History of Kenya 1895–1980.* Nairobi, Kenya: Evans Brothers, 1989.

Ogletree, Charles, Jr., and Austin Sarat, eds. *From Lynch Mobs to the Killing State: Race and the Death Penalty in America.* New York: New York University Press, 2006.

Oheneba-Sakyi, Yaw, and Baffour K. Takyi. "Introduction to the Study of African Families: A Framework of Analysis." In *African Families at the Turn of the 21st*

Century, edited by Yaw Oheneba-Sakyi and Baffour K. Takyi. Westport, CT: Praeger, 2006: 1–26.

Onuf, Nicholas. *World of Our Making: Rules and Rule in Social Theory and International Relations*. Columbia, SC: University of South Carolina Press, 1989.

Onuf, Nicholas. "Worlds of Our Making: The Strange Career of Constructivism in International Relations." In *Visions of International Relations*, edited by Donald J. Puchala, 119–142. Columbia, SC: University of South Carolina Press, 2002.

Ottaway, David, and Marina Ottaway. *Algeria: The Politics of a Socialist Revolution*. Berkeley, CA: University of California Press, 1970.

Pagden, Anthony. "Human Rights, Natural Rights, and Europe's Imperial Legacy." *Political Theory* 31, no. 2 (2003): 171–199.

Peffley, Mark, and Jon Hurwitz. "Persuasion and Resistance: Race and the Death Penalty in America." *American Journal of Political Science* 51, no. 4 (2007): 996–1012.

Perkins, Kenneth J. *A History of Modern Tunisia*. New York: Cambridge University Press, 2004.

Peshkopia, Ridvan, and Arben Imami. "Between Elite Compliance and State Socialisation: The Abolition of the Death Penalty in Eastern Europe." *International Journal of Human Rights* 12, no. 3 (2008): 353–372.

Phillips, Arthur, and Henry F. Morris. *Marriage Laws in Africa*. London: Oxford University Press, 1971.

Pinchbeck, Ivy, and Margaret Hewitt. *Children in English Society*. Vol. 1, *From Tudor Times to the Eighteenth Century*. London: Routledge & Kegan Paul, 1969.

Pinchbeck, Ivy, and Margaret Hewitt. *Children in English Society*. Vol. 2, *From the Eighteenth Century to the Children Act of 1948*. London: Routledge and Kegan Paul, 1973.

Pollock, Linda A. *Forgotten Children: Parent-Child Relations from 1500 to 1900*. New York: Cambridge University Press, 1983.

Pomfret, David. "'Raising Eurasia': Race, Class and Age in Hong Kong and Indochina." *Comparative Studies in Society and History* 51, no. 2 (2009): 314–343.

Potter, Harry. *Hanging in Judgment*. London: SCM, 1993.

Price, Richard. "Transnational Civil Society and Advocacy in World Politics." *World Politics* 55, no. 4 (2003): 579–606.

Prins, Adolphe, and Ugo Conti. "Some European Comments on the American Prison System." *Journal of the American Institute of Criminal Law and Criminology* 2(2) (1911): 199–215.

Pritchard, John Laurence. *A History of Capital Punishment*. New York: Citadel, 1960.

Pupavac, Vanessa. "Misanthropy without Borders: The International Children's Rights Regime." *Disasters* 25, no. 2 (2001): 95–112.

Radzinowicz, Sir Leon, and Roger Hood. *A History of English Criminal Law*. Vol. 5, *The Emergence of Penal Policy*. London: Stevens & Sons, 1948–1986.

Ramirez, Francisco O., Yasemin Soysal, and Suzanne Shanahan. "The Changing Logic of Political Citizenship: Cross-National Acquisition of Women's Suffrage Rights, 1890 to 1990." *American Sociological Review* 62, no. 5 (1997): 735–745.

Ramirez, Francisco O., and Marc Ventresca. "Building the Institution of Mass Schooling." In *The Political Construction of Education*, edited by Bruce Fuller and Richard Rubinson, 47–60. New York: Praeger, 1992.

Rehfeld, Andrew. "The Child as Democratic Citizen." *The Annals of the American Academy of Political and Social Science* 633 (2011): 141–166.

Reuters. "Pakistan to Continue Moratorium on Capital Punishment." October 3, 2013. http://dawn.com/news/1047193/pakistan-to-continue-moratorium-on-capital-punishment.

Rocamora, Jane. "Memo To: LSN Coordinators and Attendees of the LSN Death Penalty Meeting, Re: Minutes of Death Penalty Meeting on October 27, 1986." University of Minnesota Law School: Private Archives of David Weissbrodt, November 3, 1986.

Romilly, Sir Samuel. *Observations on the Criminal Law of England as It Relates to Capital Punishments, and the Mode in Which It Is Administered.* London: T. Cadell and W. Davies, 1810.

Rose, Nikolas. *The Psychological Complex: Psychology, Politics and Society in England: 1869–1939.* London: Routledge & Kegan Paul, 1985.

Rose, Nikolas *Governing the Soul: The Shaping of the Private Self.* New York: Routledge, 1990.

Rubin, Sol, and Irving J. Sloan. *Juvenile Offenders and the Juvenile Justice System.* Legal Almanac Series 22. Dobbs Ferry, NY: Oceana, 1986.

Ruggie, John Gerard. "Multilateralism: The Anatomy of an Institution." *International Organization* 46, no. 3 (1992): 561–708.

Ruggie, John Gerard. "What Makes the World Hang Together?" *International Organization* 52, no. 4 (1998): 855–885.

Russell, Franklin F. "The New Ethiopian Penal Code." *American Journal of Comparative Law* 10, (1961): 259–287.

Salacuse, Jeswald W. *An Introduction to Law in French-Speaking Africa.* Vol. 2, *The Legal Systems of Africa.* Charlottesville, VA: Michie Company Law, 1975.

Santos, Boaventura de Sousa. *Toward a New Legal Common Sense: Law, Globalization and Emancipation.* 2nd ed. Law in Context. London: Butterworth Lexis-Nexis, 2002.

Santos, Boaventura de Sousa, and César A. Rodríguez Garavito. *Law and Globalization from Below: Towards a Cosmopolitan Legality.* New York: Cambridge University Press, 2005.

Sarat, Austin. *When the State Kills: Capital Punishment and the American Condition.* Princeton, NJ: Princeton University Press, 2001.

Sawyer, Geoffrey. "Comment: The Death Penalty Is Dead Wrong: *Jus Cogens* Norms and the Evolving Standard of Decency." *Penn State International Law Review* 22, no. 459 (2004): 459–481.

Scalia, Justice Antonin. Dissenting Opinion, *Thompson v. Oklahoma* (487 U.S. 815). Supreme Court of the United States (1988).

Schabas, William. *The Abolition of the Death Penalty in International Law.* Cambridge, UK: Cambridge University Press, 2002.

Schabas, William. "Life, Death and the Crime of Crimes: Supreme Penalties and the ICC Statute." *Punishment & Society* 2, no. 3 (2000): 263–285.

Seidman, Gay W. "Gendered Citizenship: South Africa's Democratic Transition and the Construction of a Gendered State." *Gender and Society* 13, no. 3 (1999): 287–307.

Seidman, Robert B. "Law and Economic Development in Independent, English-Speaking Sub-Saharan Africa." In *Africa and Law: Developing Legal Systems in African Commonwealth Nations,* edited by Thomas W. Hutchison, 3–74. Madison, WI: University of Wisconsin Press, 1968.

Seligson, Tom. "Are They Too Young to Die?" *Parade Magazine,* October 19, 1986: 4–7.

Sen, Satadru. *Colonial Childhoods: The Juvenile Periphery of India 1850–1945*. London: Anthem, 2005.

Sen, Satadru. "A Juvenile Periphery: The Geographies of Literary Childhood in Colonial Bengal." *Journal of Colonialism and Colonial History* 5, no. 1 (2004).

Sen, Satadru. "The Orphaned Colony: Orphanage, Child and Authority in British India." *Indian Economic & Social History Review* 44, no. 4 (2007): 463–488.

Sen, Satadru. "A Separate Punishment: Juvenile Offenders in Colonial India." *The Journal of Asian Studies* 63, no. 1 (2004): 81–104.

Shikita, Minoru, and Shinichi Tsuchiya. *Crime and Criminal Policy in Japan: Anaylsis and Evaluation of the Showa Era, 1926–1988*. New York: Springer-Verlag, 1992.

Shivji, Issa G., Humudi I. Majamba, Robert V. Makaramba, and Chris M. Peter. *Constitutional and Legal System of Tanzania*. Dar Es Salaam, Tanzania: Mkuki Na Nyota, 2004.

Shorter, Edward. *The Making of the Modern Family*. New York: Basic, 1975.

Sikkink, Kathryn. "Human Rights, Principled Issue-Networks, and Sovereignty in Latin America." *International Organization* 47, no. 3 (1993): 411–441.

Sikkink, Kathryn. "Restructuring World Politics: The Limits and Asymmetries of Soft Power." In *Restructuring World Politics: Transnational Social Movements, Networks, and Norms*, edited by Sanjeev Khagram, James V. Riker, and Kathryn Sikkink, 301–317. Minneapolis: University of Minnesota Press, 2002.

Simmons, Beth A. "International Law and State Behavior: Commitment and Compliance in International Monetary Affairs." *American Political Science Review* 94, no. 4 (2000): 819–835.

Simmons, Beth A. *Mobilizing for Human Rights: International Law in Domestic Politics*. New York: Cambridge University Press, 2009.

Smith, Stephen F. "The Supreme Court and the Politics of Death." *Virginia Law Review* 94, no. 2 (2008): 283–383.

Sommerville, C. John. *The Rise and Fall of Childhood*. Beverly Hills, CA: Sage, 1982.

Soss, Joe, Laura Langbein, and Alan R. Metelko. "Why Do White Americans Support the Death Penalty?" *The Journal of Politics* 65, no. 2 (2003): 397–421.

Steiner, Benjamin D., William J. Bowers, and Austin Sarat. "Folk Knowledge as Legal Action: Death Penalty Judgments and the Tenet of Early Release in a Culture of Mistrust and Punitiveness." *Law & Society Review* 33, no. 2 (1999): 461–505.

Stephen, Sir James Fitzjames. *A History of the Criminal Law of England*. Vol. 1. London: Macmillan, 1883.

Stephen, Sir James Fitzjames. *A History of the Criminal Law of England*. Vol. 2. London: Macmillan, 1883.

Stevens, Justice John Paul. Judgment of the Court, *Thompson v. Oklahoma* (487 U.S. 815). Supreme Court of the United States. (1988).

Stoler, Ann L. "Making Empire Respectable: The Politics of Race and Sexual Morality in 20th-Century Colonial Cultures." *American Ethnologist* 16, no. 4 (1989): 634–660.

Stoler, Ann L. "Sexual Affronts and Racial Frontiers: European Identities and the Cultural Politics of Exclusion in Colonial Southeast Asia." *Comparative Studies in Society and History* 34, no. 3 (1992): 514–551.

Stone, Lawrence. *The Family, Sex and Marriage in England, 1500–1800*. New York: Harper & Row, 1977.

Streib, Victor L. "The Juvenile Death Penalty Today: Death Sentences and Executions for Juvenile Crimes, January 1, 1973–December 31, 2004." Ohio Northern University College of Law, 2005.

Streib, Victor L. "The Juvenile Death Penalty Today: Death Sentences and Executions for Juvenile Crimes, January 1, 1973–February 28, 2005." Ohio Northern

University College of Law, 2005. http://www.deathpenaltyinfo.org/juveniles-and-death-penalty.

Strolovitch, Dara Z. *Affirmative Advocacy: Race, Class, and Gender in Interest Group Politics*. Chicago: University of Chicago Press, 2007.

Sugarman, David. *Legality, Ideology, and the State*. London and New York: Academic Press, 1983.

Sunstein, Cass. *Free Markets and Social Justice*. New York: Oxford University Press, 1997.

Tallack, William. *The Practical Results of Total or Partial Abolition of the Capital Punishment in Various Countries*. London: Society for the Abolition of Capital Punishment, 1866.

Tamanaha, Brian Z. "The Folly of the 'Social Scientific' Concept of Legal Pluralism." *Journal of Law and Society* 20, no. 2 (1993): 192–217.

Tanenhaus, David S., and Steven. A. Drizin. "'Owing to the Extreme Youth of the Accused': The Changing Legal Response to Juvenile Homicide." *The Journal of Criminal Law and Criminology* 92, no. 3–4 (2002): 641–706.

Tanner, Murray Scot, and Eric Green. "Principals and Secret Agents: Central Versus Local Control over Policing and Obstacles to 'Rule of Law' in China." *The China Quarterly* 191 (2007): 644–670.

Taylor, David. *Crime, Policing and Punishment in England, 1750–1914*. New York: St. Martin's, 1998.

Teeters, Negley K. *Hang by the Neck: The Legal Use of Scaffold and Noose, Gibbet, Stake, and Firing Squad from Colonial Times to the Present*. Springfield, IL: Charles C. Thomas, 1967.

Teubner, Gunther. *Global Law Without a State*. Studies in Modern Law and Policy. Aldershot, UK: Dartmouth, 1997.

Teubner, Gunther. "The Two Faces of Janus: Rethinking Legal Pluralism." *Cardozo Law Review* 13, no. 1443 (1992): 1443–1462.

Thompson, Carol B. "Beyond Civil Society: Child Soldiers as Citizens in Mozambique." *Review of African Political Economy* 26, no. 80 (1999): 190–206.

Thurston, Linda M., and Amnesty International USA. "A Strategic Plan for Effective Work to Abolish the Death Penalty." University of Minnesota Law School: Private Archives of David Weissbrodt, 1995.

Tie, Warwick. *Legal Pluralism: Toward a Multicultural Conception of Law*. Aldershot, UK: Ashgate/Dartmouth, 1999.

Tsutsui, Kiyoteru, and Christine Min Wotipka. "Global Civil Society and the International Human Rights Movement: Citizen Participation in Human Rights International Nongovernmental Organizations." *Social Forces* 83, no. 2 (2004): 587–620.

Tuttle, Elizabeth Orman. *The Crusade against Capital Punishment in Great Britain*. London: Stevens & Sons, 1961.

UNICEF. *1946–2006 Sixty Years for Children*. New York: UNICEF, 2006.

UNICEF. "About UNICEF." Accessed on May 24, 2008. http://www.unicef.org/about/who/index_history.html.

UNICEF. "About UNICEF: Who Are We: Maurice Pate Biography." Accessed on May 24, 2008. http://www.unicef.org/media/media_35903.html.

UNICEF. "Annual Report 2011," (June 2012) last accessed June 1, 2013. http://www.unicef.org/publications/files/UNICEF_Annual_Report_2011_EN_060112.pdf.

UNICEF. "Annual Report 2012 Summary," last accessed October 23, 2014, http://www.unicef.org/publications/files/UNICEF_Annual_Report_2012_SUMMARY_ENG_2July2013.pdf.

UNICEF. *Child Protection: Current Status and Progress*, http://data.unicef.org/child-protection/overview.html.

UNICEF. "Facts on Children." http://www.unicef.org/media/media_35903.html. Accessed on May 24, 2008.

UNICEF. *Implementation Handbook for the Convention on the Rights of the Child*. New York: UNICEF House, 1998.

UNICEF. *The Needs of Children: A Survey of the Needs of Children in the Developing Countries*. Edited by Georges Sicault. New York: Macmillan, 1963.

UNICEF. "The State of World's Children 2013, Children with Disabilities," May 2013.

UNICEF. "United Nations Special Session on Children: The World Summit for Children." http://www.unicef.org/specialsession/about/world-summit.htm.

UNICEF, Rachel Hodgkin, and Peter Newell. *Implementation Handbook for the Convention on the Rights of the Child*. New York: UNICEF House, 2002.

UNICEF Regional Office South Asia. "Juvenile Justice in South Asia: Improving Protection for Children in Conflict with the Law." Kathmandu, 2006. http://www.unicef.org/rosa/Juvenile_Justice_in_South_Asia.pdf.

United Nations. *Legislative History of the Convention on the Rights of the Child*. New York: United Nations, 2007.

United Nations, and Secretary-General Kofi Annan. *We the Children: Meeting the Promises of the World Summit for Children*. New York: UNICEF House, 2001.

United Nations Children's Fund. "The Nobel Peace Prize 1965: History of the Organization." Nobelprize.org.

United Nations Economic and Social Council. "Civil and Political Rights, Including the Question of Disappearances and Summary Executions: Extrajudicial, Summary or Arbitrary Excutions: Report of the Special Rapporteur, Philip Alston: Addendum: Summary of Cases Transmitted to Governments and Replies Received." Commission on Human Rights, E/CN.4/2005/7/Add.1 (2005). http://daccess-dds-ny.un.org/doc/UNDOC/GEN/G05/131/17/PDF/G0513117.pdf?OpenElement.

United Nations Human Rights Committee. "Consideration of Reports Submitted by States Parties under Article 40 of the Covenant: Comments of Human Rights Committee 53d Sess., 1413th Mtg. Para. 14, at 4 U.N. Doc. CCPR/C/79/Add.50 (1995)." 1995. https://www1.umn.edu/humanrts/usdocs/hrcuscomments.html.

United Nations Human Rights Committee. General Comment 24, UN Doc CCPR/C/21/Rev 1/Add 6 para 10 (1994).

United Nations Office on Drugs and Crime. "Global Report on Trafficking in Persons," February 2009. https://www.unodc.org/unodc/en/data-and-analysis/glotip_2009.html.

United Nations Office on Drugs and Crime. "Global Report on Trafficking in Persons," 2014. https://www.unodc.org/documents/data-and-analysis/glotip/GLOTIP_2014_full_report.pdf.

United States Department of State, and John J. Charnow. "The International Children's Emergency Fund." Department of State Publication 2787. United States—United Nations Information Series. Washington, DC: Government Printing Office, 1947.

Unnever, James D., and Francis Cullen. "The Racial Divide in Support for the Death Penalty: Does White Racism Matter?" *Social Forces* 85, no. 3 (2007): 1281–1302.

Unnever, James D., and Francis T. Cullen. "Reassessing the Racial Divide in Support for Capital Punishment: The Continuing Significance of Race." *Journal of Research in Crime & Delinquency* 44, no. 1 (2007): 124–158.

Uno, Kathleen S. "Japan." In *Children in Historical and Comparative Perspective*, edited by Joseph M. Hawes and N. Ray Hiner, 389–419. New York: Greenwood, 1991.

Valenin, Karen, and Lotte Meinert. "The Adult North and the Young South: Reflections on the Civilizing Mission of Children's Rights." *Anthropology Today* 25, no. 3 (2009): 23–28.

van Bueren, Geraldine. *The International Law on the Rights of the Child*. Boston: Martinus Nijhoff, 1998.

van Bueren, Geraldine. "Multigenerational Citizenship: The Importance of Recognizing Children as National and International Citizens." *The Annals of the American Academy of Political and Social Science* 633 (2011): 30–51.

Vanderlinden, J. "Civil Law and Common Law Influences in the Developing Law of Ethiopia." *Buffalo Law Review* 16 (1966–1967): 250–266.

Vienna Convention on the Law of Treaties. 115 U.N.T.S. 331, Articles 53 and 64. 1980.

Wallace, James. "Appeal Fails; Dodd Hanged; Killer of 3 Boys Is First Felon Executed in State in 30 Years." *Seattle Post-Intelligencer,* January 5, 1993, A1.

Wang, Yuhua. "Judicial Hierarchy and Judicial Outcomes: Evidence from a Natural Experiment in China," Working Paper, Harvard University. May 11, 2015, 2. http://scholar.harvard.edu/files/yuhuawang/files/court.pdf.

Ward, Robert E. "The Origins of the Present Japanese Constitution." *American Political Science Review* 50, no. 4 (1956): 980–1010.

Watson, Alison. *The Child in International Political Economy: A Place at the Table*. New York: Routledge, 2009.

Watson, Alison. "Children and International Relations: A New Site of Knowledge?" *Review of International Studies* 32, no. 2 (2006): 237–250.

Watson, Alison. "Saving More Than the Children: The Role of Child-Focused NGOs in the Creation of Southern Security Norms." *Third World Quarterly* 27, no. 2 (2006): 227–237.

Weissbrodt, David, Joan Fitzpatrick, and Franck Newman. *International Human Rights: Law, Policy and Process*. 3rd ed. Cincinnati, OH: Anderson, 2001.

Wendt, Alexander. "Anarchy Is What States Make of It: The Social Construction of Power Politics." *International Organization* 46, no. 2 (1992): 391–425.

Weyland, Kurt. "The Diffusion of Innovations: How Cognitive Heuristics Shaped Bolivia's Pension Reform." *Comparative Politics* 38, no. 1 (2005): 21–42.

Weyland, Kurt. "Theories of Policy Diffusion: Lessons from Latin American Pension Reform." *World Politics* 57, no. 2 (2005): 262–295.

White, Owen. *Children of the French Empire: Miscegenation and Colonial Society in French West Africa, 1895–1960*. Oxford: Clarendon, 1999.

Williams, David R., and Chiquita Collins. "US Socioeconomic and Racial Differences in Health: Patterns and Explanations." *Annual Review of Sociology* 21, no. 1 (1995): 349–386.

Willetts, Peter. *"The Conscience of the World:" The Influence of Non-Governmental Organizations in the U.N. System*. Washington, DC: Brookings Institution, 1996.

Witkin, Gordon, and S.J. Hedges. "Kids Who Kill." *U.S. News & World Report*, April 8, 1991.

Wollons, Roberta Lyn. *Kindergartens and Cultures: The Global Diffusion of an Idea*. New Haven, CT: Yale University Press, 2000.

Wong, Wendy. *Internal Affairs: How the Structure of NGOs Transforms Human Rights*. Ithaca, NY: Cornell University Press, 2012.

Zelizer, Viviana A. *Pricing the Priceless Child: The Changing Social Value of Children*. Princeton, NJ.: Princeton University Press, 1994.

Zimring, Franklin E. *The Changing Legal World of Adolescence*. New York: Free Press, 1982.

Zimring, Franklin E. *The Contradictions of American Capital Punishment*. Studies in Crime and Public Policy. New York: Oxford University Press, 2003.

Zimring, Franklin E., and Gordon Hawkins. *Capital Punishment and the American Agenda*. Cambridge, UK: Cambridge University Press, 1986.

INDEX